A Torah Giant

The Intellectual Legacy of
Rabbi Dr. Irving (Yitz) Greenberg

A Torah Giant

The Intellectual Legacy of Rabbi Dr. Irving (Yitz) Greenberg

Edited by
Rabbi Dr. Shmuly Yanklowitz

Foreword by
Rabbi Avi Weiss

Introduction by
Rabbi Joseph Telushkin

URIM PUBLICATIONS
Jerusalem • New York

KTAV PUBLISHING

A Torah Giant: The Intellectual Legacy of Rabbi Dr. Irving (Yitz) Greenberg

Edited by Rabbi Dr. Shmuly Yanklowitz

Foreword by Rabbi Avi Weiss

Introduction by Rabbi Joseph Telushkin

Printed in Israel

First Edition

ISBN 978-965-524-271-3

Published by

KTAV Publishing House
527 Empire Boulevard
Brooklyn, NY 11225
www.ktav.com

Urim Publications
P.O. Box 52287
Jerusalem 9152102 Israel
www.UrimPublications.com

Library of Congress Cataloging-in-Publication Data

Names: Yanklowitz, Shmuly, 1981– editor.
Title: A Torah giant : the intellectual legacy of Rabbi Dr. Irving (Yitz) Greenberg / edited by Rabbi Dr. Shmuly Yanklowitz ; foreword by Rabbi Avi Weiss ; introduction by Rabbi Joseph Telushkin.
Description: First edition. | Jerusalem : Urim Publications ; New York : Ktav Publishing, [2018]
Identifiers: LCCN 2017038814 | ISBN 9789655242713 (hardcover : alk. paper)
Subjects: LCSH: Greenberg, Irving, 1933- | Rabbis—United States—Biography. | Jewish scholars—United States—Biography. | United States—Biography.
Classification: LCC BM755.G74 T67 2018 | DDC 296.8/32092 [B] —dc23
LC record available at https://lccn.loc.gov/2017038814

In honor of our dear friend

Rabbi Irving "Yitz" Greenberg

to whom we owe so much.

The Harold Grinspoon Foundation

Rabbi Dr. Yitz (Irving) Greenberg
(U.S. Holocaust Memorial Museum, 2002)

Contents

Foreword

Rabbi Avi Weiss

Rabbi Irving Greenberg is, without a doubt, one of the seminal thinkers of our generation. His formulation of new creative ideas – that Jesus was not a false messiah but a failed messiah; that the Covenant post-Holocaust is voluntary; that Christianity and Islam are also covenantal religions – have been carefully studied, explored deeply by rabbis and clergy of all backgrounds, and have evoked fierce criticism from more traditional circles of Judaism.

Some, like Dr. Steven Bayme, have noted that R. Yitz's ideas on modernity and *halakhah* inspired countless students during his teaching days at Yeshiva University (YU) in the 1960s. Dr. Bayme suggests that as a young, brilliant, innovative scholar, R. Yitz was suited to become the next president of YU. Had that occurred, YU may not have drifted so precipitously toward Orthodoxy's right. But alas, Yitz may have been *too* far ahead of his time. His candidacy for president was quashed and YU's doors were closed to him.

Still, Yitz persevered.

It is rare that a rabbi is both a scholar and a communal leader, but Yitz has the rare talent to combine both of these qualities. There is hardly any vital area in Jewish life that Yitz has not profoundly impacted: It was R. Yitz who pioneered and introduced the first Judaic Studies program on a college campus; it was Yitz who was the visionary for studies that focused on Shoah memory; it was Yitz who was amongst the early founders of the first national organization advocating for Soviet Jewry (SSSJ); it was Yitz who rallied for an Israel that not only could defend itself but remain a spiritual light to the world – a country that expresses its power with deep ethical sensibilities; it was Yitz who was instrumental in creating the SAR Academy, one of the great day schools in the world today, and it was Yitz who founded CLAL, bringing together Jews from across the denominational spectrum to engage in respectful dialogue.

In short, R. Yitz is a dreamer. He is the epitome of Robert Kennedy's idea that some people look at the world as it is and ask *Why*, while others look at the world as it should be and ask *Why Not*? All people dream, but Yitz stands above as a master dreamer.

R. Yitz is also a master educator; his brilliance is accessible to the masses. He has taken complicated ideas about *tzelem Elohim* (image of God) and the centrality of life and covenant, and taught them in ways that stir the soul. His thoughts are profound, and yet he's been able to popularize these ideas in ways that penetrate religious consciousness. In my travels around the country, I have met countless people who refer to Yitz as their rabbi. Single handedly, he's inspired Federations and United Jewish Appeals, the elite of Jewish leadership, and multitudes of people to engage in Torah study.

With all of his success as a leader and teacher, Yitz is the epitome of Micah's religious teaching, "Do what is right, love mercy, and walk humbly with your God." He lives the Talmudic dictum: In the place of real greatness, there is humility.

Often, it is the case that scholars of such depth and leaders of such accomplishment have little time for family. Yet the test of real greatness is one's interaction with *mishpacha*. R. Yitz models what it means to be a husband, a father, and grandfather. Together with his wife Blu – a Torah Giant in her own right – they have created a home of deep *kedushah*, deep holiness.

So many of us feel part of Yitz and Blu's family, privy to what can be called "R. Yitz stories." For me, it started when I first met Yitz. To this day, I remember him sitting opposite me, his head slightly tilted as he paid close attention. Rabbis are taught to speak. Here, for the first time, I met a rabbi who was a master listener.

And then there was the story of Yitz, together with Blu, knocking at my door at 6:30 in the morning during the days of the *rabba* ordination controversy. "We had a thought," they explained, "on how you can go forward while lessening the criticism."

Or Yitz, years back, around Purim time, offering a *Purim shpiel*, displaying, even in his humor, great genius; R. Yitz sitting in devout prayer. Indeed, one of the best "books" on *tefillah* is watching Yitz as he dialogues with God.

Or a woman in Florida who introduced me to her son. "His name," she said, "is Yitz. After Rabbi Greenberg spoke of centrality of life, I was so moved. I shared the thoughts with my husband. We decided to have another child and, in honor of Rabbi Greenberg, named him Yitz." I have little doubt that there are many other such incidents.

The Bible notes that our second patriarch is called Yitzḥak because Sarah laughed when first told she would have a child. The rabbis wonder why the name Yitzḥak is in the future tense, "will laugh," rather than *tzaḥakah* which is the past tense.

Perhaps, it can be suggested that the tense of Yitzhak teaches that in the future *Am Yisrael* will face dark times, but against all odds, *Yitzḥak* – we will prevail.

This is one of the deepest legacies of Rabbi Yitz Greenberg. Through the years, he has endured great challenges. The tragic loss of his son JJ and daughter-in-law Mindy would test even the greatest of believers. Through all of this deep pain, with dignity and belief, Yitz and Blu have endured.

We, in our community, have cried with Yitz and Blu, laughed with Yitz and Blu and now, through this volume and many more, we study and celebrate the legacy of one of the greats of our time, my teacher, my mentor, my friend – Rabbi Yitz Greenberg.

Rabbi Dr. Shmuly Yanklowitz deserves great credit for editing a critical edition of essays on the life and legacy of Rabbi Greenberg. It is, for me, an honor to write a few words of introduction as Yitz – as Rabbi Greenberg is affectionately known throughout the world – has become, over the years, the older soul brother I have always sought.

May R. Yitz and Blu be blessed for many years to come.

Yitz Greenberg: An Appreciation

Rabbi Joseph Telushkin

I PROUDLY COUNT MYSELF a disciple of Rabbi Irving "Yitz" Greenberg, the most influential teacher with whom I studied at Yeshiva University. Profound as Greenberg's impact was upon me in the late 1960s and 1970s, it has grown and grown since then. And I, of course, am one of just thousands whose thinking has been shaped by his extraordinary vision of Judaism, Jews, God, and humankind. Indeed, I believe that Greenberg's thinking is only beginning to make its impact, and that it will prove to have ever-increasing significance to Jews, theologically sensitive Christians, and open-minded secularists throughout the next century.

What distinguishes Greenberg's thinking as so consequential? For one thing, he espouses an ideology of Judaism and the human condition that is both passionate and tolerant. Passion and tolerance are not necessarily virtues. Evil ideologies, no less than good ones, have passionate adherents, while tolerance is often practiced more easily by those with no convictions at all.

However, the genius of Greenberg's passionate tolerance is that it is more than tolerant; it truly is rooted in an openness to learn from diverse people and ideologies, an openness that itself derives from his full-hearted acceptance of Judaism's teaching that all human beings are created in God's image. If each person has a spark of divinity within him or her, then many, many people will have something divine to teach.

Greenberg's openness to learning from and appreciating people of diverse orientations also stems from his ongoing reflections on the Holocaust. It is one of Yitz's great insights to realize that the Holocaust challenges and, to a certain degree, shatters everyone. For Jews, of course, the Holocaust challenges one of the most important statements made about God in the Torah: that He is a God Who acts in history. Christianity, which argued for two thousand years that it had triumphantly replaced Judaism, must confront the fact that the Holocaust was conceived and carried out in the midst of Christian Europe and by people many of whom were not Christians but almost all were children of Christians. Secularists, who might point to the Holocaust to argue that there is no protecting God, must confront the fact that the Holocaust was instituted and carried out in a secularist society. The two most powerful ideologies spawned by secularism, Nazism and communism, lacked mechanisms to stop their leaders and many of their adherents from becoming mass murderers. Indeed, Greenberg was one of the first to point out the moral dangers inherent in value-free secular education; he noted that, of the twenty-four Einsatzgruppen[1] leaders put on trial for their wholesale murder of more than one million Soviet Jews, nine were lawyers, two were economists, and one each was architect, professor, banker, high school teacher, and dentist. The Holocaust challenged religious faith because God did not stop the atrocities, and it equally challenged secularism, whose adherents largely implemented the "Final Solution."

Another important element of Greenberg's thinking is his willingness to do battle against divisions that unnecessarily separate people. While he certainly acknowledges the existence of serious differences between believers and skeptics, he also insists that, in the aftermath of the Shoah, such divisions may be less absolute than is commonly thought. For example, because of the Holocaust, few believers can assert that their faith is never plagued by doubts. Thus, Greenberg asserts that: "After Auschwitz, faith means that there are times when faith is overcome. . . . We now have to speak of 'moment faiths' interspersed with times when the flames and smoke of the burning children blot out faith, although it flickers again. . . . The difference between the skeptic and the believer is frequency of faith, and not certitude of position."

Greenberg insists that we guard ourselves against the self-righteous-

1. The German mobile killing units that followed the Wehrmacht (German army) in the former Soviet Union, murdering at least one million Jews from 1941 to 1942.

ness that denominations and religious groupings inevitably seem to inspire. This doesn't mean that people shouldn't belong to a denomination or to an organized religious grouping; on the contrary, Greenberg is a passionately affirming Modern Orthodox rabbi. But his profound awareness that all truth does not reside in any one group is reflected in one of his wittiest remarks: "It is not so important which denomination in Judaism you belong to, as long as you're ashamed of it."

The meaning behind this quip is profound. Interdenominational acrimony is largely fueled by various Jews' tendency to highlight their movement's perceived strengths and the others' weaknesses. Thus, Reform Jews commonly dismiss Orthodoxy as fanatical, and view their movement as the only truly tolerant, open-minded one. Meanwhile, Orthodox Jews often seem to think of themselves as the only ones sincerely trying to follow God's laws, and commonly view the non-Orthodox as irreligious people who change the Torah's meaning to conform to their own convenience.

But since all the movements have failed to complete Judaism's task of "perfecting the world under the rule of God," it behooves all their adherents to speak more charitably of their "opponents," and more humbly of their own accomplishments.

This insight applies to different religions no less than to different denominations. Twenty years ago, Greenberg argued with Dennis Prager and me over what he felt were our unfairly harsh criticisms of Christianity. "It's wrong," he counseled us, "to take the best of your own tradition and compare it to the worst of someone else's." The comment affected us both profoundly, and has guided us to a more comprehensive, nuanced, appreciative, and balanced understanding of Christianity.

In his openness to learning from diverse views, Greenberg hardly preaches tolerance without limits. But the boundaries he establishes are commonsensical and moral; they emanate from his deep love of the Jewish people. Thus, although a tendency has emerged in recent years in some, not all, right-wing Orthodox circles, to understand the Holocaust as punishment for Jewish sinfulness, Greenberg denounces such an explanation on moral grounds: "Now that [the victims of the Holocaust] have been cruelly tortured and killed, boiled into soap, their hair made into pillows and their bones into fertilizer, their unknown graves and the very fact of their deaths denied to them [by Holocaust deniers], the theologian would inflict on them the only indignity left: that is, insistence that it was done because of their sins."

Given polemicists' unfortunate tendency to use the Holocaust to justify positions they already hold, Greenberg offered this challenging and moving guideline for Holocaust discussants: "No statement theological or otherwise should be made that would not be credible in the presence of the burning children."

Greenberg's love for *clal Yisrael*, the Jewish people, was instilled in him in the learned Orthodox household in which he was raised in Brooklyn. Once, several years after World War II, when he was a teenager passing through an intensely religious phase, he made some highly critical comments about American Jews' irreligiosity. His staunchly Orthodox father was angered by his words: "You dare to attack Jews in the name of God? Tell me – of these two [God and the Jewish people], who should be more ashamed of their behavior over the past decade?"

This seminal exchange deeply and permanently affected Greenberg. In a powerful passage, he explains the impact of his father's rhetorical question: "Without ever saying a word about the Holocaust, my father communicated that that was what he meant. God had not saved the Jewish people from the Shoah, but the Jews had remained faithful. . . . In stunned silence, I heard the message: Don't you dare ever attack (or shame) Jews in the name of God. They deserve better from God and from you."

It is this appreciation for Jewish loyalty to the Jewish people, after God's seeming abandonment of them during the Holocaust that enables Greenberg to discern a life of Jewish affirmation even among those whom others dismiss as leading "uncommitted" lives. Jews who celebrate a child's bar or bat mitzvah even with gaudy parties, do so with an awareness that identifying as a Jew can and has, led to death, and are making a profound, if hidden, affirmation.

I remember thinking that Greenberg had gone too far when I once heard him speak of Jewish parents affirming covenant by installing wall-to-wall carpeting in their homes so that their children would not suffer unnecessary pain when they fell. This struck me as far-fetched, but when my children were born, I had wall-to-wall carpeting installed. Greenberg understands such behavior as, in part, a response to the Holocaust. Because Jews had suffered such unnecessary and extreme pain during those years and children were the greatest victims of this pain, Jews were responding by trying to do away with preventable suffering.

An awareness of this sort of "holy secularity" is what lies behind Greenberg's affirmation of the work done by Jewish federations. Operations Exodus and Solomon (respectively, the resettlement in Israel of Jews from the former Soviet Union and Ethiopia) and programs such as Meals-on-Wheels are more than kind acts of philanthropy; they are holy behavior. A half-century ago, the Nazis not only waged war on the Jewish body; they also tried to destroy the Jewish notion that human beings, because of their creation in God's image, are of infinite value. A major reason the Nazis used Zyklon B gas in murdering Jews was because it cost them less than a penny per person to do so. By expending enormous amounts of money and effort to save lives, the federation community is affirming – in the aftermath of Nazism's assault – the most important of Jewish religious values, the infinite value of human life.

Just as Greenberg's tolerance does not encompass those who would blame the Jews for the Holocaust, so it excludes those of the political left who hold Israel to standards that will ensure its destruction. After the Holocaust, the need for a Jewish homeland was so self-evident that one must question the goodness of any person who wants to see Jews deprived of sufficient military might to defend themselves ("No one should ever be equipped with less power than is necessary to assure one's dignity"). Greenberg taught me that one of the Holocaust's most important lessons is that Jews must never again be so weak that their very weakness tempts others to destroy them. And while power must be used morally, it is immoral to impose upon Israel the kinds of limits that will guarantee its destruction. "If we Jews are five percent better than the rest of the world, we can be a 'light unto the nations.' If we are twenty-five percent better than the rest of the world, we can bring the Messiah. If we're fifty percent better than the rest of the world, we'll all be dead."

Finally, Greenberg is, and will remain, famous for his radical and controversial notion of "voluntary covenant." In espousing the idea that the Holocaust broke (or wounded) the covenant between God and the Jewish people, he is willing to say what many feel, certainly on an emotional level, but are reluctant to articulate: "Therefore, morally speaking, God must repent . . . for having given His chosen people a task that was unbearably cruel and dangerous without having provided for their protection. Morally speaking, then, God can have no claim on the Jews by dint of the Covenant." The covenant, therefore, "Can no longer be commanded and subject to a serious external enforcement"; thus, it becomes voluntary. The miracle of the age, in Greenberg's view, is that "the covenant was broken but the Jewish people, released from its obligations, chose voluntarily to take it on again and renew it. God was in no position to command anymore but the Jewish people were so in love with the dream of redemption that they volunteered to carry on with its mission."

What is often overlooked is that these words, which appear harsh to some or radical to others, are, in fact, words of reconciliation and love between God and Israel. Greenberg concludes that, during the Holocaust, "the Divine Presence was in Auschwitz, suffering, burning and starving . . . ," that is, "sharing the pain in a way that only an Infinite Consciousness and Love could share." God's inaction was part of a greater divine *tzimtzum* (self-limitation) that is a call to humans to take full responsibility for the covenant. Furthermore, Greenberg insists that human voluntary acceptance of the covenant yields a loyalty that is, in fact, more internalized, more idealistic, and more steadfast than ever before. What is more, even though God is more hidden than ever, God is more present than ever. This opens the door to an explosion of holiness in the secular – further eroding the easy, but mistaken, walls and categories that separate the holy and the secular.

I am proud to count myself a disciple of Rabbi Yitz Greenberg, one of the great and seminal Jewish thinkers. Whoever reads this book will be deeply enriched. Yitz Greenberg is one of the great Jewish gifts to the world.

Preface

Rabbi Dr. Shmuly Yanklowitz

Undoubtedly Rabbi Dr. Irving "Yitz" Greenberg is one of the most significant voices of our time. His years of service in the rabbinate, as organizational leader, author, lecturer, and long-time activist for a multitude of spiritual causes has led to the perpetuation of Jewish values across the spectrum of other religious traditions and cultures. Rav Yitz is this generation's consummate bridge builder: He constructs bridges within the Jewish community, as well as between different faiths and over the vast gulf that separates tradition and modernity. While committed to Orthodoxy, Rav Yitz made great contributions across all of Jewish life, always remaining rooted within a forward-looking *halakhic* observance. He is that rare pedagogue who has demonstrated the relevance of a *modern* Judaism while assembling and nurturing the vibrant Jewish institutional landscape that we know today.

Rav Yitz's preeminence in Torah thought is but a minor aspect of his larger role in shaping contemporary Jewish attitudes towards the world. From the time he was ordained at Beth Joseph (Novardok) Rabbinical Seminary and earned a Ph.D in American history at Harvard University in the 1950s, to his tenure as a professional in stimulating the Jewish community, Rav Yitz has been a tireless proponent of a more engaged Judaism. In his understanding of Judaism, pluralism is the ideal while narrow particularism must be eschewed as a remnant from earlier, more precarious times. Rodger Kamenetz's book *The Jew in the Lotus* contains perhaps the most succinct summation concerning Rav Yitz's concern for expanding the vocabulary of Jewish social action: "There was no question in [Rabbi Greenberg's] mind that Judaism takes place in real history and that Jews had to learn from other cultures . . . [He] was particularly concerned that Orthodox Jewish culture had withdrawn into itself, shunning contact with the challenge of pluralism" (49).

While Rav Yitz is a committed pluralist, this volume reflects thinkers who have emerged from Modern (or Open) Orthodoxy. This does not mean that non-Modern Orthodox views about Rav Yitz are of a lesser status. To be sure, these other opinions are significantly valid, but I wanted this volume to focus on the extraordinary amount of work Rav Yitz has done to change the conventional assumptions in the Orthodox world, which are both more insular and more dynamic than meets the eye.

On a personal level, I appreciate Rav Yitz's contributions contributions to social justice: his advancement of Jewish ethics on a global level, his expansion of modern conceptions of T*zelem Elokim,*[1] theology and *tikkun olam* values, as well as the clarity and accessibility he has brought to epistemic pluralism. In some cases the two values of social justice and pluralism come together:

> The only way to wholeness is to heal the world and to work to take the poison out of absolutism without eroding all values and truth in the process. Post-*Shoah* (Post-Holocaust), the yearning for perfecting finitude, properly harnessed, can fuel the drive for *tikkun olam* (mending the world), politically and economically as well as religiously and philosophically (*Theology after the Shoah*).

Perhaps what matters most to so many of us is that Rav Yitz has never been merely an armchair philosopher. He has lived a life committed to serving and advocating for public service. For him, there is no worthy task without personal involvement and heavy lifting. Moreover, Rav Yitz has a unified vision of the Jewish people: We Jews have a unique ethical, religious, and moral obligation to serve our communities, and thus we must be active participants in building a more just society. "Personal service," writes Rav Yitz, "must be brought to the fore as a central value of Jewish tradition and culture":

1. The Jewish theology that all human beings are created in the image of God.

> Every synagogue, school, and organization must teach this norm. Even unaffiliated Jews recognize education and family as synonymous with Jewish values: so should personal service become known as the indispensable expression of Jewishness. . . .
>
> A Jew is commanded not just to do individual acts of *chesed* (kindness) to others but to set aside regular time for volunteering and giving personal service. . . . We must create a Jewish culture in which the final measurement of "was this life worthwhile" will be: Did one set aside regular times for nurturing other human beings? (Personal Service – A Central Jewish Norm for Our Time. CONTACT. 4.1 (2001): 3–4).

We must not be confused. This is not watered-down Judaism nor is it "Judaism-lite." It is, rather, an expansive conception of Jewish action in the world. This approach demands rejecting mindless relativism and instead, encourages respectful and empowered pluralism. One teaching from Rabbi Greenberg has always stayed with me. It goes like this:

> Pluralism means more than accepting or even affirming the other. It entails recognizing the blessings in the other's existence, because it balances one's own position and brings all of us closer to the ultimate goal. Even when we are right in our own position, the other who contradicts our position may be our corrective or our check against going to excess (*For the Sake of Heaven and Earth*, 196).

There is humility found in this pluralism, an acknowledgement that we cannot see the full picture ourselves. We need others to complete the vision, even those who are different from us in temperament and persuasion and with whom we disagree. Only when we open our hearts to all valid views of the world, can we learn from all. Rav Yitz continues:

> The essential difference between pluralism and relativism is that pluralism is based on the principle that there still is an absolute truth. . . . Pluralism is an absolutism that has come to recognize its limitations (ibid., 201–203).

Though Rav Yitz's deeds are too numerous to count, I took on this project both out of love for the man and for his ideas. I continue to find Rav Yitz's ideas, his courage, his leadership, and his emotional support to be inspirational. This *Festschrift* (collection of writings published in honor of a scholar) contains contributions from some of the greatest scholars and leaders of Modern Orthodoxy; it is meant to be a singular place where Rav Yitz's intellectual children come together in awe and respect for their spiritual father. We know that his ideas, his leadership, and his accomplishments throughout the entire Jewish world need to be sustained and transmitted not merely to the next generation, but to the many generations to come.

Throughout the process of putting this volume together, it was a delight to work with each of the talented thinkers and leaders that contributed. Each of them has been deeply affected by Rav Yitz intellectually and personally. I'm grateful for their willingness to share their thoughts and tributes.

I want to express my gratitude to Tzvi Mauer, Michal Alatin, and Pearl Friedman of KTAV Publishing House for their partnership, generosity, and guidance to make this book a reality.

I want to thank Rabbi Dr. Eugene Korn & Abraham J. Frost for their diligent editing assistance, which really helped substantially during the long process of shaping this book from a dream to a tangible collection.

Lastly, I want to thank my dear wife Shoshana and my children Amiella Rachel, Meir Lev Kook, and Maya Neshama for making everything in my life sweet and meaningful. Without their love, nothing would be worth doing. And, of course, thanks to the Creator of the World for making everyone and everything possible.

May this book inspire you, dear reader, to continue to grow deeply in all your intellectual, spiritual, and ethical pursuits.

Proceeds from this book will go toward furthering Jewish education, as this has always been one of Rav Yitz's greatest passions and life-long commitments.

I am not only grateful to Rav Yitz for these teachings, modeled and taught over many decades, but also for his personal guidance, partnership, and friendship. He gives his students time and attention. Perhaps that is his greatest gift.

Personal Tributes

Wisdom from the Gentle Giant

Dr. Erica Brown

In the trenches of Jewish education, intellect and character are woven together into whole cloth. Separating them has inevitably led to backlashes throughout Jewish history; overly *pilpulistic* study of rabbinic literature arguably birthed some of our most important movements as correctives, from the medieval pietists to early strains of Hasidut to the *Mussar* Movement.[1] The move from the brain to the heart has never been simple for those who prize the intellect. Ideally, these two organs live in symbiotic harmony, as Martin Buber reminds us in his essay "Teaching and Deeds:" "The process of education involves the person as a whole."[2] We find a similar sentiment in the introduction to Rabbi Yitz Greenberg's book, *Sage Advice*, his commentary on *Ethics of the Fathers*, where he provides insight into his choice of subject:

> . . . Torah culture [is] an ecology, designed to mold a human being of good character, who would establish ethical relationships and take caring responsibility for fellow human beings. With its focus on character traits and moral formation, Ethics of the Fathers fit this model; therefore, the book was regarded with esteem in the movement. Under the *Mussar*niks, I also became caught up in the

1. A Jewish ethical, educational and cultural movement that developed in the 19th century in Lithuania, particularly among Orthodox Lithuanian Jews.

2. Martin Buber, "Teaching and Deeds," in *The Writings of Martin Buber* ed. Will Herberg (New York: Meridian, 1956), 317.

> challenge of connecting people to Jewish tradition and making it a force shaping their lives.[3]

Anyone following the trajectory of R. Yitz's professional life understands that when he writes about connecting Jewish people to tradition as a force that shapes lives, that this could be an apt summation of his career. R. Yitz places a premium on human interaction, on identifying the uniqueness of the individual before him in a counseling moment, on creating a safe space and a bond that feels durable and tender. I experienced this on several occasions myself when I sought out his advice, unafraid to make myself vulnerable in his presence because he, without articulating it, invited me to do so. I also witnessed it as a faculty member on retreats where I observed R. Yitz, often in what was supposed to be down time, tucked into a couch beside a retreat participant, listening with laser focus and without judgment. When my copy of *Sage Advice* arrived, I smiled at the cover, thinking how perfectly it captured both him and the ideal of a teaching relationship. Those who have only read R. Yitz's works and been taken by his pithy observations or vast knowledge may not have sampled the most impactful aspects of his teaching and ministering: *his* sage advice.

A student who asks advice of a teacher takes an enormous risk of personal exposure, of confusion, of possible humiliation. He or she – in seeking the confidentiality of the other – also hands power over to the confider. A secret shared can be a secret owned by others, and this revelation can feel weighty and uncomfortable. The burden can be lifted through a compassionate ear, but whether or not one has chosen to reveal oneself to a thoughtful listener is rarely known ahead of time. We have all made mistakes in thinking that someone who appeared to be sensitive from the podium might be the same in the confessional booth. R. Yitz takes his role as counselor seriously. I asked colleagues and students to share small "Yitz" moments that illustrate the role of educator as sage counselor, as dispenser or model of wisdom.

*

3. Yitz Greenberg, *Sage Advice* (Jerusalem: Maggid, 2016), ix.

"One of the things I've appreciated most is the confidence that R. Yitz instilled in me," says one loving disciple. "From the time I met him – when I knew nothing – I wanted to be close to him, and he made that happen." This young man met R. Yitz when he was twenty. He was an undergrad at a Hillel event for the weekend and only at the beginnings of what would become the long, winding road to an intense Jewish personal and professional life. He spent the better part of the weekend speaking with R. Yitz and was, in his own words "enraptured by him." Before R. Yitz left, this young undergraduate asked him to sign one of his books. He inscribed it, "This is the beginning of what I hope will be a long friendship." This was simply bewildering to the recipient. "He wrote that to me, and I was twenty years old, and I had so little to offer him at that stage in my life." And yet, it *was* the beginning of an enduring and very magical relationship, just as the inscription predicted.

*

A mutual friend calls Rabbi Yitz the Gentle Giant. His towering height belies his humility in a counseling situation, his capacity to consider the totality of another's situation, his companionship, and his warmth. R. Yitz often communicates to an individual what he values in them, as one man shared, "He saw something special in me and continually reminded me of that in many ways." Another said that R. Yitz was always quick to tell her how much he enjoyed her sense of humor. She was disappointed that he did not, perhaps, see more in her but he explained how powerful this comic side is in relaxing others, in making teachings easier to absorb, in the power that exists in making someone laugh. Thus, she arrived at a conclusion about R. Yitz: "There is nothing simple about his observations. They are exquisite in their specificity and carefully delivered." If you pay careful attention to these aspects of his personality, you hear the tenderness and optimism in his written words as well:

> In our time, God has become even less manifest and even more present – to those who refocus their eyes and ears to listen. Thus, human beings have become even more responsible for bringing God's love and care to all creatures. They are now the supreme agents for divine liberation and redemptive activity. Human behavior and teaching – whether openly religious or presented

> as secular – have become the primary source of making God's presence visible in the world. Human actions make God believed in people's eyes and provide sanctification of His name.[4]

In this lyrical way, R. Yitz describes the role of the Jewish educator in the most profound sense: making God's presence visible in the world. In traditional settings, a teacher does this both from the front of the classroom, in spontaneous hallway conversations between formal learning and in the small, private and scheduled interactions students have with a teacher. But this emerges most organically from the way the Jewish educator models what he or she teaches.

*

> Ben Zoma would say: Who is wise? One who learns from every man. As is stated (Psalms 119:99): From all my teachers I have grown wise, for Your testimonials are my meditation.

R. Yitz often said to his students that they were his teachers, especially when responding to feedback. This humility was very striking for one of them. "He always says, 'I've learned more from my students than my teachers,' and he always reminded me of that, which is clearly ridiculous because what did I have to teach him? But it made me feel good." This student felt that this is just an aspect of his greater generosity. "He opens his home and his life in the most personal ways without any hesitations. He has spoken with me about his children, his grandchildren, about losing a child. He is always curious and continuously learning."

*

Buber spoke cogently of the role of the educator in the delicate position of bridging the generations, that teachings with universal import can cut across time and space when they are not only delivered but embodied:

> In these recurring encounters between a generation which has reached its full development and one which is still developing,

4. Yitz Greenberg, *Sage Advice* (Jerusalem: Maggid, 2016), xi.

> the ultimate aim is not to transmit a separable something. What matters is that time and again an older generation, staking its entire existence on that act, comes to a younger with the desire to teach, waken, and shape it; then the holy spark leaps across the gap. Transmitted content and form are subordinate to the tradition of existence as such, and become valid only because of it. The total, living, Jewish human being is the transmitting agent; total, living, Jewish humanity is transmitted. Tradition is concentrated in the existence of the Jew himself. He lives it, and it is he who approaches the new generation and influences it by producing the blend of the old and the new.[5]

If, for Buber, tradition is concentrated in the Jewish person, then what we find in the great Jewish educator is the capacity to live the teachings and also to inspire others to do so by bringing the old to the new.

*

At an educational retreat some years ago, there was a long and winding line at the registration desk. It was Friday afternoon, and people were frustrated. Some people pulled rank – politicians, professors and those who were Sabbath observant and needed to speed up the process on a winter afternoon. There were elderly people who found it hard to stand. Many of them simply cut the line, complaining that an hour-and-a-half was simply too long to endure. Not R. Yitz, observed one of his colleagues. And because of his height you could see him from all over the lobby, way at the back end of the line, smiling his gentle and huge smile with those shining blue eyes. He greeted everyone who came over to say hello, patiently hearing their stories and listening intently. This ordinary, indeed prosaic, moment was a source of deep inspiration: "For me, despite his tremendous insights into Torah, this was one of the deepest teachings I ever got from him."

*

Sooner or later, if you hang around with R. Yitz long enough, you will hear him state the moral imperative of continuity: all Jewish families

5. Buber: 319.

should have one more child beyond the number they had planned to make up for the lost one and a half million children killed in the *Shoah*. It is a recommendation he lives through his own large family and one he encourages others to live. If every Jewish family "compensates" in this way, we create a future that defies our past. This suggestion gave rise to what have been famously called "the Yitz babies," children born to parents who were profoundly moved by R. Yitz's teaching and acted on it. And in so doing, an optimism glimmers through our dark past, a theme that winds itself through much of R. Yitz's writings and teachings. In his commentary to *Ethics of the Fathers* 6:11, he writes:

> Long after this universe has contracted and been swallowed up in eternal darkness, void and silence, the cosmic Maker will reign and likely preside over the creation and decay of further universes. But in the moment that humans grasp the process and the Maker, they are one with infinity and eternity.[6]

Our mortality is twinned with a desire for transcendence, to touch that which will live long beyond us. On some level, having children helps us both imitate God as Creator and Redeemer, bringing light into these painful shadows. Children also ensure that some piece of our flawed and limited human selves live on when we are gone. If this is true for those of us who have fertility choices, it should be even more so for those whose lives were cut tragically short in the Holocaust, those whose very names have faded over time.

*

Hearing R. Yitz speak powerfully about our need to repopulate the Jewish world post-*Shoah*, many were inspired, but this message could also create tensions among those who felt that they should or could not expand their families or were wrestling with infertility. How should they react to R. Yitz's suggestion?

One such couple was actually pregnant, yet their oldest son was diagnosed in utero with a birth defect. It was a scary diagnosis, and they had been advised by one doctor to terminate the pregnancy. Young

6. Buber: 333 citing Genesis Rabba 3:7; Ecclesiastes Rabba 3:14.

and afraid, they had no idea what to do with this information. R. Yitz and Blu were the first people they spoke to about the situation because they had, by their admission, learned practically everything about life from this special couple. R. Yitz made them see that having a family is the biggest value in Jewish life. "When Yitz talks about the triumph of life, he lives it." Yitz heard their story:

> We spent hours with him. He gave us both the legal and the human side of this – he encouraged us to choose life but helped us understand that choosing life was not a simple decision to keep or not keep this child. While prioritizing life he also helped us understand that sometimes choosing life means making decisions that do not feel that way immediately. Had we not had this baby, it would have been the biggest mistake we could have made but either way we knew he loved us and supported our decision. When we told him we were keeping the baby, he was very supportive. And he spent time with us in the hospital, at a pretty frightening time when the baby was very sick, and he was totally present for us. He remains an important figure in our lives and in our children's lives as well.

On the flip side, another student approached R. Yitz. She did not want more children but her husband did. Their fertility disagreement was proving a strain on their relationship. She decided to approach the rabbi, knowing his feelings about the importance of family and the significance of repopulating the Jewish community to honor the memory of those children murdered by the Nazis. She heard him but was not sure she could go through with it. She wanted his insight on the struggle, yet deep down she also wanted his "permission" to be exempt from this *mitzvah*. "He helped me to put my own resistance into a larger perspective, so that I would at least thoroughly challenge myself to make sure I was not missing something important. But he responded with such tenderness and kindness and empathy and respect – embodying that in his relationship with a student was more important to him than his deeply felt imperative to grow the Jewish population." He wears his rabbinic authority lightly – using it to prod and guide, assist and affirm.

*

In the link the teacher forms with the student, Buber contends that: "The spark that leaps from him who teaches to him who learns rekindles a spark of that fire which lifted the mountain of revelation to the very heart of heaven."[7] Imagine for a moment being at Sinai, seeing the flames, hearing the thunderous sound of the Decalogue, trembling before the presence of the Holy One. Each spark off the mountain, as it were, contained and mirrored future sparks that exist when an old teaching reignites in the life of a new generation, "awakening and activating our common bond with our Father," in Buber's words. If this is true for the student/teacher relationship in a study hall, it is even truer when a teacher confronts a student in their shared humanity, in a counseling moment.

Many of us owe R. Yitz a debt of gratitude for guiding and mentoring us and for mentoring us to mentor others, often through the simple act of intentional listening. There is the gift of R. Yitz's words as an intellectual – sometimes radical, always expansive, impressive, and challenging – and then there is the gift of his silence, a penetrating silence in which he tries to capture *our* words and make us whole again with his wisdom. The great teacher not only expands the mind. The great teacher holds up the spark from Sinai, offers it to us, encourages us to become that spark and then, through loving counsel, gently lifts us across our hurdles so that we, too, can shine.

7. Buber: 324.

One Shavuot Night: Rav Yitz's "Prism of Life"

Rabbi Dr. Seth Farber

It was a Shavu'ot night in the late 1980s when we finally had an opportunity to learn with Rabbi Yitz Greenberg. Having grown up in Riverdale as best friends of the Greenberg kids, we had plenty of chances to hear R. Yitz teach. Yet that night was different.

Being raised in the Greenberg sphere gave us unique insight into Yitz's life and thinking. From age seven or eight we already knew what "the Third Era" meant. We grew up joking about the "failed messiah" before it was a blog. I never saw Yitz in shul without a book – and often the book had hundreds of paperclips in it referencing things that only Yitz understood.

We also knew a personal side of Yitz. His office in the house was a veritable file cabinet: There was a constant pile of papers and books piled up in every corner, which miraculously didn't fall down. Yitz's extraordinary powers of concentration led us to joke that he seemed to be in a constant state of "unaware." As kids, we spent hours contemplating the various qualities of our parents ("Does your Abba really know that you don't go to school every day?") and we even once bet how long it would take Yitz to notice if we went through with our plan for the Farber and Greenberg kids to switch homes one night.

We spent summers in Gloucester, Massachusetts with the Greenbergs, including one memorable trip where we travelled in a motorhome that Yitz couldn't fit into. Completely enmeshed in each other's lives, we schooled together, swam together (in the Greenberg's semi-private pool in Riverdale), played tennis and ping-pong together. We moved homes with the Greenbergs and watched them go off to Israel for a year in 1974. We watched them come back to the new house next door, and then a few years later, again next door. We went to Yeshiva together, came on *Aliyah*[1] together, partied together, and more than we should have, mourned together.

Yitz spoke at my bar mitzvah and the bar mitzvahs of my brothers, and taught us in multiple venues from the Shavuoton at Camp Ella Fohs sponsored by SAR in the early 1970s through graduations, at parties and later at our family's private celebration in honor of my *Semikhah.*[2] Though a world-renowned scholar, his personal attention to crafting the particularly right message for the occasion was striking.

And all this gave us ample opportunity to hear R. Yitz teach. During the summers in Gloucester in Yitz and Blu's country home that they had rented or purchased (it was never really all that clear) following their move to New York, we were exposed to Yitz's reading and expositions of each week's *parashah*. It never really bothered us that there was no *shul* in Gloucester, and Shabbat mornings were spent dreaming of the ocean (right over the porch) and hearing Yitz teach about the *parashah*. At our many Shabbat meals in Gloucester and in Riverdale, there was the requisite *divrei Torah* that somehow always included the words "sanctify life." Those meals also gave us an opportunity to hear R. Yitz talk to other scholars who were frequently at Yitz and Blu's for Shabbat. And of course once I became a community rabbi, a number of times I invited Yitz to speak in my shul.

There were times when I was left out of Yitz's teaching. In 1986, while I was studying at Yeshivat Har Etzion, I asked Yitz if he wanted me to arrange an appointment between him and Rabbi Aharon Lichtenstein, my *Rosh Yeshiva*. I was naïve, not fully understanding the public debates they had together towards the end of their time in Yeshiva University and subsequently Rav Yitz and Rav Aharon had written articles in the Yeshiva University *Commentator* (Yeshiva College's newspaper) in the 1960s focusing on Modern Orthodox theology and the philosophy of *halakhah* that became "must reading" for the intellectual stream in Modern Orthodoxy. They were both icons, and I was unaware of how charged such a meeting could be. (I'm not even sure why each agreed to

1. Moved to live in Israel
2. Rabbinic ordination

sit down with the other.) Either way, R. Yitz came to meet Rav Aharon at the yeshiva in 1986, but when I asked if I could join the meeting, I was refused.

Growing up with R. Yitz as a role model was inspiring. We knew he was something special, and yet, as we grew into our high school classes – where many of our rabbis were *yeshivish* and in the best case were ambivalent about Yitz and, in the worst case, disparaging – we began to understand that things were complex. When we spent our gap years in Israel, few knew about him, but those of us who went to YU and Stern knew that our rabbi from the Riverdale Jewish Center wasn't like other rabbis.

But that Shavu'ot night was different.

For us young men and women – mostly friends of Yitz's kids – R. Yitz's Torah that night wasn't a lecture, but a kind of *chavruta*[3]. The learning took place around Yitz's dining room table, and it had the feeling of a *tish*. For all of us, some in the YU *semikhah* program and some having finished two or more years learning in Israel, we were going to meet Yitz, perhaps for the first time, on territory that we considered sacred. We weren't going to study but to learn, to be engaged, to challenge and be challenged. This was going to be a unique opportunity for us to discuss Yitz's ideas for us, his children's friends. At this time, we all knew that some in the Modern Orthodox rabbinate were attempting to marginalize Yitz, some of us even understood why. Many of us were torn about what had happened to Yitz over the years, and while we were sympathetic to the man, this meeting was going to give us a couple of hours to understand Yitz ourselves.

So that Shavu'ot night, a handful of us decided to forego the "traditional" poring over *halakhah* and *gemara* that had pretty much characterized our Shavu'ot nights of learning until that point, and spend a couple of hours learning Torah with Yitz. This wasn't going to be *Gemara,* Rashi, *Tosafot,* and Rambam, but a look at a version of Orthodoxy from one of its expositors.

The text Yitz chose was emblematic of who he was, and I believe that evening provided the skeleton for an article he eventually published about Rabbi Soloveitchik, entitled something like "Five Doors the

3. Learning Torah with a study partner.

Rav Opened but Didn't Walk Through." Forever etched in my mind, that evening we learned a passage about Reb Hayim Brisker (the Rav's grandfather) from *Halakhic Man*. For many of us, R. Yitz was a link to Rabbi Soloveitchik, and his interpretation of the passage reflected his worldview through the prism of Reb Hayim.

The passage speaks about Soloveitchik's approach to the sanctity of life. Yitz pondered over the introductory section that focuses on purity and impurity, highlighting the fact that the Soloveitchiks shunned cemeteries because they reflected the antithesis of life. (For Yitz this was no issue, as he is a *kohen*). After discussing some general approaches to life and death, the apex of the evening arrived when Yitz read the passage in which Rabbi Soloveitchik discusses his family's approach toward feeding someone in need of food on Yom Kippur. Despite the fact that many *Rishonim* (rabbis during the 11th to 15th centuries) believe that such a person should be fed incrementally, so as not to violate the biblical prohibition of eating, Rabbi Soloveitchik tells a story that concludes with the remarkable statement of Reb Hayim: "When my father was about to travel to Rasseyn . . . to take up a rabbinical post, R. Hayim took him aside and said, 'I command you to follow my view regarding a sick person in danger on the Day of Atonement. It is an absolute *halakhic* truth.'"

For Yitz, this was not a theoretical statement, but a statement about the very nature of the *halakhah*. *Halakhah* must be interpreted by humanity and be its blueprint for sanctifying life. It is inconceivable any other way. The historical claims about Rabbi Yohanan Ben Zakkai's reformulation of Judaism were secondary to the understanding Torah and *halakhah* through the prism of sanctifying life, and to appreciating its beauty. Rav Soloveitchik was making a practical statement about the influence of meta-*halakhah* on *halakhic* practice. For Yitz, the prism of life was as valuable a tool as the *Mishneh Berurah* to determining our observance patterns.

I don't remember about how convinced we were that night, but it was Yitz at his best. It was who he was then and who he has continued to be throughout his entire life.

Meeting Yitz Greenberg: A Fifty Year Memoire

Rabbi Daniel Landes

My first meeting with Yitz Greenberg about fifty years ago was accidental, confusing, jarring, and illuminating. I was a junior at the Chicago – soon to be called Ida Crown – Jewish Academy. I missed the South Side school bus that took us up North to Melrose, so I took the Illinois Central train to Downtown. From there I would hop on the 151 bus, but as I waited for the bus I saw a stream of Jewish people, mostly well-dressed middle aged or older, headed to the Pick Congress Hotel. I remembered the prior day's March 11, 1967 *Chicago Tribune* front page headline announcing that former Prime Minister David Ben Gurion was to address the World Jewish Bible Society. My missing the bus was evidently a fortuitous accident. So I played hooky, skipped school, and got an education instead.

I joined about 2,000 people in listening to Ben Gurion join a lively ninety minute conversation on the first three chapters of Exodus. Brilliant, passionate, and impressive, and we all felt that we were in front of living history and a living Bible. Yet somehow, I had heard it all before – the déjà vu of a sixteen year-old with a good education. As we filed out, I read the title of a breakout session – "Biblical Theology" – and the names and titles of the presenters. I was startled to see that Rabbi Dr. Irving Greenberg, an Orthodox rabbi was one of the speakers on a topic that confused me: "Biblical Humanism." All the talks and endless sermons I heard while growing up Orthodox in Chicago had taught me one thing – that we Orthodox Jews were not humanists. But having participated with my family in civil rights issues and having read some existentialist works of philosophy and literature that my parents supplied, I knew one other thing – that along with my punctilious observance and complete faith, deep down I was secretly a humanist.

I entered and grabbed a seat. My eyes fixed upon the panel and I was certain that the short man with the carefully trimmed dark beard and black *kippah*[1] was Rabbi Greenberg, and the one sitting next to him must be the clean shaven, gangly Hebrew Union College graduate, Rabbi Prof. Steven S. Schwarzchild. I was confused. The "Orthodox rabbi" spoke first and gave a brilliant and well-nuanced talk on free will in the Torah with appropriate references to Kant and Kierkegaard, and a cautionary word about the dangerously romantic illusions of humanism. Great, but not surprising. When the "Reform rabbi" got up to speak, I was disconcerted to see that somehow his place card read Greenberg. Surely, a mistake. Well, the speaker spoke directly to the issue – my issue – of how underneath its theo-centrism, the Torah actually did reflect a profound, realistic, and encouraging sense of how to be human. This tall young rabbi with a strange, enormous bald head spoke meaningfully of topics that we now all know well belong to the Greenberg menu: inclusivity, the humanizing of slavery, the urgent need of sexual intimacy, the place of ethical sensitivity in biblical society; and he spoke of the rabbinic development of these issues, given the impossibility of putting a perfect structure in place all at once in history.

What Yitz said was strikingly illuminating for three reasons. First, it placed humanistic concerns at the center of *halakhah* and not as an act of *noblesse oblige* by the truly pious nor as anecdote fodder for sermonic barrages proclaiming how great Judaism really is. Next Yitz did not hesitate to place up front the problems of unfulfilled *halakhic* moral paradigms, such as the slowness of *halakhic* development and its sometimes tin ear to human needs. Third was his surprising understanding of the relationship of *d'rabanan* (rabbinic legislation) to *d'oraitah* (Torah legislation). I had been taught that the Torah model was of perfection and the *d'rabanan* was a way of adapting it to a general *yeridah* (moral and spiritual descent).

R. Yitz turned this on its head. In his description, the Torah was often the starting place for morality and the rabbis' task was to move it along. I was completely jarred, hearing that the Torah, in a sense, was producing

1. Jewish religious head covering.

a *be-d'evad* (post facto) that was meant to be succeeded by a rabbinic *le-ḥatchilah* (ideal) slowly but surely throughout the generations. This was a dangerous, but most compelling, ideal and process for the *frum* religious humanist, which I only later understood that I was becoming.

Yitz elucidated Torah as a shared human-God project that wasn't (only) interested in legal formalism, or even the doing of good deeds. He insisted that the Torah actually demanded getting somewhere better in the now and, even more, later on. Although in those days he sounded a lot less patient with the slow speed of the roll-out of a better Jewish and universal world, all of this was an exciting and validating universal and progressive viewpoint that seemed rooted in a profound understanding of Torah.

But was it *frum*? I was paralyzed in my seat. My anxiety at the thought that maybe in the end this Irving Greenberg really *was* a HUC rabbi was relieved when after the session Yitz put together a *minchah minyan,* which then, and in the temperament of this "secular" event, was actually audacious. (I noted that he wasn't saying a Mourner's *Kaddish).* Yitz *davened* strongly, but humbly. I felt encouraged.

Shortly after, the Six-Day War broke out and Jewish emotions burst forth. Yitz was a great hit in Chicagoland, and was back often to speak. I followed him everywhere in the area including two trips to Indiana and many North Side locations (I lived in the old far South Side, which was emptying out of Jews, along with white flight, but my parents' commitment to integration still remained). It culminated with a four day invitation-only conference at the Barat College of the Sacred Heart, a very beautiful women's Catholic college in Lake Forest, IL, thirty miles north of Chicago. It was a long trip, but my Dad (*z"l*) gave me the car, commenting, "You should know that rabbi's speeches by heart already." Not completely, but I had his main stories down. Nevertheless, Yitz's spontaneous humor and puns continued to be an unceasing fountain of laughter and insight.

The conference was for Catholic professors of religion who wanted a new way to teach Judaism, but I invited myself and somehow got in. All I knew was that this kind of ecumenicism was *assur* (prohibited). I had read the Rav's 1964 essay, "Confrontation," a number of times and had spoken to my teacher, the great Professor Rabbi Eliezer Berkovits, who had little trust in such dialogue, believing it to be a Catholic cover-up for their part in the Holocaust. My experience growing up on the South Side with Catholics, mostly Irish, had more to do with fisticuffs around Easter, and some carefully rehearsed "remarks" on a young adult public early Sunday morning interfaith TV show that I was part of. This conference was at an early stage of Christian-Jewish dialogue and the Catholic participants had never encountered an Orthodox (what they said was "a real") rabbi before. Indeed, the participants were sophisticated well-trained philosophers, theologians, and historians, mostly clergy. They were far from hostile, but yet they naively espoused opinions about Judaism that were primitive and not far from anti-Semitic. Yitz more than won them over. He was totally honest about Judaism (including its warts) and honest about his beliefs. This was dialogue at its best, and it allowed him to say pointed and direct things about Catholicism, and about Catholics and Jews. The students listened and thought, and asked many questions. The whole process was transformational: hearts and minds were deeply changed, helped by the presence of Blu Greenberg, whose beauty, brilliance, and vivacity were crucial to the mix.

This conference had its moments. Leaving on my long commute the first day, I put on the only garment left in my closet, since the day before I sent a trunk of clothes to Israel. (I was about to become the only American at Yeshivat Mercaz HaRav.) I showed up to the Barat College of the Sacred Heart wearing a black suit with a white turtle-neck, and a brown *kippah* lost in my (then abundant) curly brown hair. The bevy of nuns attending some of the formal talks dubbed me the "young Jewish Father," since they were already calling Yitz "the tall Jewish Father." That same day, during a break and meandering through the lush gardens, I discovered in a secluded arbor two of the delightful Greenberg children. They were sitting on the laps of nuns, and out of some medieval impulse I immediately lunged to save them before Blu entered and introduced the "babysitters" as Sisters Jo and Francine.

I returned from an intense year of learning (from "the Nazir," Rav Tzvi Yehudah, Rav Shaul Yisraeli, Rav Avrum Shapira, and other *Gedolim*), and entered Yeshiva College and RIETS. Soon, I realized it was imperative that I study formally with Yitz. Two of his classes became hot tickets and I did not have the seniority or the prerequisites to get in. Yitz kindly wrote a note to the dean allowing me in with undeserved praise for my abilities. Normally I would have been embarrassed, but I so wanted to attend that I swallowed it, but then discovered that he had done the same for a number of other young men, writing something unique about each one. He actually had high expectations for us.

He set a high standard in class that was the equivalent of a graduate seminar and a senior Talmud *shiur*.[2] Indeed many of my co-students were also *talmidim* in the best RIETS *shiurim*. They came because they were madly curious by what Yitz had to say with many intoxicated by his blend of analysis, literary sensitivity, and hard history. The uproarious humor and the relevance to our lives seemed dead earnest. And sometimes it was truly surprising. One of the classes was a history of the *Mussar* Movement[3] disguised as a general history course, something like "Nineteenth Century Social Thought." But the real point of conflict was that we all had had earlier experience of *mussar*[4] study and *mussar* mentors, which often left us at best cold and at worse morose and antagonistic. *Mussar*'s seemingly endless tortuous practice of self-criticism and reflection was not only at odds with a faster hipper late '60s early '70s general culture, but it also was contrary to the set religious mode of Yeshiva at that point. Intellectually, Yeshiva was decisively "Brisk": strong category building in Talmudic dialectics that penetrated theological thinking. If you wanted to be creative, then you could "synthesize" that method with literature or philosophical challenges or even return to something of *halakhic* interest. Clearly, *Mussar* was not on the radar.

Yitz offered a way to consider what was then an "alternative" way of doing Jewish practice and thinking Jewishly. He laid out the early modern secular challenges that created the need for *mussar*, a discipline of both inwardness and of moral rectitude. He showed us that *mussar* was not a given – as we experienced it in our strongly traditional Orthodox society – but a created culture and society. In so doing, he offered the tantalizing possibility that our Orthodox world could also be recreated and rethought through with its own new and unique institutions and ways of living that fit our own late twentieth century challenges. That

2. A class for studying religious Jewish texts.

3. A Jewish ethical, educational and cultural movement that developed in the 19th century in Lithuania, particularly among Orthodox Lithuanian Jews.

4. Moral conduct, instruction, or discipline.

was both enticing and fear producing. Orthodoxy at Yeshiva produced a stabile, if often fragile, middle-class way of observance and learning. It certainly had its triumphs – you could be religious and learned and get into a great medical or law school, and take from the outside culture a measured hedonism. But for many of my best classmates all this, somehow, did not seem enough. Many of the most talented were on the brink of giving up on the religious life even if their defection was quiet. What many of those right-wing critics of Yitz did not realize was that his vision of an intellectually breathing, generous, and world concerned with Judaism was what kept the potential "defectors" as vibrant members of the learning and observing Jewish world. Being part of this partnership with God through Torah to improve ourselves, our culture, and our Jewish and surrounding worlds meant a positive reengagement with our teachers who too often dismissed this whole process ironically.

The classes were full of the intense debate that R. Yitz thrives on. His course on The Holocaust, justly famous as the first academic class of its type, had great impact. Almost everyone in it (but not me) were second generation survivors. Intellectually and spiritually it was for them an encounter group in which they could begin to understand their family history. For all of us, it meant confronting the major challenge in and of modernity. Yitz taught us to see the actual historical record as the sacred story and he taught us not to flinch when confronting its implications on all levels: political, social, theological. We should be shattered and humbled and never turn away. Casual racism, mechanical theodicies, insensitivities to those oppressed became the true obscenities.

In all this, of course, we learned from the man. We saw in him the utter courage of Novardok *Mussar,* of his own teachers, who stood up through their humility to the worst Soviet oppression; and in his vision we discovered the teachings of Slobodka that testified to the human being's potential greatness. In teaching the Shoah, we saw in Yitz a true Kohen with an inherent revulsion of death and an advocate of life which is the *summa* of his ongoing theology. Those of us who studied with him learned of the prophetic use of laughter generated even by the lowliest of all puns, and we learned of the vitality, support and warmth of family life when we visited Yitz and Blu in their Riverdale home.

May his work continue to flourish.

Building Bridges

Rabbi Yitz Greenberg, Christian-Jewish Relations, and *Halakhah*: A Brief Overview

Rabbi Dr. Dov S. Zakheim

How should contemporary Jewry relate to Christianity, a religion that was its most sanguinary tormentor for nearly two millennia? Rabbi Irving "Yitz" Greenberg's answer was unequivocal: "For the first time, the 'Other' is no longer other."[1] Engagement and encounter with those who do not share his religious, political or social worldview has been Greenberg's watchword for decades. As a founder and the first president of CLAL, the National Jewish Center for Learning and Leadership, Greenberg has been an inspiration to those who would move Jewish-Christian relations in a new, positive direction. In his seminal article on pluralism, entitled "Seeking the Religious Roots of Pluralism," Greenberg asserted that "pluralism is grounded in the deep structures of Judaism and of religious life."[2] His book, *For the Sake of Heaven and Earth,* expanded on this notion, explicitly focusing on Jewish-Christian dialogue. As he put it in a subsequent interview, disagreements between the two religions "are for the sake of heaven, not be seen as denying the other side.... You don't necessarily reconcile or come to agreement. But you do understand the validity and the role of the other even when they disagree."[3]

On its face, Greenberg's view of how to relate to Christianity is

1. Alice Chasen, "Disagreeing in the Service of God," http://www.beliefnet.com/Faiths/2006/03/Disagreeing-In-The-Service-Of-God.aspx

2. Irving Greenberg, "Seeking the Religious Roots of Pluralism: In the Image of God and Covenant," *Journal of Ecumenical Studies* 34 (Summer 1997), 386.

3. Chasen, "Disagreeing."

seemingly a marked departure from long-standing Jewish view, and particularly Orthodox attitudes, to the religion that it spawned.

Christianity was long considered to be a form of idolatry. R. Tahlifa bar Avdimi's dictum in Samuel's name postulated that one could never do business with a Christian, since it was forbidden to do business on Sunday as well as three days before and after Sunday, that is, any day of the week.[4] For centuries thereafter, many of Judaism's leading lights adopted the views of Rav Sa'adyah Ga'on and Maimonides, both of whom considered Christianity to be a form of *avodah zarah* – idolatry. Rav Sa'adyah labelled as idolators those who viewed the founder of their religion to be either consisting of both body and spirit that were an outgrowth of God, or with a human body but whose spirit was an emanation from God, or as possessing both human and body and spirit but who had, as it were, an additional spirit that was a divine emanation.[5]

Maimonides conceded that the religions spawned by Jesus, and for that matter Mohammed:

> were only in order to pave the way for the king Messiah and to organize the entire world to serve God as one . . . How so? The world is already filled with the words of the Messiah and of Torah and the Mitzvot and these matters have spread to the furthest islands and many nations whose hearts are uncircumcised, and they discuss these matters and the words of Torah, some saying these commandments were true but already have been nullified in current times and have not been in force for generations while others say they have hidden meanings and are not as they seem, and messiah has already come and revealed those secrets. And when the [real] king Messiah will emerge and will arise and succeed all will immediately return and recognize that their fathers inherited falsehood and that they had been misled by their fathers and prophets.[6]

4. BT *Avodah zarah* 6a, 7b. See also A. Mishcon, trans. *Avodah zarah* (London: Soncino, 1983), 6a, fn. a9, and Ephraim E. Urbach, *The Halakhah: Its Sources and Development* trans. Raphael Posner (Tel Aviv: Modan, 1996), 218.

5. Rabbi Sa'adyah Ga'on, *Ha'emunot VeDe'ot*, trans. Rabbi Yehuda Ibn Tibbon, 2:7.

6. Rabbi Moses ben Maimon, *Mishneh Torah, Hilkhot Melakhim* 11:4. This passage was censored and does not appear in standard version of *Mishneh Torah*. It is cited

Despite this seemingly favorable attitude towards Christians, as well as Muslims, Maimonides actually was far more explicit and vituperative regarding the idolatrous nature of Christianity than R. Sa'adyah had been. Maimonides asserted that:

> Jesus the Nazarite, who thought himself to be the Messiah ... caused the extermination of Jews by the sword, brought about the scattering and debasement of their descendants, and mutated the Torah and misled the majority of the world to serve a god other than the Lord.[7]

Other medieval decisors and expounders of the Talmud (*Rishonim*) took a more liberal view of Christianity, however, arguing that while it did represent a syncretic belief that was forbidden to Jews, it was not idolatry. This argument was first put forward by the twelfth century Tosafist, Rabbeinu Tam, Rashi's grandson, who also was Maimonides' older contemporary. Rabbeinu Tam made his case in the context of a Talmudic dictum by the father of the *Amora*[8] Samuel that it was forbidden to enter a business partnership with a heathen. Samuel's father argued that in the event of a dispute between the partners, a not uncommon occurrence in his times as well as ours, the heathen would be required to take an oath. He would do so in the name of his deity, thereby violating the Biblical verse: "Make no mention of the name of other gods, neither let it be heard out of thy mouth."[9] In what

---

verbatim in R. Shlomo Zalman Havlin, "*Nusach HaRambam Besof Perek Yud ALef Me'Hilkhot Melakhim: Amiti or Mezuyaf*" (The version of Maimonides at the end of the Laws of Kings: Authentic or a Forgery," *Yeshurun* 29 (Elul 5773/August/September 2013), 789. R. Havlin makes a strong case that this passage is indeed authentic. This passage prompted a major debate regarding the nature of Christianity's paving the way for the widespread acceptance of Torah when the true Messiah arrives. See the comments of R/ Yechiel Michel Schlesinger, in ibid. 799; and R. Zvi Gertner, R. Haim Gedaliah Zimbalist, and R. Shlomo Koshelevsky in *Yeshurun*, 30 (Nisan 5774/April 2014), 544–52.

7. Rabbi Moses ben Maimon, *Mishneh Torah, Hilkhot Melakhim* 11:5. This passage likewise does not appear in standard versions of *Mishneh Torah* but is cited verbatim in Dror Fiksler and Gil Nadel, "*Ha'im Notzrim Beyomeinu Ovdei Avodah Zara Hem?*" (Are modern day Christians idolators?), *Teḥumin* 22 (5762/2002), 77–78.

8. A Jewish scholar of the period from about 200 to 500 CE.

9. BT *Sanhedrin* 63b; the verse is Ex. 23:13.

was a remarkable ruling, given his maltreatment by French crusaders who broke into his home, robbed him of everything except his books, dragged him into a field, insulted him on account of his religion, and hit him on the head five times to avenge the five blows that Jews had given Jesus, Rabbeinu Tam ruled that Samuel's father's ruling did not apply to Christians. He asserted that despite vowing in the name of their saints, Christians did not view them as divine, "and this is not a form of idolatry and [when swearing] they have in mind the Creator of heaven."[10]

A century later, Rabbeinu Yonah cited Rabbeinu Tam and accepted his argument.[11] So too did his near-contemporary, R. Yaakov ben Asher in his major work, *Arba'ah Turim*. R. Yaakov stated in his volume on *Oraḥ Hayim* that R. Shlomo Yitzḥaki – Rashi – permitted partnerships with Christians, "since they are not idolators today"[12] and did so again in *Yoreh De'ah*, this time citing a dictum by R. Samuel ben Meir in the name of his grandfather Rashi, that "today . . . all is permitted for they are not idolators and followers or believers."[13]

The fourteenth century rabbinic scholar, Rabbeinu Nissim took a half step back from Rabbeinu Tam's position, however. He too acknowledged that it was true that when Christians took a vow "they have in mind the blessed Creator." Still, Rabbeinu Nissim averred that their inclusion of their saints in the vows they took was an aspect of idolatry.[14]

R. Moshe Isserlis (known by his acronym Remah) whose glosses on the *Shulḥan Arukh* have been the foundation for virtually all subsequent decisors, ruled that Christianity was not idolatry but a form of syncretism (*shituf*), and thus permissible to Christians, who were not prohibited from syncretic religion if it incorporated belief in [the] one [true] God.[15] Indeed, for many decisors, both medieval and modern, the issue was not whether Christianity was a forbidden form of idolatry if practiced by Christians, but rather, as Rabbeinu Tam had emphasized,

10. *Tosefot*, s.v. *Assur*, BT *Sanhedrin, ad. loc.*

11. Quoted in Zvi H. Zakheim, *Zvi HaSanhedrin*, IV (New York: Gross, 1994), 170–71.

12. *Tur: Oraḥ Hayim*, 156.

13. *Tur: Yoreh De'ah*, 148.

14. *Sefer Hidushei HaRaN Al Masechet Sanhedrin* (New York: S. Goldman, n.d.), *BT Sanhedrin* 63b s.v. *Assur*.

15. R. Moshe Isserlis, *Oraḥ Haim* 156:1.

it was forbidden as idolatry insofar as Jews were concerned. As a result, the limitations that *halakhah* placed upon Jews with regard to the idolatry in ancient times applied just as much to modern Christianity even if it appeared that present-day Christians had a much different view of their religion than did their forefathers.[16]

Nevertheless, some *halakhists* throughout the centuries went even further. They considered Christianity an unalloyed form of idolatry forbidden to Jews and non-Jew alike. Specifically, those who worshipped the trinity were idolators whether they were Jewish or not.[17] As for Rabbeinu Tam's ruling, it was meant to be narrowly construed, addressing only the specific question of a vow, which, when taken by a Christian, did not indicate that he had a deity in mind.[18]

This is also the opinion of the overwhelming majority of modern and contemporary *Haredi poskim*.[19] The views of this group are exemplified by R. Eliyahu David Rabinowitz-Teomim (known as Aderet) who described a Lithuanian Catholic shrine as "an idol dedicated to worship by idolators" (*elil mukdash l'ovdai avodah zarah*). Aderet asserted that not only should Jews refrain from providing pilgrims to the shrine with food, drink and other supplies, but argued that Jews should be prepared to sacrifice their lives in order to avoid offering any support to the Christians.[20]

R. Moshe Feinstein, post-World War II Ashkenazi Jewry's leading

---

16. See comments of Rabbi Yaakov Ariel in Fiksler and Nadel, "*Ha'im Notzrim Beyomeinu Ovdei Avodah Zara Hem*?, 77–78.

17. See for example, the eighteenth century decisor R. Yeheskel Landau, *Noda B'Yeuda Mahadura Tinyana: Yoreh De'ah*, no. 148, cited in J. David Bleich, *Contemporary Halakhic Problems* vol. II (New York: Ktav, 1983), 213, fn. 36. See also the responsum by R. Yosef Shaul Natansohn, one of the leading decisors of the nineteenth century, in *Sh"ut Sh"oel U'Meishiv, Mahadura Tenina* 1 no 51. R, Natansohn initially seems to support Remah's view but concludes by arguing that syncretic religion, such as the trinity, was forbidden to non-Jews as well. Bleich, *loc. cit.*, offers an exhaustive though not complete list of decisors who took a position on the nature of Christianity.

18. See, for example, the seventeenth century halakhist Rabbi Ephraim b. Jacob ha-Kohen., *Sh"ut Sha'ar Ephraim* (Jerusalem: n.p., 5741/1981), no. 24.

19. Among twentieth century *Haredi* decisors who did not consider Christians practicing their religion as being idolatrous was R. Barukh Halevi Epstein, author of the *Torah Temimah* commentary on the Pentateuch.

20. R. Eliyahu Dovid Rabinowitz-Teomim, *Sh"ut Ma'ane Eliyahu*, ed. R. Aharon Bak (Kfar Etzion: Or Etzion, 5763/2003), 322–23, no. 107.

decisor, likewise averred that, in practice, Christians were idolators. Among his many rulings on matters pertaining to Christianity was one that explicitly forbade students from taking holidays during the period from December 25 to January 1st, on the grounds that these were days that Christians celebrated their *avodah zarah*.[21] Other leading Ashkenazi decisors, such as R. Mordechai Breisch, have applied the terms for non-Jew (*goy*) and idolator interchangeably when referring to Christians in particular.[22]

Sephardi decisors, who follow in the wake of Maimonides and take a similar view, include Yitzḥak Nissim, the former Sephardi Chief Rabbi of Israel. In addressing the question of using the dates of the secular calendar, R. Nissim ruled against doing so if at all possible, since what seemingly appeared to be secular dating actually derived from idolatrous Christian beliefs regarding the year Jesus died.[23]

The opinion that Christianity is a form of idolatry is not limited to *Haredim*, but is shared by Modern Orthodox scholars and decisors as well. For example, R. David Zvi Hoffmann, the leading decisor of pre-World War I Germany, and a noted leader of the Modern Orthodox movement, emphatically ruled that from a Jewish perspective, Christianity was idolatry, even though it was not forbidden to Christians.[24] More recently, R. Aharon Lichtenstein, in a discussion of the conver-

---

21. Moshe Feinstein, *Sh'ut Igrot Moshe: Orach Hayim* part 4 (Bnei Beraq: Yeshivat Ohel Yosef, 5741/1981), 328, no.85. In an earlier responsum addressing donations to a church, Reb Moshe (as he is colloquially known) employed language that could indicate that he only would go so far as to state that Christianity might be idolatry (*she'ulai gorem bi-netinato she'ya'avru hanokhrim al issur avodah zarah*) but that could equally be referring to one who donates to a church who thereby causes Gentiles to commit idolatry. Moshe Feinstein, *Sh'ut Igrot Moshe: Yoreh De'ah* part 1 (New York: Moriah, 5720/1959), 298, no. 149. In any event, it is clear that he took a harder line on the issue in the responsum that appeared over two decades later, and which is cited in the text.

22. See, for example, R. Mordechai Yaakov Breish, *Helkat Yaakov* vol.1*: Oraḥ Hayim* (Tel Aviv: n.p. 5752/1992), no. 33:4; vol. 2: *Yoreh De'ah* no. 53:5 and f.n. 1, and 55:2–5. See also R. Haim Moshe Yehuda Ortzel, "*B'Inyan Limud Sheva Mitzvot D'Vnei Noaḥ L'Goy*," (In the matter of teaching the seven Noahide Laws to a Non-Jew), *Tzohar* 12 (Tevet 5764/December2003–January 2004), 439–41 *passim.*

23. Yitzḥak Nissim, *Sh'ut Yain Hatov: Oraḥ Haim* (Jerusalem: Cohen, 5739/1979) 33–34, no. 8.

24. David Zvi Hoffmann, *Sh'ut Melamed L'Ho'il* (Jerusalem: Feldheim, 5770/2020), 234–35, no. 55.

sion to Judaism by a Catholic priest, distinguished between Catholicism and Unitarianism, the former being a polytheistic faith. R. Yehuda Herzl Henkin, whose rulings are a major influence on Modern Orthodoxy, has stated explicitly that:

> Christianity is to be treated as idolatry for several reasons: (1) the belief in a trinity of the father, holy spirit and son, by which they consider Jesus to be god . . . had they considered Jesus the son of God, God forbid, but not God Himself, and had they not worshipped him, this would have been *minut* (heresy) but not idolatry and if they had considered him the messiah but not God, nor the son of God, this would have been an error and stupidity but not idolatry . . . (2) they believe that their bread is converted in the celebration of the mass to the body of Jesus (3) they kneel to idols and icons and in the course of falling to the ground they make the sign of the cross.[25]

Like R. Lichtenstein, R. Henkin distinguishes between the Catholic, Orthodox and Anglican (in America, Episcopal) churches on the one hand, and, on the other, other Protestant denominations. Indeed, he goes so far as to assert that as long as Protestant worshippers do not kneel before the image of Jesus on the cross, their service is not considered idolatrous.[26] On the other hand, he rules that since, apart from Unitarians and other, similar denominations, the majority of Protestant denominations believe in the trinity, celebrate mass, and accept Jesus as divinity, it is forbidden to enter their churches.[27] Finally, though he did not explicitly address the question of whether Christianity is a form of idolatry, Rabbi Joseph B. Soloveitchik's manifest hostility toward any form of theological engagement with the Catholic Church testifies to his shared belief with other decisors that its tenets, if perhaps not those of other Christian denominations, are indeed idolatrous.[28]

---

25. Yehudah Herzl Henkin, *Sh'ut B'nei Banim* vol. 3 (Jerusalem: 5758/1998), 116, no. 35.

26. Ibid. 35.

27. Ibid. 117.

28. See for example, his reactions to Vatican II, as documented in Rabbi Joseph B. Soloveitchik, *Community, Covenant and Commitment: Selected Letters and Communi-*

The attitudes described above are certainly not unanimously shared by all decisors, however, nor were they so in previous eras. Greenberg actually is building upon a different set of views regarding Christianity that can trace their roots back nearly seven centuries, a time when the Church's persecution of Jews was widespread throughout Europe. Indeed, even Maimonides was not consistently negative about Christians. Maimonides was asked for a ruling as to whether Rabbi Yoḥanan's Talmudic dictum that it was a capital crime for a non-Jew to study Torah, and whether a Jew could teach a non-Jew the *mitzvot* other than the seven that were binding on non-Jews. His response was surprising, given his view of Christianity. He replied that it was permitted to teach the *mitzvot* to Christians and to "attract them to our religion" because "the uncircumcised accept that the text of the Torah has not changed, but derive it falsely with their faulty interpretations . . . and if they interpreted it properly perhaps they will return to what is good. And even if they do not, it will not undermine us, because nothing in their text will be found different from ours."[29]

Later *halakhists,* both pre-modern, modern, and contemporary, acknowledged that the Christians of their era simply were different from their ancient predecessors. The thirteenth century Talmudic commentator Rabbi Menachem HaMeiri, whose early life overlapped with Rabbeinu Yonah's later years, went furthest in distinguishing between Christians and idolators. In his view, those who were "to an extent, fenced off from the ways of [false] religion and idolatry, even if their beliefs were far removed from ours, are not in the category of [idolatry], even if their beliefs are distant from ours."[30] Elsewhere, Meiri addressed

cations, ed. Nathaniel Helfgot (New York: Ktav, 2005), especially 260–61 and 263–65. On the other hand, Eugene Korn points out that R. Soloveitchik "never issued a formal halakhic ruling on the status of Christianity for Christians," see Eugene Korn, "Rethinking Christianity: Rabbinic Positions and Possibilities," in Alon Goshen-Gottstein and Eugene Korn, eds., *Jewish Theology and World Religions* (Oxford and Portland, OR: The Littman Library of Jewish Civilization, 2012), 201, f.n. 52.

29. David Yosef, ed. *She'eilot U'Teshuvot Rabbeinu Moshe ben Maimon: Pe'er Hador* (Jerusalem: Machon Yerushalayim, 5754/1994), p.123, fn. 4. On the other hand, Maimonides did enforce Rabbi Yohanan's ban when it came to teaching Torah to Muslims, who, he argued, completely distorted the Biblical text, and, unlike the Christians, denied its divinity.

30. Kalman Schlesinger, ed. *Rabbi Menahem Hameiri's Commentary Beth Habehira*

the term *notzri*, the medieval term that Jews reserved for Christians, and argued that the Talmudic prohibition against doing business with a *notzri* on Sunday referred not to Christians and their day of rest, but rather to sun worshippers who treated Sunday as the first day of the week.[31]

Meiri's approach to Christians was nothing short of revolutionary, extending far beyond granting Jews permission to engage them economically. In contrast to earlier rabbinic rulings with respect to idolators, Meiri permitted Jews to maintain a variety of social contacts with Christians, such as greeting them affectionately, or entering their homes to greet them on their holidays[32] and preparing food for them on Jewish holidays.[33] He also ruled that laws regarding paternity applied to Christians, whereas they did not apply to idolators.[34] Finally, he ruled that one could desecrate the Sabbath in order to save a Christian's life; one could not do so to save that of an idolator.[35] Meiri did not argue that Jews could participate in Christian sacraments or any other religious ceremonies; for him too, such practices were forbidden to Jews. Yet, he drew upon the distinction between Christianity and idolatry that

---

on the Talmudic Treatise Baba Kamma (Jerusalem: n.p, 1963), 330.

31. Abraham Schreiber, ed. *Menachem HaMeiri's Beit Habeḥirah al Masekhet Avodah zarah*, 3rd. ed., (Jerusalem: Kedem, 1964), 4 and see 59. R. Yehuda Herzl Henkin argues that even according to Meiri, Christians who celebrate mass and kneel before the crucifix are indeed idolators; *B'nai Banim* vol. 3, 122, no. 35. His view appears to be a solitary one, however.

32. R. Menachem ben Shlomo HaMeiri, *Beit Habeḥirah al Masechet Gittin*, ed. Kalman Schlesinger 4th ed. (Jerusalem: n.p., 5724/1964), 257–58. For a detailed analysis of these and Meiri's other views cited in this paragraph, see Moshe Halbertal, "'Ones Possessed of Religion'": Religious Tolerance in the Teachings of the Meiri," *The Edah Journal* 1:1 (Marcheshvan 5761/October 2001), 1–24.

33. Meiri, *Beit Habeḥira al Masechet Beitzah*, ed. Yitzhak S. Lange and Kalman Schlesinger (Jerusalem: n.p. 5729/1969), 117–18.

34. Meiri, *Beit Habeḥirah al Masekhet Yevamot* (Jerusalem: *Machon Hatalmud Hayisraeli Hashalem*, 5722/1962), 354. He points out that the absence of paternity among non-Jews applies only to idolators and not those within "the bounds of religions."

35. Meiri, *Beit Habeḥirah al Masechet Yoma*, ed. Joseph Hacohen Klein, 2nd. ed. (Jerusalem: *Machon HaTalmud HaYisraeli Hashalem*, 5735/1975), 212. Meiri reasons that the Talmudic dictum that there is no commandment to save an idolator on Shabbat is due to the fact that "they have no religion." Halbertal concludes from Meiri's statement that there is a mandate to violate Shabbat in order to save a Christian. See Halbertal, "Ones Possessed," 9.

other decisors had identified to justify a far broader relationship with Christians than most others were willing to accept.

It is clear that Meiri was not writing to placate censors; as R. Shlomo Aviner pointed out, had that been Meiri's motivation, he would have dealt with Christianity with far greater brevity and, it might be added, in a considerably more *halakhically* restricted fashion. Instead, he expatiated on the subject at some length, and at various points in his commentary. His position clearly influenced that of R. Abraham Isaac Kook, who wrote that "the essential position is that of Meiri, namely, that [the populations of] all nations are constrained by proper interpersonal conduct (*bein adam leḥavero*) and they are already considered to be observant of the seven Noahide laws (*geirim toshavim*) with respect to all human obligations."[36]

This view, drawing on that of Meiri and the tradition begun with Rashi and Rabbeinu Tam, colored those of later decisors and *halakhic* analysts who have taken a more lenient, and at times more generous view of Christianity. Thus, for example, R. Shabtai Cohen (known colloquially by his acronym Shakh), asserted that one could even sell incense to ordinary Christians, although it was used in their rituals, because "their intentions were directed to the creator of heaven and earth."[37] Two centuries later, R. David Zvi Hoffmann emphatically ruled that from a Jewish perspective, Christianity was idolatry, even though it was not forbidden to Christians.[38]

Similarly, R. Isaac Herzog, the first Chief Rabbi of the State of Israel, writing in the course of an essay regarding the permissibility of allowing Christians to have a chapel above the Tomb of David, noted that "contemporary Christians, *even Catholics* [my emphasis] do not consider their statues, or even the cross, as deities, as they simply venerate them, and it is unclear whether these statues have the status of idolatry."[39] In another essay regarding the rights of Christian minorities in the new

36. Rabbi Shlomo Aviner, "Judaism's Attitude toward the Christian World," (*Yachas Hayahadut el Ha'olam HaNotzri), Teḥumin* 8 (5747/1987), 368–69.

37. Shakh, *Yoreh De'ah* 151:7.

38. David Zvi Hoffmann, *Sh'ut Melamed L'Ho'il* (Jerusalem: Feldheim, 5770/2020), 234–35, no. 55.

39. Yitzhak Isaac Halevy Herzog, *Pesaqim U'Ktavim* vol. 1*: Sh'ut B'Dinei Oraḥ Haim* (Jerusalem: Mossad Harav Kook, 5749/1989), no. 27.

Jewish state, R. Herzog again asserted that "contemporary Christians, even Catholics, are not idolators in the essential sense of that concept, but their hearts are toward Heaven, even if they cannot comprehend the contradiction between unity and trinity." He did go on to point out, as others previously had done, that because of their syncretism it was forbidden to enter their houses of worship and, more generally, avoid anything relating to their religion.[40] Nevertheless, he concluded that because syncretism was permitted to non-Jews, Christians were entitled to full rights in the State of Israel.

R. Haim David Halevi took a more lenient position than R. Herzog, asserting that the changed nature of Christianity meant that many of the stringencies applied to it in previous generations. R. Halevy cited R. Yaakov ben Asher, noted above, as well as R. Yosef Karo, who, writing in *Beit Yosef*, explained this statement as essentially negating the various strictures that the Talmud had imposed with respect to idolators. R. Halevi then argued that these views actually applied to idolators whose practices had evolved over time. As for Christians, he asserted that the essence of their religion had never been idolatrous. Their syncretic form of religion was not forbidden to them, though it was not permissible to Jews, and therefore, laws such as those forbidding the sale of homes to non-Jews, praying for the health of non-Jews, returning the losses of non-Jews, or doing business with them on their holidays, simply did not apply to Christians.[41] In fact, he even went so far as to assert that Maimonides would no longer have classified Christians as idolators.[42]

R. Eliezer Berkovits likewise did not contend that Christianity was anything other than a syncretic religion. Nevertheless, he too was prepared to relax at least one long standing rabbinic prohibition, which many of his contemporaries continued to support, namely, that of entering a church. As he put it: "The prohibitions because of the strin-

40. R. Yitzhak Isaac Halevy Herzog, "*Zechuyot Hamiutim Lefi HaHalakhah*" (The rights of the minorities according to Halacha), *Teḥumin* 2 (Summer 5741/1981), 175.

41. R. Haim David Halevi, "*Darkei Shalom B'Yahasim Sh'Bein Yehudim L'Sheiainam Yehudim*" (The Ways of Peace in Relations between Jews and Non-Jews, *Techumin* 9 (5748/1988), 73–78.

42. Halevi, *Aseh Lekhah Rav* vol.8 (Tel Aviv: n.p. 5748/1988), 194 no. 68.

gency of the law of idolatry . . . are not applicable with respect to entry into the holy places of Christianity."[43]

R. Naḥum Rabinovich, conceding that Christians practice a syncretic religion, nevertheless favorably quoted R. Zvi Hirsh Chajes who asserted that "Christians who believe in religion and that Torah is from Heaven . . . are certainly treated in our laws as *gerei toshav* [proselytes who are not idolators and adhere to Noahide laws], despite their syncretism." Accordingly, R. Rabinovich, like Rabbis Halevi and Berkowitz, has gone beyond other rulings that accepted Christians as syncretists yet applied to them various Talmudic strictures that had originally intended for idolators, in this case, the prohibition on violating the Sabbath to save an idolator. Addressing the question of whether soldiers in the Israel Defense Forces could do so to assist a wounded Christian, R. Rabinovich answered in the affirmative.

R. Joseph Ehrenkrantz addressed yet another long standing prohibition, that of Jewish-Christian dialogue. R. Ehrenkrantz argues that not only is it permissible to engage in Jewish-Christian dialogue, but it is actually a *halakhic* obligation to do so.[44] In support of his case he cites many of the decisors mentioned above, but also, somewhat surprisingly in light of his opposition to dialogue in the context of Vatican II, R. Joseph B. Soloveitchik. R. Ehrenkrantz asserts that R. Soloveitchik gave "tacit approval" to the participation by "out-of-town" rabbis – whom he had ordained – in interfaith organizations, in order to foster peace (*mipnei darkhei shalom*).[45] R. Soloveitchik explicitly drew a line between interfaith cooperation on social issues and theological interaction. R. Ehrenkrantz went further, however, and did engage in dialogue with Christians, notably Catholics in the aftermath of Vatican II, though within what he has termed "the constraint of Jewish law."[46]

43. Quoted in Melekh (Marc) Shapiro, "*Ha'im Muttar L'Hicanes Li'Kneisiah?: Pirsum Rishon Shel Tehsuvat Ha'Gaon R. Eliezer Berkovits Benidon*," (Is it Permitted to Enter a Church?: First Publication of a Responsum by the Gaon R. Eliezer Berkowitz on the Issue, *Milin Havivin* 4 (5669–5770/2008–2010), 49. Shapiro also notes the differing views on this issue on the part of leading Haredi decisors, including R. Moshe Feinstein, R. Ovadiah Yosef, and R. Eliezer Waldenburg, ibid. 43.

44. Joseph Ehrenkrantz, "The Halakhic Obligation of Jewish-Christian Dialogue," *Conversations* 20 (Autumn 2014/5775), 129.

45. Ibid. 133.

46. Ibid. 135–38.

Finally, although it has been generally accepted that Maimonides did consider Christians to be idolators, Dror Fiksler and Gil Nadel followed R. Halevy in arguing at length that according to Maimonides, today's Christians are not idolators in any sense. In their view, Maimonides applied two criteria that led him to conclude that the Christians of his time were idolators. First, they worshipped an exogenous being apart from God, believing that he was the messiah. Second, their ritual, namely, the sacraments, was directed toward this exogenous being. Fiksler and Nadel assert that for almost all Christian denominations, one or the other of these two criteria no longer is being met. For example, Unitarians do not accept the trinity, while Protestants no longer conduct the sacraments. Fiksler and Nadel therefore conclude that even according to Maimonides, only Catholics and the Orthodox Church would qualify as idolators, while for other decisors, even those branches of Christianity no longer practice idolatry.[47]

R. Yitz Greenberg, like R. Ehrenkrantz, a student of R. Soloveitchik, pursued a path-breaking course that drew upon Meiri and the like-minded decisors who have followed him. Indeed, Greenberg has gone as far, if not further than that of R. Ehrenkrantz in advocating a relationship with Christians based on dialogue and mutual respect. As he noted, "I began to realize the true power, and the values and the strength of true Christianity. And so I began to ask myself, is Judaism fair and proper in its understanding of Christianity? That's how I moved into . . . pluralism, because I came to see the power of the other's side."[48] In Greenberg's view:

> The emergence of pluralism is a breakthrough for the fundamental, hitherto suppressed, category of the image of God. Historically, justice to the image of God of the other has been denied as a consequence of the lack of contact . . . good systems, holy faiths, deliberately and systematically self-perpetuated by degrading others . . . It is a moral breakthrough, then, when one encounters the other and is "forced" to rearrange the universe of meaning, that is, to get to know the limits of one's absolutes. . . . Nevertheless . . .

47. Fiksler and Nadel, *"Haim Notzrim,"* 71–76.
48. Chasen, "Disagreeing in the Service of Gd."

> pluralism does not mean that there cannot be genuine disagreement and conflict between faiths . . . another faith can be wrong objectively (or wrong by my standards) and it may yet be treated as legitimate.[49]

Greenberg further argues that Jewish law mandates that one must entertain the views of "the other" even when one disagrees with them, even if they are inherently incorrect. As he puts it, "the law is teaching us to respect ideas that otherwise might be dismissed as false (or suppressed) as being the views of a system that is wrong . . . These ideas get a hearing – and are treated with respect or even considered as truth – thanks to the sheer weight of the dignity of the speaker. This is the *religious* [my emphasis] basis of the pluralist right for "wrong views . . . to be granted a hearing and to be advocated in the face of other "established" truths."[50] Finally, Greenberg argues that: "Ultimately, all humans and the Divine are partners in the perfection of the world. This partnership can only be carried out successfully by allowing room even for those who are wrong – even those whom I believe are wrong – to argue, to propagate, and to share their truth and their encounter with the Absolute."[51]

Greenberg's vision regarding other religions is a generous one. It is of a piece with his views of *tikkun olam*, which he sees not as a substitute for *halakhah* and its implementation, but as its complement. It is a reflection of the man's intellectual integrity, and also of his courage. For, as might be expected, he has had to withstand severe criticism, usually of the *ad hominem* variety, from those for whom fundamentalism, accompanied by intolerance, are the essence of Judaism. Greenberg rose above such pettiness. Instead, he has for many decades served as a model of what Orthodoxy can and should be in the world we live in.

49. Irving Greenberg, "Seeking the Religious Roots of Pluralism: In the Image of God and Covenant," *Journal of Ecumenical Studies*, 34:3 (Summer 1997), 389–90.

50. Ibid. 391.

51. Ibid. 394.

Idolatry and the Covenantal Pluralism of Irving Greenberg

Rabbi Dr. Eugene Korn

Some years ago, a group of Jewish thinkers met at University of Scranton to discuss how to begin building a Jewish theology of other religions that would be credible in contemporary society where Jews come into frequent contact with Christians, Muslims, Hindus, Buddhists, other Asian believers and secularists.[1] Of course, a central issue was what to do with the *halakhic* category of *avodah zarah* – worship often identified with idolatry: What does it mean in our world where few pray to the stars, sun or other material objects? To whom, if anyone, does it apply today? How can Jews today accept the unmitigated intolerance – to the point of annihilation of idolatrous persons and cultures[2] – that the Bible and *halakhah* demand of Jews? In practice and theory, *avodah zarah* functions in rabbinic discourse as the domain of the intolerable. It defines the line at which tolerance is to end and intolerance is warranted.[3]

Surprisingly, one Orthodox professor of philosophy urged us to disregard the concept entirely. "*Avodah zarah* has no relevance to-

1. The conference resulted in *Jewish Theology and World Religions*, edited by Alon Goshen Gottstein and Eugene Korn (Littman Library of Jewish Civilization, 2012), many of whose essays explore this issue in depth.

2. "You shall not leave one soul alive" (*Lo tiḥayeh kol nishamah)* is the biblical command to Jews regarding the idolatrous Canaanite nations. (Deut. 20:16). See also Maimonides, *Mishneh Torah*, Laws of *Avodah Zarah*, ch. 10.

3. See the trenchant analysis of *avodah zarah* and its function in *Idolatry* by Moshe Halbertal and Avishai Margolit (Harvard University Press, 1994).

day," he insisted, "and the sooner we get rid of it the better." To me and many others at the conference, this suggestion seemed eminently reasonable. The idea of wreaking violence upon another person for his variant theological convictions, however incorrect or objectionable, seems unjustifiable today – particularly to Jews with a keen awareness of the suffering Jews endured for their dissident beliefs during the long night of our exile.

Not long after the conference, I discussed this issue with one progressive Jewish theologian. He passionately disagreed with the idea of dropping *avodah zarah* from our deliberations, insisting that we need *avodah zarah* in our contemporary theological worldview. Idolatry has significance today, he claimed, and we would not be able to honestly fashion contemporary Jewish theologies toward others without considering *avodah zarah*.

That theologian was Rabbi Irving (Yitz) Greenberg.

Technically, *avodah zarah* means worship deemed illicit by Jewish law, both in its idolatrous and non-idolatrous manifestations.[4] While often identified with the pagan idolatry that the Bible condemns, it is in fact a wider category that also includes some non-pagan forms of worship.

Fundamentally, two competing conceptions are prevalent in rabbinic discourse, and both are inferred from the Bible. The Torah sometimes describes intolerable idolators as people who worship celestial bodies, stars, and trees[5] (i.e. finite physical objects) understanding them to be divine. At other times, idolators are portrayed as people with abominable immoral practices.[6] The first conception – that of intellectual error – was emphasized by rabbis with philosophic bents, most prominently Maimonides in twelfth century Spain and Egypt. As the greatest *halakhic* authority in Jewish tradition, Maimonides exerts prodigious influence over the Jewish canon. And as a rationalist philosopher steeped in Aristotelian metaphysics, Maimonides understood *avodah zarah* to be the conceptual confusion of mistaking something

4. For a fuller analysis of this claim, see my "Rethinking Christianity," in *Jewish Theology and World Religions*, op cit. 189–215.

5. Deut. 4,12,16.

6. Lev. 18; Deut. 12.

finite for God, Who is infinite in being and essence.[7] For Rambam, an idolator is anyone who believes that God is physical, plural, has emotions, or is subject to change, since all these properties indicate limits and imperfection.

As a result, Maimonides considered not only ancient sun worship, star worship, and polytheism to constitute idolatry, he also concluded that Christianity was full-fledged *avodah zarah* because of its doctrines of the Incarnation and the Trinity. He ruled that Christians who held these beliefs were idolators and were subject to all the same strictures of alienation and intolerance as the pagans of the biblical and Talmudic eras. Maimonides was consistent: he also believed that Jews who harbored personalistic conceptions of God were worse offenders than gentiles who believed that God was physical.[8] But Rambam was no exclusivist. He considered Muslims to be legitimate believers because Islam insists on absolute monotheism (similar to Judaism) and Islam's conception of Allah is free of any corporeal dimension. It is important to note here the influence that life experience had on Maimonides. He never lived with Christians and learned about Christianity only from books. Except for his brief stay in Crusader Palestine, he resided all his life in Muslim societies. As far as we know, he never engaged personally with Christians and thus it was psychologically easy for him to categorize Christianity and Christians as the intolerable Other; nor did he have to grapple with the practical *halakhic* obstacles that Jewish law would impose upon Jewish-Christian interaction in his society, were Christians indeed idolators.

Rabbi Menachem ha-Meiri, living in thirteenth century Christian Provence, emphasized the other biblical identification of idolators as primitive immoral pagans with abominable ethical, religious and sexual practices. He conceptualized idolatry in moral terms: Idolatry is any religion that does not impose on its adherents the fundamental moral restraints against murder, theft, sexual wildness, lawlessness[9], that is, the foundations of orderly civilized society. Thus, according to Meiri,

7. Because Maimonides understood *avodah zarah* as intellectual error, he codified its laws in the Book of Knowledge (*Sefer Madda*) in the *Mishneh Torah*.

8. *Guide of the Perplexed* I:36.

9. See Jacob Katz, *Exclusiveness and Tolerance*, (Schocken, 1962) Ch. X. and Moshe Halbertal, *Bein Torah L'Hokhmah*, (Hebrew University, 2000) Ch. 3. For an English

even a polytheist and a corporealist who subscribed to fundamental moral principles belonged to the domain of valid believers – *ba'alei dat.* In his eyes, the Torah requires pure monotheism of Jews, but not of gentiles. Meiri interacted with Christian priests and understood them to be moral, sophisticated, and spiritual persons. One Christian cleric even inspired him to write his book on repentance, *Hibur ha-Teshuvah.*[10] Meiri had no theological or practical problem with Christianity or with any other civilizing religion of which he was aware.[11] In fact, he restricted idolatry in his day to the far-flung corners of the earth – i.e. only places where Jews did not live. In doing so, Meiri relegated Judaism's mandatory intolerance of idolators to the realm of theory.[12]

R. Yitz Greenberg offers a third definition of idolatry:

> Idolatry is the partial, created or shaped by humans, that claims to be infinite. Idolatry mimics the divine and claims the absolute status of the divine, yet it is in fact finite.[13]

Rabbi Greenberg's definition is at once traditional, drawing on the two cited traditional rabbinic conceptions, and modern, because it is fashioned in light of twentieth century history, the *Shoah* and our awareness of different religious traditions in the contemporary pluralistic world.

Greenberg's definition most obviously resembles Rambam's understanding of idolatry as cognitive error, as mistaking the finite for the infinite, the limited for the absolute. Absolutizing our own limited theological, political or philosophical ideas betrays the infinite nature of God. Even religious beliefs based on a conviction in God's revelation

---

translation of Halbertal, see "Ones Possessed of Religion: Religious Tolerance in the Teachings of Meiri" in *The Edah Journal* 1:1, *Marheshvan* 5761 at www.edah.org.

10. As Meiri indicates in his introduction to the work.

11. That is, such belief systems were not *avodah zarah* for gentiles, and perhaps even not for Jews.

12. Meiri never addressed how he would evaluate atheists, and this is an important issue for Jewish theology today. I suspect that Meiri required belief in and submission to a transcendent God because, like nearly every other thinker in the Middle Ages, he assumed that any moral code lacking a punishing and rewarding divine authority could not be sustained.

13. "Pluralism and Partnership" in *For the Sake of Heaven and Earth* (Jewish Publication Society, 2004) 210.

are grounded in our human perception and cognition of that revelation, and hence are subject to human epistemological limitations. This awareness led rabbinic tradition to assert that revelation at Sinai had 600,000 "faces," one for each male Jewish adult present at Sinai.

Yet, Rabbi Greenberg's conception also bears a close relation to Meiri's ethical conception of *avodah zarah:*

> This pseudo-infinite cannot contain the infinity of life (or of human dignity). In fact, we know that idolatry is the god of death and that it creates a realm of death. . . . All human systems (even those that are given by Divine Revelation) that claim to be absolute, exercise no self-limitation and leave no room for the other turn into idolatry, i.e. into sources of death. . . . It is no accident that Nazism which sought perfection and eliminated all restrictions and limitations created a realm of total death – the kingdom of night. . . . All political systems and all religions that allow themselves to make unlimited absolute claims are led to idolatrous behaviors. They often generate death-dealing believers. . . . All social systems that "other" the other and absolutize their own host culture turn idolatrous and then degrade or destroy others.[14]

More important than idolatry's cognitive error is its horrific moral consequences: Absolutizing our limited ideas leads to imposing them on others which, as history has shown, inevitably produces persecution, destruction, and death. And this moral problem turns theological: it is theologically abhorrent because it annihilates the Image of God present in human beings and thus eliminates the presence of God in the world – literally *Hillul ha-Shem* (the absence of God). Jews understand this viscerally. As victims of the absolutist doctrines of the medieval Church, the Nazi Final Solution, and Stalinist Communism, this truth has been burned into our flesh. These monistic systems sought to impose imperial truth on the world, ultimately crushing all dissenters and murdering millions of Jews.[15]

---

14. "Pluralism and Partnership" in *For the Sake of Heaven and Earth* (Jewish Publication Society, 2004) 210.

15. As an absolutist, Maimonides taught similar intolerance and violence toward

Written in 1999, Rabbi Greenberg's insight was prophetic, accurately describing the jihadist slaughter wreaked by Al-Qaida, ISIL, and other Islamist zealots that was to emerge in the first decades of the twenty-first century. In their absolute quest to purge the Middle East of all vestiges of non-Islamic life and culture, these extremists now bring chaos, destruction, and death to the countries and peoples of the region. Their absolutism has become a savage murderous idol, and their absolutist worship has shown itself to be the enemy of the God of Creation who brought order out of chaos and sanctified each human being with the Divine Image.

Nor are Jews immune from this modern idolatry. As Yehudah Halevi noticed already in the tenth century, Jews have been tolerant of other religions historically, but that may have been only because they lacked the capacity to act out any intolerance.[16] As a powerful majority in Israel today, however, some religious Jews have absolutized their beliefs and have begun to practice intolerant exclusivism in Israel. These monists deny the legitimacy of religious pluralism, advocate restricting Israeli residence to Jews, and, at times, physically assault Muslims and Christians in their midst – all on allegedly religious grounds.[17]

Only non-absolute systems or religions that allow room for the other can succeed in protecting the dignity of human beings and seeing the *Tzelem Elokim* (Divine Image) in every person. It is our commitment to self-limitation (human *tzimtzum*: imitating God's act of creation, according to kabbalistic teaching) and our awareness of the finitude of our religious and political conceptions that ensure human life can flourish. All absolutist systems are destined to produce only "oceans of blood,"[18] and violate God's love for His children as well His covenantal

---

idolators. See *Mishneh Torah*, Laws of *Avodah Zarah*, ch. 10 and Laws of Kings and their Wars, 8:10.

16. *The Kuzari*, I:113–115.

17. In 2009, Rabbis Yitzhak Shapira and Yosef Elitzur, two Jewish religious extremists, published *Torat Hamelekh* ("The Teaching of the King"), which justifies killing innocent gentiles in war. In 2010, a number of Israeli nationalist rabbis wrote a public letter prohibiting selling Israeli land to gentiles. In 2015, Jewish nationalists set fire to the Church of Loaves and Fishes in the Galilee, claiming it to be a house of idolatry. And frequent incidents continue today of Jewish religious extremists defacing church properties in the ancient part of Jerusalem and assaulting Armenian priests living there.

18. Another trenchant pluralist, Isaiah Berlin, put it this way: "Few things have done

plan for humanity.[19] In the end, the greatest witness to the Creator of Life is the covenantal pluralism that protects religious co-existence and promotes human partnership.

Covenantal Pluralism and Relativism

The most troubling aspects of modern culture for traditional theologians are empirical pluralism, social equality, and the expansive awareness of other cultures gained through global travel and internet communication. Three hundred years ago, a New Englander could believe that the Boston State House was the hub of the solar system and that his church had a monopoly on God's truth.[20] Today, our universe has expanded exponentially on scientific, cultural, and religious levels. We know there are multiple solar systems, and we regularly meet, come to value, and learn from those who believe differently from us. No longer can a rational person believe that his group is the exclusive center of humanity, moral excellence or theological truth – and returning to

more harm than the belief on the part of individuals and groups (or tribes or states or nations or churches) that he or she or they are in sole *possession* of the truth. . . . It is a terrible and dangerous arrogance to believe that you alone are right, have a magical eye which sees *the* truth, and that others cannot be right if they disagree. This makes one certain that there is one goal and only one for one's nation or church or the whole of humanity, and that it is worth any amount of suffering (particularly on the part of other people) if only that goal is attained – even "through an ocean of blood to the Kingdom of Love" as said Robespierre. Hitler, Lenin, Stalin, and, I daresay, leaders in the religious wars of Christian vs. Muslim or Catholics vs. Protestants sincerely believed this: the belief that there is one and only one true answer to the central questions which have agonized mankind and that one has it oneself – or one's Leader has it. This belief was responsible for the ocean of blood. No Kingdom of Love ever sprang from it, nor could it." *Liberty* (Oxford U. Press, 2002) 345.

19. I am using the masculine "His" in reference to God only as a linguistic convention. I do not wish to imply any gender or gender preference to God. In Jewish theology, God transcends gender, although in attempting to understand God, Jewish sacred literature has found it helpful to ascribe to God traits associated both with masculinity (e.g., authority and punishment) and femininity (e.g., compassion and nurturing). This has significant pedagogical implications: *Imitatio Dei* demands, then, that human beings also strive to develop a combination of personality traits as an ideal religious and ethical model. According to Jewish mystical thought, in the eschaton all these traits will merge into a perfect unity – both in God and His creatures.

20. Abraham Joshua Heschel, "No Man is an Island" reprinted in *Moral Grandeur and Spiritual Audacity*, edited by Susannah Heschel, (Ferrar, Strauss, Giroux, 1996) 237.

pre-modern innocence means turning one's back on God's universe and His creatures. Often, this attempt at willful blindness generates cognitive dissonance, frustration and uncontrolled rage when God's real pluralistic universe inevitably intrudes.[21]

Rabbi Greenberg's acknowledgement of the validity of other religions and advocacy of covenantal pluralism has led some traditionalists to see him as a relativist, accusing him of violating normative Jewish belief. Evidently his recognition that other religions can also possess spiritual worth and theological truth, i.e. that Judaism does not have monopoly on God's revelation, is too much for some traditional Jews to accept.

Yet, religious pluralism is not a foreign idea to rabbinic thought or *halakhah*. Long before modernity, the rabbis of the Talmud taught a version of covenantal pluralism: *Torat Moshe,* the Sinaitic covenant with Moses with its 613 *mitzvot* applied to the Jewish people, while the Noahide covenant containing seven *mitzvot* applied to gentiles. Importantly, the rabbis acknowledged that just as the Torah is valid and sufficient for Jews, so too is the Noahide covenant and its *mitzvot* valid and sufficient for non-Jews, and that there is no need for gentiles to enter the Mosaic covenant for them to be loved by God or to gain a share in the world to come.[22] This covenantal pluralism is simply classic Judaism and time-honored *halakhah* devoid of any hint of relativism.

Moreover, according to many *halakhic* authorities the definition of *avodah zarah,* too, is pluralistic: Most *hakhmei Ashkenaz*[23] accepted one definition of *avodah zarah* for Jews (i.e. the violation of absolute monotheism) and a different one for gentiles, since they ruled that any *shituf* (associationism) like the Trinity that includes the Creator of Heaven and Earth – which constitutes *avodah zarah* for Jews – is not *avodah zarah* for gentiles, but is a valid form of belief for them.[24]

---

21. This is Bernard Lewis' explanation for current Islamic frustration and violence. See *What Went Wrong?* (Oxford University Press, 2002)

22. See *Tosefta, Sanhedrin* 105a, and Maimonides, *Mishneh Torah,* Laws of Kings and their Wars, 8:11.

23. Referring here to rabbinic authorities from the 16th century up to the present.

24. See "Rethinking Christianity," op cit. 195–204 for a fuller explanation of this point.

Further still, the dialectical nature of *halakhah* also exhibits pluralistic logic. Though there exists a procedural need to decide on one *halakhic* position over its opposition, in fact both are considered to possess truth: *Elu v'elu divrei Elokim Hayim* ("Both are the words of the living God"). And finally, Isaiah tells us of a pluralistic understanding of God's elect and blessed: "Blessed be my people Egypt, My handiwork Assyria and My very own Israel" (25:19). In all these instances traditional Judaism endorsed pluralism regarding covenant, acceptable theology and religious standards without any vestige of impermissible relativism.

Conflating Rabbi Greenberg's covenantal pluralism and relativism is conceptual confusion. Relativism is the doctrine that points of view have no absolute truth or validity, only subjective value according to perception.[25] Thus relativism easily leads to the loss of the capacity to affirm any truth or standard. Yet Greenberg makes clear that for him (and for other Jews) Judaism is absolutely true and objectively binding. Judaism is a non-subjective truth for Jews, but one that stands alongside a plurality of other absolute truths in the universe. Greenberg has not been seduced by Plato's ghost, who insists that what is true for me must be true for everyone at all times.[26] Unlike relativism, Greenberg's theological pluralism does not give up on absolutes or undermine their authority. It limits them so that they do not turn into instruments of intellectual, political or religious oppression. As God is infinite, so is His truth open to manifold understandings. And as human beings are unique, so are their understandings of God unique. To know God perfectly – to define God definitively – is to make God a mere object of human cognition and subordinate Him to our finite intellects.

The difference between principled pluralism and cognitively weak relativism was dramatically articulated by another pluralist theologian: Rabbi Abraham Joshua Heschel. He was at the forefront of building cooperation and mutual appreciation between Christians and Jews during the Second Vatican Council in the early 1960s, and saw both Christianity and Judaism as valid ways to understand and worship God.

---

25. *American Heritage Dictionary*

26. This is Rabbi Jonathan Sack's formulation in *Dignity of Difference* (Continuum, 2002) 49.

He believed that "God is a pluralist" – i.e. that God wills for people to worship Him in different ways. Yet Heschel never wavered in his commitment to Judaism as the only true way for Jews to worship the God of Abraham, Isaac, and Jacob. He even traveled to the Vatican during Catholic deliberations over the correct formulation of *Nostra Aetate*, the Church document that was to lay out the new Catholic teachings about Jews and Judaism. Heschel firmly denounced any hint of conversion to Christianity appearing in the document or in proper Jewish-Christian relations. He poignantly – and bluntly – announced to Vatican officials, "If faced with the choice of baptism or the crematoria of Auschwitz, I would choose Auschwitz."[27] Greenberg's insistence on the absolute correctness of Judaism for Jews augers for the same choice.

Idolatry Again

Greenberg's covenantal pluralism stands, then, midway between the relativism of no absolute truths and the absolutist monism that insists on only one religious truth for everyone. As a moderating position, it functions as the corrective to the evils of both extremes that lead to either theological anarchy or brutal repression.

In *The Brothers Karamazov*, Dostoevsky claimed that "without God, all is permitted." Without one absolute God determining good and evil, morality is impossible. Analogously, today's religious thinkers should ask: "Without universal religious truth is every conception of God permitted?" Under the pluralist principle, we must allow others to form their own idea of God without imposing our own limits upon them. Yet if every form of worship is potentially legitimate – even if only for others – do we not forfeit the right to criticize those who believe differently, even when they worship the God of death and destruction?

How can theological pluralism not destroy itself by being so open that it accepts as legitimate even beliefs in religious violence?

It is here that we can see the need for Rabbi Greenberg's concep-

27. Judith Hershcopf, *American Jewish Year Book,* 1965, 128; Reuven Kimmelman, "Rabbis Joseph B. Soloveitchik and Abraham Joshua Heschel on Jewish-Christian Relations," *Modern Judaism*, 24, 2004, 255.

tion of idolatry and the centrality of *Tzelem Elokim*[28] in his religious worldview. His concept of idolatry as human systems that claim to be absolute, that exercise no self-limitation and that leave no room for the other, establishes the limit of legitimate theological pluralism – and in doing so it saves theological pluralism from becoming a false idol of its own. Without Greenberg's concept of idolatry, there would be no logical way to distinguish between a valid religious worldview promoting the sanctity of every person and one that destroys the Other in the name of God. Without the idolatry-limit, a principled pluralist would have no rational grounds for critiquing the religious imperialist who strives to violently impose his intolerant views on others.

Ultimately, it is not idolatry's logical function that makes it essential to Greenberg's religious world or ours. It is its role in steering persons away from delegitimizing others and the brutal carnage that absolutism brings in its wake. Insisting that idolatry is an evil that must be avoided directs religious people to the path of God Who loves His creatures.

In a prophetic key, idolatry's inverse of covenantal pluralism teaches us to be partners with others who work to realize the biblical vision, the one where human beings flourish, where peace and cooperation reign and where different peoples recognize the Creator of Heaven and Earth – by whatever names they call Him and in whatever forms they worship Him:

> It shall be in the end of days that the mountain of the Lord shall be established on top of all mountains and shall be exalted above the hills. And peoples shall stream onto it. Many nations shall come, and say, 'Come let us go up to the mountain of the Lord and to the house of the God of Jacob; and He will teach us His ways and walk in His paths. For the Torah shall go forth from Zion, and the word of the Lord from Jerusalem.' They shall beat their swords into plowshares and their spears into pruning hooks. Nation shall not lift up sword against nation, nor shall they learn war anymore. But every man shall sit under his vine and his fig tree; and none shall make him afraid. . . . *For let all people walk, each in the name*

28. The Jewish theology that all human beings are created in the image of God.

> *of his God* and we will walk in the name of the Lord our God for ever and ever (Micah, 4:1–5).

Both Micah and Rabbi Greenberg teach that combining conviction and pluralism is no contradiction. On the contrary, it is spiritually necessary in our experience of God's diverse world, and in God's larger plan for sacred history.

Irving Greenberg stands with three other great modern Jewish pluralists, all of whom have had a profound effect on modern thinking. Isaiah Berlin taught us the necessity of political pluralism for a free and open society. Abraham Joshua Heschel's poetic pluralism sensitized us to the essential role of spirituality in modern scientific material culture and Jonathan Sacks has shown us the virtues of philosophic pluralism in a Jewish mode. For this alone, Jews today are profoundly indebted to Rabbi Greenberg and his Torah.

Genius Theologian, Lonely Theologian: Yitz Greenberg on Christianity

RABBI DR. ALON GOSHEN-GOTTSTEIN

Overview and Method

Rabbi Irving (Yitz) Greenberg is arguably the most engaged Jewish thinker to have rethought the meaning of Christianity for contemporary Judaism and to have put forth a carefully constructed notion of their relationship. Certainly, he is the Orthodox Jewish thinker who has thought hardest and deepest about the meaning of this relationship. For Greenberg, the question of Jewish-Christian relations goes well beyond formulating a *halakhic* ruling or a community policy; it is also not merely a theological challenge that needs to be overcome. It is, rather, a deep personal spiritual quest to come to terms with Christianity and its spiritual message. Greenberg strives to gain a higher vision of the purpose of Christianity and of what kind of relationship Judaism and Christianity should enjoy.

An appreciation of Yitz's theological contribution requires us to not only refer to positions he takes on specific issues, but also to consider his theological method and how it sets new standards for a Jewish theology of other religions. One of the novelties of Greenberg's method is the quest to affirm Christianity on its own terms, not only in Jewish terms. He is willing to examine issues such as the crucifixion, the incarnation, and Jesus' messianic status as part of his attempt to affirm Christian self-understanding.[1] Needless to say, Yitz would not affirm the truth of

1. Interestingly, the doctrine of the Trinity seems to fall beyond the scope of his

any of these theological positions as true in the sense that the faithful might proclaim. Nevertheless, he seeks to view these faith claims as valid and as somehow faithful to Judaism's own faith foundations. To do this, he evokes a notion of models or depth structures. Accordingly, even if the incarnation is contradictory to some biblical principles, the model itself is operating out of classic biblical modes.[2] Biblical faith provides a frame of reference that defines the grammar common to both faith traditions, even if what they say may seem contradictory.[3] A deep theology or a comparative theology therefore provides a means for affirming Christianity as a whole and the possible legitimacy of particulars of Christian faith.

A central notion in Greenberg's attempt to validate Christianity is the appeal to Christian experience. The approach is one of validation. If Christians have experienced something significant we must seek to accommodate their feeling and their self-understanding within a Jewish framework, without necessarily subscribing to their truth claims. This is a fine line to walk. But Greenberg is able to apply it in some important contexts. For instance, he is willing to validate Christian experience of spiritual regeneration through faith in Jesus as a messianic figure who forgives sins and launches a new reality.[4] The beauty of his approach is that rather than affirming the truth claim of such a faith experience he is content to validate that experience, but only as relevant to those who had it. Jews, by contrast, at the time of Jesus and in later generations,

---

efforts. Is this a function of deep seated Jewish attitudes to idolatry or is it that one theologian cannot cover all bases? Significantly, the one time that Greenberg injects his own preference into Christian theological debates, rather than accepting Christianity on its own terms, has to do with the divine status of Jesus. Irving Greenberg, *For the Sake of Heaven and Earth: The New Encounter between Judaism and Christianity,* Jewish Publication Society, Philadelphia, 2004, 92, 232. All references below to page numbers only are to this work.

This discussion is disturbing in some ways and not fully in keeping with Greenberg's own theological approach. It would seem, in this discussion, that affirmation of the same God would be contingent on adopting certain non-classical views of the Christian godhead. This is in marked contrast to the tone and method that governs most of his work and may be a later development or an expression of theologizing that does not meet his own standards.

2. 232.

3. 43.

4. 65.

had a different experience. They did not experience, through Jesus, the deliverance they had been awaiting. Christian experience is therefore only relevant for Christians and has no claim on Jews.[5]

Other expressions of the approach of validating Christian experience are found in validating the Christian experience of the resurrection, which he suggests should be viewed as an expression of God's closeness, following the biblical claim that God is close to all.[6] Greenberg goes as far as to affirm that: "Christianity's birth is a triumph of human fidelity in the face of tragedy that was rewarded with such powerful religious experiences as to enable the steadfast to know God's presence in the midst of the faith community."[7] Christian experience of election is valid. Christians have experienced God's love that singles out the beloved and transforms and revivifies life.[8]

Yitz is willing to go to the heart of Christian religious experience and validate it from a Jewish perspective. This is a deeply empathetic approach that seeks to accommodate Christian experience from within a Jewish framework. He is thus able to state that "The Kingdom of God is within you" is a true statement, at the same time as recognizing the ways in which its application tended to move into a spiritualized realm, while ignoring concrete reality.[9] This sympathetic view of Christianity based on recognition of the validity of the experience of the faithful leads Greenberg to recognize the faithfulness of the early Jesus believers who reacted to Jesus' death out of loyalty to their Jewish understanding.[10] For Greenberg, dealing with issues such as the incarnation (discussed below) "allows faithful Jews to respect the distinctive theological claims of Christianity – and not just the models and values that Jews and Christians hold in common."[11]

The issues that Greenberg engages have been the focus of Jewish

5. Ibid.
6. 66.
7. ibid.
8. 233.
9. 79.
10. 149.
11. *The Relationship of Judaism and Christianity: Toward a New Organic Model, Twenty Years of Jewish/Catholic Relations*, ed. E. Fisher et al., New York, Paulist Press, 1994, 206.

polemic, the basis of rejection, and at times even of mockery for millennia. Hence it is a significant breakthrough that a Jewish theologian is prepared to engage, in detail, the faith of a religion that until yesterday was a rival religion.

There are three faith principles of Christianity that are addressed in the framework of Yitz's discussion: faith in Jesus as Messiah, the incarnation and the crucifixion, though the latter receives much less attention than the former. Let us review the novelty of Yitz's approach in relation to each of these foci of faith.

Jesus as Messiah

The messianic status of Jesus is possibly the biggest theological stumbling block in Jewish-Christian relations. At the heart of the divide is the question of whether Jesus was the Messiah awaited by Israel. The question has obvious implications for the question of whether Jews should have recognized Jesus and whether they should accept him today. The question lies at the heart of Christian missionary efforts to this day, though it must be made clear that none of Greenberg's conversation partners, or their churches, engage in missionary work towards Jews.

We have seen that Yitz adopts a hermeneutic of empathy, in which he seeks to understand the religious reality and experience of early Christians and to validate it. This hermeneutic also informs his approach to the question of the messiahship of Jesus. The question for him is not one that can be answered by a yes or no, true or false. Rather, the question should be addressed from the perspective of the faith and experience of the respective communities. Each faith community responds differently to the same events and to the existence, if you will – the coming – of Jesus. Both responses are legitimate, and make sense within the historical and experiential framework of the respective faith community. Greenberg's task is, therefore, not to argue that Jesus is not Messiah, or that he could be. Rather, it is first to validate Christian experience. Secondly, he seeks to translate such validation into classical Jewish terms that do not compromise the classical Jewish position that refused to recognize Jesus as Messiah.

Greenberg makes the argument by shifting the focus from the person of Jesus to the fact that a claim for messiahship is being made. He appeals to the vitality, and therefore to the continuing emergence, of messianic movements within Judaism. The discourse shifts, then, from the Jesus movement to what may be called messianic phenomenology in the course of Jewish history. Jewish vitality, argues Greenberg, is expressed in its ability to generate messianic movements:

> The test of Judaism's vitality is that it will continue to generate further movements toward Messianic redemption. As long as Judaism generates Messiahs, one can be certain that it is alive. When Judaism stops generating Messiahs, it is no longer faithful to its own tradition. That does not mean that every Messiah is the final one or even a true one. It does mean that the Messianic impulse is a fundamental test of Judaism's own integrity. In that sense, Christianity is not a mere deviation or misunderstanding; it is an organic outgrowth of Judaism itself.[12]

These words rely on an important phenomenon in the course of Jewish history. Messiahship is claimed time and again, though in fact no single individual has been recognized as *the* Messiah, at least not by all of Israel. Jesus must therefore be seen in the framework of the broader workings of Jewish history and the place that messianic expectation holds within it. If messianic aspiration is a constant present of Jewish history, claims for Jesus' messiahship are simply one more case of such a claim being made, in and of itself no more harmful or problematic than other cases. And, the implied argument continues, if we can come to terms with other instances of messianic ascription that did not justify itself, we should be able to extend the same accommodating attitude to claims of Jesus' messiahship. Moreover, in a paradoxical way, there is something healthy, not a deviation, in the ascription of messianic title to an individual. It is a sign of spiritual vitality and authenticity. Thus, seen from the perspective of Jewish history and the history of messianic movements, Christianity's messianic claims may be considered normative, an organic outgrowth of Judaism, all the while bypassing any discussion of their truth value.

12. 175

Just how "Jewish" the recognition of someone as Messiah is, emerges from the following passage:

> Like good, faithful Jews, the early Jewish followers of Jesus were looking for the Messiah, particularly in a difficult century. Lo! And behold! In Jesus' life they recognized his arrival. To recognize that the Messiah has arrived, and to respond, is a very faithful response on the part of a Jew. Therefore, a Jew does not initially forfeit the state of faithfulness by recognizing someone as Messiah – even if he or she has erred.[13]

The process, then, is more important than its content. It is the faithful response that counts more than the specific identification of the messianic figure. And therefore even the mistaken identification of Jesus as Messiah is profoundly Jewish. Greenberg goes further, making the point that error in the identity of the Messiah is not some fundamental error in faith. He has much of Jewish history to back this claim. And in our own times, he is surely aware of the most recent iteration of Jewish faith in a deceased Messiah, in the person of the late Rabbi Menachem Mendel Schneerson of Lubavitch.[14] By switching the focus of attention from Jesus to the religious response that belief in him represents and by contextualizing such response within the history of Jewish messianism,

---

13. 149.

14. This would have not been the case in 1986, when the article was first published. In terms of fidelity to Jewish history and its great currents, I believe Greenberg's forgiving and accommodating stance towards errors in messianic identity is much truer than the attempt to castigate Lubavitch messianism in light of the history of Jewish objection to Jesus' messiahship, as argued by David Berger (David Berger, *The Rebbe, the Messiah and the Scandal of Orthodox Indifference,* Littman Library, London 2001). Note Greenberg's striking statement, 149: "I once wrote that I was ashamed of the fact that, in this generation, there was not at least a false Messiah. A false Messiah would show that the Jews were truly living up to their vocation, which is to hope and expect the Messiah, particularly in such tragic times. If one hopes for the Messiah and a false one shows up – well, it is regrettable but at least one has tried. Not to generate even a false Messiah is a sign that people are complacent; they have either lost hope or do not care." It is worth noting in this context that the State of Israel does not seem to have messianic overtones, at least not in terms of the present discussion that focuses on Messiah as a person. Greenberg approaches it more in terms of responsibility than in terms of fulfillment of messianic expectations. See his discussion, 159–161.

Greenberg is able to lay foundations for a novel approach to a Jewish view of Christian messianic claims.

Yitz's approach to Christian messianism does not stop with an appreciation of the overall intentionality and expression of faith. In seeking to provide a positive framework for appreciating Christian messianic claims, he puts forth a novel, daring, and easily misunderstood suggestion. Aware of the long history of messianic claimants and of the fact that such messianic claims, in and of themselves, do not lead to the delegitimization of the claimant or his followers (to date there have been no women claimants), Yitz proposes a new category by means of which to describe the messianism of Jesus. There are two variations to the proposal and, despite the different ring, they seek to achieve the same goal, namely to address Christian understanding of Jesus as Messiah in a respectful and accommodating way, while at the same time upholding Jewish refusal to recognize Jesus as Israel's Messiah. The one way of speaking of Jesus, in this context, is as "would-be Messiah."[15] Such a description refers to the self-understanding of either Jesus or his followers. It suggests potentiality, and at the same time also signals that the potential was not fulfilled, at least not according to Jewish standards. A description of "would-be Messiah" is consonant with the classical *halakhic* formulation of Maimonides concerning the testing and verification of a true Messiah;[16] it has served in recent times with reference to the Lubavitcher Rebbe.[17]

Greenberg's appeal to Jesus as would-be redeemer is particularly irenic:

> [T]he two communities owe special help to each other. One feels special rejoicing in the achievement of fellow citizens. Therefore, Jews who always yearned for a universal redeemer and who ac-

15. See 149, dating to 1986.

16. See Maimonides, *Yad Haḥazakah,* Laws of Kings 11:4.

17. Significantly, while alive, the teaching emphasized his messianic potential based on this ruling of Maimonides. In an utter reversal of this logic, most of his followers continue to uphold his messianic status, despite failure to meet the criteria cited in his lifetime, thereby making his case all the more similar to that of Jesus. Greenberg's later reference to messianism consciously relates the cases of Jesus and the Lubavitcher Rebbe. See 48.

> cept little of Jesus' message should nevertheless appreciate Jesus' service as a spiritual messiah to gentiles; he is not a false messiah, but a would-be redeemer for the nations.[18]

If Christianity is the means of fulfilling Judaism's latent universalism, Jesus must be valued positively. It is not fully clear what the "would-be" status of Jesus for gentiles is. "Would-be" suggests potentiality, and such potentiality hinges on the criteria for messianic work. If Christians apply different criteria to the Messiah than those of Israel, then, in fact, they have redefined what Messiah is, and argued for Jesus' successful fulfillment of the expectations of a Messiah. If so, Jesus' status is no longer that of a "would-be" messiah. Rather, he has fulfilled some aspect of messianic work, following different criteria. To speak of Jesus as a "would-be" Messiah, is to apply Jewish criteria to Jesus' status as Messiah, while upholding the positive benefits that Jesus brought to those who have faith in him. Greenberg seems to not be able to go all the way. His attempt at a positive evaluation of Jesus as Messiah for gentiles falls short of full acceptance of such claims, in terms suitable for gentiles. All the positive outcomes of Jesus' work are viewed through a Jewish lens that provides the criteria for messianic legitimacy, leaving Jesus as "would-be" Messiah, while rejoicing in his achievements and in how a deep Jewish universal vision is fulfilled through him.

There is a second formulation by means of which Greenberg seeks to affirm the Christian view of Jesus as Messiah. This is to speak of him as a failed Messiah:

> The general Jewish position has been that Jesus was a false Messiah. Why? Would it not be more precise to say that a false Messiah is one who teaches the wrong values and who turns sin into holiness? A more accurate description from the Jewish perspective would be that Jesus was not a "false" but a "failed" Messiah. He has not finished the job but his work is not in vain.[19]

The claim that Jesus was a false Messiah grows out of a view of Mes-

18. 100.
19. 177.

siah as a zero-sum game, assuming there is only one Messiah and that therefore Jesus either is or is not Messiah. Greenberg seeks to stretch the category. A failed Messiah, by this reading, refers to someone who has participated in the messianic process and has advanced it, but has not completed it. One might almost have said Jesus was part-Messiah, or more readily one who played a part in the messianic process, thereby removing the focus from his person to the process in which he participated. With the focus on Jesus as person, the best Greenberg can do is to acknowledge him as "failed." The failure may not be the result of his person, but simply indicates the process has not come to its end.

Once again, Greenberg's criterion is Jewish. If the view was fully pluralist, one could have imagined multiple Messiahs for multiple purposes and multiple communities. At one point, in fact, Greenberg experiments with ideas of multiple Messiahs, appealing to the notion of Messiah son of Joseph, a rabbinic tradition that recognizes at least two messianic figures, the son of Joseph and the son of David:

> This concept of a "failed" but true Messiah is found in a rabbinic tradition of the Messiah ben Joseph. The Messiah ben David (son of David) is the one who brings the final restoration. In the Messiah ben Joseph's idea, you have a Messiah who comes and fails, indeed is put to death, but this Messiah paves the way for the final redemption.[20]

To speak of Jesus as Messiah ben Joseph is to affirm his messianic status by identification with a messianic figure who is different from the ultimate figure to which Jews look. It is, nevertheless, a powerful means of affirming Jesus as a Messiah (not *the* Messiah), from a Jewish perspective. The notion of "failure" is, for Greenberg, a characteristic of many Jewish heroes, and not something to be ashamed of. Moses, Jeremiah, and many of Judaism's great heroes were "failures."[21] Therefore, Jesus is viewed in continuity with Israel's great ones. One may augment Greenberg's reading further by affirming that the status of Messiah son

20. 153.
21. ibid.

of Joseph, or a failed Messiah, is itself a title that allows us to relate to a long list of messianic claimants.

The distinction between false and failed messiahs is a reading of history. Such a reading is not divorced from the history of Jewish-Christian relations. In an interesting note to a previously quoted passage,[22] Greenberg makes the distinction between false and failed Messiah hinge on how Christians treat Jews. When Jews are persecuted, hated, and degraded in Jesus' name, then, in fact, it turns out he is a false Messiah. By contrast, the term failed Messiah points to the benefits of love and consolation brought to hundreds of millions in Christianity's name.

It is obvious that tying messianic achievement and status to the moral dimension of how Jesus' followers act towards Jews introduces an extraneous category to the discussion. This is an indication of the fine line that Greenberg has to walk, both within his community and in relation to Christians. He cannot ignore the history; he is not oblivious to criticism levelled by Jews against Christianity, operating in Jesus' name, and what it has done to Jews. At the same time, he cannot overlook all the good that Christianity brought to the world in Jesus' name. While these differing perspectives are acknowledged independently of messianic titles, Greenberg struggles with how to speak of Jesus as Messiah, also in terms of the moral consequences and historical relations between Jews and Christians. Whether this is germane to his core argument or not, a fact witnessed by the relegation of this argument to a footnote, it gives us a peak into the workings and struggles of his mind and heart as he seeks to be faithful to his community and its history as well as to the reality he encounters in Christianity.

The notion of "failed" Messiah seeks to construct a positive view of Jesus as Messiah. As argued, it does so from exclusively Jewish ground, rather than moving towards a more pluralistic notion of Messiah. In viewing Jesus from the perspective of a Jewish view of messianism, one wonders how successful this attempt is. Greenberg himself acknowledges that this suggestion is one that has been readily misunderstood. "Failed" Messiah is not a classical Jewish category, and therefore would not have much resonance with a Jewish audience. For Christians, it is hard to imagine settling happily for faith in a "failed" Messiah, even if

---

22. 177.

the terms is loaded in the most positive way by Greenberg.[23] Greenberg himself admits this much[24] and I have heard similar criticism from Jewish colleagues.[25] While still not fully pluralistic, the parallel formulation of "would-be" Messiah ultimately serves Greenberg's interests better than the notion of a "failed" Messiah.

While a consideration of the messianic status of Jesus is obviously a central concern for Jewish-Christian relations, from another perspective it is not, or should not be, a major deterrent to the advancement of relations. At the end of the day, what counts is not a consideration of the past, as much as the proper orientation for the future. Greenberg shares with many other Jewish thinkers a practical emphasis that is oriented towards the future rather than the past:

> Let us side-by-side, then, bring the Messiah instead of arguing whether it is the first or second coming. Instead of the fighting and the belittling and the denying that delays the coming, let there be mutual activity and love that hastens it.[26]

Note that the emphasis is not, as some often express it, that rather than debating the first coming, we should focus on the second coming. The point is that the emphasis should not be upon the debates about the coming, but upon common action. Such common action is itself a means of hastening the coming of the Messiah. This is, of course, a Jewish view of how to relate to Messiah's coming. While a typical Christian attitude is one of awaiting, within Judaism, especially within the kabbalistic school, a much more active awaiting is found, wherein our actions provide the conditions and circumstances for the coming

---

23. One could make the argument that faith in Messiah gave way to faith in the son of God, thereby making Jesus' status as Messiah secondary. If so, reference to him in terms of failed Messiah may not undermine Christian faith as much. Still, for the faithful, this is a very counter-intuitive way to speak of the subject of their faith.

24. 32.

25. At a recent gathering, where I referenced Greenberg's work, Deborah Weissman, a foremost teacher and activist in Jewish-Christian relations, and former president of the International Council of Christians and Jews, shared a conversation she had with Greenberg, where she expressed admiration for his overall theological oeuvre, with the major exception of the idea of a failed Messiah, that she considered a failed idea.

26. 197.

of the Messiah. This attitude is extended as an invitation to both faith communities to act for the common good. The kabbalistic worldview of *tikkun olam,* which initially saw ritual activity as a means of hastening the coming of the Messiah, has been adapted by contemporary Jewish thought to good actions meant to heal the world.[27] Greenberg extends this approach as an invitation to both Jews and Christians to engage in common actions for the ultimate common good, the coming of the Messiah.

In the most recent iteration of his thought, Yitz bases the call to common action on Judaism's affirmation of the falsity of Christian claims of the world already having been redeemed, standing such affirmation on its head and turning it into a call for collaboration:

> Jews now have to understand that their triumphant assertion that the Messiah has not come is not a victory for Judaism. There can be no complacency about the fact that the world was not redeemed – as claimed by Jesus' followers – for this flawed reality bred evil forces that threatened Jewry's very existence. Thus Judaism needs to reach out to every movement that hopes to bring the Messiah, jointly working to temper the absolutist, utopian elements in this commitment, while seeking to attain redemption as soon as possible.[28]

Moving away from a model of competition between the religions, Yitz considers the need for redeeming the world a common need for both faiths. In this context, he does not even leave room for the faith of Christians that they have experienced redemption or for the power of their subjective testimony spilling over into objective, historical reality. Likely, the forces of evil in the world make it hard to uphold such a Christian view. Attaining redemption is the more urgent the task. There is a messianic urgency in Greenberg's writing, one that cuts across the divide between faiths and that becomes an invitation to work together

27. See Lawrence Fine, "Tikkun": A Lurianic Motive in Contemporary Jewish Thought, *From Ancient Israel to Modern Judaism: Essays in Honor of Marvin Fox,* ed. J. Neusner et al, Scholars Press, Atlanta, 1989, Vol. 4, 35–53.

28. 91.

to heal the world and transcend those portions of our religions that are obstacles to its eventual, and speedy, healing.

The Incarnation

A second site of Christian faith to which Greenberg devotes his attention in a movement of accommodation is the incarnation of Jesus. Theologically, this is a much more challenging view to affirm. If messianic faith is a constant in Judaism and if a history of failed Messiahs provides the backdrop for a reevaluation of Jesus as Messiah, the incarnation seems to be a much harder concept to justify in Jewish terms. It is, after all, a claim the likes of which is not made with reference to other figures in Jewish history and which stands at the heart of the theological divide between the faiths. Moreover, it touches on concerns as central as the view of Christianity as idolatry.[29] It therefore requires much theological will and ingenuity to affirm the validity and legitimacy of faith in Jesus' incarnation for Christians.

There are two strategies one can identify in Yitz's writing. The first relates to the religious experience of the early Christians and legitimates it. The other is to consider the incarnation as an extension of the faith of Israel, even if it crosses a line that the Jewish tradition itself would not cross. Appeal to the depth structure of biblical faith is accordingly deemed more important than affirmation of the particular boundaries and theological positions that served for centuries as demarcations distinguishing one faith from another.

Let us begin by noting the reference to the faith of Christian believers:

> As Christians brought the message of hope to Hellenized gentiles, the new audience heard the proclamation about Jesus, the son of God, bringing them closer to God. According to the Jewish tradition, metaphorically, all people are the children of God. The

29. Note that even authors that are willing to come to terms with the Trinity, have a hard time justifying the incarnation. See my "Judaism and Incarnational Theologies: Mapping Out the Parameters of Dialogue," *Journal of Ecumenical Studies*, 39, 3–4, 2002, 242–3.

> newcomers understood the message in a more literal way. They accepted with gratitude the news that God sought to close the gap between humanity and the divine by crossing over and sharing human experience in the flesh. God sharing human experience was an established Jewish idea, but the conclusion that this identification took the form of Divine Incarnation, literally, was ultimately deemed by Jews to be in conflict with the monotheistic idea. . . . Historically, Judaism rejected what it saw as the divinization of a man. Many Jewish sages rated the Trinitarian teachings as idolatry or, at best, as the dilution of the monotheistic principle. Yet, the Trinity represents Christianity's effort to honor the Jewish normative understanding of God's oneness. . . . (To be fair, one should add that it is also trying to be faithful to its religious experience with the one God it worships).[30]

Greenberg cannot affirm Christian faith, either the incarnation or the Trinity. But he can affirm the religious experience of believers and their efforts to keep their faith somehow tied to its Jewish roots. Christians take the Jewish teaching of divine sonship and make it literally an expression of God sharing human experience in the flesh. And it is in the nature of their religious experience that Christians recognize in the one God also the presence of Jesus, who is himself experienced as divine. Greenberg neither affirms the validity of Christian faith nor its normativity, from the perspective of the history of Jewish views. He does, however, defend the integrity and authenticity of the intention of Christian faithful, both in recognizing Jesus as God and in seeking to contain such recognition within the bounds of classical Jewish monotheism. This defense suggests that somehow intention is ultimately more significant than the eventual theological stance taken by Christians. Christian religious experience is self-validating at least in terms of legitimation for upholding positions that are foreign to Jewish theology. We note the significant primacy of religious experience over doctrinal correctness. One cannot divorce such an approach from the modern and post-modern sensibilities that privilege subjectivity and individual, or collective, experience, over "truth" that is conceived in a

30. 72.

hard and fast way. From this perspective, understanding how Christians concluded as they did and appreciating the depth of their religious experience should be grounds for accepting and respecting them, even while maintaining distance with reference to their actual beliefs.

The above passage already makes reference to one sense in which Christian faith in the incarnation has biblical roots. It considers the biblical notion of sonship to have been extended from a metaphor to reality, and from all people (or perhaps all Jews) to the one unique son of God. This move is repeated in several different ways, in an attempt to ground even the seemingly idolatrous idea of the incarnation, in a Jewish way of thinking:

> Christianity is a commentary on the original Exodus, in which the later event – the Christ event – is a manifest, "Biblically" miraculous event – God becoming incarnate and self-validating through miracles. Obviously, many Jews will argue that closing the Biblically-portrayed gap between the human and the divine, between the real and the ideal, by Incarnation, is idolatrous or at least against the grain of the Biblical way. But even if Incarnation is contradictory to some Biblical principles, the model itself is operating out of classic Biblical modes – the need to achieve redemption, the desire to close the gap between the human and the divine which includes divine initiatives, etc. Thus, a faithful Jew can affirm that Incarnation is improbable and violative of other given Biblical principles and that it is unnecessary in light of the continuing care of the Jewish people; yet such a divine gesture is not destructive of the original covenant if it was a divine act intended for the salvation of the Gentiles and "broadcast" to them rather than to the Jews. This . . . allows faithful Jews to respect the distinctive theological claims of Christianity – and not just the models and values which Jews and Christians hold in common.[31]

The goal is stated in the final sentence: respecting Christianity in its

31. The Relationship of Judaism and Christianity: Toward a New Organic Model, *Twenty Years of Jewish/Catholic Relations*, ed. E. Fisher et al., New York, Paulist Press, 1994, 206. The text was slightly toned down in *For the Sake of Heaven and Earth.*

distinctiveness and theological particularity. Several strategies combine here. One is the biblical grounding of the incarnation, as an extension of the Exodus story. The combination of miraculous action and closing the gap between human and divine, itself a biblical movement, brings the incarnation into the realm of the possible. Significantly, Greenberg does not reject the actual claim out of hand. It is improbable, but not impossible, and the claim is made further possible at least theologically, if not metaphysically, when its intended audience are gentiles.

In another discussion, Yitz makes a similar effort to accommodate faith in the incarnation:

> Judaism denied the occurrence of Divine Incarnation; it needed to be authentic to its own religious life. This tempted it to overlook the genuinely Jewish dimension of this Christian attempt to close the gap between the human and the divine. Even while rejecting the model, should Jews not recognize that it grows out of the tormenting persistence of a great distance between the divinely sought perfection and the human condition? One can conceive of a divine pathos that sent not only words across the gap but life and body itself. I say this not as a Jew who accepts this claim, but as one who has come to see that it is not for me to prescribe to God how God communicates to others.[32]

Greenberg does not depart from Jewish refusal to recognize the incarnation, but he significantly weakens opposition to this idea. Greenberg can speak of "the genuinely Jewish dimension" of this belief. Jews are called to be empathetic to the religious sensibilities and causes that generated this faith, assuming that somehow understanding the motivation and genealogy of the belief compensate for significant substantive differences with it. Greenberg appeals to religious imagination, imagining divine pathos going one step beyond speech as the bridge of the chasm of human-divine. Finally, Greenberg remains open to the theoretical possibility of such an occurrence. The issue with incarnation is not its metaphysical impossibility, as classical Jewish polemicists might claim. Rather, it is a matter of belief not shared. It is already a big step that

32. 180.

Greenberg leaves it to God to decide how to communicate with others, without imposing his own faith's constrictions on God's actions.

However, there are limitations of another nature. Immediately following this quote, Greenberg states:

> Our task is to find ways for humans to hear God. We should measure religions by the criterion of how people act after they hear the word in community. If the Incarnation and Resurrection of Jesus lead to Christian triumphalism, to persecution, and idolatry, then Christianity proves itself to be false. If it leads to deeper compassion and understanding and a grasp of the human realities and human needs, and motivated covenantal action, then it validates itself as a channel of the Divine.[33]

This is a hugely important quote, and may be the core of Greenberg's theory of religious pluralism. What matters in religion is not the faith one upholds, but how it translates into action in the life of the community. What makes incarnation, as well as resurrection, and in theory any other aspect of the Christian faith, valid or not is not the actual content of faith, but how it is lived in the community. The reason why Greenberg is willing to affirm the biblical roots of incarnation is not because this is a good or valid application of biblical principles; rather the truth value of the faith claim is proven by the life that Christians lead. Because Greenberg has come to know Christians whose faith led them to compassion and to taking what he calls covenantal action in response to human needs, he validates their faith. Once validated in terms of its fruit, Greenberg makes the additional move of grounding such faith in biblical precedent and practicing humility or agnosticism in relation to how God might communicate with other communities. The reverse is true as well: Triumphalism and persecution provide testimony to the falsity of faith, rather than actual theological correctness.[34]

---

33. Ibid.

34. I am hard pressed to account for "idolatry" in the above quote. Idolatry is not a moral virtue, and certainly does not relate to Christian treatment of Jews. It is thus out of place in the present discussion. Appeal to it in this context begs the question around which this paragraph is constructed, namely whether belief in the incarnation is idolatrous.

One final discussion suggests Judaism and Christianity apply the same biblical principles, but through alternative strategies for achieving the same end:

> Whereas Jewish tradition affirms that the final goals can be attained under the leadership of a human avant-garde, Christianity adds the claim that God became the human model that leads humans into the final state. Thus Christianity also concedes that only a human model can bring out the fullness of humanity. Once the triumphalist distortion is removed, Christians can begin to recognize the Incarnation model is profoundly Jewish, albeit rejected by Judaism. Jews can begin to recognize that the Incarnation concept should not be dismissed as some bizarre import from Hellenistic culture but viewed as an extension of the use of human exemplars to evoke maximum covenantal behavior. It is not that Jews and Christians will accept each other's views on this issue, but they can come to realize that both positions grow out of strategies for achieving the goals of the covenant held in common.[35]

Speaking of theological differences as alternative strategies is a marvelous way of minimizing them; a strategy is an interim step taken towards some ultimate goal. Judaism and Christianity, in this view, share the same story and participate in the same covenantal processes. This fundamental identity overrides all those differences that throughout the centuries have been highlighted as means of differentiating one religion from another. In Greenberg's view, we should not be looking at the details of faith, but at the broader common participation in the common covenantal structure, or even in the common covenant. Details are then to be subsumed under this fundamental similarity.

At the end of the day details are no more than alternative strategies for fulfilling the common covenantal aspirations. In this reading, faith in the incarnation is simply a strategy that takes biblical faith in following a human leader and identifying this human leader with God himself.[36]

---

35. 166.

36. In a later formulation, Greenberg suggests Jews need not insist on the relevance of the truth of their historical experience to another faith community. "It is sufficient

But the model is Jewish, not Hellenistic, inasmuch as it echoes the fundamentals of Jewish faith and seeks to realize the biblical covenantal model.

The Crucifixion

The crucifixion poses much less of a theological challenge than the articles of Christian faith covered previously. After all, it is a fact and is not, in and of itself, one that is contested between Jews and Christians. Whereas with reference to Messiahship and Incarnation, Greenberg spoke to his Jewish audience, in an attempt to make it more accepting of Christian faith, with reference to the crucifixion he addresses a Christian audience, and engages it in the question of meaning.

> I have argued elsewhere that the true lesson of the Crucifixion had been misunderstood by Christians because of their past triumphalism. In the light of the Holocaust, one would argue that the true lesson of the Crucifixion is that if God in person came down to earth in human flesh and was put on the cross and crucified, then God would be broken. God would be so exhausted by the agony that God would end up losing faith, and saying, "My God, my God, why have you forsaken me?" If God could not survive the cross, then surely no human can be expected to. So the overwhelming call for both religions is to stop the Crucifixion, not to glorify it.[37]

It takes deep engagement in dialogue with another religion to tell its believers what the meaning of their fundamental religious symbol is and what lesson should be drawn from a formative religious moment. The explicit appeal to the Holocaust is the context for such a daring statement, providing the moral justification for telling Christians what the crucifixion *really* means, or at least what it ought to mean today. It is not a sign of love, a great offering, a redeeming sacrifice. It is a teaching

---

for Jews to affirm that they have no interest in restricting Gods' choice of tactics and method of revelation." 67.

37. 158.

of how deep humanly-inflicted suffering can operate. It operates even on God's self, causing God himself to lose faith. Greenberg takes the Christian faith in incarnation and resurrection and delivers them to a Christian audience as a moral teaching, in the relational space of both communities. The crucifixion is God going to the extreme in order to show us how not to act towards one another. It is a moral lesson that we, and all religious communities, must learn, whether they affirm their faith in the saving power of the cross or not.

The crucifixion also provides us with a view of another side of Greenberg's approach to Christianity. He is as capable of criticizing it as he is of being empathetic and accommodating:

> The narrowing of its messages that grew out of its unconditional rejection of Judaism penalized Christianity itself in no small measure. The focus on Crucifixion strengthened ascetic tendencies and devalued the spiritual significance of pleasure. The model of self-abnegating sacrifice as the key relationship to God generated fideism, sometimes at the expense of reason; it also nurtured the self-image of a powerless human, dependent on a mediator, unable to help himself or play a fully dignified role in the covenant.[38]

This is powerful criticism of Christianity. But it does not seek to devalue Christianity itself as much as to view it from the perspective of checks and balances provided, in Greenberg's view, by the existence of multiple covenantal communities. From the perspective of a true pluralism, one can ask whether all that has transpired as a consequence of key Christian symbols and moments of faith has been beneficial. Gone from this passage is the appeal to the faith of Christians or a deeper drive by means of which their belief can be justified, experientially or biblically. Instead, Greenberg considers how symbols and beliefs can distort a spiritual path. Implicit in this critique is the view of Judaism's alternative choices as superior to those made by Christians in light of the cross. Here, as in other instances, Greenberg is less concerned with the truth or falsity of a belief than with its impact and fruits in the lives of believers. The ultimate issues are the meaning and the practical

38. 224.

consequences of the Crucifixion. Some of the consequences of faith in the resurrection are undesired, especially when weighed against Greenberg's ultimate standard of humans taking their dignified role as partners in a covenantal relationship with God.[39]

Conclusion: Greenberg as Model of Engagement

It is hard to gauge Greenberg's impact within the Orthodox Jewish world, or for that matter within the broader Jewish world in relation to Christianity. My sense is that his impact has not been extensive, certainly not commensurate with the depth of Greenberg's engagement and the valiant spiritual and intellectual efforts in which he engages as he reviews Christianity and Jewish-Christian relations. The discussion above of how Greenberg engages contested issues is only one aspect, and possibly not the most important aspect of his engagement with Christianity.[40] Some readers may wish to adopt Greenberg's positions on any of the specific points covered above. However, I would submit that Greenberg's contribution is far more significant than the individual positions he takes on this or that Christian doctrine. More than individual positions, Greenberg teaches us theological audacity, grounded in an empathetic listening to the other, and an attempt to accommodate the faith of the other within one's own faith structures.[41] This, in turn, is grounded in personal relationships that invite a serious listening to the spiritual reality of the member of another tradition. What Green-

39. This passage dates to 2000. I therefore suspect that this critical note is part of a later Greenberg.

40. I am presently preparing a full review of Greenberg's approach to Christianity, to appear in a volume tentatively titled *Heschel, Greenberg, Sacks – Jewish Thinkers Face World Religions*. The extensive discussion of Greenberg that led to the eventual crystallization of this volume grows out of the mandate of the present essay. As this essay expanded I have had to make a choice of what to present for the present collection of essays. The full treatment of Greenberg on Christianity will await the said volume. Looking back, I am truly grateful to Rabbi Shmuly Yanklowitz for the invitation to contribute to the present *festschrift*. Without this invitation I would have never entered as deeply into the world of thought of Irving Yitz Greenberg.

41. Technically, this would be seen as an inclusivist move. Greenberg, however, is much more of a pluralist. This is obvious from other parts of his theology of religions. Given Christianity's growth from Judaism, some measure of inclusivism is inevitable, even if the broader spirit is pluralist.

berg models, first and foremost, is process. His process extends from openness of heart, to creativity of mind, and, ultimately, to openness of spirit to a higher vision that is common to both Judaism and Christianity. In reviewing the various discussions here, it is a mistake to approach them simply from the perspective of whether one agrees with Greenberg's stance on crucifixion, incarnation or Jesus as Messiah. It is similarly a mistake only to argue whether his stance is legitimate and why one might find fault with it. His novel and radical ideas manifest a deeper spirit, and to focus on these details at the expense of the spirit is, to some extent, to miss the point.

Internalizing the deeper spirit driven by the depth of human relations and the heights of spiritual vision provides a different vantage point on the specific positions taken by Yitz in relation to contested theological issues. A consideration of how he visits classical sites of Jewish polemic from a new vantage point and the openness of mind and heart he brings to them is skewed when it fails to take into account the broader spirit from which his individual positions are taken. As much as Yitz challenges us to consider the boundaries and parameters of various theological doctrines, he challenges us to consider the very vantage point and the attitudes of heart and mind we bring to such a view.[42] Whether this or that detail of his theology will be upheld may be secondary to the broader invitation issued to us all by Rabbi Yitz Greenberg's profound engagement with Christianity, an invitation to reposition ourselves and open up new avenues of inquiry from a novel openness of heart and mind.[43]

42. I leave it for further reflection to consider whether appreciation of this openness of heart and mind requires buy-in to some of Greenberg's positions. It may be that one can applaud and even emulate his openness without relying or accepting any of the individual positions he adopts.

43. The full extent of that invitation will become evident in my forthcoming monograph.

Between Soloveitchik, Greenberg, and Meir: The Evolution of Interfaith Thought

Tanya White

A Personal Reflection

I first encountered Rabbi Yitz's work when I read his book, *The Jewish Way*. I was struck by how an introductory book to Judaism could be so philosophically profound. The way in which Rabbi Greenberg weaved deep theology and thought into the basic principles and tenants of Judaism in such a way that a layperson or even a gentile reader would be able to appreciate, astounded me. The more I read his works – in particular his post-Holocaust thought and his concept of the Voluntary Covenant – the more drawn I became to his way of thinking. Having written a Master's degree thesis on Emil Fackenheim, I was interested to see the parallel between the two thinkers, and Greenberg's visible influence on Fackenheim's rethinking of history.[1]

R. Greenberg's thought is not just an elusive academic encounter for any reader. It touches the depths of one's personal religious being. In it I hear echoes of those who fell in the Shoah. I see the face of my grandfather *z"l*, who lost his entire family to Nazi brutality but was still a deeply religious man, though wrought with conflict. I recall his

1. It was with deep interest that I made this discovery. I had assumed the influence was from Fackenheim to Greenberg. Having asked Rabbi Greenberg if this was the case, I discovered the direction of influence was in fact in the reverse. Though Fackenheim never explicitly states as such, he alludes to it in his foreword of *God's Presence in History* (Fackenheim, Emil L. *God's Presence in History: Jewish Affirmations and Philosophical Reflections.* New York: Harper & Row, (1970).

anger on *Leil ha-Seder*[2] at *Vehi She'amdah*,[3] how he would scream to the Almighty. "It is not true, You didn't save us, You didn't save that generation. It's a lie." As a child, I could not understand the dissonance between the man who wrapped himself in a *tallit*[4] and prayed with fervor to the God who so enraged him. As Rabbi Greenberg exactly describes: "After Auschwitz faith means there are times when faith is overcome."[5] Only many years later when reading Rabbi Greenberg's thought did I begin to understand the dialectical faith my grandfather must have lived with. Only with time am I beginning to comprehend that as a nation we are living in an era of the Voluntary Covenant.

Rabbi Greenberg's work is not only important for its place in Holocaust theology in that it allows us to live and believe without having to justify or validate the evil. It is important because though we may naturally despair of mankind after the Holocaust, through the voluntary covenant, Greenberg once again endows human beings with the crown of creation. We are called upon to work with our creator in perfecting an imperfect world. For me, this demand on humanity in general and the Jewish nation in particular is the essence of our being. It is a call we must adhere to, as Greenberg insists, without denouncing, denying or justifying through theodicy, the evil that we endured during our darkest period in history. Thus, ten years after first encountering R. Greenberg's work, I am beginning my doctoral studies that focus on his notion of covenant. As part of my preliminary studies, I participated in a course focused on interfaith dialogue that led me to explore at depth R. Greenberg's book *Between Heaven and Earth*.

I feel fortunate for the chance to spend the coming years studying and analyzing Rabbi Greenberg's thought, and also privileged to have met him and his wife Blu several times, and experienced the presence of his pure goodness and idealism. The prospect of bringing his thought

2. Passover *seder* night.

3. A passage from the Passover Haggadah indicating that God will save the Jewish people.

4. Jewish prayer shawl.

5. Irving Greenberg, *Cloud of Smoke Pillar of Fire: Judaism, Christianity and Modernity after the Holocaust* Auschwitz: Beginning of a New Era? Reflections on the Holocaust. Ed. Eva Fleischner. New York: Ktav, 1977, 7–55; 441–46.

to a wider audience in this *festschrift* and advancing to new levels of understanding his philosophy from which every Jew may benefit is both humbling and exciting. I feel blessed to be able to participate in this *festschrift* and thank all who made it possible.

Introduction

This essay focuses on three thinkers. Rabbi Joseph B. Soloveitchik, known by many simply as "The Rav," Professor Irving Greenberg (a student of R. Soloveitchik), and Professor Ephraim Meir of Bar Ilan University. This chapter proposes that each of these thinkers forms a particular paradigm of interreligious dialogue.

Writing in the 1960s, R. Soloveitchik penned a highly provocative and controversial work entitled *Confrontation* in which he suggests that any theological encounter with another faith should be discouraged because of the numinous nature of each faith community. This incommensurability implies that any attempt to universalize or rationalize one's personal faith experience will reduce the totality of one's individual truth to relative terms and thus must be avoided at all costs. In his view there is an unbridgeable gap between Judaism and Christianity. The philosophical underpinnings of this chasm are based on a model of alterity that sees the self as incommensurate with the "other." Hence, the private existential faith experience will be beyond the grasp of another and any attempt to find commonality must result in the subjugation of one of the subjects in the encounter.

Professor Rabbi Irving Greenberg is an eminent American Jewish thinker best known for his post-Holocaust thought that expresses most profoundly the dialectical religious experience after the Holocaust. R. Greenberg has also been a great promoter of Jewish-Christian mutual understanding. Ultimately, he came to the realization that dialogue with Christianity is imperative today. His initial interest in interfaith dialogue was to purge Christian theology of its supersessionist and triumphalist claims, which lie at the heart of much of its anti-Semitic teaching. As his journey continued Greenberg became engaged in a deep dialogue with Christianity that led him to renounce all absolute truth claims. In many ways Greenberg echoes the thought of Abraham Joshua Heschel. He is committed to showing how both Christianity and Judaism are authentic expressions of God's will,[6] and must find common ground and a unity of differences. The Greenberg paradigm fits well into the classic category of religious pluralism that views the individual expression of faith as but one path to the absolute truth.

Greenberg interprets his revered teacher's polemic on interfaith theology as a kind of "Marrano writing,"[7] in which the surface text conveys one meaning, but the substantive depth expresses something very different.[8] This understanding allowed him to advance theological dialogue with what he perceived as the consent of his teacher. In doing so, he faced opposition and adversity from his Orthodox colleagues in the Rabbinical Council of America. Yet, in many ways, this opposition fired his passion even further. Greenberg's theology advanced interfaith dialogue throughout the seventies, and in particular helped expose the religious community to the importance of such advances.

Lastly, I outline in this paper the "trans-difference" paradigm of Professor Meir that both integrates and goes beyond the numinous thought of R. Soloveitchik and the pluralist paradigm of Greenberg. I attempt to show that Meir's approach allows us to reframe certain elements of R. Soloveitchik thinking on interfaith theology that could open the door to a new more conciliatory interpretation of Soloveitchik's thought on the subject.

Confrontation: An Introduction to the Controversy

Rabbi Joseph B. Soloveitchik was the intellectual and *halakhic* leader of American Modern Orthodoxy. His interfaith position is characterized by his strong opposition to communal, and organizational interfaith theological dialogue. His arguments were, in part, predicated upon the

6. Heschel contends in *No Religion is an Island* that the diversity of religions is "the will of God." 14

7. Greenberg. I, *For The Sake of Heaven and Earth: The New Encounter between Judaism and Christianity,* The Jewish Publication Society Philadelphia (2004) 13.

8. This interpretation is not far from Hartman's "political" interpretation of "*Confrontation*" that sees it as a means to limit theological dialogue to those that are equipped to undertake it rather than allowing everyone to pursue it. Its pursuit should be done only by those that understand the tension of the double confrontation and not by those who acquiesce the particularity of Judaism for a more universal understanding.

fear that in search of common ground or a shared theological language, Jews and Christians might each sacrifice absolute and exclusive truth claims and by doing so negate part of their religious faith. At the heart of R. Soloveitchik's ethos on interfaith dialogue, which he set out in the 1964 article "Confrontation" published in *Tradition – A Journal of Orthodox Thought*, lies a deep antipathy towards any attempt to translate the faith experience into universal or absolute categories.

There are three important things to note about this article: (1) its rhetoric is as important as its content, (2) there is no *pesaq halakhah* at the end, which means it is more polemical and recommended policy than statutory, and (3) it may hold potential for reinterpretation with regard to future interfaith dialogue, since the Christianity that R. Soloveitchik spoke of was one that was generally adversarial to Jews and Judaism.

At face value, R. Soloveitchik rejects the religious legitimacy of the theological interfaith encounter. The reasons he offers are less important than the tone set throughout the essay, and due to ambiguity the text has lent itself to contrary interpretations. Though the classic understanding of the article is as a critique of theological dialogue, thinkers such as Irving Greenberg and Shlomo Riskin[9] see the article as a means to permit rather than prohibit interfaith theological dialogue; hence there is much revisionist thinking of Soloveitchik. Due to the complexity of his position R. Soloveitchik's approach cannot easily be subsumed into classic categories of "pro" or "anti" interfaith theology or definitions of whether he was tolerant or pluralistic in regards to other faiths. I argue here that *Confrontation* presents a subjective phenomenology that lends itself nicely to the current trend of interfaith theology as purported by Meir – a position R. Soloveitchik could not have foreseen.

An Analysis of *Confrontation*

For R. Soloveitchik, it is the unique self-understanding of each religion that makes it distinct and unavailable one to the other. He begins *Confrontation* with the biblical account of the creation of man and utilizes

9. *Makor Rishon,* May 2012.

typological categories to create a philosophical anthropology. He outlines three stages:

(1) In the first stage, man is "happy mindedness," unaware of the tension between himself and his environment:

> This man is a "non-confronted being," neither aware of his existential otherness nor of an external call from his creator. In modern terms he is the hedonistic pleasure-seeking individual who searches only for aesthetic satisfaction.

(2) At the second stage, man becomes "confronted," conscious of his separation from nature and discovers his own "I":

> In this mode of existence man discovers the dichotomy of his existence and thus his tragic mode of existence begins to unfold. Happiness and serenity is replaced by perplexity, fear and loneliness. At this stage man still confronts the outside world as a subject confronts an object. He seeks to dominate through creativity and intelligence rather than hedonistic power.

(3) In the third stage, another confrontation takes place where the two subjects engage in a form of communication: the word. But the word itself is limited in its efficacy. Though we communicate, the act itself makes us even more painfully aware of our uniqueness and our inability to attain existential unity. I quote the text here in its entirety as this description will be important later when I analyze Meir's trans-different theology:

> For, in all personal unions such as marriage, friendship, or comradeship, however strong the bonds uniting two individuals, the *modi existentiae* remain totally unique and hence, incongruous, at both levels, the ontological and the experiential. The hope of finding a personal existential equation of two human beings is rooted in the dangerous and false notion that human existence are abstract magnitudes subject to the simple mathematical processes. This error lies at the root of the philosophies of the corporate state and of mechanistic behaviourism. In fact, the closer two

> individuals get to know each other, the more aware they become of the metaphysical dance separating them. Each one exists in a singular manner, completely absorbed in his individual awareness which is egocentric and exclusive. The sun of existence rises with the birth of one's self-awareness and sets with its termination. It is beyond the experiential power of an individual to visualize an existence preceding or following his.[10]

For R. Soloveitchik, the community is born through the lonely, helpless solitude of the individual searching for redemption through the act of communication.[11] But as described here, the word is limited and hence any hope of finding total redemption through the encounter with the other is in vain.

At this point in the essay, R. Soloveitchik describes a "double confrontation" that faces modern, westernized Jews. He argues that these Jews see themselves engaged in a double confrontation from which any reconciliation is impossible. In reality, Jews are called upon to undertake a double mission – the universal human one and the exclusive covenantal one. The exclusive covenantal one cannot be equated with any other faith community, and is by nature totally unique:

> The possibility of the double confrontation does not come through sharing our unique covenantal experience, but through the universal human mission where man sees himself as a member of a cultural-creative community.

However, the reason this double confrontation has been unsuccessful is that the defiant attitude of non-Jewish society sees Jews as objects to subordinate and dominate. It approaches Jews using the single confrontation model. For this reason, it was impossible for Jews to participate fully in the great universal creative confrontation.[12] Despite the pessi-

10. Ibid. 15.

11. This description is reminiscent of Adam II in The Lonely Man of Faith written soon after this essay, and perhaps forms the foundation from which his typology of Adam 1 and Adam 2 developed.

12. *Makor Rishon,* May 2012, 20.

mistic tone, there is a definite, though admittedly limited, authorization given here to dialogue with those of other faiths:

> Involvement with the rest of mankind in the cosmic confrontation does not, we must repeat, rule out the second personal confrontation of two faith communities, each aware of both what it shares with the other and what is singularly its own.

Thus, he concludes that interreligious dialogue can take place at the second level but not the third.[13]

It is clear from this analysis that R. Soloveitchik does not prohibit interfaith dialogue. Rather, he sets a limit on its feasibility and productivity, in particular with regards to the theological component of any debate.

This paper argues that though R. Soloveitchik aligns interfaith dialogue with the second of his three typologies, due to historical suppositions about Christianity's relationship to Judaism, it is possible to adopt a radical and novel paradigm of interfaith dialogue that can be placed in the third category of confrontation: the encounter between subject and subject. In this encounter, which in Meir's language lies in the mode of "trans-difference," interfaith dialogue is possible for R. Soloveitchik not just on the human-ethical level but also on the theological level if we apply a different mode of reference. I maintain that by utilizing Meir's trans-difference theology, we can develop Soloveitchik's thought to incorporate a paradigm for interfaith dialogue that fits into his third level of the total ineffable faith experience. Moreover, though Soloveitchik's thought does not go far enough, it provides a starting point with which interfaith dialogue can evolve into a new radical model.

I will now outline how Greenberg interprets R. Soloveitchik's stance on interfaith dialogue. While himself undergoing an evolutionary transformation in terms of his own ideology, Greenberg presents a classic case of interfaith theology as pluralism without relativism, but does not remain true to R. Soloveitchik's phenomenological existentialism as presented in *Confrontation*. Greenberg is the midpoint between

13. Ibid. 24.

R. Soloveitchik and Meir in the evolving paradigm shift in interfaith models.

Irving Greenberg: *For the Sake of Heaven and Earth*

Developing a Pluralistic Position

Greenberg is perhaps most well-known for his post-Holocaust thinking that understands the *Shoah* as a unique event demanding a unique response. His dialectical approach to Judaism is for many (myself included) the only authentic way of living with faith in light of the horrors of the Holocaust. Less discussed, but still of paramount significance, is his approach to interfaith theology. In his book *Between Heaven and Earth* he begins with an essay entitled, "On the Road to a New Encounter between Judaism and Christianity: A Personal Journey." By his own admission it is an autobiographical account of the development of his thought. In it we find the two main influences on Greenberg: the Christian theologian Ronald Niebuhr and his teacher R. Soloveitchik. Through the essays we can see why he became a controversial figure in traditional Orthodox circles. Greenberg does not shy away from stating some far reaching claims about Judaism and Christianity, which arguably tread on the claims of the particularity of each religion.

I will outline the basic tenets of his thought showing where he diverges ontologically and theologically from R. Soloveitchik, especially in regards to his existentialist leanings.

By his own admission, Greenberg is deeply influenced by the events of the twentieth century. He argues that the Holocaust created a total rupture in Jewish thinking.[14] He also admits that his realization of the need to engage with his Christian counterparts arose out of,

> . . . the absolute need to prevent a recurrence of just such behaviors. . . . It insisted that the teaching of contempt goes straight back to the original gospel accounts. The holocaust had revealed

14. Greenberg. Irving, *Cloud of Smoke, Pillar of Fire Judaism, Christianity and Modernity after the Holocaust Auschwitz: Beginning of a New Era? Reflections on the Holocaust.* Ed. Eva Fleischer. New York: Ktav, (1977) 22–27.

> that at the very heart of Christianity a shelter for evil existed that must be razed.[15]

Thus, Greenberg's initial motives for interfaith dialogue were internal, his thought rapidly evolved to emphasize change and the openness of each religion to the other. He admits that his engagement through dialogue with his Christian counterparts beckoned a new mode of understanding another's faith. To view the other in his intrinsic human dignity was not enough. Ultimately, one has to recognize that religion must give dignity to the character and values of other faiths:

> If religions turned out to be as valid and dignified as their practitioners were, one must come up with a new conceptualization of the nature of absolute truth that would allow for the existence of two or more valid yet contradicting faiths. My response was the image of a shift from a Newtonian universe, in which there is only one absolute centre point, to an Einsteinian universe, in which many absolute centre points exist, each absolute centre point defined relative to the system in which it was embedded. It seemed important to me that the Einsteinian physics did not invalidate the Newtonian system but turned it into a limited case that existed side by side with other systems in a multifarious universe marked by plural and alternative realities.[16]

Greenberg's metaphor of a shift from a Newtonian universe to an Einsteinian one explains not only the shift in his own thinking on faith encounters, but also a general shift in the project of interfaith dialogue that allows for a pluralistic worldview.[17] In this worldview, there exists

15. Greenberg. I, *For The Sake of Heaven and Earth,* 23.

16. ibid., 10.

17. This idea is bought forth originally in Soloveitchik, *Halachic Mind*. See also Jonathan Sacks, "Rabbi J. B. Soloveitchik Early Epistemology: A Review of the Halachic Mind," *Tradition: A Journal of Orthodox Jewish Thought,* Vol. 23, No. 3 (Spring 1988), 75–87, where he outlines the idea of "epistemological pluralism" (79) that has emerged after Galilean-Newtonian physics was surpassed by relativity, quantum mechanics and non-Euclidian geometry, which in turn affected terms of reference in regards to philosophy.

many truths that not only exist side by side, but that can be the trigger for advancing and developing one's own particular faith. His view of the Jewish-Christian relationship is radical, particularly for an Orthodox Jew, which goes far in explaining Greenberg's controversial status within American Orthodoxy. He insists that Christianity is as much the will of God as is Judaism.[18] He claims that Christianity had to grow out of Judaism and that the resurrection and incarnation were purposely ambiguous and subtle so as to allow for multiple interpretations. It should not threaten a Jew, rather both Jews and Christians should surrender their bitter fight to hold a monopoly on Divine Presence and revelation. He concludes: "The triumphalism, the rejectionism, the cruelty, and the mutual defamation all came out of the human need for reassurance that 'indeed I am the favorite child.'"[19]

Greenberg's insistence on theological pluralism is emphasized time and again in his book. His view is a pluralism that retains the uniqueness of each position, but whose faith is enriched by the encounter with another faith.

> Pluralism also bespeaks of God's love of variety and uniqueness. In pluralism we do not filter out the differences or turn everything gray. We encounter the full intensity of distinctive positions, witnessing in our uniqueness without distorting in our passion. By this token, pluralism is not relativism, for we hold on to our absolutes, however we make room for others as well.[20]

By defying the relative nature of a pluralistic philosophy, Greenberg aims to preserve certain absolutes within one's own particular religion but be equally open to differing alternatives as presented in the religion of the other. His theological standing walks a narrow bridge between a pluralistic and a relative theology. It is an uneasy balance that can

---

18. This was expressed recently in the statement by a group of Orthodox rabbis: "To Do the Will of Our *Father in Heaven: Toward a Partnership between Jews and Christians*" found at www.cjcuc.com, of which R. Greenberg is a principal author. Ironically, this idea is also alluded to in Soloveitchik, *Halakhic Mind: An Essay on Jewish Tradition and Modern Thought.* New York: Seth Press (1986).

19. Greenberg, *For the Sake of Heaven and Earth,* 195.

20. ibid., 196.

quickly slip into the abyss of either relativism or absolute truth-claims at any moment. Hence, one must constantly reassess the framework of one's own individual religion in light of new encounters if one wants to retain this balance. If not, there is an inherent danger of fundamentalism:

> Fundamentalism emerges when people find that old absolutes have lost their power once they are brought into the presence of the other. The fundamentalist fears (correctly) that this erosion raises the threat of the loss of all values. Therefore the fundamentalist proposes bringing back old values in the only way he or she knows i.e. in the absence of alternative voices. . . . Pluralism is made possible by the ability of a religion or a truth system to maintain its vitality and to continue to move its own adherents, even in the presence of the other. . . . The pluralist affirms absolute values but has come to know their limits. The absolute values do not cover all possibilities. Pluralism is an absolutism that has come to recognize its own limitations.[21]

Reflections on Greenberg's Thought

The advantage of this position is that not only can we co-exist peacefully with other religions but that we also make possible a radical re-reading of our own religion. In doing so religions will evolve, develop, reinterpret and engage in debate both internally and externally, something which Greenberg insists is an essential component of any religious system.

Furthermore, the dialectical tension between pluralism and particularity is reminiscent of the dialectical elements of his post–Holocaust thought. A thread runs through his theological thinking whose foundation rests on a fragile marriage of seemingly counter-values, but through which Greenberg, to his immense credit, manages to create a rich religious and human experience.

The problem in Greenberg's position is rooted in Soloveitchik's typological categories. Within Judaism, there obviously exists an accepted

21. Ibid. 202.

position of particularity that cannot necessarily be translated into the universal language of pluralism. As R. Soloveitchik emphasizes, the second level of the faith experience allows for interfaith communication based on accepted universal categories of shared humanity but the third level deals with the existential faith experience that can never be translated due to its unique individuality. For R. Soloveitchik, faith possesses an ontological facet that defies universal or objective categorization and hence resists the project of pluralism.

Greenberg and Soloveitchik: A Reinterpretation

We may ask how Greenberg, a devoted student of Soloveitchik, reconciled his pluralistic approach with the more conservative one of his teacher. The answer may be found in a conversation between him and his teacher. Greenberg recalls:

> I went to see Rabbi Soloveitchik to clear away his objections for myself. First I said: "Rebbe, you taught me that in the *halakhic* worldview, life is spiritually seamless. But then there is no real distinction between the areas of social action and theology/doctrine." After a moment's pause, he said: "Greenberg, you are right." (To me, the implication was that if dialogue was permitted in matters of social concern, then it was permitted in all areas.) I judged *Confrontation* to be a piece of "Marrano writing" – that is to say the surface words conveyed one message while the substantive depth expressed a very different meaning.[22]

The significance of Greenberg assessment of R. Soloveitchik's position cannot be emphasized enough. As we have noted earlier R. Soloveitchik's stance on interfaith dialogue was presented primarily in *Confrontation,* and the plethora of interpretations makes it arguably his most contentious and enigmatic essay. Greenberg adds to the confusion by suggesting that the writing, much like that of Maimonides' *Guide,* possesses a certain esoteric element that when understood correctly

22. Greenberg, *For the Sake of Heaven and Earth,* 13.

can lead to a different conclusion than the classical interpretation provides.[23]

This esoteric interpretation opens the door for interfaith dialogue done by an elite few, who possess the tools and knowledge to engage in such an enterprise. It also, as we discussed earlier, may allows us to revise our original reading of *Confrontation* to include the potential of the double confrontation. R. Soloveitchik wrote on this immediately before a great transformation in Christian-Jewish relations,[24] and the project of interfaith dialogue itself has undergone a transformation. The definition of pluralism has also evolved and advanced. In light of these changes and Greenberg's claims about his teacher, can we reinterpret R. Soloveitchik double encounter? Could we claim that the singular encounter rooted in superiority and dominance of one over the other no longer applies to Christian-Jewish relationships because in its place we now find ourselves in the double confrontation, facing the other, each in our own individual and unique faith experience? In this confrontation there is no desire for assimilation or supersession, rather an authentic and genuine wish to simply "meet" the other in all of his/her distinctiveness, on both a human-ethical level and on a theological level.

The "conflict" inherent in the double confrontation that R. Soloveitchik describes as a choice for the western Jew between being "confronted human beings or confronted Jews" contains according to the thinker an inner contradiction. Yet, these are not necessarily mutually exclusive. Perhaps today the westernized Jew can live in a dialectical tension between these two positions. Is it possible that instead of having to understand the other through universal, objective ontological

---

23. It is interesting to note that in another essay *("Shtei Dlatot Patach HaRav Soloveitchik – v'lo Avar Bahem: al Atidah Shel HaOrthodoxiah Ha Modernit." RAV BA'OLAM HACHADASH*: Iyunim B'Hashpa'ato Shel HaRav Yosef Dov Soloveitchik al Tarbut, al Chinuch v'al Machshavah Yehudit. Ed. Avinoam Rosenak and Naftali Rotenberg. Jerusalem: Magnes Press, (2010) 245–277). Greenberg makes a similar claim concerning the Rav in terms of his pluralistic leanings. He reads the Rav's writings as a lesson in pluralist theology.

24. In 1965, the Vatican II under the leadership of Paul VI produced the landmark document *Nostra Aetate* that repudiated in part the Jewish role in the death of Christ. It represented a new starting point in the relations between the Church and Judaism.

categories, we can remain fixed in our "singular normative gesture"[25] and still engage in a confrontation with the other? If we answer in the affirmative, can R. Soloveitchik's double confrontation be reinterpreted to contain a profound possibility for interfaith dialogue that reaches beyond even the claims of his students such as Greenberg and David Hartman?

The answer to this question finds its expression in the work of Ephraim Meir, who argues that interfaith dialogue must move beyond classic pluralism as portrayed by Greenberg to a new dimension where we address the other, not through mutual categories of understanding but through our "trans-difference." By outlining Meir's work, I will show that his approach moves us beyond the classic terms of pluralism and interfaith dialogue to a new dimension based on a dialogical rather than a theological interpretation of the faith encounter. This new approach marks a distinctive evolution in the interfaith project that can shed new and radical light on previously understood concepts of faith, dialogue and encounter.

Ephraim Meir: "Trans-Difference"

Reflections on the Self

In recent years, Ephraim Meir developed a new paradigm for relating to interfaith theology. His work is based on a novel approach to selfhood, as stated in the introduction to his book,[26] that despite our difference to the other and also to self, there is a real possibility and even imperative for interfaith dialogue. His book enlists the philosophy of dialogical philosophers such as Rosensweig, Levinas, and Buber to build a new philosophy of identity and alterity. His theory traces an evolving "I" that moves from self-transcendence to self-difference and finally trans-difference. Through these categories he frames his theory of interfaith theology. Meir rejects Heidegger's model of the isolated "I," as conveyed in the thought of R. Soloveitchik, arguing instead that though "each person is unique and irreplaceable in his

25. Soloveitchik, *Confrontation.*

26. Ephraim Meir, *Dialogical Thought and Identity: Trans-different Religiosity in Present Day Societies,* De Gruyter Magnes (2013).

inescapable interconnection with the 'non-I'", there is still a possibility for trans-difference or relation with the other. Meir views the self in two ways: "primarily as a self that extends to the other, at the same time retaining an element of individuality, of difference from the other." Thus, he concludes, "Between the self and the other, trans-difference is possible."[27]

Meir warns against the conclusion presented by R. Soloveitchik in *Confrontation.* He contends, justifiably, that it leads to a regressive attitude towards the other that "avoids communication and remains nomadic, within the own, without windows and without empathy and solidarity with others, remains real."[28] In such conditions, the other is seen as a threat and hence the potential for indifference and even violence exists. Similarly, Greenberg's pluralism does not grant enough significance to the genuine uniqueness and numinous nature of the "I." In Meir's paradigm, the other comes neither to threaten the "I" nor to be integrated into part of his *Weltanschauung.* Instead, the encounter between the two individuals leads to a new understanding of self. Meir contends, "that alterity or permanent changeability in favor of the other makes up the very identity of the always changeable I." [29]

It is here that the significance of the difference between their positions unfolds. R. Soloveitchik offers the direction. Meir actually enters the space that R. Soloveitchik suggests, a space opened up through dialogue and propelled by Levinas' insight that the "I" is constituted by the other. Thus, the incommensurable divide is bridged by the awareness that:

> . . . the absolute limit posed by the awareness of incommensurability is in fact also a mirror . . . a mirror whose surface is composed by one's projection of the other's conception of me. But this other is not simply a solipsistic construction, for it is formed from actual engagement with an other.[30]

27. Ephraim Meir, *Dialogical Thought and Identity: Trans-different Religiosity in Present Day Societies,* De Gruyter Magnes (2013), 2.

28. ibid., 160.

29. ibid.

30. One can always attack this position with the foil of Kant's (or Heidegger's) isolated ego. To this one can retort that if one cannot define the qualitative difference

Interfaith Dialogue through Trans-Difference Methodology

For Meir dialogue with the other is not of secondary consideration to the needs of "I." It comprises, rather, a necessity forming an integral element of the "I" identity. While both R. Soloveitchik and Greenberg view dialogue with the other as utilitarian, encompassing a secondary stage in the development of the self, for Meir it is of primary importance. As was discussed earlier, the self, especially the religious self, cannot be defined without the dialogical relationship. As a corollary, interfaith dialogue is not a project that is based on the need for reconciliation or social adhesion, but rather on the needs of the self in his search for both individual and collective identity. Hence the other is seen as integral to the self, but equally ineffable and immeasurable, immune to objectification and definition.

For R. Soloveitchik, the numinous "I" experience that may be redeemed through a confrontation with the other cannot be done from a religious perspective, for there is no way to 'translate' the covenantal confrontation. Hence, our encounter with the other faith will always remain at the second level of confrontation in the universal normative framework.

However, if we use Meir's analysis of the religious self, there is a way for men of faith to engage with each other without necessarily having to understand or define the faith experience. Meir states:

> In "self-difference," one refuses to reduce the other to himself and to exercise power over the other: the self in "self-difference" keeps a distance between itself and the other and the respect and awe for this distance creates the non-indifferent relationship. The difference of the other and the difference of the self do not lead to the impossibility of an encounter; on the contrary, the undeniable differences makes a "trans-different" encounter possible.[31]

---

between no dialogue and a dialogue based on respect, care, and desire to understand the other (i.e., love), then the accusation of solipsism lacks substance.

31. Ephraim Meir: *Dialogical Thought and Identity: Trans-different Religiosity in Present Day Societies,* De Gruyter Magnes (2013) 150.

By using this new paradigm of trans-difference there is a way to reassess R. Soloveitchik's conclusion. In the paradigm of self-difference there is a refusal to reduce the other to himself, or to acquiesce to the danger of syncretism.[32]

Conclusion

Soloveitchik's *Confrontation* sees interfaith theology as highly problematic due to the impossibility of moving beyond individual ontological loneliness. He perceives the "I" as a self-composed parochial unit. The "other" comes to threaten the "I," objectifying and defining him on his own terms. The other is seen as an object to be integrated and assimilated into the self. Any encounter with the other will entail a "translation" of my inner world which while possible on some level, for R. Soloveitchik is limited in its scope and hence can only be played out at the universal level of mankind and not at the covenantal level of faith.

Greenberg's interfaith theology is based on a limited view of the individual's particularity. It recognizes both the boundaries of one's own faith, since only God is absolute and infinite, and equally retains one's own integrity and truth. Knowledge of the other religion is merely another path to discovering the multi-faceted manifestation of God. Though his theory resembles classic pluralistic theology, unlike some pluralists, he does not reduce alterity to sameness and this is its strength and significance. His interfaith theology can be seen as an evolving conception of the encounter from an *I-It* to an *I-Thou* relationship.

Though he does not write about interfaith dialogue from the strictly metaphysical perspective, it is clear Greenberg rejects in many ways R. Soloveitchik's numinous ontology in favor of pluralism that recognizes the importance of the other in shaping the self.

Meir's interfaith theology must be seen through new categories of

---

32. In his paper "A Reassessment of Rav Soloveitchik Essay on Interfaith Dialogue: 'Confrontation'" (Columbus School of Law, Catholic University of America Volume 1 (2005–2006): 151–16), Marshall. J. Berger claims that one of the things Soloveitchik feared about interfaith dialogue was potential for the attempted reconciliation or union of different or opposing religious principles, or practices, by incorporating elements of one religion into another. Using the trans-difference method this fear would be immediately allayed.

definition: self-transcendence, self-difference, trans-difference. It rejects the Heideggerian approach of R. Soloveitchik that sees the self as an all encompassed unique being inaccessible to the other, instead favoring an ontology shaped by the "other" in his/her differences.

Through the other, the self becomes aware of its own difference leading to self-transcendence and hence reshaping one's own identity. In many ways Greenberg and Meir have much in common: Their interfaith theology rests on a subjectivity not confined to a parochial existentialism, but is a phenomenology whose encounter with the object moves beyond a limited definition of self into a continual re-definition of self. Writing more than two decades later,[33] however, Meir goes further than Greenberg. While for Greenberg self-renewal and redefinition may come as a result of an encounter with another faith, it is not an imperative for self-identity. For Meir the self cannot be defined without the other, i.e. the encounter with the other is a prerequisite for self-definition. Accordingly, for R. Soloveitchik it is impossible for the religious man to engage in a true interfaith dialogue, for Greenberg it is possible and preferable and for Meir it is a necessity.

This chapter claimed that Soloveitchik's *Confrontation*, containing many polemical elements particular to the period in which it was penned, may be reframed. Mindful of the fact that relations between Christianity and Judaism have changed significantly since 1964, and based only on the philosophical component of the essay, I have argued that by viewing the self through Meir's trans-difference theology, a genuine encounter with another at R. Soloveitchik's third level is possible. For both Meir and Soloveitchik, the other is numinous and unknown. But for Meir the alterity of the other does not lead to rejection but rather to an encounter with self and other at a new dimension. R. Soloveitchik describes an encounter between two individuals at the third level as:

> . . . two equal subjects, both lonely in their otherness and uniqueness, both opposed and rejected by an objective order, both

33. Many essays in Greenberg's book span over two or three decades. Hence, much of his inter-faith theology was written in the seventies and eighties.

> craving for companionship. This confrontation is reciprocal, not unilateral.[34]

For R. Soloveitchik, this is the end point of any genuine dialogue because the individual faith experience makes it impossible. For Meir, this is the starting point from which self-difference and trans-difference develop. Thus, there is a possibility that within R. Soloveitchik's thought lies a precarious foundation for interfaith dialogue, not in the classic pluralist model, but in the model of trans-difference.

34. *Confrontation*, 9.

Uniting a People in Diversity: The Thread of Tolerance in Our Rabbinic Tradition

Rosh Kehillah Dina Najman

Rav Yitz Greenberg has taught us the importance of the inclusion of multiple voices with the Torah conversation. In order to explore the foundations of his approach, I raise the following questions:

- Can a unified people have a plurality of voices?
- Is *mahloket* (difference of opinions) inherent in our learning of the Torah, or does it represent a breakdown of the transmission or *mesorah* from teacher to student?
- Finally, is it desirable to render one opinion authoritative for practical purposes?

In *Sefer Shemot*,[1] Chapter 19, we read of *B'nai Yisrael* preparing for the revelatory experience on Har Sinai. They are commanded how to position themselves and ready themselves for this quintessential moment in Jewish history. Notably, the people are described in both the singular and plural. They are members of distinct tribes forming a single people unified in purpose.

For example, in *Sefer Shemot* 19:2, the text switches back and forth between singular and plural verbs. We witness a unified people with multiple voices and at times, a singular voice. They traveled ויסעו (pl.) from Refidim, and then they come ויבאו (pl.) into the wilderness of Sinai. There is a switch to the singular, ויחן, in the description of *Bnei Yisrael* camping before the mountain. For Rashi, this encampment

1. Book of Exodus

is distinctive. The use of the singular verb reflects the people's unity. They were like one person with one heart (כאיש אחד בלב אחד), unlike all the other encampments where there was dispute and the people were divided.[2] In verse 8, we read that the people answered together (יחדו) and then said in a collective, plural voice: "We will do" (נעשה). Plurality and singularity are brought together in this verse.

Later, in *Sefer Shemot* 19:21–22, Hashem tells Moshe to tell the people and the priests to stay back. Strikingly, Moshe says, in effect, "You already told me!" He reminds Hashem that boundaries have already been established in accordance with Hashem's command. Did he really think that Hashem had forgotten? Surely not. Instead, we read this as an expression of incomprehension stemming from Moshe's famous humility. Hashem emphasized the distinction between different levels of people, a distinction that Moshe could not understand. Since Moshe was an *anav* (a humble person), he did not distinguish between himself and the rest of the people. Thus, Hashem emphasizes these different levels of experience: "You shall ascend, and Aharon with you," (*Sefer Shemot* 19:24).

As Rashi explains by quoting the *Mekhilta*, "אתה מחיצת לעצמך, ואהרון מחיצה לעצמו והם מחיצה לעצמם" "You will have a partition for yourself, Aharon will have a partition for himself and they [the priests and the people] will have a partition for themselves." Everybody was to have the experience of revelation appropriate for them, and there are multiple levels.

This demonstrates that there are both unified moments and specific acknowledgements of the necessity for different experiences. While one could understand this as hierarchical, it can also be understood as a pluralism implicit in the reception of the Torah from the very beginning. Thus the tension between the need for unity and the need for pluralism has been present since the revelation at *Har Sinai*.

What happens, however, when there is not only a plurality of revelatory experience but a plurality of voices in disagreement? Is this a realization of the ideal of *Kabbalat ha-Torah* or a decline?

In *Masekhet Hagigah*,[3] the *mahloket* is said to have taken place during

2. Rashi, *Sefer Shemot* 19:8, s.v. "ויחן שם."
3. Tractate *Hagigah*, Chapter 2, *Mishnah* 2.

the period of *Zugot* (142 BCE–40 CE) with respect to whether the designation of an animal for sacrifice (*semihat b'heimah*) should be performed on Yom Tov. The consequences of this debate are recorded in both the Jerusalem and Babylonian Talmud: Will disagreement and lack of unification of ideas be viewed as careless and harmful to the cohesion of the Jewish people?

In the Jerusalem Talmud, the following is taught:[4]

תלמוד ירושלמי (וילנא) מסכת חגיגה פרק ב

Gemara: At first, there was no disagreement in Israel, except on the issue of *semihat b'haima (designating an animal by leaning on an animal).* Shammai and Hillel had four disagreements between them. When the students of Beit Shammai and Beit Hillel increased, and they were not careful in preserving the teachings of their rabbis, disagreement increased in Israel. They disagreed about what was unfit and what was fit (*tumah* and *taharah*). Moreover, the future will not restore what it was to its earlier place (no disagreement) until the son of David (Messiah) comes.

גמ' בראשונה לא היתה מחלוקת בישראל אלא על הסמיכה בלבד ועמדו שמאי והלל ועשו אותן ד' משרבו תלמידי ב"ש ותלמידי ב"ה ולא שימשו את רביהן כל צורכן ורבו המחלוקת בישראל ונחלקו לשתי כתות אלו מטמאין ואלו מטהרין ועוד אינה עתידה לחזור למקומה עד שיבוא בן דוד

Presumably, it was not that there were no disputes beforehand, but rather, in this case the dispute was never resolved. In four pairs of leaders, the dispute seems to reflect a partisan disagreement between the *Nasi* and the *Av Beit Din*. When Shammai replaced Menachem as *Av Beit Din* alongside Hillel the *Nasi*, the positions switched, so that the *Av Beit Din*'s position now resembled that of the earlier *nesi'im*.

In Talmud Yerushalmi, *Masekhet Hagigah*, it is explained that following this five-generation-long *makhloket,* disputes began to increase within the Tannaim period. Here, *mahloket* appears opposed to the ideal. It is a *bedi'avad,* a lamentable severing in the transmission of the Torah. Having opposing views is seen as negative. The Rabbis of the Yerushalmi opine that the ideal state is unity and that having *mahloket* represents breakdown. They blame Beit Hillel and Beit Shammai for

4. Jerusalem Talmud, Tractate *Hagigah*, Chapter 2.

the proliferation of disputes, specifically regarding *tumah* and *taharah*, in the learning community.

The *Talmud Bavli*,[5] on the other hand, expresses an appreciation of many voices without any regret. Instead, a practical question is raised. Given that there is all this disagreement about *tumah* and *taharah*, what is forbidden and permitted what is *pasul* and *kasher*, the *Hakhamei Bavel* raise the question: How can one ever learn Torah, when everything seems to be open for debate? They reply as follows:

"The Masters of Assemblies" – These are the wise scholars who sit in various groups and occupy themselves with the study of Torah.

There are those scholars who declare a thing ritually impure and those who pronounce it ritually pure, those who prohibit and those who permit, those who disqualify and those who declare fit. Perhaps a person will say: How can I ever learn Torah [when everything is open for debate]? The Torah teaches: that all [the Torah teachings] were given from one Shepherd – one God gave them. One Leader proclaimed them, from the mouth of the Master of all matters, Blessed is He. As it says: "And God spoke all these words." Hence you too make your ear like a mill-hopper, and acquire for yourself a discerning heart to hear intelligently the words of those who declare something impure and those who pronounce it pure. The words of those who prohibit and the words of those who permit, and the words of those who disqualify and the words of those who declare fit.

בעלי אספות – אלו תלמידי
חכמים שיושבין אסופות
אסופות ועוסקין בתורה,
הללו מטמאין והללו
מטהרין, הללו אוסרין והללו
מתירין, הללו פוסלין והללו
מכשירין. שמא יאמר אדם:
היאך אני למד תורה מעתה?
תלמוד לומר: כולם נתנו
מרעה אחד – אל אחד נתנן,
פרנס אחד אמרן, מפי אדון
כל המעשים ברוך הוא,
דכתיב גוידבר אלהים את
כל הדברים האלה. אף אתה
עשה אזניך כאפרכסת, וקנה
לך לב מבין לשמוע את
דברי מטמאים ואת דברי
מטהרים, את דברי אוסרין
ואת דברי מתירין, את דברי
פוסלין ואת דברי מכשירין.

Here the concept of *mahloket* seems to be *l'chatchilah*:[6] It is optimal to have many teachings on a Torah idea. After all, one God gave each and every teaching. God spoke all the words. You are to acquire for yourself an ability to think intelligently about what is being taught and debated.

5. Babylonian Talmud, Tractate Hagigah, 3b.
6. Ideal from the start.

One is encouraged to be receptive to an approach which opens one up to various understandings.

This idea is further reflected in the *Talmud Bavli*, Tractate *Eruvin*,[7] where Beit Hillel and Beit Shammai are said to have debated each other for three years. A *Bat Kol* finally declared that for practical purposes we follow Beit Hillel. But it also said that, "These and those are the words of the living God" (*Eilu v'Eilu Divrei Elokim Hayim*), emphasizing that, even when there is practical unity, the opposing views nevertheless have equal value. From this source in *Eruvin*, we see one way to resolve the tension between plurality and unity implicit in the revelation of *Har Sinai*. Practically we need unity of law; but in the Beit Midrash, all voices are equal. Hillel and Shammai reflect different revelatory experiences while maintaining the unity of the people.

We see there is a *mahloket* about the value of *mahloket* between the Bavli and the Yerushalmi. Even in the Bavli however, we see the concern that differences in *halakhic* opinion may result in what Rashi calls two *Torot*.[8]

---

7. Babylonian Talmud, Tractate Eruvin, 13b.

8. For further reference, consider the discussion between Beit Hillel and Beit Shammai in *Mishneh Yevamot*, Chapter 1, Mishnah 4. There, one of the most well-known disagreements is found between Beit Hillel and Beit Shammai relating to the status and eligibility for marriage under certain conditions relating to a levirate marriage. Questions arise relating to the legitimacy or forbidden nature of the marriage resulting in children who are considered *mamzerim* (children born out of a relationship forbidden by the Torah, where these children are not allowed to marry children from a permissible relationship). Beit Hillel and Beit Shammai disagree under which circumstances the children are *mamzerim*. The Mishnah declares that "even though these prohibit and these permit, Beit Shammai did not refrain from marrying women from Beit Hillel, nor did Beit Hillel from Beit Shammai."

Consistent with the Yerushalmi's approach to *mahloket*, the Yerushalmi hesitates to accept the possibility that Beit Shammai's opinion was implemented in practice. The Amoraim in Yerushalmi limit Beit Shammai as a practical option before the general acceptance of Beit Hillel's authority. The Yerushalmi promotes a unified *halakhah*. However, the Bavli's approach is consistent with the idea that differing opinions are celebrated. The Bavli maintains that each side, Beit Hillel and Beit Shammai, practiced its own opinion. The Bavli maintains that in the view of each side, *mamzerim* were created by the other side's view. Beit Hillel and Beit Shammai were able to marry each other since they informed each other of debatable cases. Again, the *Talmud Bavli* is comfortable with differing viewpoints. The Yerushalmi attempts to do away with *machloket* as best it can. That being said, the Bavli as well as the Yerushalmi have diffi-

Rabbi Yoshiyah said: Ze'ira told me three things in the name of the Men of Yerushalayim: A husband who waived his "declaration of jealousy" – the declaration is waived; a "rebellious son" whose father and mother wish to forgive him – they may forgive him; a "rebellious elder" whose Court wished to forgive him – they may forgive him. When I came to my colleagues in the south, they conceded two of them to me, but with regard to the "rebellious elder" they did not concede to me, so that disputes would not increase in Israel?! . . .

דאמר רבי יאשיה: שלשה דברים סח לי זעירא מאנשי ירושלים: בעל שמחל על קינויו – קינויו מחול; בן סורר ומורה שרצו אביו ואמו למחול לו – מוחלין לו; זקן ממרא שרצו בית דינו למחול לו – מוחלין לו. וכשבאתי אצל חבירי שבדרום, על שנים הודו לי, על זקן ממרא לא הודו לי, כדי שלא ירבו מחלוקת בישראל . . .

We learn in a *beraita*: said R. Yosei: Originally they did not increase disputes in Israel, rather a court of seventy one sat in the Chamber of Hewn Stone, and two courts of twenty three sat, one at the entrance to the Temple Mount, and one at the entrance to the Sanctuary, with other courts of twenty three sitting in all the cities of Israel. When a matter required asking – they would ask the court in their city. If they had heard they would tell them, and if not – they would go to that closest to their city. If they had heard they would tell them, if not they would go the entrance to the Temple Mount. If they had heard they would tell them, if not they would go to the entrance to the Sanctuary, and he would say: "So I interpreted, but my colleagues interpreted so; so I learned, but my colleagues learned so." If they had heard –they told them, if not – these and those would come to the Chamber of Hewn Stone, where a court sat from the Morning Sacrifice until the Afternoon Sacrifice. (On Shabbat and Yom Tov they sat in the

תניא, אמר רבי יוסי: מתחילה לא היו מרבין מחלוקת בישראל, אלא בית דין של שבעים ואחד יושבין בלשכת הגזית, ושני בתי דינין של עשרים ושלשה, אחד יושב על פתח הר הבית ואחד יושב על פתח העזרה, ושאר בתי דינין של עשרים ושלשה יושבין בכל עיירות ישראל. הוצרך הדבר לשאול – שואלין מבית דין שבעירן; אם שמעו – אמרו להן, ואם לאו – באין לזה שסמוך לעירן. אם שמעו – אמרו להם, ואם לאו – אין לזה שעל פתח הר הבית. אם שמעו – אמרו להם, ואם לאו –באין לזה שעל פתח העזרה, ואומר: "כך דרשתי וכך דרשו חבירי, כך למדתי וכך למדו חבירי." אם שמעו – אמרו להם, ואם לאו – אלו ואלו באין ללשכת הגזית, ששם יושבין מתמיד של שחר עד תמיד של בין הערבים (ובשבתות ובימים טובים יושבין בחיל). נשאלה

culty with the Mishnah's assertion that each group was able to place tolerance above each side's concern for *mamzerut*.

שאלה בפניהם. אם שמעו – אמרו להם, ואם לאו – עומדין למנין. רבו המטמאים – טמאו, רבו המטהרין – טהרו.

Stronghold.) When a question was asked before them, if they had heard – they would tell them, if not – they would vote. If those who said "impure" were the majority, they would declare it impure, and if those who said "pure" were the majority, they would declare it pure.

משרבו תלמידי שמאי והלל שלא שמשו כל צרכן – רבו מחלוקת בישראל, ונעשית תורה כשתי תורות.

After the multiplication of the students of Hillel and Shammai, who had not served (their teachers) to the extent needed for their own development, disputes multiplied in Israel and the Torah became as two Torahs.

משם כותבין ושולחין בכל מקומות: כל מי שהוא חכם ושפל ברך ודעת הבריות נוחה הימנו – יהא דיין בעירו. משם מעלין אותו להר הבית, משם לעזרה, משם ללשכת הגזית.

From there they would write and send to all places: "Everyone who is wise and "of lowly knee" and well-regarded by the populace – he shall be a judge in his city." From there they would promote him to the Temple Mount, and from there to the Courtyard, and from there to the Chamber of Hewn Stones.

שלחו משם: איזהו בן העולם הבא? ענוותן ושפל ברך, שייף עייל שייף ונפיק, וגריס באורייתא תדירא, ולא מחזיק טיבותא לנפשיה. יהבו ביה רבנן עינייהון ברב עולא בר אבא.

They sent from there (Israel): "Who is a citizen of the World to Come? One who is forbearing and "of lowly knee," who "bends over entering and exiting," and learns the Torah constantly, and does not think of himself as deserving." The Rabbis placed their eyes on R. Ulla bar Abba.

Here, the students do not have a unity of practice. Rashi explains that without practical resolution, there will arise a general concern that two *Torot* will cause a violation of the Biblical prohibition of forming factions (*lo titgod'du*).[9]

There seems to be a difference even in the Bavli sources, creating differing practical *halakhic* observances all the while appreciating that voicing opinions has a place. On the other hand, there are passages in the Bavli that create room for a variety of *piskei halakhah*, on a specific observance. Within the Bavli, we encounter the phrase: דעבד כמר עבד ודעבד כמר עבד – If one chooses to follow one opinion, follow it. If one

9. *Talmud Bavli, Yevamot*, 13b, Rashi, sv. "*lo ta'asu agudot*."

chooses to follow another opinion, choose it. For example, when deciding which opinion to follow in *Tefilat Minchah* (like Rabbi Yehuda or the Tanna Kamma), given that Rav follows Rabbi Yehuda while Rav Huna and the Rabanan follows the Tanna Kamma, the Gemara welcomes both positions and declares: דעבד כמר עבד ודעבד כמר עבד. This demonstrates an acceptance of a variety of *halakhic* observances on one particular issue. Given the possibility of practical, not only theoretical plurality, how does one preserve the unity of Torah?

When confronted with opposing ideas, accepting positions that run counter to what is known intellectually and emotionally to be true, is challenging. Preparing one's heart psychologically is critical to this process. The *gemara* points out the failure of scholars who, while on one hand succeeded in engaging in dispute, failed in coming to terms with opposition.

In *Masekhet Shabbat,* there is a dispute between Hillel and Shammai regarding whether grapes became *tahor* or *tameh.* Instead of creating the space for differing views, Shammai abuses the rules of the game. According to this source, the dispute became personal and there was a threat of violence.

And another? When one vintages grapes for the vat [to make wine],

Shammai says: It is made fit [to become unclean – and have to be placed in a *tahor* basket]; Hillel says: It is not made fit to become defiled [and do not have to be placed in a *tahor* basket]. Said Hillel to Shammai: Why must one vintage grapes in purity, yet not gather olives in purity? Shammai said: If you provoke me, I will decree that olives will be unclean as well. They [Beit Shammai] thrust a sword into the study house and declared: "Whoever wants to enter may enter, but no one may leave!" And on that day Hillel sat in submission before Shammai, like one of the disciples, and it was as wretched for Israel as the day on which the [golden] calf was made.

ואידך הבוצר לגת, שמאי אומר: הוכשר, הלל אומר: לא הוכשר. אמר לו הלל לשמאי: מפני מה בוצרין בטהרה, ואין מוסקין בטהרה? – אמר לו: אם תקניטני – גוזרני טומאה אף על המסיקה. נעצו חרב בבית המדרש, אמרו: הנכנס יכנס והיוצא אל יצא. ואותו היום היה הלל כפוף ויושב לפני שמאי כאחד מן התלמידים, והיה קשה לישראל כיום שנעשה בו העגל.

It is not clear exactly what then took place in the study hall. According to the tradition cited in a similar manner in the Yerushalmi Talmud, there was a harsh dispute in the study hall to the point of bloodshed. Some explain that Hillel sat bowed before Shammai trying to convince Shammai through a discussion of the issues, like a student deliberating before one's teacher. However, as the *Ge'onim* explain, at that point the students of Beit Shammai outnumbered the students of Beit Hillel and the *halakhah* was established in accordance with Shammai's opinion.

Hillel, as the *Nasi* of the Sanhedrin, should have faced the people with Shammai and the rest of the members of the Sanhedrin alongside him. Motivated by humility and by a desire to avoid further disharmony, Hillel descended from his place and sat before Shammai in one of the students' places. The submission of the *Nasi* of the Sanhedrin and his humiliation was a shocking event in the eyes of the people. The situation that developed involved a certain amount of violence on the part of students of Beit Shammai, and the leader of Israel was forced to demean himself due to external pressure. This was considered a tragic event.

Why is this event likened to the sin of the Golden Calf? Religious observance, and religious strictness for its own sake, can become idolatrous; *halakhah* – Jewish law – and Torah study can become its own form of false worship when not directed toward Godly ends. When our Torah giants abuse Torah scholarship and their role as leaders, it is not only an embarrassment but a humiliation similar to the humiliation of lapsing into idolatry at the foot of *Har Sinai*. The *Luchot*[10] were broken there, displaying a rupture in the *Berit* of Torah and in the unity of the Jewish people. What should have been a spiritual height instead became a spiritual abyss.

In fact, one reason offered for why *Hazal* often rule with Beit Hillel over Beit Shammai is that Beit Hillel would always cite Beit Shammai's opinion before their own, demonstrating that they valued the other opinion not only because it was a challenge to their opinion but because they valued its otherness for its own sake, for its revelation of another aspect of divinity. Of course, this is not to say that, when negotiating, the tension between plurality and unity is easy.

Another example of mishandling the precious gift of learning the Torah that Hashem gave the Jewish people appears in the well-known account of the 12,000 pairs of Rabbi Akiva's students, who died because

10. Tablets with inscribed words of revelation.

they did not conduct themselves with respect towards one another. It is significant that the Gemara informs us that they died between *Hag ha-Pesach* and *Hag ha-Shavuot*.[11] This is the period in the calendar between the commemoration of the Jewish people's exodus and freedom from Egyptian bondage and their arrival at *Har Sinai*, where they would accept the Torah and emerge as one people – *k'ish echad, b'lev Echad* – as one person with one heart.

The death of the students emphasizes that, in the absence of respect, *havrutot*[12] will be decimated, learning will cease, and the people will not be entitled to continue learning Torah. The Jews emerge broken. Diversity cannot survive without the respect that comes from acknowledgement of unity. Even the students educated by Rabbi Akiva, who emphasized that the foremost principle of the Torah is that one should love one's neighbor as oneself (*v'ahavta l'raieha kamoha*) could not appreciate that true love comes with the foundation of respect.

After the destruction of the Second Temple, when the Sanhedrin was restored thanks to the foresight of Rabbi Yohanan ben Zakkai and the scholars of Yavneh, there was a particular need for unity and peaceful resolution. A number of *sugyot* involving the same Tannaitic personalities illustrate the difficulty of achieving unity while maintaining respect for alternative views at this crucial time.

Within the Babylonian Talmud, *in Masekhet Berakhot,*[13] *Masekhet Rosh Hashanah,*[14] and *Masekhet Bava Metz'ia,*[15] the relations among Rabban Gamliel, Rabi Yehoshua, Rabbi Elazar and Rabbi Akiva exhibit a dynamic that achieves unity at the cost of humiliation. One of the areas of *halakhah* where there is the clearest need for unity is the calendar. If different Jews observe the holidays at different times, it would appear as if there were two *Torot*. In *Masekhet Rosh Hashanah* 24b–25a, Rabbi Yehoshua disagrees about the determination of a specific month, placing Yom Kippur a day later than Rabban Gamliel's calculation. Rabban Gamliel, as *Nasi*, subjected Rabbi Yehoshua to humiliation by forcing

11. Babylonian Talmud, *Yevamot*, 62b.

12. Study partners.

13. Babylonian Talmud, *Berakhot* 27b–28a.

14. Babylonian Talmud, *Rosh Hashanah* 24b.

15. Babylonian Talmud, *Bava Metzi'a* 59b. For the purposes of this essay, only this episode will be quoted in full.

him to appear before him with a stick and money on what would have been the day of Yom Kippur for Rabbi Yehoshua. Rabbi Akiva convinces Rabbi Yehoshua to appear before Rabban Gamliel, accepting the ruling of the general assembly.

While Rabban Gamliel praises Rabbi Yehoshua's decision to appear before him, *Hazal* leaves us recognizing that the sacrifice Rabban Gamliel caused Rabbi Yehoshua to make for practical *halakhic* unity, threatened and undermined the diversity imperative within the learning culture.

In *Masekhet Berakhot,* a student asks Rabbi Yehoshua if *Tefillat Ma'ariv* is an obligation. The following day, the same student asks Rabban Gamliel, who ruled that *Tefillat Ma'ariv* is an obligation. The student reveals to Rabban Gamliel that Rabbi Yehoshua told him it was not obligatory. Rabban Gamliel, in a calculating fashion, directs the student to ask his question again. Rabban Gamliel sets Rabbi Yehoshua up. Even though Rabbi Yehoshua does not voluntarily contradict Rabban Gamliel, it is Rabban Gamliel who ultimately singles out Rabbi Yehoshua for ruling differently than he and commands the elder Rabbi Yehoshua to stand in humiliation throughout the duration of the daily learning.

Hazal describe the humiliation Rabban Gamliel causes Rabbi Yehoshua on Yom Kippur and decide to expel Rabban Gamliel from his post as *Nasi* of the Sanhedrin. Rabbi Elazar replaces Rabbi Yehoshua. In this scenario, the *Hakhamim* highlight the collective response of respecting Rabbi Yehoshua's opinion and position as a necessary contributor to the Torah conversation. They will not tolerate the misuse of Rabban Gamliel's power.

While the case in Rosh Hashana leaves us with the unsettling conclusion of one *p'sak* at the expense of Rabbi Yehoshua's dignity, the episode in *Masekhet Berakhot* teaches us to appreciate that there must be protection for opposing voices in our learning tradition.

Ultimately, Rabban Gamliel, after causing Rabbi Yehoshua to submit to his authority, rises and praises Rabbi Yehoshua for all he did in the name of unifying authority. Yet, *Hazal* leave the reader with a distaste for the process by which Rabban Gamliel achieved his unity of this ruling. With differing opinions, there will be varied *piskei halakhah* (*halakhic* rulings). The question is how to appreciate each view even with those in conflict with the ultimate ruling. The *gemara* presents Rabban Gamliel as a flawed leader who opts to humiliate a colleague for purposes of unified *p'sak*. His repentance and apologetic behavior towards Rabbi Yehoshua demonstrates Rabban Gamliel's capacity to shift his behavior. Yet, the reader is left disappointed in the process of issuing this *p'sak*.

In the third of these scenarios, Rabbi Eliezer debates Rabbi Yehoshua about a specialized oven. Rabbi Eliezer adduces all the evidence he can, but Rabbi Yehoshua rejects his opinion. Becoming quite desperate, Rabbi Eliezer tries to bring proofs outside the realm of the laws of the *beit midrash* to prove his point. Rabbi Yehoshua rejects this as merely being an external miracle, arguing that the proof of a *bat kol* has no place in the *beit midrash*; the majority opinion is followed.

These three stories can be examined as a unit. They are not about what is the ultimate truth: "*Lo ba-Shamayim hi*" ("The Torah is not in Heaven"). The system in the Beit Midrash follows the rules of those who have been given authority to adjudicate and present their opinions, even when flawed. The leaders may battle, but it should never be to the point of embarrassment. It is a struggle about how to resolve disputes while giving voice to various opinions. The tension between unity and plurality, implicit since Sinai, comes to the fore.

The difference between the Yerushalmi, which seems to regret disagreement, and the Bavli, which seems to celebrate plurality while struggling with its practical implications, is repeated throughout the development of rabbinic tradition. The Mishnah is a first attempt at the codification of *halakhah*, although it preserves some minority opinions. Historically, after the School (*Metivta*) of Yavneh, there is a restoration of the Sanhedrin and the Beit Midrash. Yet, for every move that promotes unity, there is a counter-move that emphasizes diversity. Perhaps in response, the Tosefta includes traditions of the *Tannaim* omitted by R. Yehuda ha *Nasi*.

The Tosefta, *Masekhet Sotah*,[16] celebrates the multiple perspectives:

16. Tosefta, *Sotah*, Lieberman, Chapter 7, *halakhah* 12.

A person might think: 'since the house of Shammai declare unclean and the House of Hillel clean, this one prohibits and that one permits, how, then, can I learn Torah?'
Scripture says: 'words . . . the words . . . these are the words. . . .'
All the words have been given by a single Shepherd, one God created them, one Provider gave them, the Lord of all deeds, blessed be He, has spoken them. So make yourself a heart of many rooms and bring into it the words of the House of Shammai and the words of the House of Hillel, the words of those who declare unclean and the words of those who declare clean.

הלכה יב
שמא יאמר אדם בדעתו הואיל ובית שמיי מטמין ובית הלל מטהרין איש פל' אוסר ואיש פל' מתיר למה אני למד תורה מעתה ת"ל דברים הדברים אלה הדברים כל הדברים נתנו מרועה אחד אל אחד בראן פרנס אחד נתנן רבון כל המעשים ברוך הוא אמרו אף אתה עשה לבך חדרי חדרים והכניס בה דברי בית שמיי ודברי בית הלל דברי המטמאין ודברי המטהרין

In fact, there is a similarity to the *beraita* cited by the statement in the Bavli: "*kol ha-G'darim nitnu b'Dibur echad*" – There is no indication here of regret for diversity. However, the Tosefta directs us to actively seek out these disputes and alternative views.

Compiling the Talmud of the *Amora'im* is another attempt at promoting unity. Yet there are of course two students and, as we have seen, the Yerushalmi and Bavli differ, *inter alia*, on the value of difference itself.

In later generations, during the period of the *Rishonim*, the most ambitious and radical attempt to promote unity is Rambam's *Mishneh Torah*. In the work, he actively removes *mahloket* for the purpose of establishing clear *halakhic* practices for the Jewish people.

The general rule is so that a person will not need another compilation at all in the laws of Israel but rather this compilation combines the entire oral law with enactments and customs and rulings which were made from the times of our teacher Moses until the compilation of the Gemara, and as the *Ge'onim* explained for us in all of their works which they compiled after the Gemara. Therefore, I called this work Mishneh Torah (Second Torah). Be-

כללו של דבר כדי שלא יהא אדם צריך לחיבור אחר בעולם בדין מדיני ישראל אלא יהא חיבור זה מקבץ לתורה שבעל פה כולה עם התקנות והמנהגות והגזירות שנעשו מימות משה רבינו ועד חבור הגמרא וכמו שפירשו לנו הגאונים בכל חיבוריהם שחיברו אחר הגמרא. לפיכך קראתי שם חיבור זה משנה תורה. לפי שאדם קורא בתורה שבכתב תחלה

cause a person reads the written Torah first and afterwards reads this and knows from it the entire oral law, and doesn't need to read another book between them.

ואחר כך קורא בזה ויודע ממנו תורה שבעל פה כולה ואינו צריך לקרות ספר אחר ביניהם.

Rambam intends to be the authoritative guide of practice. He maintained that it is best to have an authoritative voice, trimming all the other opinions and eliminating diversity. Rambam goes back to an anti-dispute model to allow for a unified people. This is *l'chatchilah* – an ideal – for the Rambam.

A few centuries later, Rav Yosef Karo (sixteenth century), offers another, less exhaustive but more practically inclined codification of Jewish law. Interestingly, his commentary on the Tur, Beit Yosef, presented rulings and customs from Jewish communities all over the world. However, he composed a simplified version, the *Shulhan Arukh*, his codification of Jewish law, out of necessity. Unlike the Rambam, he did not see codification as the optimal approach, but as a *b'di'avad*,[17] an ex post facto approach. Once a less than ideal situation has occurred, then law can be codified.

I see in my heart that it is good to gather the roses of the sayings in a concise way with a clear and comprehensive language which is beautiful and pleasant, so that God's Torah will be complete, fluent in the mouths of each person of Israel.

ראיתי אני בלבי כי טוב ללקוט שושני ספירי אמריו בדרך קצרה בלשון צח וכולל יפה ונעים, למען תהיה תורת ה' תמימה שגורה בפי כל איש ישראל

Only due to the expulsion from Spain when the Torah was not fluent in the mouth of each person of Israel was this code necessary. In another place in his introduction, Rav Yosef Karo is clear that his major work was the Beit Yosef. The *Shulhan Arukh* is merely the Cliff Notes for those who are not scholars. It is only for those individuals requiring an authoritative voice. In the immediate aftermath of the expulsion from Iberia, the scattering of Spanish Jewry and the disruption of tradition.

The counter-movement of anti-codification is simultaneous with the movement towards unity. Already within the Rambam's lifetime, the

17. After the fact okay.

Ra'avad, Rav Avraham ben David, in the twelfth century, was extremely critical of the Rambam's perspective.

The Ra'avad claims that the Rambam seems to be abandoning the entire legacy of debate and diverse opinions which strengthen a people. He maintains that unifying a voice will strengthen the nation. The Ra'avad is astonished that Maimonides does not present the various perspectives surrounding his rulings. The Rambam's legal decisions cannot be presented in a vacuum. The Ra'avad would prefer "to duke it out" intellectually in the *beit midrash*; Rambam would like a unified voice.

Two generations later, it is interesting that the Ramban, who was a student of the Ra'avad's son – uses positively the phrase that Rashi had used negatively: "two *Torot*." In a comment on *Hulin* 45b, Ramban makes a bold statement. He teaches that, when presented with a debate among individuals or groups where the Torah leaders are authoritative, a person may follow whichever leadership speaks to him or her:

Ramban questions a *beraita* that says one may follow Beit Hillel or Beit Shammai providing that he or she follows the stringency as well as the leniency within each opinion. Should not one judge each disagreement on the merits of each participant and not declare oneself the follower of one school?

That which the *beraita* says "one who wishes to follow Beit Shammai – their leniencies and stringencies – may do so, or he may follow Beit Hillel – their leniencies and stringencies," is difficult to me – don't we rule that "if one says impure and the other says pure, one permits and the other forbids, if one of them is greater in wisdom and number follow him, and if not, in Torah matters follow the more stringent and in rabbinic matters follow the lenient," as it says in the first chapter of *Avodah Zarah*! I can respond that because the dispute between the students of the House of Shammai and the (students of the) House of Hillel was large, and all the sages of Israel were subsumed within it, and the Torah

הא דתניא "הרוצה לעשות כב"ש – כקוליהון וכחומריהון – עושה, או כב"ה – כקוליהון וכחומריהון," קשה לי – והא קיי"ל ד"אחד מטמא ואחד מטהר, אחד מתיר ואחד אוסר, אם היה אחד מהם גדול בחכמה ובמנין הלך אחריו, ואם לאו בשל תורה הלך אחר המחמיר, בשל סופרים הלך אחר המיקל," כדאיתא בפ"ק דע"ז!?

ויש לי לומר: מתוך שמחלוקתן של תלמידי ב"ש וב"ה גדולה, וכל חכמי ישראל נכנסין תחתיה, ונעשית להם תורה כשתי תורות, הרשות לכל אחד לעשות כדבריהם, כדאמרינן ביבמות (י"ד

became for them as two Torahs, everyone has the right to follow either, as we say in *Yevamot* (14a). As a result, he who wishes to become a member of the group of Beit Shammai is always permitted to do so.	א›). וכיון שכן, זה הרוצה להיות מכת ב"ש ולעשות כדבריהם לעולם רשאי הוא.

Ramban explained that the dispute between Beit Shammai and Beit Hillel was so extensive, involving all the sages of Israel, that there are two *Torot*. Everyone has a right to follow the Torah of Shammai or the Torah of Hillel, provided that he or she is consistent and is not acting merely for the sake of convenience.

Shortly thereafter, the Ritva (Rav Yom Tov ben Avraham Asevilli, 1250–1330), makes explicit the view that may have underwritten the Ra'avad's objection to the Rambam's codification project and the Ramban's appreciation of diversity. For the Ritva, there may be more than one correct answer to a question. In major questions the rule of the majority in making a decision is followed. However, the minority view still has validity.

These and these are the words of the Living God. They asked the rabbis of France *z"l*, how it is possible that both of them are the words of the Living God when this one prohibits and this one permits, and they answered that when Moses ascended on high to receive the Torah, on each and every saying were shown to him 49 facets to prohibit and 49 facets to permit. He asked the Holy One Blessed Be He about this and He said that it will be transmitted to the scholars of Israel in each generation and the decision will be according to them. And this is correct homiletically and there is a reason and a hidden meaning for it according to the way of truth [*kabbalah*].	אלו ואלו דברי אלהים חיים. שאלו רבני צרפת ז"ל היאך אפשר שיהו שניהם דברי אלהים חיים וזה אוסר וזה מתיר, ותירצו כי כשעלה משה למרום לקבל תורה הראו לו על כל דבר ודבר מ"ט פנים לאיסור ומ"ט פנים להיתר, ושאל להקב"ה על זה, ואמר שיהא זה מסור לחכמי ישראל שבכל דור ודור ויהיה הכרעה כמותם, ונכון הוא לפי הדרש ובדרך האמת יש טעם וסוד בדבר.

The Ritva maintained that even Moshe Rabbeinu received conflicting views on *Har Sinai*. In other words, the tension between plurality and unity that we saw in *Sefer Shemot* was present not only in the receipt of the Torah by different members of the people but by Moshe's experience. *Mahloket* went from Moshe to *Hakhmei Yisrael*.[18] Fundamentally, the Ritva recognizes that there is a divine nature to this plurality. Distinct views can emanate from the Ultimate source simultaneously. Consequently, each generation has a plurality of voices and each one is still the truth. We do have to be *makhria* – ultimately we have to decide. He follows the principle that "*lo ba-Shamayim hi*," that it is ultimately the Torah in our hands. But the Ritva never suggests that ideally there should be only one opinion and that diversity exists only because of the decline of the generations.

Opposing the codification activity of the *Shulhan Arukh*, the Yam Shel Shlomo, Rav Shlomo Luria, sixteenth century, takes this idea of the Ritva one step further:

> The kabbalists wrote a reason for this, because all of the souls were at Mount Sinai and received [the Torah] through 49 conduits. This is seven times seven, purified sevenfold. And these are the sounds which they heard and also saw. "And all of Israel saw the sounds" – these are the ideas which were distributed by conduit. Everyone via his/her own conduit, according to their grasp. And received it according to the ability of his/her supernal soul, according to its level of elevation or diminution. One may be distant from another, to such an extent that one arrives at [a judgment that something is] pure while another arrives at [a judgment that the same thing is] impure, and a third is in the middle, far from the extremes. And all is truth. Understand it.

> והמקובלים כתבו טעם לדבר, לפי שכל הנשמות היו בהר סיני, וקיבלו דרך מ"ט צינורות. והן שבעה פעמים שבעה, מזוקק שבעתיים. והן הקולות אשר שמעו וגם ראו. וכל ישראל רואים את הקולות הן הדיעות המתחלקות בצינור. כל אחד ראה דרך צינור שלו לפי השגתו. וקבל כפי כח (נשמת עליונו) [נשמתו העליונה], לרוב עילוייה. או פחיתותה, זה רחוק מזה. עד שאחד יגיע לטהור. והשני יגיע לקצה האחרון לטמא. והשלישי לאמצעות, רחוק מן הקצוות והכל אמת והבן.

Rav Shlomo Luria said that *mahloket* was inherent even in God's transmission of the Torah to Moses. Each member of *Am Yisrael* experienced the revelation at *Matan Torah* differently and everyone has an equal claim to the truth. In conversation, Paul Franks, Professor of Philosophy and Jewish Thought at Yale University explained that "for the Yam

18. Jewish scholars.

Shel Shlomo, revelation occurs by means of divine contraction that attunes revelation to the unique power of each individual, enabling each to constitute Torah in a unique manner."

Two generations later, Rav Isaiah Horowitz (the Shelah) gives a further explanation of the plurality implicit in Torah from the beginning. The main point of the introduction to his *Shnei Luhot ha-Brit* is that God, the Torah and *Am Yisrael* are intimately interlinked in such a way that each has some version of any characteristic of any one of the three. One example is free will. Each of the three has multiple possibilities at any given time. While the attribution of free will to God and to *Am Yisrael* is standard, the ascription of free will to the Torah is not. But R. Horowitz uses this idea to explain the statement that these and those are words of the living God: "The Torah is not determined by one point of view, but includes many points of view."[19]

Later, in the nineteenth century, the Netziv, Rav Naftali Tzvi Yehuda Berlin, returns to the *mahloket* of the Beit Midrash described in texts quoted above from the Bavli.[20] The Netziv explains that the rabbis of the Second Temple were righteous and well versed in Torah yet not upright in the ways of the world. Filled with baseless hatred, they suspected those who disagreed with them and failed to open up a heart of many rooms. For the Netziv that is the meaning of *Yashar*. To be upright, you must enable different views to come in the Torah conversation. Failure to consider views of others, even for the purpose of Heaven, breaks our people and causes destruction – *harisut Yishuv haAretz* (obliterates the settling of the land). Even righteous people must learn to open their hearts to let other voices in, to open up intellectually and psychologically.

As Jews, we must rise above the overwhelming but terribly destructive temptation to vilify those who disagree with us, either religiously or politically. We have other leaders of the generation who advocate unification through codification. Moreover, we should not merely tolerate but deeply value each participant in debate for his or her otherness. It is this deep respect that unifies a people.

Rav Yitz Greenberg *sh'lita* has taught that "part of every truth is

19. *Shnei Luhot ha-Brit* (Amsterdam, 1648), 19a.
20. Haemek Davar, *Hakdamah l'Sefer Bereishit.*

the fact that an image of God is speaking it; that is to say, a being of infinite value, equality and uniqueness is speaking it." But, he has been a principal advocate for the side of rabbinic tradition that emphasizes diversity, not merely *b'di'avad*, but *l'chatchilah*.

I am thankful to Rav Yitz for enabling a rebirth of a *beit midrash*, inviting in the perspectives of many and for allowing each one of his students to witness a person who follows Torah in a way that is *yashar* and upright.

In the spirit of the Tosefta, the Ra'avad, the Ramban, the Ritva, the Yam shel Shlomo, the Netziv, the Shelah and Rav Yitz, I welcome an alternative approach to the texts considered in this essay. That would certainly be an appropriate tribute to our teacher, Rav Yitz Greenberg, *sh'lita*.

New Intellectual Paradigms

Rebuilding the Covenant Through Self Obligation:

Rabeinu Tam and Saying the Blessing on Hallel on Israel Independence Day

Rabbi Asher Lopatin

Over thirty years ago, Rabbi Yitz Greenberg electrified the Jewish world with his theory of "*Voluntary Covenant*" (*Perspectives*, October 1982). In Rav Yitz's own words, "What happened to the Covenant? I submit that its authority was broken [ed.: after the Holocaust], but the Jewish people, released from its obligation, chose voluntarily to take it on again. . . ."

For Orthodox Judaism, a voluntary covenant was a revolutionary idea. Even for more liberal streams of Judaism, it was novel as well: The idea that, at one point, the Covenant between the Jewish people and God had been obligatory upon the Jews, was not consistent with personal autonomy of Reform Judaism. On the other hand, the idea that because of a world gone awry – most poignantly during the Holocaust – the Covenant could not be imposed on the Jews anymore, was challenging for traditional Jews because they always understood the *mitzvot* as obligations whose authority was derived from the Divine Covenant with the Jewish people. If the Divine Covenant was no longer obligatory, then how could the *mitzvot* be obligatory? The ideas of obligation and standing under Divine authority are central to Orthodox Judaism, so wouldn't a voluntary covenant be the opposite of this tradition of obligation?

The concept of the Voluntary Covenant has been discussed by many over the years. In this article, I focus on the second part of the Voluntary Covenant theory: that the Jewish people voluntarily took on the Covenant, i.e., the Chosen People validated the Covenant out of their own free will. It would seem that the claim of the theory is that the Jewish People obligated themselves to the Covenant, and hence obligated themselves, voluntarily, to the *mitzvot* as well. This might seem like a contradiction in terms, but it actually fits well with established Jewish tradition. In this chapter I will discuss three ways the Voluntary Obligation element of the Voluntary Covenant theory makes sense within the context of our tradition, and in particular, I would like to focus on the parallel theory of the Tosafists in the Talmudic tractate *Arachin* 10a.

The Blessing of Obligation – *Vetzivanu* – "God commanded us"

The classic blessing over a *mitzvah* contains the language, "Blessed are you God . . . who has sanctified us and commanded us. . . ." The Talmud, in tractate *Shabbat,* questions our use of this blessing for *mitzvot* that God did not directly command. The key example is the *mitzvah* of lighting Hanukkah candles, which is rabbinic in origin, and was not directly commanded by God in the Torah. The answer is that since the Torah says *Lo tasur* – thou shalt not veer, understood to mean that "thou shall not veer from the words of the Rabbis" – the Talmud says that we are justified in saying that God commanded the candles of Hanukkah because God authorized the rabbis to make obligations upon the Jewish people. In one way, this is a precedent for turning voluntary actions – not obligated by God – into actions considered obligated by God. In other words, the Talmud, and the blessing, go beyond saying that our rabbis obligated us to do certain things. Rather, what was voluntary and not commanded by God is transformed into a commandment of God by the actions of our rabbis.

Therefore it is not a contradiction that the Jewish people can choose to create a Divine Obligation. In this case, it is the great rabbis of the Talmudic and pre-Talmudic period who did so, but they did so as representatives of the people. Rav Ahron Soloveichik, a believer in democracy, frequently declared that the Sanhedrin got their authority as representatives of the Jewish people, not as an outside force obligating the Jews to something. So with these rabbinic enactments, the Jewish People is seen as obligating itself, enabling the people to declare something not previously commanded to be a full Divine Obligation.

Yet this "voluntary obligation" is, at first, limited to the era of the Second Temple and Talmudic period, at least 1,500 years ago. More importantly, even though the rabbinic enactors are seen as representing the Jewish people then, they are representing the people as a whole. This is not a case of individuals choosing to make something voluntary an obligation. It is the people choosing to make that transformation. The individual has no choice regarding Hannukah or Shabbat candles or other rabbinically transformed commandments. His or her people have chosen to make them obligatory for them 2,000 years ago. This is not a model for an individual taking on the Voluntary Covenant for his or her self as an obligation. A transformation from the non-obligated to the obligated occurred, but it was not an individual's transformation.

A second way of looking at voluntary obligation is the concept of *minhag*.[1] One solid example is the evening service (*ma'ariv*). The ruling of the Talmud is that *ma'ariv* is voluntary: even the rabbis who determined the times and order of the services did not make it obligatory. Yet the Jewish people themselves, even more directly than the Sanhedrin and over presumably a longer period of time, obligated themselves to the prayer. According to the vast majority of decisors, *ma'ariv* is now *halakhically* obligatory, not because of a special enactment of the court or the rabbis, but because the people took it on as a custom, a *minhag*, to make it obligatory. *Minhagim* do not have the time specificity that changing the blessing had: they come about much more because of self-obligation than any formal process. Yet here, too, the contemporary individual is taken out of the equation. True, at some point, or over a period of time, individual Jews chose to create the tradition of the obligation of *ma'ariv*, but contemporary Jews are born into a tradition with customs and, in the *halakhic* world, they are not given the decision to choose this Covenant with its built in obligatory customs or not. Over time individuals have voluntarily accepted the obligation, but the individual today is not given a choice to accept or reject the customs accepted a long time ago.

Another difference in the *minhag* model from the first model is that a *minhag*, while becoming obligatory for the community and those who dwell within it, is still recognized as coming from the people, rather

1. Jewish custom.

than from God. In a sense, the *minhag* is outside the Covenant. It is not an obligation that God puts on us, rather it is an obligation that we put on ourselves. It never rises to the level of divine commandment, and, therefore there is no blessing of "who sanctified us and commanded us . . ." before performing a *minhag* since God did not actually command the *minhag*.

Tosafist Model Combining *Minhag* with Divine Obligation Through Voluntarism

In medieval Franco-Germany, the Tosafists found a brilliant way of combining the first two of these "voluntary obligations," thus enabling the individual to make the decision whether they wanted to obligate themselves to the *mitzvah* or not. In their theory most clearly expressed by Rashi's grandson, R. Yaakov ben Meir Tam (Rabbeinu Tam), an individual can take on a specific action voluntarily, and since that person makes it a personal obligation, it becomes a commandment of God.

This formulation by Rabbeinu Tam is used by the early twentieth century authority, Rav Yisrael Mayer Kagan, the Hafetz Hayim, in his *Sha'ar Ha'tzion* in the laws of *Rosh Chodesh* (*Shulkhan Arukh, Orakh Hayim*, 422:13). *Shulkhan Arukh* 422:2 says that even though one says the selection of Psalms called *Hallel* on Rosh Chodesh, the practice is not to say the blessing that God "sanctified us and commanded us to read/finish the *Hallel*" on *Rosh Chodesh* based on the opinion of Maimonides. The *Mishneh Berurah* (Rav Kagen) explains that the opinion that there is no blessing is because it is only a *minhag* to say *Hallel* on *Rosh Chodesh*, and "for a *minhag* one does not say a blessing" (#14). This is consistent with the idea that even a widespread, accepted custom is only a reflection of the people's self-obligation, and it does not recreate the Covenant or the Divine Obligations that go with it. Therefore it is not correct to say that God "commanded us to say/finish the *Hallel*" when it was not God who really did the commanding.

Nevertheless, the Ashkenazi source in the *Shulkhan Arukh*, Rav Moshe Isserles, wrote in his gloss: "Some say that even an individual [saying *Hallel*] should say the blessing on it." How could the individual say that God commanded him or her to say the *Hallel* when it is only a custom? Enter Rabbeinu Tam, quoted in the Hafetz Hayim's *Sha'ar*

Hatzi'un footnotes: "The Tosafists wrote in the Babylonian Talmud *Arachin* 10: 'In any case, hold the opinion of Rabbeinu Tam in your hand that it is good, even as an individual, to say the first *berakhah*[2] of *Hallel* (even though it says that God commanded us to say the *Hallel*) because even though of course he is not obligated to say it, but still, since he (voluntarily) obligates himself to this, it is not a wasted blessing, just as women (who are not obligated) say the blessing over taking the *lulav*[3] . . . even though they have no obligation, they can voluntarily do so'. . . ." In other words, if the individual takes on a *mitzvah* that is completely voluntary, they can recreate the Divine Obligation through this self-obligation. Hence, even though *Hallel* on Rosh Chodesh is merely a custom, if the person feels that custom as an obligation, then, as it were, the voluntary *mitzvah* becomes obligatory again.

Interestingly, the era of the Tosafists – some eight hundred years before the Holocaust – was a traumatic time for European Jewry. The first Crusade, that left the slaughter of thousands of Jews in its wake, occurred in the lifetime of Rashi. But massacres and Crusades continued throughout the twelfth to fourteenth centuries, and the Tosafists made important rulings regarding martyrdom and the pressures of the gentile world. Yet, what the Tosafists saw were Jews who were pious and zealous in their obedience to God. They saw women go far beyond the letter of the law, in their observance of the non-obligatory positive time-bound laws of *lulav* and *shofar*.[4] They saw men slaughtering their children so that the Christians would not force them to be baptized (see *Da'at Zekeinim Miba'alei Tosafot*, Genesis 9:5), even though this went beyond the law. Even the *berakhah* for lighting Shabbat candles, "God . . . who commanded us to light Shabbat candles" is a practice that was codified at this time. Lighting Shabbat candles may go back to Talmudic times, but the blessing, the people's embrace of God's commandment, appears only in this era. There certainly were instances of conversions out of Judaism to Christianity, but these were rare, representing individuals, not entire communities.

---

2. Blessing.
3. One of the four species that is used for a ritual on the Jewish holiday of Tabernacles.
4. Ram's horn used for Jewish ritual.

Jews of this era, despite the unprecedented massacres and attacks, did not feel the covenant was broken or that God's authority was broken because of all the horrors of the time. There is no evidence that they subscribed in those centuries to the first part of Rabbi Yitz Greenberg's idea of the Voluntary Covenant. It does seem, however, even from examining only the evidence from the writings of the Tosafists, that European Jewry embraced the second part of the Rav Greenberg's Voluntary Covenant: Even voluntary actions could become divinely commanded *mitzvot* if we choose to take them on again. For European Jews of the days of Tosafot and the centuries that followed, it made perfect sense to say that God has obligated to do the customs and voluntary *mitzvot* as long as we ourselves see them as obligatory for us. Even though the Hafetz Hayim quotes language from nearly a millennium before his time, it is clear that the ability to transform something voluntary into a divine commandment resonates with him both *halakhically* and, it would seem, emotionally. He quotes Rabbeinu Tam at such length and with such conviction that it feels in some mystical way he is preparing us for the challenges of the post-Holocaust era, which occurred less than a decade after his death.

Yet the Hafetz Hayim, not himself a Zionist, also prepares us for one reaction to what Rav Greenberg calls, "the greatest biblical symbol validating the Covenant: the State of Israel." We cannot speculate what the Hafetz Hayim would think of the founding of the Jewish State in the aftermath of the Holocaust, but we can connect with his *halakhic* ruling regarding reciting Hallel on Israel Independence Day, *Yom Ha'atzma'ut.* The Hafetz Hayim himself may have ruled that one should not recite *Hallel* at all on *Yom Ha'atzma'ut,* however if we look to the religious Zionist camp, who all say *Hallel* (or Half *Hallel*), there are many discussions regarding whether *Hallel* should be said with a *berakhah* or without a *berakhah* on *Yom Ha'atzma'ut*. Some see it as an obligation, based on the Meiri or other authorities, some see it as just a custom that lovers of the State of Israel have taken on, and others see it as purely voluntary. What the chain of *halakhah,* from Tosafot to Remo to the Hafetz Hayim seem to be saying, is that if a person feels passionately that they must say *Hallel* on *Yom Ha'atzma'ut* – how could they not praise God for the State of Israel? – that person has transformed the Voluntary Covenant back to an Obligatory, Divine Covenant, and, hence, the *berakhah* of "God . . . commanded us to read the *Hallel*" is the correct blessing to say. Through our own voluntary actions, we create not only a human, personal obligation, but even more significantly, we recreate the Divine Obligatory Covenant.

There are many more profound implications to the Tosafist theory regarding transforming the voluntary into Godly obligation, but perhaps this one example of the blessing over *Hallel* for *Yom Ha'atzma'ut* resonates most with Rav Yitz's Voluntary Covenant theory because it connects with the re-establishment of the Jewish State after two thousand years. Rav Greenberg writes, in *Voluntary Covenant*: ". . . The bulk of Jews . . . acted to recreate the greatest Biblical symbol validating the covenant, the State of Israel." Millions of Jews see the State of Israel not as just a voluntary gesture, nor as just a human act. Zionism may be a "bottom up" movement of human beings shaping a new theological reality of God giving the Jewish people an opportunity once again to have a state and restore the covenant. However, a Tosafist interpretation of Voluntary Covenant theory would argue that the Jewish blood and tears that went into establishing the Jewish State and that still goes into maintaining it in a hostile environment effects a theological change in the relationship of the Jewish people and God. Those who are "obligating themselves" to supporting and strengthening the State of Israel make it once again a Divine Obligation. For those of us who believe, like Rav Greenberg, that the existence of a Jewish State reflects the Divine Covenant restored, Israel also has transformed – or affirmed – the Divine Covenant to be an Obligatory Covenant.

Rav Yitz Greenberg's theory of a Voluntary Covenant is challenging and controversial for Jews who have grown up in a tradition of *mitzvot* – commandments and obligations from God. Much has been written and much more will be written debating how to fit the voluntary part of the theory into the *halakhic* tradition. Nevertheless, when we focus on the restorative aspect of *Voluntary Covenant,* that the Covenant can be validated and even restored to its former position of the obligatory, there is a rich *halakhic* tradition from Franco-German Europe of the Medieval Tosafist era which speaks forcefully to that process.

Just as we do not know what the Hafetz Hayim would have done on Yom *Ha'atzma'ut,* we also cannot know what Tosafot would have done had they read Rav Greenberg's *Voluntary Covenant.* I am convinced that the historical realities Rav Greenberg dealt with would have resonated with the Tosafists, and that Rabbeinu Tam would have a lot to say about how the Jews, through their own voluntary sense of obligation, could transform the Divine Will, and create Divine Obligation. This transformation, voluntary obligation from humankind to God, happens under the worst circumstances – the slaughter of entire towns during the Crusades or six million Jews during the Holocaust – and in the most elevating times – the creation of the Jewish State. Whether God gives up obligating us to God's Covenant can be debated fiercely; but the ability of human beings to create an obligatory Divine Covenant through their love and devotion to God and God's Torah cannot be denied.

God is waiting; will we embrace God's *mitzvot*? Will we give meaning to the *berakhah* of "God . . . commanded us"? Whether it is a *minhag*, a voluntary law or a law that used to be obligatory but is not seen that way, the answer needs to be: *Hineini*! – We are here, and we are ready for the challenge God has given us to make God's Will and our wills intertwined with one another.

Visions of the Secular and the Impact of Rabbi Yitz Greenberg's Vision

Rabbi Dr. Ariel Burger

Two Types of Modern Orthodoxy

To say that Modern Orthodoxy stands at a crossroads is redundant. Modern Orthodoxy *is* a crossroads, a way of holding tension between tradition and creativity, *halakhah* and moral intuition, history and unfolding new realities. All Jewish streams have had to deal with these tensions. What makes Modern Orthodoxy unique is its celebration of, and stark refusal to abandon the struggle, as well as its particular and unique set of enduring methodological commitments. Inspired by the best of our *halakhic* tradition and its most brilliant proponents and *Poskim*,[1] Modern Orthodoxy has claimed the mantle of Yisrael – the ones who wrestle, who avoid easy answers, who are not afraid of the hard path.

Yet this vibrant vision does not always translate into reality on the ground. Modern Orthodoxy "as it is often practiced" looks like a compromise, like an attempt to ease or avoid creative tension rather than celebrate and work with it. Evincing neither devotion to the details of *halakhah* nor fervor for justice, Modern Orthodoxy sometimes seems to be defined by the absence of these qualities and the unwillingness to face fully the demands of tradition and the moment.

The exceptions we encounter are all the more inspiring for being rare. Of course there are rabbis, scholars, and laypeople dedicated to

1. Jewish legal authorities.

a Modern Orthodoxy that is creative and unafraid of facing competing claims. These teachers speak of the lived conflict between the guiding directives of the text and the reality of the street, between *halakhah* and personal moral intuition, between the written tradition and lived experience, and the need to hold onto both sides of that conflict in search of deeper responses. These teachers, and to some extent the communities they lead, want to feel the presence of the Living God, they want lives of depth and devotion, and they want Torah to *say something* urgently relevant to what is happening in every dimension of life. They grapple honestly and constantly with difficult matters, never giving up on their commitment to Torah, and never refusing responsibility for the world and the time in which they live. We might call this approach a Modern Orthodoxy of Presence, because it deals not only with the issues raised by modernity (historicity, autonomy, Zionism, etc.), but it expands to encounter all aspects of the present moment. "Staying present" is also the psychological posture we must adopt in order to manage those difficult moments when we feel caught between competing values and claims. A Modern Orthodoxy of Presence both rests on and supports this posture. Finally, we shall see that a key element of this attitude is the recognition that God is present in every moment and in every encounter, even those that are most challenging.

A Modern Orthodoxy of Presence represents a fierce commitment to dealing with the theological difficulties raised by new categories of thought and philosophy. Rather than seeking reconciliation, this Modern Orthodoxy seeks to accept the tension and to celebrate and work with the unresolved issues that define our moment. Its proponents offer great hope for Modern Orthodoxy to thrive and flourish as a relevant and passion-inspiring pathway in Jewish life today and in the future. One of the most impactful of these teachers in my life – as well as in the lives of countless others – is Rabbi Dr. Irving "Yitz" Greenberg, or "Rav Yitz" as he is affectionately called by many students.

Those readers who do not recognize the first approach from their own experience of Modern Orthodox life should consider themselves fortunate. But even for those of us who do, and who are not satisfied with a Modern Orthodoxy of compromise, we must ask: What is our method? How might we explain to our children and students the ways in which we choose to hold the creative tension between our roots and the ever-changing world around us? Rav Yitz provides cogent answers to these questions, ones that appeal and are credible to not only committed Modern Orthodox Jews, but to anyone concerned with the future of religion and religious communities. At the heart of his argument is the notion that Modern Orthodoxy can serve as a bridge, a unifying conduit between the world of Torah study and practice, and the world in which the vast majority of Jews today inhabit: the secular. As we shall see, Rav Yitz's theology is driven by the urgent quest for a credible response to the Holocaust, and this has led him to new thinking about the secular and hidden holiness in what he calls "the Third Era" of Jewish history. It is the place of the secular that I explore here.

Two Views of the Holy in Jewish Thought

The distinction between a Modern Orthodoxy of compromise and a Modern Orthodoxy of Presence reflects an earlier distinction in Jewish teachings about holiness. In much of classical Jewish literature, holiness is associated with separation (for example, Shabbat is separated from the week, the *Mishkan/Beit HaMikdash* is separated from other spaces, and the act of *kedushin* is to set one person aside).[2] Rambam went further and defined holiness as *perishut*, separation.[3] To be holy is to make distinctions, *havdalah,* clear boundaries between sacred and profane. In this view, Judaism does not celebrate the liminal, it resolves the discomfort of the in-between, and helps us to clarify: impure or pure, kosher or not, forbidden or permitted. From this perspective, the realm of *reshut* is just a *p'saq* waiting to happen. Ambiguity is dangerous and impure. The realm of service of God is in the holy, in holy space and holy time, while the outside world is a distraction or a threat, unless and until it is rectified by *halakhah.* Because holiness is a separate arena meant to be protected from interference, the religious posture that naturally follows is conservative and reactive.

2. See also Rashi on *parashat Kedoshim,* quoting the Midrash that "In every place we find sexual boundaries we find holiness." Also see Ramban on *Shemot* 12:1 for his discussion of *Kiddush haChodesh.*

3. Ramban, *parshat* Kedoshim. Rashi, too, associates *Kedushah* with *Perishut,* but he specifically addresses separation from *arayot,* while Ramban expands the category to include all areas of living.

This is not the entire story. Many Jewish teachings, from the rabbis on, recognize the importance of the liminal. An alternative view of *re-shut* as neither command nor transgression, but an open arena of choice, does exist in the commentaries. Indeed, the role of *Aggadah* can be seen as a necessary corrective to the either/or, *p'saq*-oriented approach of *halakhah*, a way of describing the contours of the liminal in ways that help us navigate complexity and unresolvable issues. For example, we find the notion, developed at length in the *kabbalah* of the Arizal, that every moment is filled with potential, everything composed of sparks of light, as well the shards from which they must be freed. In more recent Jewish history, the Hasidic movement expanded this approach, with sometimes radical results. I turn now to that movement's founder.

A Hasidic View of the Secular

The Ba'al Shem Tov ("The Besht"; 1700?–1760) taught his followers the concept of *avodah be-gashmiyut*, serving God through the material, and that everything – eating, drinking, working, marriage – could become sacred devotional activity.[4] By rendering porous the distinction between holy and profane, he opened new possibilities for Jewish religious life – and opened himself to critique from other Jews, to whom such talk posed an existential threat to Judaism. That he based himself in part on earlier sources did not appease his critics, who feared the masses would translate the Besht's teachings into a complacent spirituality devoid of discipline – or worse, would end with antinomian horror, as the Sabbateans had not too long before. Yet, despite the dangers, his softening of the rigid distinction between sacred and secular in Jewish life allowed the isolated Jewish innkeeper or unlearned farmer to find meaningful and vibrant Jewish expression, and to see that as a positive and not as an unfortunate compromise. The idea that we can find holiness in the everyday is not new. But the Besht's stark expressions and examples, and the stories and teachings he used to instantiate the claim were new.

4. For simplicity's sake I focus on *avodah b'Gashmiyut* here, but I have in mind other concepts as well, from what has been described as the panentheism evident in early Hasidism, to the concept of *shoresh neshamah*, to the more challenging notion of *averah lishmah*. Each of these, in different ways, challenges the more normative world of distinctions implied by holiness as separation.

Ultimately, this element of Hasidism had great theological weight and personal resonance for many, changing the life of Jews across Eastern Europe, and later in America and Israel.

Following the Besht, each Hasidic school developed the idea further, in diverse ways. I will point to one: the teachings of the Besht's great-grandson, Rebbe Nachman of Breslov.[5] Let us look at two sources, a teaching and a tale. The teaching, from *Likutei MoHaRaN* 33:2:

> And one must know that "the entire world is filled with His glory" (Isaiah 6), and "no place is empty of Him" (*Tikunei Zohar* 57).... and even someone who is working among Gentiles [far from Jewish community] cannot justify giving up on devotions/religious life.... For our sages have already revealed to us that in every material object and in all foreign languages one can find Godliness....
>
> And this is what our Sages revealed and opened for us, so that one who is wise will know and understand, that in all material objects there exists Godliness and God's life-force, as they taught: "TaT is Caspian for 2, and PaT is Afrikan for 2." [The biblical word commonly translated as "phylacteries," *Totafot*, is unidentifiable as a Hebrew word. The rabbis explain its etymology as derived from two words in two foreign languages – languages associated with idolatry. "TaT" and "PaT" come together to form the word "*ToTaFoT*," which means the *tefillin* worn on the head, which has four compartments (two plus two).] This is to teach us that in all foreign languages God's life-force is present as a sustaining force....[6]

It is clear from this lesson, based on rabbinic literature but presented in a more explicitly radical way, that this is confident theology and not apologetics. The nature of the universe is God-filled. No place,

5. I choose Rebbe Nachman not only because he emphasized the secular in particularly creative ways, but because if he received the mantle of leadership through any lineage at all, it was that of his mother and grandmother, the Besht's daughter Adel. A female Jewish spiritual lineage is a fitting well to plumb in honor of Rav Yitz. This is also a modest tribute to his nephew Rabbi Natan Greenberg, my Rosh Yeshiva, who introduced me to this and many other Breslov teachings.

6. I believe that "language" here refers to culture as well.

thing, situation, *not even foreign idolatrous culture,* is empty of Divine Presence and meaning. Although this is a mystical and not a *halakhic* claim, its profound implications for Jewish life share characteristics with a Modern Orthodoxy of relevance. Whether beginning from Rebbe Nachman's teaching or from Rav Yitz's (as we shall see), we are led to a claim of universal access to holiness. Nothing is unredeemable, not Caspian, not Afrikan, not feminism, not post-modernism. Every cultural development has something to contribute to the religious perspective. Of course, every ideology also demonstrates what Rebbe Nachman later refers to as "garments and constrictions," elements that hide God's presence, elements in need of raising up. He does not argue for an uncritical encounter with ideas, but neither does he countenance their easy dismissal. In a similar way, a confident Modern Orthodoxy of Presence is unafraid of both challenging and being challenged by contemporary ideologies, and as it engages it purifies them, removing layers to reveal the holiness hiding within them.

A tale that further illustrates this theme of the secular concerns Rebbe Nachman's brother Reb Yechiel, who visited his brother for Shabbat:

> The Friday night meal was filled with Torah teachings and sacred songs. The lunch meal, however, consisted of conversations about current events. (This was the time of the Napoleonic wars, and Rebbe Nachman was known to be always thirsty for news of the world.) After Shabbat, Reb Yechiel came to his brother's room. "I don't understand," he said. "Friday night was beautiful, holy, filled with exalted teachings. But at the second meal, you just discussed matters of this world with your followers! It didn't look so holy to me!"
>
> Rebbe Nachman said, "Do you remember all the details of what was discussed at lunch?" Reb Yechiel shook his head. Then Rebbe Nachman walked over to the door and locked it. And until the morning, he proceeded to review the conversation at lunch in every detail, but this time revealing the secret teaching each thread of conversation was hiding.
>
> After that Reb Yechiel became his brother's follower.[7]

7. *Chayei MoHaRaN, Yegiaso b'Avodas Hashem,* 11.

The rabbis taught that "the worldly talk of the sages requires learning," yet Reb Yechiel still held to the hierarchy of sacred discourse over secular. After all, isn't a *d'var* Torah a more significant contribution than a discussion of current events, especially at a Shabbat meal? Rebbe Nachman agreed that simply discussing the news is not enough, but he showed his brother that it is possible to find meaning – spiritual, educational, religious significance – in such discussions. Our children respond to such a claim, they too look for universal meaning, for openness to all areas of life, for nothing human to be foreign to us.

The Secular – A Vision of Relevance

Back to our two Modern Orthodoxies. In a post-Holocaust era we have been at least subconsciously shaped by the encounter with ultimate evil. A theology of distinction, which states that God can only be found in certain arenas and that sees holiness only as *perishut* is no longer credible. In order to be redeemed, our conception of the God who allowed Auschwitz must now demonstrate universal relevance and presence. A God who lives in the synagogue is no longer enough; we need to see God in the streets, the slums, and the front-lines of human conflict. A Torah that circumscribes religious life is not enough; we need a Torah that speaks to, sheds light on, every aspect of human life.

The most articulate proponent of such an approach is Rav Yitz. In our time, driven not by mystical insight but by theological re-evaluation after the Shoah, he describes and models an approach that reignites a passionate Modern Orthodoxy of Presence, which benefits far beyond our own community. He has publically articulated a vision for incorporating passionate devotion and passionate progressivism, theological depth, and tactical canniness in a creative dialectic. His is an attitude that cares deeply about living out the details of a *halakhic* life and being immersed in Torah, while being turned toward the world. Ultimately, it harnesses creative tension as an engine for dynamic growth.

Rav Yitz has written at length of his encounter in the '60s with the Shoah, and the resultant recognition of the inadequacies of previously held positions, both theological and *halakhic*. Many people, in having their dearly held convictions and inherited beliefs challenged in this way, would have collapsed the problem, choosing either to leave tradition and *halakhah* or circling the wagons and adopting a *chumrah*-driven approach in order to avoid the danger of the theological challenge. Rav Yitz did neither. Perhaps drawing on his early years studying and practicing *mussar*[8] in Yeshivas Eitz Chaim-Novardok, he was able to remain in the discomfort of serious re-evaluation.

This re-evaluation led to a new vision of Judaism with several key components: the Triumph of Life as an all-embracing narrative with meta-*halakhic* implications (*kelal gadol*); a serious coming to terms with modern challenges from feminism and the encounter with other religious traditions; a new understanding of covenant as evolving, and as voluntary after the Shoah; and – in short – an articulation of a deeply relevant Judaism that spoke to generations of leaders in mainstream settings like Federations as well as rabbinical schools.[9]

While each of these aspects deserves further study, at the heart of this articulation is Rav Yitz's description of the Third Era of Jewish history, beginning with the Shoah, in which older categories and constructs are no longer credible. A major aspect of this is his description of the secular in Jewish life, and the ongoing evolution of the covenant between God and humankind: "At every stage in the maturation, the Divine partner in the covenant becomes more hidden, and the human becomes more active and responsible."[10]

Building on the rabbinic idea that as history unfolds, the prophet gives way to the scholar, messages from God give way to human leaders wrestling with competing claims to arrive at contingent truth. But this truth (as evidenced in many examples within *halakhah*, from *Kiddush ha-Hodesh* to *Anan Sahadi to Bitul* in *Basar b'halav* and *Ta'arovet*) however contingent and flawed it might be, represents God's will.

> The rabbi's appearance is secularized in comparison to the priest and the prophet. After all, anybody can be a rabbi. . . . The word

8. Moral conduct, instruction, or discipline.

9. It has been noted that Rav Yitz's impact has been felt outside the Modern Orthodox community more than within. It is my hope that those in the Modern Orthodox community will study his writings in a more serious way, one that can deepen our theological conversation and practical approach to difficult issues.

10. *Living in the Image of God: Jewish Teachings to Perfect the World, Conversations with Rabbi Irving Greenberg*, (Jason Aronson, 1998) 293.

> of God comes through human activity and interpretation, which is a "hidden" voice of God. In the past, the prophet declared, "Thus says the Lord." In contrast, the rabbi says, "In my best judgment, applying past models of divine instruction to this moment, this is what God wants of you or of me."[11]

Thus far, we have Rav Yitz's elaboration of the rabbinic dictum *Hakham adif mi-Navi,* the sage is better/more effective – or, in Rav Yitz's terms, more credible, than the prophet. But he extends this teaching to a post-Shoah era:

> Today, we live in a time of even greater "hiddenness" of God. The Divine is calling on humans to take a greater role in creating or uncovering holiness. The sacred realm is even more masked; it is more widely present, but it needs to be uncovered by deeper digging. In these circumstances, what would be the model of the best teacher? Logic suggests that the teacher would also be more hidden. The rabbi today, especially when the rabbi speaks with rabbinic authority and style, often sounds like the priest or prophet did after the destruction of the Temple. They talk, but you do not hear them. The holiness is too visible. The self-evidence is in dissonance with the hiddenness of actual holiness today.[12]

There are many implications of this outlook. Rav Yitz examines one here, namely, new models of leadership. Broadly, however, the notion that history, and particularly history after the Shoah, necessitates a new paradigm in which holiness is more ever-present, yet more hidden, offers a new way of thinking about Modern Orthodoxy and its role. Rather than a compromise between *halakhah* and Torah life on the one hand, and modern values like feminism, Zionism, or involvement in the sciences on the other, Rav Yitz's Modern Orthodoxy is the embodiment of Third Era holiness. It finds holiness everywhere – in *shul*, yes, but equally (or perhaps even more credibly) in the boardroom, the art studio, an encounter on the street. Because it views the sacred as hidden

11. Ibid.
12. Ibid. 294.

in every field of life, it willingly engages with phenomena that on the surface do not appear to hold religious meaning. It elucidates the Torah within even the most seemingly remote situations, so that Torah and moral intuition, rather than ideological opinion, informs our response to controversial issues. Though originating with different concerns, Rav Yitz's view comes very close to that of the Besht and Rebbe Nachman, both inspired by the statement of the *Tikunei Zohar* that "No place is empty of God." The result of this view is, indeed, a Modern Orthodoxy of Presence, a serious religious affirmation of God's presence in all things. And, just as those great luminaries made Judaism relevant for so many two centuries ago, Rav Yitz's vision continues to do so in our time.

Implications

Modern Orthodoxy faces crisis after crisis, of infighting, of the inability to find *halakhic* solutions to our most pressing dissonances, including *agunot* and *giyur*, the loss of our youth to the right and to the left, the lack of self-confidence that leads to circling the wagons and adopting a protective rather than a proactive stance. Why is this? What is at the root of these problems? Each of them has its own conditions, its proximate causes. But what lies behind all of them that might account for all of them, the root cause?

I believe it is a loss of our "Why." For Modern Orthodoxy to continue to exist, to attract our passionate support and our students, to develop and blossom as a movement, it requires more than self-perpetuation as a *raison d'etre*. Rav Yitz has provided one of the most cogent articulations of a "Why" for Modern Orthodoxy, one that not only justifies its continued existence but sheds light on its very definition.

His vision of Modern Orthodoxy is as a way of Jewish living that leaves nothing behind, that serves as a champion of unity, a bridge between the depth of Torah and those to whom it is foreign, between the beauty and power of a *Tosefot*, and the impact of new culture. It is a model of inclusiveness both for all people and for all aspects of each person: Everyone welcome, and everything worthy of thoughtful consideration and examination; allowing Torah sources to critique and correct our errors as we stumble our way into an uncertain future; allowing new insight and moral developments to raise new questions and challenges as we read our sacred texts; bringing Torah into everything; allowing moral intuition and acute historical sensitivity to inform *halakhah* and allowing *halakhah* and Torah to inform policy; and lastly, being unafraid of the secular, indeed, recognizing that what we call the secular is in fact the primary locus of hidden holiness.

If there are two ways of instantiating a Modern Orthodox life, the first is a Modern Orthodoxy of compromise that seeks a resolution of the struggles inherent in Jewish living. The second is, a Modern Orthodoxy of Presence that seeks to play up and work with those struggles, then which has more to offer the Jewish people and the world? A compromise solution between the demands of tradition and the realities of contemporary life, driven by social trends as much as by theology, is simply not a compelling vision for the twenty-first century. Its goal seems to be the maintenance of a *halakhic* community in the face of new challenges, and our children need more than a vision of maintenance. Its responsiveness to new realities mainly focus on changes in *metzi'ut* – new technologies, political, and sociological trends, and the fact that we are more acutely aware of other, more internal and fundamental, changes of worldview and philosophy. It is fundamentally reactive, and at its best attempts reconciliation, and an easing or minimizing of tension, and our children demand our honesty when we don't have answers to difficult questions.

By contrast, a Modern Orthodoxy of Presence, the Modern Orthodoxy articulated by Rav Yitz, offers a way of engaging with the world as it is lived in every moment, celebrating unresolved questions even as it seeks workable solutions, and continuously evolving even as it deepens its roots in Torah. Just as two centuries ago, the Hasidic insistence on God's presence even in the secular led to spiritual revival and inclusion, Rav Yitz's creative reading of Jewish history, covenant and the secular helps us achieve similar results. At a moment in Jewish life when we need unity and inclusion more than ever, such an open all-embracing Jewish theology is a necessity.

Personally, this approach allowed me to embrace Modern Orthodoxy as a vibrant path and identity. Yet, far beyond one person's experience, I believe it holds promise for Modern Orthodoxy as a bridge between Torah and the world and as a meeting place for Jews across the denominational spectrum, far and beyond.

Living the Jewish Way: The Lofty Dreams of Rabbi Yitz Greenberg's Judaism

PROFESSOR ARNA POUPKO FISHER

WHEN I FIRST ENCOUNTERED Rabbi Irving (Yitz) Greenberg's first book, *The Jewish Way: Living the Holidays,* shortly after its publication almost thirty years ago, I cried – how beautiful is this work! How beautiful is this man! How fortunate is his wife, of whom he writes in the dedication, "To Blu, who taught me the meaning of covenantal love."[1] Still now, for me, when the outcomes of Jewish communal life disappoint and bring a certain sadness or malaise, Rabbi Greenberg's words breathe the love of Judaism back into me and re-awaken my romance with it:

> Living *The Jewish Way* means dreaming a dream of total perfection so vivid that you can almost touch it, while affirming and working with what *is* in order to make the dream come true. The lifestyle designed to teach the hope and pass it on – the specific acts and images needed to nurture the people who must live out this challenging way.[2]

And, as a teacher, like so many in Jewish education, whether in the college classroom or adult learning setting, I turn to the work again and again.

Many years later, while teaching the *Tanakh* unit of the Wexner Her-

1. Irving Greenberg, *The Jewish Way: Living The Holidays* (New York: Touchstone, 1988). (Henceforth: *TJW.*), 6.
2. Ibid. 33.

itage Program (a Jewish learning and leadership development program for volunteer leaders in North America) to students in Dallas, I assigned readings from *The Jewish Way*. There is no other example of contemporary Jewish writing that so effectively connects a grand vision of Judaism with the details of Jewish life, practice, and ritual. While *The Jewish Way* is ostensibly a treatment of the history and practice of the major and minor Jewish holidays, in one of the few reviews it received, Michael Rosenak reflected that it is, "by no means simply a description of the Jewish year and 'what you should do when': it is an interpretation of '*The Jewish Way*', a Jewish religious world view."[3] And so, with only six sessions devoted to an overview of the Hebrew Bible, I knew that there was no better way to bring my Dallas students beyond not just the "what" to the "why," but more essentially, to an understanding of the deeper existential reasons for the content and direction of Jewish life; what it is one must understand about Judaism and its history in order to fully appreciate its meaning and relevance for Jews and for all of humanity.

Standing in that classroom, I was filled with excitement and confidence as I prepared to read several passages from *The Jewish Way*. Piquing the anticipation of my students, I fanned the pages of my personal copy of the book, which held too many Post-it note flags to render any of them useful, and more highlighted sections than not. While I typically have the students read selections from the assigned readings aloud in class, this time I grabbed the opportunity. I had chosen an excerpt from the chapter, "The Dream and How to Live it: Shabbat," where Rabbi Greenberg elegantly situates the narrative and legal portions of the Bible and subsequent rabbinic laws within the framework of his Jewish vision of how the world will look, once perfected and redeemed (thanks to human intervention); a kind of *ta'amei ha-mitzvot* (purposes of the commandments) writ large. I knew this particular passage nearly by heart and could feel my heart beating faster as I began reciting aloud:

> Shabbat creates a time in which the freedom becomes the rule of all life. The earth is free from exploitation, servants and beasts are

3. Michael Rosenak,"On Ways and Visions: The Theological and Educational Thought of Irving Greenberg," in *The Melton Journal*, Spring 1992, 3.

> free from servitude; and workers are liberated from work. Then liberation radiates and grows. Freedom is a dynamic force; once unleashed, it is bound to spread. The mood of redemption gets stronger and stronger as the Shabbat wears on.[4]

I read a few more passages along similar lines, concluding with:

> On this day Jews are central to the drama of salvation instead of being the marginal outcast people of the weekday universe. All week long the ghetto Jew might have been a pariah pack peddler. On this day he takes off his stained commoner's clothes, dons Shabbat finery, and reenacts his "true" role – that of cosmic royalty, the bearer of salvation.[5]

I paused; my voice filled with emotion, and looked up from the book. I waited for what I anticipated would be a kind of revelatory response. Instead, one student, who actually observed the Sabbath and was a serious thinker, simply blurted out: "Arna, it's just not like that!" I responded somewhat dismissively, lamely joking, "I know, I know, don't try this at home . . .," and continued reading from the section which followed: "The Limits of the Dream:"

---

4. *TJW,* 151–152.

5. Ibid. 132. As an aside, this passage had always reminded me of an excerpt from Isaac Rosenfeld's, *Passage From Home* (New York: Meridian, 1961) that Ruth Wisse includes in *The Modern Jewish Canon* (Chicago: University of Chicago Press, 2000):

For as a Jew, I was acquainted, as perhaps a Negro might be, with the alien and divided aspect of life that passed from sight at the open approach, but lingered, available to thought, ready to reveal itself to anyone who would inquire softly. I had come to know a certain homelessness in the world, and took it for granted as part of nature; had seen in the family, and myself acquired, a sense of sadness from which both assurance and violence had forever vanished. We had accepted it unconsciously and without self-pity, as one might accept a sentence that had been passed generations ago, whose terms were still binding though its occasion had long been forgotten. The world is not entirely yours and our reply is: very well then, not entirely. There were moments, however, when this minor world was more than universe enough; times such as when grandfather would be raised to nobility, or when the family, gathered of a holiday, would distil so rare and joyful a spirit that all the assurance which had been lacking would rush back in a flood, and one could feel the presence of God in it, and one could cry, "This is reality, truth, beauty and freedom! What has the rest of the world to compare?"

> A dream without limits is an illusion. The Jewish dream is not an illusion, but neither is it reality yet. In offering hope of perfection, the Jewish tradition, takes the countervailing evidence of reality fully into account. The party of hope fully admits the possibility of defeat but does not yield the dream. Rather, it offers a method to make the dream come true.[6]

But I knew I had not really addressed the source of my student's objection – the soaring, poetic, creative, covenantal, messianic, perfected, redemptive Jewish endeavor Rabbi Yitz Greenberg describes is simply not the Judaism she knows. It is not even a Judaism of which she dreams.

In one of the great understatements in the publishing world, a "review" of *The Jewish Way* in the *Library Journal Review* states:

> The diverse, non-delineated material in this book precludes its easy use as a handbook, distinguishing it from such works as Leo Trepp's traditional Complete Book of Jewish Observance or Arthur Waskow's innovative Seasons of Our Joy. **Indeed, Greenberg appears to use the holidays as a vehicle for expressing his own philosophy of Judaism** (bold is mine).

Indeed, he does. Written with "[a] heart filled with joy and gratitude," *The Jewish Way* unflinchingly lays out Rabbi Greenberg's central thesis as to the meaning of Judaism and the Jewish people. While it is true that it does not present itself as a "handbook," it is highly readable and, at least for the intellectually curious, with the inclusion of personal anecdotes, contemporary events and engaging prose, remarkably accessible. It is the combination of some of the "best of" Judaism (the wonderfully colorful, imaginative, evocative and amusing Jewish holidays) with Greenberg's own historical, philosophical, and theological framing that makes this work thoroughly original and still irreplaceable.

While *The Jewish Way* is organized around an exploration of the origin of the holidays – including the modern commemorations of *Yom Hashoah* (Holocaust Memorial Day) and *Yom Ha'atzma'ut* (Israeli Independence Day) – and the interpretation of their significance and rituals,

6. Ibid. *154*.

the Jewish calendar is used as a template for Greenberg's conceptualization of the meaning of the Jewish people in history. Steven Katz's elegant and authoritative synopsis of *The Jewish Way* declared that: "[it is a] theology of Judaism, interpreted through the holidays, [which] traces Judaism's attempt to transform the world in history and the impact of great events on the unfolding of the religion."[7] It is with fresh and stunningly holistic thinking, that Greenberg partners traditional religious constructs with "*The Jewish Way* to get humanity from the world it is now to the world of final perfection."[8] The notion of *Tzelem Elokim* (human beings created in the image of God) is linked with the obligation to maximize creativity in order to eradicate human suffering and the *mitzvot* related to three pilgrimage festivals are described as expressing the underlying humanistic values of freedom, redemption and liberation. Fundamentally, *The Jewish Way* is a synthesis of commentary, philosophy, theology, and political advocacy. Yet, perhaps most importantly, it is a work of deeply energetic pedagogy – a way to communicate, to many kinds of Jews (though not for the intellectually lazy) the brilliant capacity of Judaism (in this case through the holidays) to capture the totality of the human experience:

> A hope is a dream that has accepted the discipline of becoming a fact. Jewish faith is the communal commitment to work at realizing the hope. Passover states Judaism's goal, which is defined by hope. Shavuot confirms the covenant, which is the commitment to persist until the goal is reached. Sukkot addresses the third dimension of Judaism's religious core: how to get there.

Rabbi Greenberg's ability to capture the "ways" of Judaism in language that moves Jews of so many backgrounds and makes Judaism feel compelling, relevant, and above all else, necessary is at the heart of his success as an educator. As a Harvard trained historian and ordained rabbi who is engaged at the highest levels of Jewish communal and institutional life, Rabbi Greenberg is a disarmingly credible admixture

7. Steven T. Katz, "Irving (Yitz) Greenberg" in *Interpreters of Judaism in the Late Twentieth* Century, ed. Steven T. Katz (Washington: B'nai Brith, 1993), 59–89, here 87.
8. *TJW*, 24.

of theologian and public intellectual. In his doctoral thesis dedicated to the earlier years of Rabbi Greenberg's life and scholarship, Joshua Feigelson writes: "[He is able] in writing and in person, [to connect] with American Jews thirsty for a teacher and a teaching that was both 'religious' enough to feel authentic and academic enough to feel intellectually credible." Rabbi Greenberg's dialectical framing of Judaism comes across as both honest and reasonable; a helpful response to the practical bewilderment of the Jew with little or no knowledge of *halakha* or history and the theological disappointment/confusion of the Jew with broad and deep knowledge. Feigelson continues that:

> Greenberg aimed to escape the either/or choice of absence or presence, history or memory, the past or the present [and was] relentlessly dialectical in his thought and his teaching, insisting on an orientation that was both – and: noting God's absence (in modernity in general and the Holocaust in particular) and God's presence (in the "holy secularity" of modernity in general, and the holy secularity of the state of Israel in particular), the study of history as he objective study of the past (e.g. an academic study of the Bible) while simultaneously engaging it as collective memory that lives through tradition in the present (e.g. in yeshiva study of the Bible.)[9]

Ten years later, Greenberg says of his own work:

> I wish I had *The Jewish Way* in my university days. The combination of presenting the philosophical basis of the Jewish religion and combining this with the valid account of what it is to experience life, to really live as Jews in accordance with the Jewish calendar, makes it, I think, perfect for young questioning minds.[10]

Among the most vital contributions of Rabbi Greenberg to Jewish

9. Joshua Meir Feigelson, *"Relationship, Power and Holy Secularity: Rabbi Yitz Greenberg and American Jewish Life, 1966–1983,"* (Ph.D Diss., Northwestern University, 2015), 28; 37.

10. Rabbi Irving Greenberg and Shalom Freedman, *Living in the Image of God: Jewish Teaching to Perfect the World* (North Vale: Jason Aronson, 1998), 19.

thought is the way he re-constructs redemption and covenant. His novel re-conceptualization of redemption allows for a framing of a Jew's obligation to be engaged with the ethical, political, and societal demands of contemporary life as a necessary outcome of the ethical imperative that emerges naturally and organically from Jewish religious life. Relatedly, his definition of covenant equips readers with the philosophical tools to reconsider and negotiate the significance of the major eras of Jewish history, as well as the profound theological disappointments of the Holocaust. On redemption, he writes:

> The central paradigm is redemption. According to the Bible, the human being is created in the image of God. According to the rabbis this means that every single person is unique and equal. Endowed with the dignity of infinite value. But in history most humans have been degraded or denied their due. Judaism affirms that this condition should never be accepted; it must be and will be overcome. The ultimate goal will be achieved through human participation [. . .]. The whole process of transformation will take place on a human scale. Human models, not supernatural beings, will instruct and inspire humankind as it works toward the full redemption.[11]

As for the meaning of covenant in a post-Holocaust world:

> Both the unreconstructed traditional view (for our sins we are punished) and the radical view (the covenant is finished; it was an illusion) have resolved the incredible tension between the Holocaust experience and the covenantal one. [12] One (by disobedience) and one (by despair) have released the dialectical spring that throws us back and forth between faith and doubt, hope and despair, triumph of life and victory of death. Evoking the broken paradigm image [. . .] one can argue that both views

11. *TJW*, 18–19.

12. In a previous section of *TJW*, the covenant is defined as "Jews (giving) their word to go on living as a people in a special way so that their loves testify to something greater than themselves. With that testimony they bear witness to a final, universal redemption" (19).

err because they account for everything. [. . .] It is not so much that affirmation (and denials) cannot be made but that they can be authentic only if they are made after working through the impact of the Holocaust, which is ceaselessly tormenting and dialectical. In the same sense, the relationship to the God of the covenant cannot be unaffected.[13]

13. *TJW, 324.* In Greenberg's theology, "God self limits and makes a covenant so that human beings may become partners – to improve the world. It is pedagogic relationship that presents differently in accordance with the particular era in history. In the first era, Biblical, God is the dominant partner." As restated by Rabbi Greenberg in a lecture, *"Tradition and Innovation: Rabbis Yitz Greenberg and Shai Held Discuss God, Torah Pirke Avot and the Jewish Future,"* lecture, New York, 19 June 2016*:* Greenberg quips, quoting Sam Levinson, that in the Biblical era, "When God wants our opinion, He gives it to us." He further states that:

[In] the second [Rabbinic] era, God is more hidden (but comes closer as *Shechinah*, is less controlling in history, no more visible miracles (only hidden ones), [there is] no more prophecy and the rabbis establish what are God's instructions. At this moment, the paradox is that God has come closer. *Shechinah* is at the table, in the home, in the bedroom, at the head of the sick bed, when people learn together etc. – but must be discerned. So while the visible God of the Biblical period is unmistakably present, God's presence in this era must be discerned and the central role of *Talmud Torah* is to equip people to encounter God and to discern *Shechinah* everywhere. Since God restrains the divine intervention in history, human behavior becomes more responsible for the outcome. Hence the sins of the second Temple's destruction are not the sins against God, but the sins against humanity [. . .] Part of this shift to the (rabbinic stage) is God asking humans to grow up and move from visible reward and punishment in this world to delayed gratification *(olam haba)* and to more mission driven and relationship driven covenantal behaviors. Finally, I contend that there has been a third *tzimtzum* [contraction], starting with modernity. God is now totally hidden, but is found everywhere, especially in the secular. Humans are fully responsible – all divine miracles are completely done through human agents, utilizing natural laws, acting as partners in the brit. This is accompanied by asking humans to become more mature – fully mature in the covenant. Thus, they are asked to give up the miracle/magic of a *ness* in response to-a-prayer and instead to live the good life and the love of *Hashem*, love of fellow human beings, love of tikkun olam – and the *chizuk* that comes from God's total closeness (*imo anochi b'tsara)* sustaining love. . . . It is equivalent to the shift of God from the loving, controlling parent in the first [biblical] stage who self limits as the child grows. God loves them more and truly wants them to internalize values and take on full responsibility. This divine third *tzimtzum* occurred at the onset of modernity – indeed human beings responded by stepping up and taking power to repair life and the world (which is what modern civilization is all about). The Holocaust is the outcome of this divine self-limitation and [the] commitment work only through humans and natural law which was responded to by a broad scale human failure to take responsibility. The

He continues:

> What then happened to the covenant (post Holocaust)? Could it be that the covenant was broken, but the Jewish people, deeply committed to the partnership, chose voluntarily to take it on again? [. . .] When the Jewish people originally accepted the covenant, they had no way of knowing what the cost would be [. . .] The Jewish covenant is a commitment, out of faith, to achieve a final perfection of being [. . .] In the generation after the Holocaust, the staggering costs were never clearer, yet the Jewish people did not yield their dreams [. . .] After the destruction of the temple, the people of Israel moved from partial participant to full partner in the covenant. After the Holocaust, the Jewish people were called upon to become the executive partner in the mission of redemption.[14]

Rabbi Greenberg concludes his expansive chapter, "The Shattered Paradigm: Yom Hashoah," by noting that:

> [In] Jewish tradition, the mourner is asked to say *Kaddish*, the prayer for the speedy coming of the messianic redemption. If a person who has just experienced absurdity and deep loss through death and who is in despair of mourning can nevertheless express the hope of final perfection that is incredibly powerful testimony. It means that life is strong enough to overcome death and that the Jewish hope is no illusion.[15]

In this way, Rabbi Greenberg creates a kind of cooperation between the evolving nature of the covenant and redemption, binding the Jew to the obligation to work towards a perfected society and improve the

---

Nazis use their freedom to kill without limit. The allies used their freedom to stand by and do nothing. The world Jewish community failed to take on more responsibility, etc.

Rabbi Greenberg, correspondence with the author, June, 2016 Note: while this theological formulation has been expressed by Rabbi Greenberg in many written works and lectures, the above articulation of it is from a recent conversation via email.

14. Ibid. 320.
15. Ibid. 372.

predicament of her fellow Jew and non-Jew alike; and through a newly defined covenant as neither static or unchanging, transforms the Jew from, in a sense, the "victim" of a broken covenant to one entering into a powerful partnership with God that has the capacity to change the world. Through this re-imagining of the role of covenant and redemption, Rabbi Greenberg achieves what feels virtually impossible: an honest grappling with the crushing outcome of the Jewish experience that then results in the penultimate ennobling and empowerment of the broken Jew. This dialectic, of hope and defeat; triumph and disappointment; success and failure, is, for Greenberg, the real rhythm of the Jewish calendar.

When *The Jewish Way* was first published, students of Rabbi Greenberg certainly recognized many of his ideas from exiting articles and lectures.[16] Sometimes, these ideas were most powerfully expressed in personal anecdotes and observations, where one could feel the extent to which Greenberg was committed to demanding, in particular, a deeper understanding of the function of *halakhah*. In the famous interview published in 1966 in *The Commentator*, the Yeshiva University newspaper, Rabbi Greenberg laments the inability of many *halakhah*-abiding Jews to truly understand the essential intent of Jewish law. He observes:

> Boys who keep *Shabbat* will still measure a person by how much money a person makes. Yet, *Shabbat* is supposed to teach us the intrinsic values of existence independent of what we can make or produce. In other words, the YU student doesn't take the principle out of the *halakhah*; he draws few implications from *halakhah* as far as human behaviors and attitudes are concerned.[17]

In *The Jewish Way*, this personal lament finds expression in his plea that we understand that "all *halakhic* behaviors [are] dramatic/mimetic ges-

16. For a comprehensive collection of the titles of Rabbi Greenberg's publications, see the website: "Home – Rabbi Irving Greenberg," Rabbi Irving Greenberg, accessed July 07, 2016, http://rabbiirvinggreenberg.com/.

17. Harold Goldberg, "Dr. Greenberg Discusses Orthodoxy, Y.U. Vietnam and Sex," *The Commentator*, 28 April 1966.

tures articulating a central metaphor of living. Grasping the metaphor adds depth to action and joy to life."[18] And that:

> Jewish faith is the communal commitment to work at realizing the hope [. . .]. Despite all the good intentions and intentions and commitments, there is still an enormous gap between the hope and reality of the world [. . .]. *Halacha* is the art of the possible, the divine science of the doable.[19]

For Rabbi Greenberg, the *mitzvot, halakhot,* and customs of Jewish holiday observance are not ends in and of themselves, but vehicles for the highest level of human expression, namely, the reflection of the intent of the Divine:

> The Holy Days are the unbroken master code of Judaism. Decipher them and you will discover the inner sanctum of this religion. Grasp them and hold the heart of the faith in your hand [. . .] each holiday has one central metaphor that orchestrates myriad details into one coherent whole. By understanding a few key models one can hear and interpret the central messages of Judaism and its development over the course of history.[20]

---

18. *TJW,* 13.
19. Ibid. 94.
20. *TJW,* 17. This view is reflected in the writings of Rabbi Elisha Ancselovits, a sample here from his doctoral dissertation:

> In a religious culture that had no formal way to modify its traditional laws and rarely articulated its theoretical principles, leading legal authorities viewed themselves as sages rather than as scholars. As such, they carefully studied the legal sources, empathetically viewing them as a multiplicity of narratives, of grounded intents, of insights on the human condition. This enabled them to develop an intuitive sense of what Jewish law considers right and wrong. They then applied these intuitions to contemporary conditions so as to maintain the critical connection between law and concrete reality and thus achieve good laws. But always, they thought, and expressed themselves, in the terminology of those internalized norms, addressing the contemporary situations in the language of the earlier norms.

"Towards a New Theory of Halakhic Development," (PhD Diss., Liverpool Hope University, 2011), 1.

This was a critically important contribution to the field of the philosophy of *halakhah* as it flips the paradigm on its head; insisting that law be observed because of the value it brings to the world. This, in turn, orients the application of Jewish law toward innovation; insisting that the *Posek* (a scholar whose efforts were concentrated on determining the law in practice), when rendering a decision regarding the application of the law, carefully consider its fundamental and ultimate purpose.

As Greenberg continues to develop his theology, his construct of the "power" of humans, as it relates to covenant and partnering with God, gains prominence. In a June 2016 lecture, "Tradition and Innovation: Rabbis Yitz Greenberg and Shai Held Discuss God, Torah, *Pirkei Avot*, and the Jewish Future," held in honor of Mechon Hadar and the launching of Greenberg's book on *Pirkei Avot,*[21] Rabbi Held inquiried into Greenberg's notions of "God's hiddenness" and the challenges of moderns to believe in a God they cannot discern as well as the nature of prayer in this era. Responding to these questions, Rabbi Greenberg stated that:

> This takes us to prayer today. I said that prayer no longer (or in much reduced form) focuses on *bakashot*, cures for ailments, etc. We shift from the prayers of the powerless (i.e. the doctors cannot help anymore, "I need a miracle") to prayers of the powerful. The surgeon prays: steady my hand. The doctor prays: inspire my brain and diagnostic power, strengthen my mind and will to make night rounds and calls to patients; the businessperson prays: Keep me focused on constructive activities and products that improve the world and sustain it (*metaken* [fixes] not *mekalkel* [destroys]) instruct me to be honest with labor and in work; the general prays: inspire my strategic creativity. Judge me and hold me accountable morally; give me the inner strength to order people to go to battle (necessarily) and die. The teacher prays, draw me closer to you and your Torah, give me the inner strength to be *metzamtsaym* [reserved], for the benefit of my student.[22]

21. Irving Greenberg, *Sage Advice: Pirkei Avot* (Jerusalem: Maggid Books, 2016).

22. Rabbi Greenberg, in conversation with the author, June 2016. Note: due to logistical constraints, it was not possible to transcribe the exact wording of Rabbi

And then, in a stunning moment, Rabbi Greenberg describes his response to a devastating phone call from Israel, learning that his son, J.J. Greenberg, had been struck by a car while riding his bicycle:

> After twenty-five years of working on this new understanding of God's behavior and the rules of the covenantal interactions, when the call came from Israel and it suggested that the doctors likely could not save him, I jumped out of bed, ran to *shul* for an *aliyah*, made a *mishebayrach* (prayer of healing), and changed his name, adding Chayim to Natan Yosef. Even as I did that, I knew in the back of my mind that God does not work that way anymore. However, the yearning for my daddy to bail me out, the desperate need not to lose him, overpowered my awareness. I understood that this was a long shot, but prayed for the miracle. I needed and wanted that miracle and like a helpless child, I turned to my parents and to all the habits and beliefs of my childhood. That closeness, that magical saving way, I fully understand why it is so powerful and so hard to give up, and why the *haredi* way is so appealing and comforting.[23]

The audience in the lecture hall, already listening intently, fell silent. We realized we had been given a gift, albeit an excruciatingly painful one. When I followed up with Rabbi Greenberg about whether or not he had ever shared that story before, he responded, "The story was an admission of the continuing yearning and response to the 'magic/ Father': 'save me' – but it was also a critique. I have never published it. In fact, I only said it publicly one other time in my life."[24]

Greenberg's statements during the actual lecture. The above quotation has been gleaned via informal conversation and follow-up email correspondence with Rabbi Greenberg. Thus, although it may not reflect his original comments *verbatim*, they nonetheless reflect Rabbi Greenberg's current thinking.

23. Ibid.

24. On Sept. 13, 2002, Jonathan Joseph "J.J." Greenberg, the executive director of the New York based Jewish Life Network, 36, died in Tel Aviv on Saturday, one day after being struck by a car while riding his bicycle. Five of Greenberg's organs were donated for transplants, as he had requested. After the funeral and *shiva*, Rabbi Greenberg and his wife, Blu, visited four of the six recipients..

Rabbi Greenberg's story brought me back to a time when I had reached out to him to say a prayer on our behalf. At the time, our granddaughter was sick. Only one year old, she had been diagnosed with a devastating and incurable genetic disease. We did not go out of our way to put her name on *tehilim* (Psalms) lists recited by groups who dedicate themselves to such efforts (though we always appreciated the sentiment and concern), nor did I personally ask any rabbis to recite a *meshebayrach* on her behalf. But while in Rabbi Greenberg's presence on a visit to New York, and he so genuinely asked how I was – as he always does – I shared the story of our granddaughter and wrote down her Hebrew name. Over the course of that year, I admit it brought me great comfort to know that Rabbi Greenberg, every morning, was praying on her behalf.

Many months later, I once again saw Rabbi Greenberg. The first thing he did upon seeing me was to inquire about our granddaughter. I was startled he did not know she had died, and he was devastated, shaken, and mortified. I did my best to console him, assuring him that this spoke well of him – he was not on social media and it had been my responsibility to convey this news. The knowledge that he continued to pray on her behalf filled me with a kind of religious wholeness, a certainty and clarity that, felt rare and precious. His words in Manhattan that evening, helped me understand my reaction:

> Yet, I believe that *Hashem* wants the prayers of the powerful. They come from a place of equality, out of the capacity to turn to *Hashem* out of relationship and love. Power and dignity free me much more to work at loving *Hashem* and learning *Torah lishmah* [Torah for its own sake]. Now when I say a *mishebayrach* or pray for individuals – and often I do this – it is like friending on Facebook. The knowledge that others care and will be with me no matter what (As *Hashem* will be) is strengthening. It actually improves cure rates, but this is the natural miracle, not the reward miracle of having prayed to God and getting this special prize from the divine vending machine. In short, this stage when humans take full power to achieve the goals of the covenant, involves a much more mature religiosity, driven by relationship and love growing

> out of capacity. I believe that God treasures such a relationship, he is asking for it out this third *tzimtzum.*[25]

In my exchanges with Rabbi Greenberg concerning his address that evening, particularly with regards to the story he shared about his son, and about prayer and the powerful, there was a scribble at the very bottom of the pages of notes he had scanned and sent to me: "Arna, P.S., what does this have to do with *The Jewish Way?*" I laughed out loud when I read it. He had really nailed it. My honest response is: I'm not completely sure. What I am certain of, however, is that I (and so many others) have found in Rabbi Greenberg's first book, *The Jewish Way*, a way to think about our Judaism that feels truthful and daring and, above all, loving.

And that is what I hope, at the end of her Wexner studies, my student in Dallas understood. That even if she and we never experience a glimmer of the *Shabbat* of *The Jewish Way,* we are existentially moved by the idea that there is hope; and that there is a Jew who finds this vision within reach. It brought me immeasurable comfort to know that Rabbi Greenberg was praying for my daughter's life – not because this would save little Ayelet, but because it meant there was at least one Jew among us who is in an actual relationship with God, one that is raw and real and complicated and powerful and overflowing with love; a relationship that, like all authentic and vibrant relationships, is always being re-defined. This, Rabbi Greenberg, is *The Jewish Way* you continue to show us.

25. In conversation with author, June 2016.

For and Against: A Consideration of David Hartman and Jonathan Sacks in Relation to Irving Greenberg

Rabbi Dr. Darren Kleinberg

Irving Greenberg was not the only personality to address the issue of pluralism in the American Jewish community, but he was certainly its most outspoken voice. While he could always find partners across the denominational aisle in the likes of Eugene Borowitz, Harold Schulweis, and many other non-Orthodox thinkers, Orthodox communal and thought leaders were more critical of Greenberg and his theology of religious pluralism than they were supportive. Those that comprehended the full implications of Greenberg's thinking were vocal and sustained in their disagreement. One notable exception was David Hartman.

Greenberg and Hartman partnered in the 1960s to create groundbreaking cross-denominational meetings in Canada and they remained close friends until Hartman's death in 2013. As Simon Cooper has correctly observed, Greenberg "shares the same mid-century American intellectual background as . . . Hartman." His "Orthodox education under Soloveitchik mirrors that of Hartman" (Cooper 187) and that the "similarities with Hartman's thought are marked" (Cooper 188).

Hartman's 1999 book, *A Heart of Many Rooms: Celebrating the Many Voices within Judaism*, expressed a multiculturalist orientation in the title and called on Jews to "celebrate" their differences. In part three of the book, entitled "Celebrating Religious Diversity," Hartman posed the problem that "It has often been claimed that belief in revelation and divine election is incompatible with religious pluralism" (153). He then asked, "Given the competing claims of Judaism, Christianity, and Islam[1] being the true heir to Abraham's legacy, the crucial concern of faith must be: Which faith community mediates God's vision for history?" (ibid.). Hartman answered that "The messianic dream [is that] of a world in which all human beings realize that they were created in the image of God, that they owe their existence to God, and that therefore all of life is sacred" (Hartman, *Heart,* 163). Hartman described a vision of redemption that, like Greenberg's, began with the creation of human beings in the image of God.

According to Hartman, the bookends of creation and redemption are separated by the stages of revelation and election, thus outlining the four stages of Hartman's conception of religious pluralism. Following the stage of creation (in the Image of God), Hartman wrote that a belief in revelation could also permit an expansive pluralism. He suggested that "Revelation is not addressed to humanity in general, but to a particular individual or community. And because of this inherent particularity, it need not invalidate the faith experience of other religious communities" (Hartman, *Heart,* 164). Echoing Greenberg's understanding of Christianity as a parallel covenant,[2] Hartman rejected the notion that revelation in the Jewish tradition exhausted the opportunity for other revelations.

Moving from revelation to election, Hartman addressed concerns regarding the presumed chosen status of the Jewish people and its implications for the status of other religions. His response was to distinguish between two aspects of the divine. He wrote that:

> Election represents a particularization of God's relationship to humankind by virtue of divine involvement in history, without the

1. Hartman did not consider any other religions in his treatment of religious pluralism. In a footnote to another essay, Hartman wrote that "From a Jewish viewpoint, pluralism in the broader sense as including the other major world religious necessarily raises the question of idolatry, since those other religions do not acknowledge exclusively the God of Israel" (Hartman, "Possibilities" 101).

2. Greenberg has written that, "In my view, Christianity itself is another one of the particular covenants that God has called into being in order to engage more and more humans in the process of *tikkun olam* [repairing the world]" (Greenberg, *For the Sake* 44).

> implication that there is only one exclusive mediator of the divine message. Consequently, theologians who claim that worshipping the universal God is incompatible with election are making a "category mistake." The universal God is the God of creation. But it is God as the Lord of history who enters into specific relationships with human beings and who is therefore loved in a particularistic manner. All intimate relationships claim exclusivity by their very nature (Hartman, *Heart,* 164).

Hartman's distinction between "the universal God" and "the Lord of history" allowed him to make a claim for the universal and the particular at the same time. The result was that, "The distinction between creation and history enables biblical faith to admit the possibility of religious pluralism without neutralizing its passionate commitment to the biblical Lord of history" (Hartman, *Heart* 164). Returning to the theme of creation, Hartman made the implications of his system explicit:

> . . . the concept of creation, not the concepts of community and history, must nurture the dream of a universal ethical awakening of human consciousness. The Jew, the Christian, and the Muslim are all one, insofar as they are creatures of God. One thus acknowledges the sacredness common to all human beings irrespective of their ways of life and modes of worship (Hartman, *Heart* 165).[3]

This brief sketch of Hartman's approach to religious pluralism highlights the similarities between Greenberg's and Hartman's thinking. In another parallel to Greenberg, this time on the practical plane, Hartman would also engage in sustained cross-denominational work in the Jewish community through the Shalom Hartman Institute in Israel, which he established after emigrating there in 1971. In many ways, Hartman and Greenberg were two sides of the same coin; one based in the United States and the other in Israel.

3. Of course, it is here that the narrow treatment of only Christianity, Islam, and Judaism becomes most problematic. Hartman refers to the "sacredness common to all human beings" but limits his observations only to those of the three faiths under consideration.

Hartman represented one of the few prominent Jewish intellectuals still associated with Orthodoxy to express support for Greenberg and for religious pluralism.[4] More often, the response of Orthodox rabbis and community leaders was rejection. One of Greenberg's most articulate Orthodox rejectionists was the former Chief Rabbi of the United Hebrew Congregations of the Commonwealth, Jonathan Sacks. Sacks served as Chief Rabbi for more than twenty years (1991–2013), during which time he became a significant public figure and established himself as a thought leader in the Jewish world and beyond.

In his role as an Anglo-Jewish communal leader, Sacks regularly found himself embroiled in controversy, often taking stringent positions on questions of intra-Jewish pluralism. The most public of these controversies was what has become known in Anglo-Jewry as "The Hugo Gryn Affair." Gryn was a survivor of Auschwitz who eventually made it to Britain to become the senior minister of the Reform movement's West London Synagogue. According to *The Independent* newspaper, Gryn was "probably the most beloved rabbi in Great Britain" (Persoff, 91). Gryn passed away in 1996 and, to the disdain of many, Sacks failed to attend the funeral. After months of conflict over the issue, and Sacks' decision to attend a subsequent memorial service for Gryn, the *Jewish Chronicle* newspaper published a leaked copy of a damning letter that Sacks had written to Chenoch Padwa, then head of the Jewish court of the Union of Orthodox Hebrew Congregations. The letter reassured Padwa that Sacks was not giving credibility to Reform Judaism by participating in the memorial service for Gryn, hosted by The Board of Deputies of British Jews. In Sacks' words:

> The leaders of Reform, Liberal and Masorti movements know that they have no enemy and opponent equal to the Chief Rabbi, who fights against them intelligently and defends the faith in our holy Torah in his writings, articles and broadcasts; that he has in this respect achieved considerable standing in non-Jewish eyes; and that he does not accord them any gesture of recognition. . . . There

4. Hartman was treated with similar disdain to Greenberg by the centrist and *haredi* communities. It is also the case that Hartman was based in Israel, where denominational politics play out in a different manner than in the United States.

> would be no greater victory for Reform and for pluralism that that there should be two Chief Rabbis, one Orthodox and one Reform, at every ceremony and national or communal gathering. If such were to be the situation, then in the eye of the whole community time after time the impression would emerge that there are two kinds of Torah, two kinds of faith, two kinds of rabbi, that they are equal in their standing in the eyes of non-Jews and the community, and there is no greater shame and falsehood that that. My sacred task is to prevent this absolutely, and thankfully we have succeeded thus far . . . (Persoff, 105).

Sacks' opposition to both non-Orthodox Judaism and pluralism was unmistakable.[5] But what was the philosophical basis of Sacks' opposition? A Cambridge-trained philosopher, Sacks was certainly more than equipped to address this question, and did so in the pages of his book, *One People?: Tradition, Modernity, and Jewish Unity* (1993).

Writing seven years after the publication of Greenberg's influential essay, "Will there be One Jewish People in the Year 2000?" Sacks addressed a similar topic. Like Greenberg, Sacks noted the transformative influences of modernity, the Holocaust, and the establishment of the State of Israel. According to Sacks, the impact of these events on Judaism included, among other things, the development of the concept of Jewish peoplehood. He wrote that,

> Jewish peoplehood has emerged as a key component of identity. . . . Its adherents are "Jews who seek to be Jewish through identification with the Jewish people as a corporate entity, its history, culture and tradition, but without necessarily accepting the authoritative character of *halakhah* [Jewish law] or the centrality of *halakhah* in defining their Jewishness." (Sacks, *One People?* 10)

For Sacks, the notion of peoplehood, so popular in recent decades,[6]

5. For a complete analysis of the "Hugo Gryn Affair" and other aspects of Sacks Chief Rabbinate, see Persoff, *Another Way, Another Time: Religious Inclusivism and the Sacks Chief Rabbinate*. Brighton: Academic Studies Press, 2010.

6. For example, see Pianko, Noam. *Jewish peoplehood: An American Invention*. New

was not native to Judaism. Instead, Sacks claimed, it was a response to the Jewish encounter with modernity, and the seismic events of the Holocaust and the establishment of the State of Israel, rather than a traditional commitment to norms as prescribed by Jewish Law. As such, peoplehood's attendant desire for Jewish unity was also a foreign element. As Sacks put it:

> Recent history – the Holocaust, and the sense of involvement that most Jews throughout the world feel in the fate of Israel – has convinced us that the Jewish destiny is indivisible. We are implicated in the fate of one another. That is the substantive content of our current sense of unity. But it is a unity imposed, as it were, from outside. Neither antisemitism nor anti-Zionism, we believe, makes distinctions between Jews. But from within, in terms of our own self-understanding, the Jewish people evinces no answering solidarity. External crisis unites Jews; internal belief divides. (Sacks, *One People?* viii)

In this telling, the Jewish call to unity was a reactionary one that resulted either from the historical tragedy of the Holocaust or from the uncertain fate of the State of Israel. However, when these negative motivators were removed, Sacks suggested that what remained would be a fundamental division between traditional Judaism and a Judaism that embraced modernity. Rather than offer a case for overcoming these divisions, Sacks presented a manifesto as to why they were necessary. Ultimately, Sacks claimed that "both tradition and modernity have adequate ways of resolving conflict, but *that they systematically exclude one another*" (Sacks, ix).

Sacks' orienting understanding of modernity was similar to Greenberg's in its recognition of the postethnic nature of the open society. Sacks began by describing what he referred to as "traditional societies" in this way:

Brunswick: Rutgers University Press, 2015. See also, The Center for Jewish Peoplehood Education, http://jpeoplehood.org/.

> In traditional societies, the individual is identified by his or her membership of a variety of social groups and by occupancy of a set of roles. In a stable and long-standing culture, these roles – of spouse, parent, child, occupation, social class, and so forth – carry with them established duties and responsibilities. The scope for individual choice, sometimes even with respect to marriage partner, is relatively circumscribed . . . in such traditional communities 'the moral life does not spring from the consciousness of possible alternative ways of behaving.' Instead, 'we acquire habits of conduct in the same way as we acquire our native language.' The self is largely defined by society (Sacks, 154).

In this context, one's identity is defined by one's place in society. Choice is limited and the range of options even more so. Individuals are born into socially determined responsibilities. According to Sacks, this traditional society is contrasted with our modern reality in which:

> . . . the individual in the contemporary urban setting typically occupies a series of roles that are experienced as not given but chosen. Nor are they definitive of personal identity. Sociologists have observed that modern identities are peculiarly 'open-ended, transitory, liable to ongoing change.' As a result, 'biography is . . . apprehended both as a migration through different social worlds and as the successive realization of a number of possible identities.' Religious or ideological commitments too become forms of role of which we may choose several, successively or simultaneously. No longer universes we inhabit, they become positions we adopt (Sacks, 154).

Here, writing two years prior to the publication of David Hollinger's *Postethnic America* (1995), Sacks anticipated Hollinger precisely. Identity is no longer circumscribed or fixed; it is voluntary and variable. Furthermore, individuals are free to "try-on" different identities in this new open society. According to Sacks:

> This mode of discourse and consciousness collides with classic Jewish assumptions at several points. First there is the constitu-

> tive idea of Judaism itself, that Jews are *born into obligations*. . . . Secondly, within Judaism itself there are *distinctions* of obligation which follow from birth rather than choice. . . . Thirdly, the specificities of Jewish law conflict with what, on liberal assumptions, would be deemed to be matters of personal choice. . . .[7] So modernity and Jewish tradition seem to conflict in their deepest assumptions about the self (Sacks, 156).

For Sacks, speaking presumptively on behalf of Orthodoxy,[8] the postethnic assumptions of modern society were in direct opposition to traditional Jewish commitments. It is birth and not choice, law and not the self, that are at the center of one's identity in Sacks' traditional Jewish reality. Put simply, "Tradition postulates an objective order . . . while modern ethical theory makes the self its own legislator" (Sacks, 156). While Greenberg welcomed the realities of the open society, Sacks rejected them outright.

Turning specifically to the question of pluralism, Sacks began by sketching a historical backdrop to the rise of the denominations in nineteenth century Germany. Listing off the impacts of the European Emancipation and Enlightenment, and the impact of secularization – or privatization – of religious life in Western Europe, Sacks recounted the origins of German Reform and Positive Historical Judaism.[9] Turning to the American Jewish context, Sacks offered that "Reconstructionist, Reform, and Conservative Judaism were all responses not to secularization as such but to the particular form in which it confronted Jews: economic and cultural integration into newly open societies" (Sacks, 30). Sacks referred to the innovations of non-Orthodox Judaism that resulted from their cultural integration as "the accommodationist strategy" that "accepts one of the most striking features of modernity, what sociologists have described as the 'plurality of life worlds'" in which the "lifestyles and beliefs are vastly different from his own [and] are accessible to him if he chooses to adopt them" (Sacks, 30). Even

7. Sacks offered homosexuality and intermarriage as two such examples.

8. Orthodox Judaism has no formal spokesperson as does the Catholic Church, although the office of Chief Rabbi does command some respect, even if more from the non-Jewish community than the Jewish.

9. The progenitor of American Conservative Judaism.

though, as Sacks put it: "he may choose not to; but then his own lifestyle is the result not of necessity but of choice" (Sacks, 30–1). Here, we see the application of Sacks' understanding of the open society to the unfolding of Jewish denominationalism: "The denomination is the institutional equivalent of this consciousness. It announces itself as one way, but not the only way, of being religious; in this case, of being Jewish" (Sacks, *One People?* 31). This conclusion was unacceptable for Sacks, for whom any portrayal of "Orthodoxy, Conservatism, Reform, and Reconstructionsism . . . as the four denominations . . . imports *pluralism* into Judaism" (Sacks, 31); however, as he made clear:

> Orthodoxy does not, and cannot, make this accommodation. It recognizes pluralism along many axes. It recognizes at least some other faiths as valid religious options for non-Jews.[10] It recognizes, within Judaism itself, different *halakhic* traditions: Ashkenazi and Sephardi, for example, or Hasidic and *Mitnagdic*. Beyond *halakhah*, it legitimates a vast variety of religious approaches: rationalist and mystical, intellectual and emotional, nationalist and universalist, pietist and pragmatic. But it does not recognize the legitimacy of interpretations of Judaism that abandon fundamental beliefs or *halakhic* authority. It does not validate, in the modern sense, a plurality of denominations. It does not see itself as one version of Judaism among others (Sacks, 31).

Sacks made his ironic point in unequivocal and unself-conscious terms: there is only one type of Judaism that can rightly claim that title, and that is Orthodoxy, *in all its varieties* (!). Sacks devoted a chapter in *One People?* to the question of why Orthodoxy should be able to maintain an internal pluralism even as it rejects all expressions of Judaism external to it. For him, the abiding commitment to "fundamental beliefs" and Jewish law are the key factors that are shared across all versions of Orthodox Judaism and that undermine sectarianism in the Orthodox

10. Interestingly, Sacks has himself been called a heretic and his books have been put under the ban by Orthodox rabbis who have seen his openness to religions other than Judaism as going too far. See Shapiro, "Of Books and Bans." *The Edah Journal.* 3:2 (2003) 1–16.

community. Sacks made the limits of his internal (Orthodox) pluralism clear, with Irving Greenberg as the external boundary marker.

In *Living in the Image of God*, the collections of his conversations with Shalom Freedman, Greenberg recalled a brief episode with Sacks. According to Greenberg's recollection, "On my 1987[11] trip [to the UK], Jonathan Sacks, who had been a good friend, invited me to speak at Marble Arch Synagogue.[12] This took some guts, since Rabbi Jakobovits[13] had decided that no chief rabbinate institutions should give me a public forum" (Freedman, 150). Evidently, Greenberg's reputation as a radical thinker and activist had even reached the shores of Anglo-Jewry. Two years after the visit to speak at Marble Arch synagogue, Greenberg was invited and then uninvited to a conference on the future of Orthodoxy due to pressure from a member of the faculty of Yeshiva University. Greenberg pointed out that "Sacks was somewhat apologetic because he realized that he was collaborating with those who were delegitimating me. . . . Unfortunately, Sacks was under political pressure. He was running for the Chief Rabbi's post" (Freedman, 151). However, Greenberg's assessment that Sacks was bowing to political pressure may have been too generous.

By the time *One People?* was published, four years after the episode recounted above, Sacks seemed to have not only succumbed to political pressure, but also to have reevaluated Greenberg's place in the Orthodox community.[14] Sacks discussed Greenberg a number of times in the book, specifically with regard to his Holocaust-influenced covenantal theology and its implications for pluralism. While Sacks went to great lengths to make the case that there is great latitude within the Orthodox community, Greenberg was left on the outside looking in. In what is a tellingly implicit statement in the book, Sacks never once referred to

11. Sacks had not yet been elected to the office of Chief Rabbi.

12. This was the synagogue where Sacks served as rabbi prior to taking the post of Chief Rabbi.

13. Immanuel Jakobovits (1921–1999) was Chief Rabbi of the United Hebrew Congregations of the Commonwealth from 1967 to 1991, and Sacks' immediate predecessor in the office of the Chief Rabbi.

14. Had Sacks originally understood Greenberg's ideas in the terms he would later outline in *One People?*, it is hard to believe that he would have invited him to speak at Marble Arch Synagogue in the first place.

Greenberg by the title rabbi; something he did for every other "mainstream" Orthodox rabbi. In this act of omission, Sacks subtly placed Greenberg in a separate group from centrist Orthodox figures such as David J. Bleich, Norman Lamm, and Joseph B. Soloveitchik, each of whom is referred to by the title "rabbi" every time they are mentioned in the book and in their listing in the index.

Turning to Sacks's specific treatment of Greenberg's ideas, he began by summarizing the three stages of his covenantal theology. Accurately reflecting Greenberg's ideas, Sacks wrote that:

> The first, the biblical era, was marked by the immediacy of God, intervening in the human situation through miracles and prophetic revelation. In the second, rabbinic era, God was more hidden. He was found not in prophecy but through study, and not in the Temple but through prayer . . . The third era, that of modern Judaism, was born in the Holocaust. The Holocaust marked a yet deeper 'hiding of the face' of God, so much so that it has become impossible to have any theological certainties any more (Sacks, 37).

At the conclusion of his summary, Sacks wrote that "Greenberg's thought involves a radical secularization of the key terms of Judaism. The idea of covenant between God and Israel remains, but it has been transposed into a new key" (Sacks, 38). Most troubling for Sacks was the idea that, "Religious pluralism necessarily follows. As long as one could speak of theological certainties, there could be Orthodoxy on the one hand, heresy on the other, but after the Holocaust there are no certainties. The very basis of covenant has become voluntary" (ibid., 38).

As we have already seen, this result – a post-ethnic orientation towards identity – was unacceptable for Sacks. Not only did these ideas place Greenberg outside of Orthodoxy but, according to Sacks:

> Its revolutionary thrust is unmistakable. It is far more radical than, for example, Reform or Conservative Judaism. For while they concede that Orthodoxy is a viable contemporary option, it follows from Greenberg's premises that Orthodoxy is strictly speaking impossible in a post-Holocaust world. Religious *certainty*

> and *halakhic authority*, the key categories of rabbinic Judaism, are cognitively and socially unavailable to the modern Jew (Sacks, 38).

Here, Sacks made explicit what was only implied in Greenberg's covenantal theology and he concluded that it was thoroughly outside of Orthodoxy, because it denied *Orthodoxy* in its literal sense. i.e., correct belief.

Recalling Sacks's two key factors that unite all forms of Orthodox Jewry – "fundamental beliefs" and "*halakhic* authority" – Greenberg's third great cycle of Jewish history, in which the Jewish role in the covenant is voluntary and any expression of Judaism is valid, would necessarily be at odds with Sacks's conception of Orthodoxy. Put simply, "... Orthodoxy cannot subscribe to pluralism in the contemporary sense, for Orthodoxy is the decision to continue to understand tradition *in the traditional way*, as objective truth and external authority" (Sacks, 148). Furthermore, "Pluralism, then, proposes a mode of the Jewish unity acceptable to modern consciousness. But it is *ipso facto* unacceptable to Orthodoxy. It succeeds only if the terms of Orthodoxy are false" (ibid., 151). In this way, Greenberg was determined by Sacks to be other than Orthodox and his ideas unacceptable to Orthodox Judaism.

In place of pluralism, Sacks proffered 'inclusivism' in its place. In Sacks's definition:

> Inclusivism understands the present alienation of many Jews from Torah as neither a mandate to fragment the covenant (pluralism) nor justification for a clash of competing exclusive truths. Instead it is evidence of the overwhelming force of a secular culture in which many of Judaism's truths are unstable. It does not accord this culture the status of revelation. But neither does it regard it as non-existent. Judaism demands of Jews, now as always in the past, that they go against the current of the times (ibid., 215–6).

Sacks concluded that "Pluralism conceives Jewish unity in terms of modern consciousness. Inclusivism conceives it in terms of traditional consciousness" (ibid., 167). For Sacks, pluralism is a function of *modernity* while (Orthodox) Judaism, by contrast and by definition, is a rejection of *modernity*.

Sacks is but one example of those Orthodox thinkers that have rejected both pluralism and Greenberg as wholly un-Orthodox. As Michael Berenbaum correctly observed in 1991: "Only two current thinkers, Irving Greenberg and David Hartman, present a case for religious pluralism. Both are publicly identified – though not necessarily accepted – as part of Orthodox Judaism, and both seem to define its limits. The fate of either thinker may well determine the boundary of the movement" (Berenbaum, 111). Little has changed since those words were written and even as Greenberg and Hartman have grappled with theologies of pluralism that would call for greater inclusivity they have themselves been treated as outsiders by many in their own Orthodox community.[15]

Berenbaum, Michael. *After Tragedy and Triumph: Essays in Modern Jewish Thought and the American Experience*. Cambridge: Cambridge University Press, 1991. Print.

Cooper, Simon. *Contemporary Covenantal Thought: Interpretations of Covenant in the Thought of David Hartman and Eugene Borowitz*. Boston: Academic Studies Press, 2012. Print.

Freedman, Shalom. *Living in the Image of God: Jewish Teachings to Perfect the World*. Lanham: Rowman & Littlefield Publishers, Inc., 1998. Print.

Hartman, David. *A Heart of Many Rooms: Celebrating the Many Voices within Judaism*, Jewish Lights, 1999. Print.

Hollinger, David. *Postethnic America: Beyond Multiculturalism*. New York: Basic Books, 2005.

Persoff, Meir. *Another Way, Another Time: Religious Inclusivism and the Sacks Chief Rabbinate*. Brighton: Academic Studies Press , 2010. Print.

Sacks, Jonathan. *One People?: Tradition, Modernity, and Jewish Unity*. Oxford: The Littman Library of Jewish Civilization, 1993. Print.

15. One is reminded of the biblical story of the high priest that becomes impure in the act of sacrificing the red heifer to purify the nation.

Ethics

The Ethical Implications of *Tzelem Elokim* Theology

Rabbi Dr. Shmuly Yanklowitz

Introduction: Rav Yitz Greenberg's Ethical Development

As has been acknowledged repeatedly in this volume, Rabbi Dr. Yitz Greenberg is one of the most significant voices shaping an ethical Modern *Orthodox* movement within Judaism. His contributions to the field and theological innovations have influenced countless disciples, me among them. I was drawn to Rav Yitz's work for its spiritual elegance and nuance, its fascinating superstructure, and how it connects the wisdom of the ancient sages to the complexities of a post-modern Jewish society

As an Open Orthodox rabbi and as someone trying to cultivate a deeply-rooted sense of moral obligation in my community, I naturally turn to the work of Rav Yitz. Early in his rabbinical career, R. Yitz was influenced by the profound desire to help humanity, not merely by ritual Judaism. He points to two compelling influences for this desire. The first stems from his yeshiva experiences: "In my study years at Bais Yosef (a *mussar*[1] yeshiva that grew out of Rabbi Israel Salanter's nineteenth-century renewal movement for Orthodoxy), the yeshiva stressed character-building and ethics" (*Living in the Image of God*, 33). The second came from his father: "My father's burning commitment to help people, especially the oppressed and the underdog" (ibid.). But Rav Yitz didn't settle for maintaining the ethical impulse of his youth.

1. A moral conduct, instruction, and discipline.

Rather, he wanted to develop his positions intellectually, so that they would be as fundamental and spiritually faithful to Judaism as possible.

Tzelem Elokim Theology

The concept that human beings are created *b'Tzelem Elokim* (in the Image of God) is the foundation of Rav Yitz's theology. He explains that this principle implies that humans are endowed by God with three intrinsic and ineradicable qualities: infinite value, equality, and uniqueness. His proof text for this is the *Mishnah* found in *Sanhedrin* 37a. For Rav Yitz, this is not an abstract truth relegated to a certain human experience, but a living truth that must permeate our existence. He writes:

> The principles of human infinite value, equality, and uniqueness not only regulate the realm of society and collective behavior. They are equally the ethical principles that are meant to govern all human relationships (31–32).

We are able to actualize our human potential filled with dignity only because God engaged in *tzimtzum* (giving space to humans to exercise free will). Our covenant with God and our partnership with the Divine makes a difference because every person has a different, unique role to play in repairing the world. *Tzelem Elokim* theology tells us not only about the essence of humanity but also about God, which we can discern from studying the Holocaust and its ramifications:

> After the Shoah (Holocaust), the value of *Tzelem Elokim* – of nurturing the infinite value, equality, and uniqueness of every person – is crucial. Such confirmation is the only credible statement about God one can really make. This is the true glorification of God in an age when God is profoundly hidden, in a time where there has been a serious assault on the credibility of faith because of the great destruction of human life (37).

In the world today, God is hidden. We do not witness Divine Providence (*hashgachah*) the way some used to. We can only look back at God's action in history. "God now acts primarily, at least on the visible level, through human activity – as is appropriate in a partnership whose human participant is growing up" (38). Although God does not act for us, we feel God's closeness:

> *Hashgachah* means that God is with us; God is interested in and concerned about every detail of our lives. There is not a moment in life that is cut off from God. But *hashgachah* is not to be interpreted as meaning that God is doing the fighting and, therefore, is guaranteeing the outcome for us (39).

Our human responsibility is greater than ever, as God continues to retract from participation in this world. We no longer look toward the heavens to find divine intervention, rather to the Divine Image for human solidarity in fulfilling our covenantal mission.

Character Development

For Rav Yitz: "The whole system of *mitzvot* is dedicated to *tikkun ha-adam*" (71). Yet as this theology makes major demands on our civic duties, it also places moral responsibilities upon our individual character development: "Perfecting the human being – *tikkun ha'adam* – is part of the process of making the world whole" (70). Each of us must work on ourselves. The model for this is *imitatio Dei* (*halakhtah b'drakhav*) as we try to emulate the compassionate ways of God. All of Judaism aims at this goal:

> To live a life of *kedushah* (holiness) is to bring out those qualities in myself and vis-à-vis others. This is the basic purpose of every *mitzvah*. The *halakhot* are actually designed to train, to bring out in the individual or in the structure of society the maximum of life, e.g., the maximum of holiness (72).

For Rav Yitz, this ethical commitment includes legal decisions; indeed, it must permeate *halakhah* (Jewish law) itself. "It follows that this consideration should be given a heavier weight in *halakhah* or *p'sak* (legal rulings) than in the past" (37).

Of course, *Tzelem Elokim* theology extends universally to our relationship with gentiles and particularistically in our understanding of *halakhah*. Yet, it also resides in Jewish peoplehood. Because the image of God is contained within every person, the truths of every person emanate from a kernel of Truth. Thus, there is value present in other religions and within the different Jewish denominations. Honoring each other's commitments is not merely a pragmatic form of tolerance to ensure collaboration and combat violence. It leads to something much deeper: epistemic humility. We work on our character trait of humility to emulate the will of God. To do so, we honor different truths and different kinds of people with identities different from our own. This is no relativism that makes all truth claims equal. Instead, we embrace our absolutes while creating space for other's absolutes. This is also emulation of God's *tzimtzum*.

The Sphere of Politics

Commitment to channeling the Divine into the mundane arenas of the world extends from the interpersonal realm to politics as well. That *Tzelem Elokim* theology translates into political advocacy is a uniquely "Greenbergian" innovation:

> The definition of the state of *tikkun olam* – the arrival of the messianic kingdom – is when the actual legal, political, social institutions in the world will be structured so that each human being will be sustained and treated as if he or she is an image of God. The world must become rich enough to spend an unlimited amount of money to save one life. The world must be reorganized so that there cannot be systematized degradation or discrimination against people; there must be no inferiority imposed by law or by practice (69).

Furthermore, as religious people, this is the dream that we must work toward each day:

> *Tikkun olam*, then, is the process whereby humans transform the world or improve it to the point where it truly sustains each image of God in appropriate dignity. Part of the process involves upgrad-

ing the economy. If the world is poor, it cannot support people at the needed level of dignity. Similarly, to reach the messianic stage, humans have to overcome war because wars take lives; armies kill and waste images of God. If the society, by law, opposes equality, then there will be no equality. If people are equal, then every vote should count just as much as every other. This is what democracy is all about (ibid.).

A Personal Example

Rav Yitz affirmed this teaching in his personal life:

> I have always set my goal to try to act covenantally with people, to listen to their own distinctive voice, to recognize their personal qualities, and to learn from their unique insights, (ibid. 32).

Having interacted closely with Rav Yitz over the years and watched him interact with others on countless occasions, I can say, unequivocally, that I have never seen him stray from this.

Going Forward

It seems that, more than ever, human affairs are undergoing a breakdown in community, respect, and civil discourse. Many retreat into solitude rather than engaging with others who are different from them. The process of *othering* based upon gender, sexual orientation, race, nationality, and religion is rampant.

Binary thinking is an early stage of intellectual development. In today's political discourse, we cannot elevate those committed to binary thinking. Vituperation does not bring elucidation. Sadly, even talking common sense might not work. They don't need more liquid poured into the container but rather a larger container – that is, a new developmental stage.

We need to progress from binary thinking to stages of plurality that ultimately lead to unity. To do so, we must re-think education in America. This requires more than just good schools, which are, of course, crucial. It requires the business sector, government, media, religion and all partners who can contribute to the intellectual development of citizens and help us to re-think how we talk about others' ideas. We can learn to hold our complex narratives and truths and still honor those of others. Given the resurgence of extremists who imagine that only their own needs, truths, and narratives alone are valid, every institution and person is now more responsible than ever for this work of modeling critical thinking and instilling empathy.

With the resurgence of deeply hateful political rhetoric, we must double-down. Each of us needs to work personally to rebuild the fabric of a healthy, trusting, inter-dependent cross-cultural society that some are trying to destroy. Some have sown fear by spewing (or just ignoring) malicious rhetoric against those who are different. Those with friends only of the same race, same religion, same origin of birth, or same sexual orientation need to triple-down and make the conscious efforts to go beyond their limited social circle to build new relationships. Now more than ever we have to rebuild social trust and empathy for others. If not, the threats of fear-mongering, *othering,* and shaming will prevail. We cannot allow this to happen.

The problem with *othering* is the dehumanizing of people created in the Divine Image. Many try to fuel nightmare narratives by insisting that the "others" are coming for us and that they are taking over. This was done toward Jews fleeing the Holocaust, and toward Muslim refugees fleeing from Syria since 2011, toward people of color and toward immigrants in America. How can we collectively ensure that all adult citizens come to value plurality, complexity, and difference? Indeed, the future of our country is at stake. Lives are at stake.

We owe sincere gratitude to Rav Yitz for helping the Jewish people deal with the complexities of the twenty-first century. He has rooted us in Jewish tradition and our particular identities while also fortifying us intellectually and ethically to engage successfully and respectfully with other people and their ideas.

Rabbi Yitz Greenberg and a Postmodern *Mussar*

Rabbi David Jaffe

"A proponent of *mussar*"[1] is the way the original *Encyclopedia Judaica* describes Rabbi Dr. Irving "Yitz" Greenberg. That Rabbi Greenberg was so described for his activities in the 1960s and early '70s may come as a surprise to the many who know him for his groundbreaking work on pluralism and covenantal theology. This chapter demonstrates how Rabbi Greenberg's early *mussar* training in the Novardok Beit Yosef Yeshiva in Brooklyn had a profound and direct influence on central elements of his life work. In particular, this article explores *mussar* parallels to Rabbi Greenberg's critique of Judaism's encounter with modernity, his innovative Torah teaching in secular environments, his emphasis on human dignity, and his ability to withstand withering criticism from his own Orthodox community. The goal of this chapter is to raise awareness of Rabbi Greenberg's work among the growing audience of *mussar* practitioners in North America as well as demonstrate to the broader Modern Orthodox and Jewish communities the importance of *mussar* learning and practice to meeting the challenges of Judaism in the postmodern era.

Introduction to the Mussar Movement

The *Mussar* (ethical development) movement was founded by Rabbi Israel Salanter in the late 1840s in Lithuania. While *mussar* literature dates back to the tenth century, it only became an organized

1. Moral conduct, instruction, or discipline.

movement for ethical and spiritual improvement in this later period with specific schools and techniques. Rabbi Salanter wielded great authority in the Lithuanian Jewish world due to his outstanding and widely recognized Torah scholarship. In response to the encroaching Western enlightenment, R. Salanter realized his community needed to improve both its ethical behavior and internalize more deeply its Jewish commitments. His main innovation involved understanding and mobilizing unconscious forces for character development using Jewish study, chanting, and ethical practice. He also understood the need to bring authentic Jewish experiences to secularized Jews and spent the latter decades of his life working to this end in Germany and France.

Through his students, R. Salanter and *mussar* had a deep and lasting impact on the Torah world. The three main "*mussar*" *yeshivot* – Kelm, Slobodka, and Novardok – provided training to many of the twentieth century's leading Ashkenazi Torah scholars. Each of these three *yeshivot* had a different feel, emphasizing different aspects of *mussar* teaching. At the risk of oversimplifying, Kelm emphasized responsibility for the other, Slobodka the dignity of humanity, and Novardok extreme trust in God. It was Novardok *mussar* that had the biggest impact on R. Greenberg from his years studying at the Novardok Beit Yosef yeshiva in Brooklyn. Novardok was founded by Rabbi Yosef Yuzel Horowitz around the turn of the twentieth century. R. Horowitz was a Torah scholar-businessman who dedicated himself to full-time learning after an encounter with a student of R. Salanter's. An intense spiritual personality, R. Horowitz spent close to a decade in seclusion dedicating himself to building his trust in God. After coming out of seclusion he founded the Novardok yeshiva, which became famous for instilling an unshakeable inner moral compass in its students. Against tremendous obstacles, graduates founded over one hundred *yeshivot* throughout Poland before World War II, using their training to overcome fear and opposition. This yeshiva network was destroyed during the Shoah, but its few survivors founded Novardok *yeshivot* in Jerusalem, France and Brooklyn after the war. It was in the new Novardok Beit Yosef yeshiva that young Greenberg got his introduction to *mussar*.

R. Greenberg describes his first visit to the yeshiva with his father as a teenager:

> We went to the third seder at night. We sat and learned together so I had no real experience except that it was full at night. Thirty minutes before *Maariv* they learn *B'hispailus* (fervent and emotional learning). I had no idea what was going on. Someone clapped. Someone next to me jumped up and screamed the teaching from *Pirkei Avot,* "Jealousy, lust and seeking honor removes you from the world." And someone else was clapping. Another was calling out Torah verses and crying and screaming. Thirty or so people were doing this. When this was over I said to my dad – this is what I want!

From 1949 to 1953, R. Greenberg learned *mussar* at Beit Yosef under the auspices of Rosh Yeshiva Rabbi Avraham Yaffen, and developed a special relationship with *Mashgiaḥ Ruḥani* (Spiritual Advisor) Rabbi Yehuda Leib Nekritz. Rabbi Nekritz provided R. Greenberg with a living example of a *mussar* personality modeling both spiritual intensity and thoughtful compassion for others. R. Nekritz became R. Greenberg's personal mentor, introducing him to the world of *middot* development. At the same time, R. Greenberg attended Brooklyn College in the morning, adding a first-rate secular education to an intense yeshiva experience. It was this combination of secular and religious studies in a *mussar* environment that would have a definitive impact on R. Greenberg's later projects.

Responses to Modernity

Among R. Greenberg's major contributions to contemporary Jewish thought is his analysis of Judaism's encounter with modernity. Central to this analysis is his critique of ultra-Orthodoxy for rejecting modernity and Reform, Conservative, and Modern Orthodoxy for assimilating *too much* modernity. His solution is what he calls "synthesis," or a dialectic relationship between Judaism and modernity that demands a high level of Jewish engagement while also participating in the best of modernity. Direct antecedents to this approach can be found in the writings and personality of Rabbi Israel Salanter. The Enlightenment of the late eighteenth century presented Ashkenazi Jewry with a profound challenge: Medieval Judaism was characterized by a high level of group affiliation and identity and little social mobility or positive interaction outside the group. Modernity and the offer of citizenship to the Jews of Europe changed all this. Modernity, with its offer of individual rights, economic and scientific advancement, and a vision of universal peace aligned well with Judaism's messianic vision.

Assimilationists found modernity irresistible and completely abandoned Judaism. Classic Orthodoxy, agreeing that modernity was irresistible, built a wall of separation and completely rejected modernity. Reform, Conservative, and Modern Orthodoxy all made different kinds of compromises with modernity. No matter what the approach, modernity created opportunities but also posed a major challenge to Jewish survival. In mid-nineteenth century Lithuania, Rabbi Salanter confronted the challenge of the *maskilim*, the "enlightened" Jews who wanted to modernize their traditionalist brethren by persuasion or force. In the second half of the twentieth century, Greenberg faced a North American Jewish community deeply absorbed in modernity and headed toward full assimilation.

R. Salanter and R. Greenberg both critiqued the uninspired, conformist nature of their communities, calling for deeper internalization of Judaism as a necessity for responding creatively to the aggressive challenge of modernity. In the following letter to his student, Elijah Levinsohn of Cartinga, Rabbi Salanter names weak observance as a problem and calls for his people to develop a more personal and authentic relationship to Judaism through *mussar*:

> ... [concerning] the matter of *Mussar* study – to strengthen it with immovable nails, to strengthen weak hands [so as] to give the way of life, and to give them strength to wage the battle that is a *mitzvah*, the battle of the Lord. Particularly in these times, when the everyday habit [that is, of observance of Torah and mitzvot] grows weaker from day to day and from hour to hour, where can one find Torah and Divine service? And who shall put a stop to it [this fall] and reinvigorate [Torah study] seeing that it has fallen so drastically from the status which it formerly held.... If we are silent and thereby sin, who knows whether we will not be required to give an accounting for our failure to seek out the collective good by strengthening the Divine service. And what can

> they, the flock, do? The battle surrounds them from every side and corner, [even] if they have the strength of stones and their flesh is bronze, how can they not be tempted by the foolish [counsel] of these people who sin against their own souls to deflect them from God and His service. [Unless] those who have been given by God a greater share of wisdom and understanding then their brethren . . . spread their understanding and extend wings in whose shade those weak of mind and understanding may take shelter, to build a rampart and to construct an embankment, in order to strengthen the Torah like a fortified city. . . .

Professor Immanuel Etkes writes that, "This letter clearly reflects Salanter's great fear in the face of the challenge to the hegemony of the tradition among his contemporaries. He describes activity to fortify the fear of God among his contemporaries by establishing circles of *mussar* students, whose activity would be concentrated around *mussar* houses, thereby immunizing them against the dangerous influences of those who sought to deflect them from the Torah – that is, the *Maskilim*."

For R. Greenberg, a century later in North America, modernity had already won the hearts of most Jews but the question remained the same: Can Jews live an authentic, invigorating Judaism flexible enough to engage modernity and survive? Notice the similarities between R. Salanter's letter and R. Greenberg's assessment of the challenge of Jewish survival in this 1968 article about campus life and the Jewish future:

> We will have to develop a new style of Jewishness. It would have to be considerably more open yet committed, more intellectually sophisticated and critical. It will have to be less organizational and more individual. It will demand greater self-fulfillment in Judaism and Jewishness and less working so that others can be Jewish. We will have to be more willing to concentrate our efforts on committed Jews and on particularistic activities. This does not mean exclusion or narrowness. But it means an end to mindless non-specific Jewish loyalty and activity. Such a deepening would make Jews more capable of participating constructively in American society without thereby assimilating.
>
> The Jewish community has been depending on a nominal Jew-

> ishness combined with neighborhood and social concentration to carry it through. College is destroying this possibility socially and culturally. Only a major upgrading in informed Jewish commitment and deepening of Jewish knowledge can save the day.

This "mindless non-specific Jewish loyalty" was a twentieth century parallel to the weak habits of observance pointed out by R. Salanter, while the call for "a major upgrading in informed Jewish commitment" echoes the advocacy for *mussar* learning among nineteenth century Lithuania and Poland's Jews. Indeed, R. Greenberg attributes his sensitivity to the Jewish community's need for deeper internalization and reform to his *mussar* background. Beit Yosef was his first experience with "unfiltered Judaism" and it exposed the weaknesses of Modern Orthodoxy at confronting the temptations of modernity.

According to R. Greenberg, the Modern Orthodoxy of his day was a "domesticated religion that didn't offer raw religious experiences and serious attempts at character reconstruction. While at Beit Yosef, Judaism was emotionally charged and we talked about God. We were not intimidated and overawed by spiritual or physical threats. I had very deep experiences along those lines." In addition, it was clear that:

> You needed to be a *ba'al middos*. Rabbi Salanter was dealing with modernity. Change was coming and people needed to shift from being other-directed personalities to inner-directed. If Judaism stayed other-directed people would assimilate because observance was weak. Rabbi Salanter developed an internalized religious experience in life. He said interpersonal mitzvot also needed to be stepped up and made as important as mitzvot between people and God. This was part of the internalization. Torah was to develop a personality.

Beit Yosef gave R. Greenberg a visceral experience of the type of Jewish experiences that can help Judaism modernize without losing itself in modernity.

In addition to this personal religious experience, R. Greenberg's views on modernity were also influenced by R. Salanter's work as an internal revolutionary within Orthodoxy. He first came to understand how radical R. Salanter's *mussar* project was during a seminar early in his doctoral studies at Harvard in the mid–1950s. Perry Miller, the great colonial intellectual historian, taught his students to see how Puritan preachers transformed Orthodox Calvinism into liberal Protestantism over time by looking for the questions the preacher was trying to address in his sermon. On the surface, the sermons sounded like traditional presentations of Calvinist theology, but a closer look at what was bothering the preacher revealed how he was making the religion less about predetermination and more voluntary. R. Greenberg describes how this was a transformational experience for him:

> I said, 'oh my' – I never asked myself – what is Rabbi Salanter's question and what was he really saying? Up to that point I thought of him as simply trying to uphold the tradition. I went back and reread *Ohr Yisrael* and stories about him. I realized for the first time he was much more critical of Orthodoxy and I understood why there was so much opposition to him. It wasn't about learning *middot*. It was about the conformity and the external focus of Judaism at that time. He was critical of a *frumkeit* that was oblivious to the distortion of personality and *middot*. At 59 years old the secular government approached him to set up an official rabbinic seminary that would promote assimilation. They approached him because they sensed he was critical of the Orthodox establishment. He escaped because he was also against assimilation. This is what I came to see. Orthodoxy couldn't handle modernity and if you tried to do anything, they would tell you that you are ruining it. He went to the West where there was openness to new approaches. He told Rabbi Azriel Hildesheimer, "I wish I had your portion in *Olam Habah* for teaching girls, but in the East they would excommunicate me for doing that." This became a transformational moment for me.

The second similarity in approaches to modernity involves synthesis – or how both R. Salanter and R. Greenberg challenged their communities to embrace the best of modernity while still being grounded deeply in traditional Judaism. The following passage from Etkes describes how R. Salanter advocated synthesis in regards to the economic situation of

Torah scholars. The nineteenth century Lithuanian Torah world looked down on manual labor as the occupation of the poor and unlearned. Finance and commerce were the chosen means of earning money for those that needed to work. Trade and money lending among Jews was popularly thought of as contributing to the poor ethical practices rampant in the community. The *maskilim* were highly critical of this and advocated that Jews become artisans and laborers to improve their ethical behavior to a level befitting of "enlightened" society. Despite the fact that manual labor and ethical improvement was associated with the dreaded *maskilim*, R. Salanter advocated the same approach, but with one important difference: Torah study always comes first.

Salanter sought to make physical labor, which was generally associated with the masses and the ignorant, into an acceptable, respected source of livelihood for one who was an outstanding Talmudic scholar. Moreover, Salanter's critique of commerce partly coincided with that of the *maskilim*. The *Haskalah's*[2] demand for the productivization of Jewish economic activity and the inclusion of vocational training within the system of Jewish education also argued that commerce, and particularly petty commerce, was an inadequate source of income and entails exploitation and deceit. Salanter was evidently aware of the similarity and took pains to stress the points of disagreement between himself and the position of the *maskilim*: While the latter demanded the implementation of vocational training already in the early stages of education, Salanter insisted that it must be preceded by the acquisition of the basic fundamentals of Torah study, and that vocational training be postponed to a later stage. His consideration was not only ideological, but also pedagogical. He wrote:

> ... So long as the son can find his way in the study of Talmud, one ought not to assist him [to learn] a trade, for the study of craft has no fixed time, and may be acquired in maturity just as in youth. ... But this is not true of the study of Talmud, which is the basis of our lives and protects our souls; its foundation can only be laid in the days of childhood; let us not move from it.

2. Jewish Enlightenment movement.

This is a good example of what R. Greenberg calls *synthesis*. R. Salanter advocated that the Jewish community align with the best ideals of the general culture, while staying firmly rooted in the particular aspects of Judaism – Talmud Torah and rejecting general culture's dismissal of this aspect of Judaism. The *maskilim* were the Jews of his time who were buying too fully into modernity and needed a corrective. Unlike the Orthodox of his time, R. Salanter was willing to innovate by developing neglected aspects of the tradition and simply trying new things. We can see similarities in the following prescription from R. Greenberg about the next stage of Jewish history:

> To move to this next stage will mean that all the groups [Reform, Conservative and Modern Orthodox] must turn and do *teshuvah*. Part of that repentance is to recover the whole tradition: not to be afraid to consider the possibility of a personal God or a God who redeems, despite the embarrassment such views cause by modern criteria. In a generation where redemption takes place it is necessary to have the courage to reformulate, to go beyond modernity and, therefore, to go beyond traditionalism as well. . . .
>
> Such a policy points to more radical *halakhic* redevelopment than Reform has ever considered on some issues. In still other cases, it demands a traditionalism and a going back to tradition far beyond that which the right wing Orthodox might dare ask. The synagogue thus becomes an alternative community, making demands and creating ways of life, not just drifting along in the grip of outside cultural forces. The goal is a coherent set of Jewish values and models imprinted on every area of life, able to override modern values where they contradict or do not do justice to the Jewish perspective.

R. Greenberg goes on to offer the Zero Population Growth movement of the 1970s, in which Jews were prominent leaders and participants, as an example of modern values that contradict Jewish interests. True synthesis would mean Jews would emphasize the highest interpersonal ethical values, something also promoted by modernity while at the same time rejecting movements like Z.P.G. that do not align with Jewish values. In R. Greenberg's own words: ". . . Jews relate dialectically to every host culture; they are in it, but not totally of it. They resist being absorbed fully, for no partial culture deserves absolute loyalty. Also, were Judaism totally integrated, this would mean that Judaism would be dragged down when the local culture comes to its inevitable end. We are committed to outlast each civilization and to be reborn as often as necessary to reach the kingdom of God. . . . The goal is to successfully synthesize modernity and Judaism; this means preserving Judaism's millennial vision and direction and ensuring that it is the active shaping force in this new civilization." For R. Salanter, *synthesis* meant adopting manual labor as a goal to help ethical improvement, but not at the cost of Torah. Torah always comes first, which is his assertion of Judaism being an "active shaping force in this new civilization." R. Salanter's bold, yet traditional approach to change was an inspiration for R. Greenberg's model of synthesis as the answer to the challenge of Judaism and modernity.

The reality of subjectivity is the third of R. Salanter's innovations that influenced R. Greenberg's approach to Judaism and modernity. Probably his most radical innovation, R. Salanter explored the power and influence of unconscious forces in human affairs, particularly in *halakhic* decision-making. Until that time, it was accepted wisdom that, through great effort, Torah scholars could come to an objective understanding of the truth of any piece of Torah. R. Salanter undermined this key assumption with his revelation of human subjectivity. The following excerpts from his seminal Letter 30 in *Ohr Yisrael* and the introduction to his journal, *Tevunah* (Letter 29), express the implications of subjectivity:

> . . . He thus remains saddled with emotional forces and does not have the ability to detach his intellect from them. There, man does not have the capacity to apprehend true wisdom, absolutely purified and divorced from human emotion. The Torah, however, was given to man to make judgments according to the human intellect. Matters are clarified by accumulating proofs and evaluating them. . . .
>
> All men are equally fit in their intelligence to determine which side has the greater quantity of proofs, providing that the heart accurately understands them. However, concerning the evalua-

> tion of the quality of proofs, each person's spirit differs from the next. These are the value judgments we have been discussing, and there is a vast difference in people's analytic abilities.

In other words, we do our best to understand a matter intellectually, but at the end of the day, even if we can calm our emotions, we have a spirit that is subjective and colors the way we see a matter. Later in this letter, R. Salanter claimed that this is the reason the voice from heaven declares that both the words of Beit Shammai and Beit Hillel are the words of the living God. The fact of human subjectivity necessitates that God communicates in multiple truths. One implication of subjectivity is the need for others to provide a corrective to our thinking. If emotions or some essential subjective spirit colors how we see reality, than sharing our ideas with others for correction can help us see other angles on the truth and reduce our own distortions. R. Salanter relates to this in Letter 29:

> Additionally, the language in matters of *middos* is different than the language of scholarship. In the intellectual realm, flowery speech and rhetoric is unacceptable. However, the opposite is true concerning character traits; it is essentially impossible to present or explain them without expressing a rhetorical conceptualization – for the purpose of such language is to awaken emotional forces, which are dependent on *middos*. [Of course, there is danger in this as well,] . . . for the more a man is able to employ rhetorical language to correctly explain a concept, the greater potential there is for him to err by cloaking falsehood with the mantle of rhetoric. An effective strategy against this is to present one's proposition [to a number of people who are unfamiliar with it]. By exposing part of his essay to the light of day, "the public will review his words with sharp critique, [and he will be able] to polish and refine its every measure [constructive criticism] being a vital foundation for success in both physical and spiritual endeavors. Then it will be a beacon of truth for all who wish to seek it."

Rabbi Salanter's exploration of subjectivity and the extent to which the unconscious controls our thinking were important factors in R.

Greenberg's embrace of postmodernity. A postmodern Judaism is one that accepts multiple paths to truth and encourages the encounter between different systems such as Judaism and modernity. R. Greenberg describes that, "... Jews have entered into each local (historical) culture, lived within it and revised it to move it toward the values that the Torah upholds." This "revision" is a type of critique or corrective. The corrective goes the other way as well. Judaism at times needs a corrective from other cultures. The idea of the need for "sharp critique" became a foundation of his understanding of the necessity of pluralism, both in the Jewish community and between faiths.

Zikui Rabim – Bringing the Many to Righteousness

The second major area of *mussar* influence on R. Greenberg's life work concerns public service, or teaching Judaism to the masses. Bringing deeper Jewish awareness and learning to secular Jews is one of R. Greenberg's great achievements. Through the CLAL: The National Center for Learning and Leadership, R. Greenberg pioneered both intra-denominational study and bringing Torah learning to the, mostly, secular world of Jewish Federations. This commitment to spreading Torah was not a given early in his career. Back in the late 1950s, R. Greenberg was most concerned with figuring out his own personal solution to the tension between Judaism and modernity. He was going to be an American academic, teaching secular history while living a deeply passionate, personal Jewish life. Thankfully for the Jewish world, his *mussar* training pushed him away from this personal solution towards Jewish public service. Rather than find a teaching position at a secular university, R. Greenberg took his first job with Yeshiva University in 1961. Although he was teaching secular history, he had an opportunity to influence Jewish students. Over the years, he took on more and more Jewish-oriented projects, particularly as his interest in the *Shoah* grew. He also served as a congregational rabbi during the 1960s and eventually decided to fully serve the broader Jewish community by founding what became CLAL.

Mussar has a strong tradition of encouraging public service to the Jewish people. R. Salanter decided as a young man to forego living as a hidden *tzaddik* and serve Lithuanian Jewry (and later served Western

Jewry) at great personal sacrifice. Many of his letters encourage his students to teach others *mussar*. While in Lithuania, he encouraged the practice of gathering unlearned manual laborers on Shabbat to study the basics of Jewish law. In describing his decision to stay in Germany, far from his base of influence, R. Salanter compared the contemporary situation to wild horse at the top of a hill:

> When the horses begin to gallop wildly . . . down the hill, it is totally impossible to stop them in the middle of the mountain . . . but only after the horses have gone all the way downhill can they be stopped and calmed down. The same is true of the direction of communities. . . . In the great cities of Russia, the communities are galloping down the mountain, and are now in the middle of the descent, so it is impossible to bring about any order in them. But the communities abroad have already reached the bottom of the hill, so that it is now possible to halt them and to put them in place.

Rabbi Salanter was a communal leader driven by a calling to help his people. If the best way to do this was to go West, that is where he would go. Etkes describes some of his specific innovations aimed at bringing the nourishment of Torah and Judaism to secularized, Western Jews:

> Salanter's tendency to develop skills and activities appropriate to the circumstances of time and place was expressed in his program regarding the teaching of Talmud among the Jews of Germany. His concern was how to interest enlightened youth, who had never received a traditional education, in the study of Talmud. Salanter originally toyed with the idea of composing a lexicon of Talmudic Aramaic, and to this end consulted some scholars who lived in Memel, but after a period of time, he conceived of a more far reaching plan: the composition of a new commentary to the entire Talmud. He thought in terms of a commentary in Hebrew, which would explain the course of reasoning of the Talmudic argumentation in such a manner that even novice students could study on their own.

R. Greenberg demonstrates the same concern and creativity for making Torah accessible to secularized Jews on college campuses. In addressing the crisis of assimilation of college campuses in the 1960s, R. Greenberg noted, ". . . the absence of serious works of a positive Jewish content and, in particular, the almost total dearth of college textbook level books in various Jewish areas. There is not a single first-rate one-volume treatment in English of Jewish history, *Halakhah*, Bible or even theology." Before the era of Jewish Studies departments at colleges across the country, Greenberg proposed, ". . . the development and publication of textbooks and college-level courses in Judaism. Such courses would be suitable for inclusion in the college curriculum." Like Rabbi Salanter, Greenberg saw the university as the bastion of modernity and the leverage point for bringing Judaism to assimilating Jews.

Novardok specialized in *Zikui Rabim*, teaching the public. As mentioned above, Novardok students were trained to create Torah institutions throughout Poland and parts of Russia, resulting in a network of over a hundred *yeshivot* in the first half of the twentieth century. The last section of Rabbi Horowitz's key work, *Madregat Ha'adam*, describes the virtues of public service. The ten chapter section is an extended argument why taking time out of yeshiva studies to connect with young people and teach them Torah is not a diversion from spiritual growth, but actually is core to spiritual growth. For example, in chapter nine, he retells the Talmudic story of Rav Preida, who was greatly rewarded for reviewing a lesson with his student eight hundred times. Rabbi Horowitz answers his student's imaginary challenge to Rav Preida:

> Why do you regard this as sacrifice and wastefulness and loss to oneself? Do you not see that just the opposite is the case? That only through his forbearance and complete commitment did he [Rav Prieda] attain to such a high level of Divine service and ennoblement of character? And as to you, who finds it difficult to commit yourself completely to community service, and who is always apprehensive as to the possibility of loss, will your end not be to be wanting both in Divine service and in perfection of character? For one cannot be successful in Torah and awe of G-d unless his heart is pure and his mind free of vain and false conceits.

> Therefore, it is precisely one's inability to part from those fancies which prevent committed service, and his quest for the easiest and nearest access to reward in this world which keep him from true greatness and wholeness.
>
> Furthermore, it is important for us to know that the most difficult aspect of Divine service is the employment of character traits in their proper place and time, an activity which is highly subject to error and fraught with stumbling blocks. This is true, however, only when one relies exclusively upon his own judgment and attempts to arrive at the truth by his own reasoning – in which case he will fail to acquire it. However, when one becomes a community servant . . . the proper character reactions are dictated by the demands of the situation.

Helping others grow spirituality is the direct route to one's own spiritual growth. It is false to think one can grow just by learning in the study hall or by contemplating character development on one's own. Service is the path to growth. This is a foundational *mussar* idea that broke with the contemporary practice since the time of the Vilna Gaon of focusing all of one's time on Torah study. R. Greenberg absorbed this communal service ethic during his four years at Beit Yosef setting his life's direction towards bringing Jewish spiritual sustenance to all corners of the Jewish world.

Tzelem Elokim and *Tikkun Olam*

Rabbi Greenberg is perhaps most known for his emphasis on the Divine Image of humanity. In his own words, he describes the centrality of this idea to his life work:

> Two core ideas in my thought are *tikkun olam* and *Tzelem Elokim* (the image of God). The term *tikkun ha-adam* is a play on the relationship between *Tzelem Elokim* and *tikkun olam.*
>
> Being in the image of God means that each human being is born with three intrinsic dignities – infinite value, equality and uniqueness. . . . The definition of the state of *tikkun olam* – the arrival of the messianic kingdom – is when the actual legal, political, and

> social institutions in the world will be structured so that each human being will be sustained and treated as if he or she is an image of God. . . . Perfecting the human being (*tikkun ha'adam*) is part of this process of making the world whole. Human beings have their own weaknesses and faults. . . . What does perfecting the human being involve? . . . Part of the task is to improve the individuals' and groups' recognition of their intrinsic dignities. This requires the creation of a foundation of religious and ethical values, as well as cultural teachings that communicate the infinite value, equality and uniqueness of every individual and the preciousness of the groups within which individuals grow. Part of the task is to get humans to want to do good. Humans are not machines: the goal is not to generate ethical robots. So *tikkun ha-adam* is not an attempt to change human nature, but rather to develop the best tendencies in people.

This emphasis on human perfection and the perfection of the world has clear precedent in R. Salanter's life and teaching. R. Greenberg describes how he was influenced by his *mussar* mentors:

> I read stories about Rabbi Salanter and his teachings on my own. The Torah came to make a *mensch*. The key question is what kind of human being are you going to be? There was a big emphasis in the yeshiva on *kavod habriyot* (human dignity) and the implications of that. These had a very strong influence on me. Rabbi Nekritz was patient and understanding and kind. He could be penetrating but it was never oppressive. This all set the tone for centrality of *Tzelem Elokim* and middos in my thinking later on.

R. Greenberg certainly encountered many stories about R. Salanter's extraordinary concern for other humans. These stories are too abundant to mention here, but the following two accounts recorded in *Israel Salanter and the Mussar Movement* give a flavor of R. Salanter's character. The first deals with the classism and elitism in Lithuanian Jewish society; the second with concern for vulnerable workers. In both, R. Salanter demonstrates his genuine Torah-based compassion. Lithuanian society honored Torah scholarship and denigrated those who were unlearned, which often correlated with being poor. To counter this, Etkes writes that R. Salanter taught that:

> . . . the knowledge that a person acquires by studying Torah must be measured against the student's own talents and the degree of effort invested therein. This relativistic approach applied to the study of Torah, while characteristic of Salanter's mode of thought, represented a striking departure from the prevailing view. Once again, Rabbi Salanter is revealed as one who does not shrink from developing and expressing unconventional positions. Within the context of Lithuanian Jewry, which was fond of the saying, "An ignorant man cannot be pious," and which related to Torah geniuses with sacred awe, Rabbi Israel declared that even an am *ha'aretz* could be considered as a perfect *zaddik*" – provided that he labor to study Torah in accordance with his own ability!
>
> Salanter is portrayed therein as a personality whose entire behavior and range of activities were motivated by a love of his fellow human being of rare intensity, by a unique sensitivity to the suffering of the unfortunate, and by a profound involvement in the destiny of society generally. However, as his concepts took from within the strict boundaries of the *halakha*, he did not perceive this unique pattern of behavior as a spontaneous demonstration of love of humanity, but simply as what was required of him by law. Such an understanding sufficed to make his behavior an example to be followed by others.

The following story is typical of R. Salanter's concern for the working poor and that employers and kosher supervisors fulfill the letter and spirit of the law regarding treatment of workers. He was especially careful to give more weight to human considerations when those conflicted with ritual observance, bucking the trend in his community:

> Once, while still living in Salant, Rabbi Israel was pressed for time during the days preceding Passover and was unable personally to supervise the baking of the *matzot,* as was his usual practice. When those close to him, who had assumed this task in his place, asked for directions concerning those things over which they ought to

> take especial care, he answered: "The only thing which I ask of you . . .[is] to be exceedingly careful that you not cause anguish to Zippah the kneader through excessive strictness (dough for Passover *matzot* must be kneaded quickly), when it seems to you that she does not knead the dough fast enough. Do not forget that she is a widow, and it is forbidden to cause anguish to a widow . . ." (168).

For the young R. Greenberg, these stories, in addition to live examples of *mussar* personalities, made a deep and lasting impression regarding the centrality of human dignity to his life work.

Internal Compass and Indifference to Public Opinion

Rabbi Greenberg suffered withering criticism from his Orthodox colleagues as soon as he began promoting intra-Jewish dialogue that recognized and respected liberal rabbis. The criticism ranged from outright public rebuke in forums and print, to more subtle non-invitations to speak on panels on which he certainly belonged. In one glaring example, recounted in *Living in the Image of God*, he was left out of a panel in England on the future of Orthodoxy organized by soon-to-be Chief Rabbi, Lord Jonathan Sacks because he had defied the then-Chief Rabbi Jakobovits and met in public forums with liberal rabbis. He explained:

> ". . . Rabbi Sacks organized a conference on the future of Orthodoxy. He invited people from a broad spectrum (including, from the right, Rabbi J. David Bleich of Yeshiva University). Bleich told him that he would not come if I participated. He cited my work with the Reform and liberal groups, and Sacks caved in. I was not invited." This type of incident repeated itself many times over R. Greenberg's career.

Fortunately for him, and for the Jewish world, his Novardok training helped him build a strong internal compass. The goal of the Novardok method was to break the ego and become indifferent to public opinion. R. Greenberg comments:

> I think that really helped me stick to my guns and not give in or be over-swayed by Orthodox or other conventional consensus." Novardok was famous for training its students to be fearless. A story is told about Rabbi Yisrael, the official *Mashgiaḥ* of Beit Yosef in Brooklyn, who worked at the yeshiva while it was in Poland. They were learning in the Beit Midrash when the Nazis rolled into town at the beginning of the Second World War. The Nazis saw a Jewish star on the building and began to fire as they drove by. Bullets were flying through the door and everyone panicked and jumped to the floor. Rabbi Yisrael, because he was trained not to get excited or intimidated, was the only one who calmly closed his book and got to the floor.

Rabbi Greenberg explains that Novardokers ". . . had an inner gyroscope that was not affected by external stimuli." While R. Salanter recommended a number of techniques, including fervent chanting of verses and special focus on behavior to improve *middot*, most yeshivas focused more on learning and less on actual practice. Novardok was the exception. Rabbi Horowitz was incredibly intense and Beit Yosef maintained its commitment to deep, transformative practice. R. Greenberg describes the discipline that helped him develop such a strong internal compass and ability to withstand criticism:

> We had a *va'ad* (*mussar* group). We kept a spiritual diary of the week that tracked where you failed. Then the group would tear you apart and tell you where they thought you were off.
>
> Some of the boys got in private conversations with the *Mashgiah*. The *va'ad* was the next inner level. The inner, inner level might have been more extreme. On the one hand, you get this tremendous critique in the *va'ad* and reshape your behavior patterns. On the other it only matters what God thinks of you. If you are intimidated or moved by their criticism or moved by their praise, it is a problem for you. It is only about you and God. Nekritz Beit Yosef had a very strong influence on me – they took God seriously and growth seriously.
>
> We had Talmud *shiur* a couple of times a day. Three days a week we had a *mussar* schmooze from the Rosh Yeshiva, which was

> more intellectual. The Mashgiah gave a more emotional schmooze. Rabbi Nekritz would talk *mussar* at the end of talmud *shiur*. He would also talk with me one-to-one, which included everything from diagnosis to *middot* development. The most powerful thing was seeing Rabbi Nekritz in action talking with his children and *talmidim*[3] and having personal conversations. Every night we had learning *B'hispailus* (fervent chanting) before *maariv* . . .
>
> [These were] remarkable human characters. They were not driven by *kavod* and were very sensitive to other people. They were mellow in terms of *middot* and not looking for pleasure in this world or praise.

This training served Rabbi Greenberg well as he went on to create new institutions and tried to move Orthodoxy and the broader Jewish community towards a positive, more generative encounter with modernity.

Conclusion

A high level of synthesis between Judaism and contemporary culture is needed as much today as fifty years ago when R. Greenberg first promoted this idea. As it was for R. Greenberg himself, *mussar* remains a potent tool for living this synthesis. The process of assimilation R. Greenberg observed gaining momentum during the 1960s has reached its full expression with 90 percent intermarriage rates in some cities. Nearly all Jews attend college and many assimilate to secular campus culture. Postmodern identity challenges any tribal loyalties that remain. Deep, internalized Jewish spirituality is needed to give those connected to Judaism the grounding and confidence to engage fully with the options out there. For those already fully assimilated into the general culture, *mussar* offers a point of connection that is deeply universal and also grounded in authentic Jewish spirituality. The Modern Orthodox community could use *mussar* particularly well, since most members of this community have high levels of Jewish knowledge and commitment, but often lack a deep sense of spirituality. Fortunately organizations like The *Mussar* Institute are creating the infrastructure

3. Students.

to support a broad engagement in *mussar* learning and practice across the denominational spectrum in North America.

It is my hope that Rabbi Greenberg will write more on *mussar*'s role in his life work and how *Mussar* learning and practice can be part of the realization of his vision of *tikkun olam and tikkun ha'adam.* With deeply internalized Judaism, a commitment to service, a vision of *tikkun olam,* and unshakeable inner confidence, we could actually fulfill our covenantal mission.

Modern Orthodoxy & Halakhah

Needed: Redemptive Halakhah: How Halakhah Must Transcend Itself

RABBI DR. NATHAN LOPES CARDOZO

IT SEEMS A CONTRADICTION IN TERMS that for a people who introduced arguably the greatest idea ever to appear in this world – monotheism – the Jews have produced few theologians.[1] And it is not by chance that those who may be defined as such have frequently found themselves at odds with the conventional Orthodox community. To mention only a few: Philo, Maimonides, Franz Rosenzweig, Abraham Joshua Heschel, and David Hartman – all clashed, to a greater or lesser degree, with mainstream Judaism.

This is not surprising. It is difficult for great minds to be confined by pre-existing criteria and patterns of thought. They will always glimpse broader horizons within sacred texts and ideas than their forerunners had the capacity or willingness to do.

Unconventional, radical, and innovative thinking is commonly found in the non-Jewish philosophical world. At times, it has profound consequences for the development of various legal systems, such that the ideological interpretations of the law deeply influence the practical outcome of a legal decision. The modern development of Orthodox *halakhah*, however, displays scant evidence of any major role played by philosophy, theology or ideology in the process of *halakhic* decision making.

1. This essay first appeared in *Conversations, The Journal of the Institute for Jewish Ideas and Ideals* (NY: September, 2015).

Practical *halakhah*, especially over the past hundred years, has been developed exclusively by great *halakhic* authorities; the influence of theologians and philosophers has been minimal at best. The latter are not part of the community of *halakhic* innovators. They deal with the non-*halakhic* aspects of Judaism, such as *emunah* (belief in God), *Torah min ha-shamayim* (the question of the divine authorship of the five books of Moses), and more. They might delve into the *philosophy* and *ideology* of *halakhah*, but this barely makes a dent in the practical application of *halakhah* itself.

Not that the *halakhists* overlooked theological issues; many responsa indicate that they did discuss these. But their philosophical ideas were incorporated only on a sporadic basis into their practical *halakhic* decisions. It is extremely rare to discover in a responsum a lengthy theological-ideological treatise intended to actually *answer halakhic* questions. Matters such as the divine need and purpose for creation, the meaning of life, or the concept of the chosen people and its mission scarcely enter the *halakhic* debate. The teachings of the Prophets are almost never quoted (*Hakham* Ben-Zion Uziel's responsa are exceptional, typically so). And even when such great talmudists as Rav Avraham Yitzhak Kook and Rabbi Joseph Dov Soloveitchik did discuss these matters or imbued new meaning in *halakhah*, they either left the practical *halakhah* as such untouched, or we find their philosophy of *halakhah* actually colliding with their practical *halakhah*. Far-reaching concepts found in *The Old Will be Renewed and the New Will be Sanctified* and *Catharsis* did not, for all intents and purposes, translate into practical *halakhah*.

In former times, one could find great *halakhists* such as Maimonides incorporating their philosophy in their *halakhic* rulings. With rare exception, today this is no longer the case. *Halakhah* is now often perceived as an independent edifice functioning according to its own rules, absolutely separated from matters of theology. One reason for this is that *halakhists* are no longer trained to think in terms of ideology and worldview. That *halakhah* is frequently treated as a system without a profound *Weltanschauung* is not only a tragedy but also a danger, inasmuch as it has been cut off from its very source and consequently has become detached from real life.

Due to all the above, the time has come for today's Jewish theologians to interfere in practical *halakhah* and no longer leave this to *halakhists*. They may not possess the knowledge and expertise that pure halakhists do, but they are armed with invaluable knowledge concerning the nature and ideological workings of the *halakhah* – knowledge that halakhists often lack. It is not that they know *less*, but that they know *differently*.

To a much greater extent than the *halakhists*, they understand how to read the *halakhah* via a philosophical and ideological lens. They are able to uncover the great ideas which gave birth to practical *halakhah*; and hence better equipped to recognize when *halakhah* no longer lives up to its ideological foundations. If *halakhic* ideology is forgotten or denied, the results may be the undermining and obstruction of *halakhah*, even though the latter is being presented as authentic. And is will be theologians, not the *halakhists*, who will become the guardians of our most precious treasure.

No doubt, different readings of the *Weltanschauung* of *halakhah* are possible, and these may result in divergent, and even opposing, decisions. But to deal with *halakhah* as if it has no *Weltanschauung* whatsoever is a major tragedy. The beauty of *halakhah* lies in its representing a magnificent outlook on life. The question of what that outlook entails is precisely what keeps it alive, as we can deduce from the Talmud's well-known teachings, "The Torah is no longer in Heaven," and "These and those are the words of the living God." It is this fact that marks out Judaism as unique.

Our teacher Rabbi Dr. Irving Greenberg is one of the prominent Jewish theologians of our time. He challenges us to reconsider many accepted notions in Judaism, dealing with the thorniest of topics, such as our relationship with God after the Holocaust and the breaking of the covenant between us. While he has not written specifically on practical *halakhah*, one can see in many of his essays how much this topic is in the back of his mind and how much he is disturbed by the fact that today's mainstream Orthodox *halakhah* is out of touch with a new world order and no longer responds to the many challenges of our days. Issues such as *infinite value*, *equality*, *uniqueness*, our relationship to non-Jews, the State of Israel and *tikkun olam* have substantial consequences for the development of *halakhah*. Theological halakhists may not always agree with his ideas but the issues Rabbi Greenberg touches on need to be part of the *halakhic* discourse and must be translated into practical *halakhah.* This will not happen overnight but we must make sure that over the years to come they will slowly find their way into *halakhah.* This is a major challenge and we better make sure we will live up to it.

Rabbi Greenberg's membership in the club of thinkers considered highly controversial in the Orthodox world only speaks to the excellence of his work. His boldness proves his integrity. Unless you enter the tiger's den you cannot take the cubs, say the Japanese.

In honor of Rabbi Greenberg, I offer herewith an essay on the topic of Judaism's *Weltanschauung* and the impact it ought to have on practical *halakhah.*

The Yayin Nesekh Incident

Some time ago I had a long talk with my only brother, Dr. Jacques Lopes Cardozo, two years my junior. We spoke about our early years, growing up in our parents' home in the Netherlands. Although we were children of a mixed marriage (Jewish father, non-Jewish mother), we took a keen interest in Judaism. Our father was a proud Jew, and our mother was raised in a strong Jewish cultural milieu in Amsterdam where she felt completely at home. If not for her "Jewishness," my father would probably not have married her. In fact, our mother was in many ways more Jewish than some members of my father's family who were *halakhically* Jewish but completely disconnected. I decided to do *giyur*[2] at the age of sixteen, and my mother followed suit many years later. After 27 years of married life our parents remarried, this time by the same rabbi who officiated at my wedding three months later. Both *ḥupot*[3] took place in the famous Esnoga, the Portuguese Synagogue in Amsterdam.

This put my brother in a strange position. From then on, all members of his immediate family were Jewish, and while he did not have the *halakhic* status of a Jew, he continued to feel Jewish. This was, to say the least, an atypical Jewish family.

During our conversation, my brother referred to a particular *Pesach*

2. See my essay, *Lonely but Not Alone: An Autobiography by a Jew Who Should Not Have Been, Conversations,* Spring 2013/5773, 1–35.

3. Weddings.

Seder that I conducted at our parents' home when I was about seventeen years old. An incident took place that profoundly shocked him and caused one of the most painful moments in his life. Fifty years later, with great emotion, and tears in his eyes, he told me that he had taken a bottle of kosher wine to pour for our many guests. He felt very much a part of the Jewish tradition and immersed himself in this religious experience, wanting to participate fully. After all, those who had left the bondage of Egypt that very night and would cross the Red Sea a few days later were also *his* ancestors! But instead of realizing my brother's enormous religious dedication to that experience, I snatched the wine bottle from his hands and told him he should not touch it since he was not Jewish, and that when a non-Jew touches the wine, according to Jewish law it could be cursed. The latter statement proved my complete ignorance. As a newcomer to Judaism, I had been told that the *halakhah* determines that non-Jews should not touch our wine, and I probably concluded that this meant the wine would be cursed. Our sources state nothing of the sort. The only thing indicated is that the wine is no longer permissible to drink.[4]

My brother froze, and then sat down without uttering a word.

Now a dental surgeon of fame and a man of great integrity, my brother told me that to this day he is deeply hurt by the incident and, although he forgave me for what I had done, he could not emotionally make peace with it. Not only because he considered himself to be very Jewish and could not imagine that this law would apply to *him*, but also because he could not believe that such a law would be part of this beautiful tradition called Judaism, which he dearly loved.[5] My gut feeling tells me that this incident played a huge role in his decision not to covert, though he came very close to doing so.

---

4. *Shulḥan Arukh Yoreh De'ah* 124:11; *Mishneh Torah, Hilkhot Asurot* 11:4.

5. Once my brother told me about this incident, I realized there are other laws as well that are very disturbing, such as *bishul akum* (the prohibition of eating food that was cooked by Gentiles), the saving of non-Jews on Shabbat, the institution of the "shabbes goy," and the prohibition of doing a favor for a non-Jew. This is not the place to discuss each one of them, but it will become clear to the reader that all of these laws, or customs, are the result of circumstances that prevailed in ancient times, and they should no longer apply today.

The Absence of the Problem

Although I studied for more than twelve years in *Hareidi* (Ultra-Orthodox) *yeshivot,* which are hardly, if at all, concerned with the non-Jewish world, I admit that I may be more sensitive than others about matters relating to non-Jews. After all, how could I not be? My own background, as well as my brother's situation, forces me to confront this issue on an almost daily basis.[6] At the same time, I am fully aware of the fact that more and more thinking religious Jews are becoming highly uncomfortable with this and similar laws and are asking why these rulings are necessary. What is it about non-Jews that makes their touching kosher wine forbidden for us to drink?

During the almost forty years I've lived in *Yerushalayim,* I have discussed this law with yeshiva students, both *Hareidi* and *Dati Leumi* (National Religious). Most of them were born in Israel and have had almost no exposure to non-Jews besides the Arab population. When I challenge them and ask whether they are uncomfortable with this law, and whether they feel that it is discriminatory and perhaps racist, they do not understand my question. Their argument is straightforward: Since according to Judaism non-Jews are secondary inhabitants of this world, and most if not all are anti-Semitic, they should definitely not touch our wine.

Moreover, it is their task to serve the Jews, and the law makes it clear who are the servants and who are the masters. When I tell them that billions of non-Jews around the world are living in countries where they never meet a Jew and therefore cannot serve Jews, their response is either complete silence or that these non-Jews have nothing to live for and are sadly unable to fulfill their mission on earth. When I press them further and ask whether they believe that God treats all His creatures fairly and whether His failure to allow these non-Jews to fulfill their mission would not highly compromise this belief, they are dumbfounded. Their astonishment increases when I explain that since there are so few

---

6. Human subjectivity is a major factor in *halakhic* decision making. See Dr. Aaron Kirschenbaum, *Subjectivity in Rabbinic Decision Making,* in *Rabbinic Authority and Personal Autonomy* by Moshe Z. Sokol, ed. (Northvale, NJ, London: Jason Aronson, 1992) 93–123.

Jews and there are billions of non-Jews, it would mean that every Jew would have a few thousand non-Jews as servants and that I wonder whether this would not be a little overdone! Moreover, doesn't our tradition teach us that one of the functions of the Jewish people is to aid gentiles and be concerned about their spiritual and physical welfare?[7]

The Awkward Halakhah

Surely some readers will argue that when I snatched the wine bottle from my brother's hand, I did the right thing *halakhically*. After all, this law appears in the *Shulhan Arukh*: One may not drink kosher wine that was handled by a non-Jew. This prohibition is called *issur yayin nesekh*[8] or, more accurately, *issur maga nochri* – loosely translated as the prohibition of using wine that has been handled by a non-Jew, meaning the bottle is not only touched but moved as well. The law applies only when the bottle has already been opened.[9]

The big question is: How did this law ever become a part of Judaism?

Looking into the history of this prohibition, we clearly see that the reason why the Sages forbade the drinking of wine after it was handled by a non-Jew is that most non-Jews of that time were idol worshippers. This worship is identified with evil and immoral behavior, not much different from that of the Nazis, or the terrorists of today. In fact, the same law applies to a wicked Jew; we are also forbidden to drink wine that *he* handled.[10]

---

7. It's true that certain sources, many of them kabbalisitic, seem to point out that non–Jews should serve the Jews, but such notions are much debated and not generally accepted. These beliefs may be the result of historical developments. When the Talmud states that gentiles will serve the Jews in the messianic age, it means they will do it voluntary, out of respect for the Jews, but not because it is their duty. See *Yeshayahu* 49: 22, 23; *Eruvin* 43b, Ben Yehoyada's commentary. See also Nathan Lopes Cardozo, "*On Jewish Identity and the Chosen People*," *Between Silence and Speech* (Northvale, NJ, London: Jason Aronson, 1995) 35–75.

8. *Halachic* category for wine that has been poured to an idol.

9. See *Shulḥan Arukh, Yoreh De'ah* 124:11. Wine that has merely been touched by a non-Jew is not prohibited. "*Maga*" means handling. Two actions have to take place: touch and movement. See *Yoreh De'ah*, ad loc. When the non-Jew touches the bottle without intent, the wine is permitted for the purpose of drinking. *Mishneh Torah, Hilkhot Asurot* 13:11; *Yoreh De'ah* 124: 7, 24.

10. The wicked Jew is foremost identified as a *mumar* (an apostate), one who de-

It is clear, then, that the motive for this prohibition was one of the great principles behind Judaism: *protest.* Protest against the kind of abomination that was an integral part of idol worship. The Sages wanted to ensure that Jews would never come close to this sort of behavior or to these kinds of people, and as a protest they forbade the drinking of wine that had been handled by them. It reminds me of the Dutch who after World War II refused to have anything to do with Germans, or even bring German-made products into their homes. It was taboo.

It is important to understand that the Sages were not so much concerned with idol worship per se. Had idolatry not led to such excessive abominations, they would most likely not have made such an exacting decree concerning wine. What really prompted them to issue these rulings were the accompanying loathsome and abhorrent acts, particularly gluttony and orgies.[11]

---

liberately rejects Judaism and violates its demands. Nowadays, many authorities are of the opinion that this term no longer applies, since it is not malice that motivates him but ignorance, as well as the lack of revealed Divine Providence, which would convince him of the Torah's truth. See *Chazon Ish* on *Yoreh De'ah Hilkhot Shechitah* 2:16, 28. See also Yaakov Ettlinger, *Responsa Binyan Tzion Ha-Hadashot,* no. 23; David Zvi Hoffman, *Responsa Melamed Leho'il,* no. 29; Rav Ovadia Yosef, *Yabi'a Omer,* vol. 1, *Yoreh De'ah* no. 11.

11. Some of my *halakhic* "opponents" may claim that I am overstating the case of wickedness and immorality as the reason for the law concerning *yayin nesekh,* while the only real reason is idol-worship and its libations. However, this seems to me incorrect. What really bothered the Torah and Sages about idol worship were the abominable, immoral acts that were inherent to paganism and their accompanying libations. Under those circumstances, ethical monotheism could never succeed and flourish. For a careful study of this topic, see Menachem Meiri (1249–1316, France), *Beit Ha-Behirah* on *Avodah Zarah,* 15b, 22a and 26a. Much literature has been published on the Meiri's understanding of the gentile world. See Dr. Marc Shapiro, *Islam and the Halakhah,* in *Judaism: A Quarterly Journal of Jewish Life and Thought,* vol. 42, no. 3, Summer 1993. See also Dr. David Berger, *Jews, Gentiles and the Modern Egalitarian Ethos: Some Tentative Thoughts,* in *Formulating Responses in an Egalitarian Age* by Marc D. Stern, ed. (Lanham, MD: Rowman and Littlefield, 2005) 83–108. Whether or not ongoing libations and immoral acts actually took place is a matter of dispute. See Sacha Stern, *Compulsive Libationers: Non-Jews and Wine in Early Rabbinic Sources,* in *Journal of Jewish Studies,* vol. 64, no. 1 (Spring 2013). See also *Sanhedrin* 63b.

Assimilation and the Stereotype

Yet another reason for this prohibition is that drinking wine with non-Jews increases familiarity, which could then lead to assimilation. It seems, though, that the proscription was more symbolic than practical, since other drinks, even alcoholic, are not included in this prohibition.[12] In the olden days, wine was by far the most popular alcoholic drink, and was used specifically in religious settings. The fact that a person could become intoxicated and lose control increased the possibility that boundaries between Jews and non-Jews would be blurred.[13] The Sages decided to apply this law only to bona fide wine, not to kosher wine that was pasteurized or cooked (known in *halakhic* literature as *yayin mevushal),*[14] because once wine was boiled[15] it was no longer used for idol worship and therefore no longer considered "real" wine.[16] The fact that the *berakhah "al pri ha-gefen"* is still recited over *yayin mevushal,* and it remains an alcoholic drink that could still lead to familiarity in social settings, clearly indicates that this law is mostly symbolic.[17]

While too much familiarity is still one of the primary causes of assimilation, one can hardly argue today that drinking wine plays any role in this unfortunate situation. Religious Jews would not marry non-Jews

12. It is most revealing that several early commentators on the Talmud were at one time not concerned about mixed marriages, since the non-Jews prohibited such marriages. See Ramban on *Avodah Zarah* 35b. See also *Encyclopedia Talmudit,* vol. 18, s.v. "Chatnut," 362–366.

13. There was some discussion about beer, which was also very popular in ancient times, but the Sages did not prohibit it probably because it was a life sustainer and safer than water! See *Encyclopedia Talmudit,* ibid.

14. Cooked wine.

15. See *Avodah Zarah* 29a. For a discussion on when wine is considered to be *yayin mevushal,* see RaN on *Avodah Zarah* 30a; *Yoreh De'ah* 123:3; Rabbi Moshe Feinstein, *Igrot Moshe Yoreh De'ah* 2:55 and 3:31.

16. On whether boiled wine is permitted for *Kiddush,* see *Shulḥan Arukh, Oraḥ Hayim,* 275:8.

17. For a general overview, see *Encyclopedia Talmudit,* vol. 24, s.v. "Yayin Shel Goyim," 330–498 and vol. 18, s.v. "Chatnut," 362–366. See also the following three works by Prof. Haym Soloveitchik: *Yeinam: Sachar Be-Yeinam Shel Goyim al Gilgulah shel Halakhah Ba'Olam Ha-ma'aseh* (Tel Aviv: Alma, 2003, Hebrew); *HaYayin BiMei HaBeinayim: Yayin Nesekh* [*Wine in Ashkenaz in the Middle Ages: Yayin Nesekh – A Study in the History of Halakhah*] (Jerusalem: Zalman Shazar Center for Jewish History, 2008, Hebrew); "Can Halakhic Texts Talk History?" *AJS Review,* vol. 3 (1978) 153–196.

even if they would drink wine with them, while those who run the chance of assimilating are the ones who don't care about this law. So what does this prohibition really accomplish? It would seem that its only claim is to remind us Jews of our special status.

Over the years, however, this law has taken on a life of its own. It has created a psychological condition among many religious Jews that exceeds by far what the Sages wanted to accomplish. Since the law was never officially abolished, it created an ontological view of non-Jews. No matter what their beliefs, non-Jews are by definition idol worshippers and depraved people. This is their nature, and they cannot escape it. This view on the part of many religious Jews is not conscious and deliberate, but it is deeply ingrained in the Jewish religious psyche. It points to a kind of Jungian archetype. What this means is that many religious Jews believe not only that the law concerning wine should not be changed but also that non-Jews are not meant to and are unable to change. After all, this law reflects Judaism's authentic view of non-Jews. In other words, there is nothing wrong with the Jewish tradition for still applying this law. On the contrary, there is something wrong with the non-Jewish world for changing and no longer fitting the description that the Jewish tradition attributes to them.

While all this may sound very foreign to those living in *hutz la'aretz* (diaspora), this view is widespread in Israeli religious communities, whether *Hareidi* or *Dati Leumi*, with few exceptions.[18]

This attitude is tragic and extremely dangerous. It completely contradicts one of the most important teachings of the Jewish tradition, that man – both Jew and gentile – can and must change. In fact, this belief is not only a misrepresentation of Judaism; it is the very antithesis of all that Judaism stands for. If non-Jews will always be looked upon as idol worshippers, no matter how far behind they have left that world, then Jews cannot be a light unto the nations, nor do they have anything to offer them. That would mean that Judaism was doomed to fail from the start.

18. I refer here to native Israelis, not to those who came on *aliyah* from Western countries.

Heilsgeschichte

To understand the danger of this unfortunate development, we need to take a broad look at Judaism and its vital mission. Several questions come to mind. Why does the world need a Jewish nation and what is its purpose? Why do the Jews need to be separate, and why is assimilation seen as one of the most destructive forces within Judaism throughout the ages?

What lies at the core of Judaism?

While many opinions prevail, there are some basic beliefs concerning the existence of the Jewish People and its mission. With perhaps the exception of Maimonides,[19] all the classic Jewish philosophers claim that the ultimate reason for Israel's existence is to be part of the unifying thread in a kind of *Heilsgeschichte* (redemptive history). Its purpose is to move humankind forward on its spiritual journey both to full recognition of God as the ultimate Master of all existence and to supreme ethical behavior. This noble role demands exemplary conduct on the part of the Jews. To fully understand this, we must realize that God is not merely the Creator and God of the universe but primarily the God Who is deeply involved in human history. God is not a philosophical idea advanced by Greek philosophers, totally separate from and beyond all human existence. He is an almost touchable Being Who dresses Himself in human emotions to make His point known to mankind:

> God appears to experience all the human emotions: love, anger, involvement, indignation, regret, sadness, and so on. By so doing, He gives the seal of divinity to the very essence of our humanity. He implicitly says to man: "You cannot know what is above and what is below, but you can know what is in your hearts and in the world. These feelings and reactions and emotions that make up human existence are, if illumined by faith and rationality, all the divinity you can hope for. To be humane is to be divine: as I am holy, so you shall be holy; as I am merciful, so you shall be

19. See David Hartman, *Israelis and the Jewish Tradition: An Ancient People Debating Its Future* (New Haven and London: Yale University Press, 2000).

> merciful." Thus, there is only one kind of knowledge that is open to man, the knowledge of God's humanity.[20]

God, then, becomes a specific and historic personality. He becomes a player in the history of man, together with all the players in the human race. This makes Him the most tragic figure in all of human history, because He cannot appear in His authentic form, which would require Him to be far beyond all human limitations and characteristics. Would He do so, He would be meaningless to mankind. He must appear in opposition to His very Self. Not as a philosophical idea beyond all human resemblance, but as a Redemptive God within history. This means that He had to become a God of compromise for the sake of man's limitations. Precisely for that reason He often fails in His ultimate goals. He *has* to fail so as to connect with man. His objective is to allow man to fail so that redemptive history becomes a reality. Nothing can be redeemed if all is perfect.

To achieve His goal, God requires a specific people who are destined to carry out the redemptive nature of history. Universal ideas cannot be relied upon, because they are impersonal, and what is impersonal is beyond history. Furthermore, an impersonal entity cannot carry a commitment, a moral assignment; for if *all* are committed to a particular mission, there is no one to be persuaded and therefore no mission to implement. Redemptive history then becomes impossible.

More important, however, is that the God of history can work only within time and space. This allows for a personal encounter with Him solely in the context of life and history. And only in that way can there be a mission of redemptive and God-centered history. It is through particularism that this universal mission can be accomplished.

And yet, those who are called on to carry out this mission must have an element of universality and eternity. They cannot be completely distinct, as that would lead them to becoming self-absorbed and unable to redeem and help mankind on its spiritual journey. So, paradoxically, this group must to some degree be a-historical. It must be unique and incapable of being sociologically or ethnologically categorized. It can-

20. Dr. Yochanan Muffs, "A Jewish View of God's Relation to the World," *The Personhood of God* (Woodstock, VT: Jewish Lights Publishing, 2009) 177.

not belong to a particular race, culture or even a conventional religious domination. Nor can it be a nation in the traditional sense of the word. It must transcend all these definitions and represent something that is a mystery, an anomaly and even a contradiction, so that it can stand at the center of history. Through its uniqueness, all of human history must be expressed. It has to carry the true history of mankind in a world that has an origin and a divine goal. This group of people, then, must identify with all of mankind while remaining separate.

Only "Israel" fits this description, for Israel is neither a race nor a nation nor a religion in the conventional sense. It violates all the criteria that "race," "nation," and "religion" stands for. Indeed, it is religion that determines its nationality, and it is nationality that determines its religion. It includes members of all races, and everyone can join to become a genuine child of Avraham and Sarah.

In addition, there is such a wide range of language, culture, and belief among Jews that no definition of these terms can accurately describe this unusual people. Yet the Jews do represent a surviving historic continuum, identifiable but consisting of constantly shifting groups.

Redemptive Halakhah

This perplexing notion of "redemptive history" stands at the very core of the mission of Jews and *halakhah*. For *halakhah* to be meaningful and eternal, it must be *redemptive halakhah*, constantly deriving its vitality and its guidelines from this notion. Redemptive history must move forward in order to be redemptive, and *halakhah* must therefore move with it. Once it has accomplished a certain goal, it must abandon the means by which it achieved this goal and move to the next stage of its redemptive goals. If, instead, it adheres to the means by which it achieved its goal, it undermines itself and becomes destructive. Instead of being redemptive, it becomes confining and harmful, turning progress into regression and reversing everything that it wants to achieve.

It is for this reason that the law of *yayin nesekh* is counter-productive. *Its objective has already been achieved.* It fulfilled its purpose and has become obsolete. As long as a good part of the non-Jewish world was deeply committed to idol worship and abominable acts, it was important and made a powerful point. But since by now, a large percentage of mankind has abandoned idol worship, is no longer dedicated to repugnant deeds, and has accepted values such as human rights, equity and equality, we can no longer ignore these developments and look the other way.

In fact, by continuing to observe this law, we deny that Judaism has had a powerful influence on our world. As a protest movement in the face of great evil, it has done extremely well. Many of its redemptive goals have been fulfilled. Franz Rosenzweig's thoughts on this subject have been right on the mark. He points out that it is not so much Judaism *itself* that is directly responsible for these achievements.[21] It required a more extroverted monotheistic religion to take on its ideals and expose them to the world. This, says Rosenzweig, is what Christianity did. With all its mistakes and anti-Semitic overtones, it paradoxically made monotheism into a powerful force throughout the world, and many Jewish values are now well known while conventional idol worship has ceased to exist. Rosenzweig adds that Judaism gave birth to Christianity for this *very* purpose, and Christianity can only fulfill its purpose if Israel is in its midst. It must take its inspiration from Israel. It cannot stand on its own feet. Christian philosopher and theologian Paul Tillich suggested that there would always be a need for Judaism because "it is the corrective against the paganism that goes along with Christianity."[22]

That is the reason why there is no point in continuing to observe a law that forbids non-Jews to touch our wine. To argue that idol worship is still alive and well and that there is still a lot of evil around is missing the point. First of all, it is questionable whether idol worship is indeed still around. Hinduism and Buddhism may well not fall into this category, and even if they would, they are definitely not prone to immorality and evil.[23] Secondly, evil behavior is no longer acceptable by any law-abiding society. This is the indirect result of Judaism's influence

---

21. Franz Rosenzweig, *Briefe* (Berlin: Schocken, 1935) 100. See also Jacob Agus, *Modern Philosophies of Judaism* (New York: Behrman's, 1941) 191–194.

22. Quoted by A. Roy Eckardt in *Christianity and the Children of Israel* (New York: Columbia University, 1948) 146–147.

23. See Alon Goshen-Gottstein and Eugene Korn, eds., *Jewish Theology and World Religions* (Oxford, Portland, Oregon: The Littman Library of Jewish Civilization, 2012) Part 3.

on civilization. In fact, Judaism introduced many other ethical laws that are not found in the Torah itself. Its redemptive qualities, which the law of *yayin nesekh* symbolizes, did the job. The same is true about assimilation, which is no longer affected by the law of *yayin nesekh*. Now that there are so many alcoholic drinks that are not forbidden after they've been touched by non-Jews, the law is meaningless. If anything, we should forbid non-Jews to touch whiskey, or beer. But to do so would be ineffective. If we want to fight assimilation, we need totally different strategies. That phenomenon has undergone a shift and it can be countered only by ideology. To believe that the law of *yayin nesekh* still has anything to do with assimilation is to bury one's head in the sand.

For Jews to remain separate, other strategies will have to be developed. It will require a novel attempt to stir a strong feeling of mission among our youth, combined with a very compelling ideology and education that would be irresistible. Paradoxically, as long as this law exists, it sends a message that the mission rooted in the concept of redemptive history is a fake, and an effective ideology cannot be developed. So the law, which should be building a strong, compelling Jewish identity, in fact does the reverse.

The Foundations for a New Halakhah

My position has been alluded to by several Sefardic *halakhic* authorities. As is well known, the famous Menachem Meiri (1249–1316, France) already stated his opinion that non-Jews are moral people who have left idol worship behind them. He therefore concluded that many discriminating Talmudic laws concerning non-Jews are no longer applicable. He was clearly a believer in redemptive *halakhah*. However, Meiri did not go so far as to abolish the law of *yayin nesekh*. The person who came closest to doing so was none other than the Remo (1520–1572), Rabbi Moshe Isserles, the foremost Ashkenazi sub-commentator on Rabbi Yosef Karo's *Shulḥan Arukh*. He brings a view that if a *ger toshav* (a non-Jewish resident) touches a bottle of wine, it is still permitted to drink that wine. Whether or not today's non-Jew, who is no longer an idol worshipper, fits the definition of a *ger toshav* is a matter of debate.[24]

24. See *Shulhan Arukh Yoreh De'ah* 124:2. See also Dr. Asher Ziv, ed., *Shu"t HaRama*

Another great *halakhic* authority who came very close to doing this was the eminent Rabbi Yosef Messas (1892–1974) from Algeria, Morocco, and later chief rabbi of Haifa. He was one of the most daring *halakhic* authorities of our days. Professor Marc Shapiro writes about Rabbi Messas: ". . . he defends drinking alcohol which contains wine that had been handled by Muslims. He quotes a responsum by an earlier Moroccan rabbi who even permitted drinking the wine itself – [Rabbi] Messas didn't go this far – and who had justified this decision as follows: 'There is no unity [of God] like the unity found in Islam; therefore, one who forbids them to handle [wine] turns holy into profane by regarding worshippers of God as worshippers of idols, God forbid.'"[25]

The Waiting Mode of Halakhah

The famous philosopher, Talmudist and *halakhic* expert Rabbi Eliezer Berkovits argues that over the last two thousand years *halakhah* has become increasingly defensive.[26] It has had to deal with aggressive anti-Semitism, as Judaism and Jews were constantly attacked in the Diaspora. Under those circumstances, rabbinical authorities built many walls between us and the gentiles. This was very understandable; it was the only way to survive. But it also meant that *halakhah* became

---

124, where Rabbi Moshe Isserles is *melamed zekhut* (judges favorably) those who drink wine produced by non-Jews.

25. See Rabbi Yosef Messas, *Otzar Ha-Michtavim* vol. 1, nos. 454, 462; *Shu"t Mayim Chayim* vol. 2, *Yoreh De'ah* no. 66. Rabbi Messas expresses a similar opinion concerning *bishul akum* (kosher food cooked by non-Jews). See Dr. Marc B. Shapiro, "Rabbi Joseph Messas," *Conversations – The Journal of the Institute for Jewish Ideas and Ideals*, Spring 2010/5770, 100–101. See also Rabbi Ovadiah Hadaya, *Responsa Yaskil Avdi*, vol. 1, *Yoreh De'ah*, No. 4. In his latest book, Dr. Shapiro states that in Italy religious Jews were used to drink non-Jewish wine and that great rabbis were among those who did or did not protest when others did. Rabbi Samuel Judah Katzenellenbogen of Venice (1521–97), a leading Italian halakhist of his time drank this wine himself. Another Italian halakhist, Rabbi Shabetai Be'er, 17th century, ruled that it is permissible to use non-Jewish wine for *kiddush* and *havdalah* but not for general consumption. See: *Changing the Immutable, How Orthodox Judaism Rewrites Its History*, (Oxford, Portland, Oregon The Littman Library of Jewish Civilization), 2015, 95–98.

26. Eliezer Berkovits, *Ha-Halakhah, Kocha V'Tafkida* (Jerusalem: Mossad HaRav Kook, 1981). A shortened English version is *Not in Heaven: The Nature and Function of Halakhah* (NY: Ktav Publishing House, 1984) ch. 4.

stagnant. It couldn't develop naturally because it had to constantly look over its shoulder to make sure that Jews wouldn't be affected by the non-Jewish world whose practices and ideologies might oppose Jewish ethical values. It had to ensure that in no way, neither directly nor indirectly, would Jews be influenced by or support non-Jewish idolatrous traditions and immoral acts. During all of these 2,000 years in exile, *halakhah* was forced into a waiting mode, in anticipation of redeeming itself when Jews would again return to their homeland and live in freedom.

While Rabbi Berkovits does not discuss the issue of *yayin nesekh*, it is clear that the law prohibiting it originated under these circumstances. It's a law that is based on fear.

But times have changed. The waiting mode has come to an end. *Halakhah*'s longtime dream, to liberate itself from its defensiveness and fear, is being fulfilled in our own days! The Jews' situation has drastically changed, specifically since the establishment of the state of Israel. We no longer have to be defensive, as we were in the ghettos. The state has given us our long-awaited independence. We run our own affairs and are no longer afraid of the anti-Semitic world. If attacked, we will strike back. And just as the Jewish state has freed the Jews from defenselessness by building a powerful army with tens of thousands of soldiers and the most sophisticated weaponry, which has made the Israeli army into the world's best, so must *halakhah* abandon its fear, take a courageous, assertive approach, and make a radical turnabout. Instead of fearing the corrupt influence of the non-Jewish world, we should now show ourselves and the world the enormous spiritual and moral power of Judaism. Instead of building high walls around us, we should create transparent partitions. It's time for the world to be awestruck by the power of Judaism. It's time for exposure, and the export of Jewish spirituality and ethics. The world needs it. The world is ready for it. Jews would find great meaning in religious Judaism, and non-Jews would be astonished and impressed. Assimilation will not come to an end by enacting laws rooted in fear and weakness, but by a *halakhic* ideology of strength and courage. Judaism has more than enough strength to face head-on the many negative powers that surround us and win the war. Yes, there will be victims, as we have in any Israeli war, but war can only be won if you take that risk, no matter how painful. Today's weak approach creates more victims, by far.

Rebellion

Even more important is the fact that all of this will have an immediate effect on our own youth. Judaism will be something people want to be part of. It will again become a mission to fight for and be proud of.

One of the great tasks of Jewish education is to *deliberately* create an atmosphere of rebellion among its students. Rebellion, after all, is the great emancipator. To paraphrase English writer Charles Caleb Colton (1780–1832): We owe almost all our knowledge and achievements not to those who agreed but to those who differed. It was this quality that brought Judaism into existence. Avraham was the first great rebel, destroying idols, and he was followed by his children, by Moshe, and by the Jewish people.

What has been entirely forgotten is that the Torah was the first rebellious text to appear in world history. Its purpose was to protest. It set in motion a rebellious movement of universal proportions second to none. The text includes all the heresies of the past, present and future. It calls idol worship an abomination, immorality a scandal, and the worship of man a catastrophe. It protests against complacency, imitation, and negation of the spirit. It calls for radical thinking and radical action, without compromise, even if it means standing alone and being condemned or ridiculed.

This reality seems lost on our religious establishment. We teach our students and children to obey, to fit in, to conform and not stand out. We teach them that their religious leaders are great people because they don't want to rock the boat. They would never think of disturbing the established religious or social norm. But these teachers don't realize that they are teaching a tradition of protest, and if they want to succeed they must communicate that message.

By using clichés instead of the language of opposition, we deny our students the excitement of being Jewish. Excitement, after all, comes from the knowledge that you make a difference, and you take pride in it, whatever the cost. It comes from being aware that you are part of a great mission for which you are prepared to die, knowing that it will make the world a better place.

When we tell our children to eat kosher, we need to tell them that this is an act of disobedience against self-indulgence, by which human beings are prepared to eat anything as long as it tastes good. When we go to synagogue, it is a protest against man's arrogance in thinking that he can do it all himself. When young couples are asked to observe the law of family purity, it is a rebellion against the obsession with sex. The celebration of Shabbat must be taught as an enormous challenge to our contemporary world, which believes that happiness depends on how much we can produce.

As long as our religious teachers continue to teach Jewish texts as models of approval, instead of manifestations of protest against the mediocrity of our world, we will lose more and more of our young people to that very mediocrity.

Judaism is in essence an act of dissent, not of consent. Dissent means renewal. It creates loyalty. It is the stuff that world growth is made of.

But all of this can be achieved only if we re-establish *halakhah* as an ideology and practice by which courage and determination will lead to great pride and a strong feeling of mission.

Purification and De-Codification

We must now make sure that *halakhah* can once again develop in its original, innovative way and come back to itself. We don't need to reform or update it. We need to simply take it back to the point where it had to turn against its own self because of our *galut* experience, and we must get it back on track. We have to cut off the many foreign branches that have for centuries concealed its ancient roots. It requires a purifying process so as to bring it to complete spiritual fulfillment.

Yes, it has to be done slowly, with great care, and in a way that doesn't harm the core. I haven't the slightest doubt that we'll discover a beautiful canvas with many diverse but harmonious colors that will deeply impress our fellow Jews and make Judaism irresistible.

To achieve this goal, we have to de-codify Jewish law and dispense with the official codes of law by which Judaism was able to survive in past centuries. Codification stagnates.[27] While it was necessary in order to overcome the enormous challenges of exile, it has now become an obstacle, outdated and unhealthy, which to a great extent blocks the natural development of *halakhah*. Jewish law must move and grow, taking into account various developments in our world and giving them guidance. And that can happen only if it is fluid and allows for a great amount of flexibility, which codification cannot offer. Certainly, some conformity is necessary, such as in the case of civil law, but unlike non-Jewish codifications, Jewish law is foremost a religious and spiritual tradition. As such, it can never be translated into immutable rules to be applied at all times, under all conditions, and for everyone, without considering the personal, religious and practical components. These elements vary drastically, as can be seen by the many differing and even opposing opinions in the Talmud, which the Sages were not only aware of but seem to have actually encouraged.[28]

Prophetic and New Age Halakhah

What we need now is *prophetic,* new age *halakhah,* dedicated to the great, authentic, ethical mission of the Jewish people as conveyed by the prophets, and combined with the demands of the Torah. The prophets preached a rare combination of particularism and universalism. They strongly advocated Jewish particularism, so as to keep the Jews separated from the rest of the nations. But they always viewed this in terms of universalism.[29] There was a need for a central driving force, full of spiritual and moral energy, that would enable the Jews to inspire all of mankind and be "a light unto the nations," conveying the oneness of God and the significance of justice.

---

27. See Rabbi Shlomo Luria (Maharshal), *Yam Shel Shlomo*, introduction to *Bava Kama* and *Hulin*; Rabbi Yehudah Löw ben Betzalel (Maharal), *Netivot Olam* 16, end; Rabbi Chaim ben Betzalel, *Vikuach Mayim Chaim*, 7. See also my essay *On the Nature and Future of Halakhah in Relation to Autonomous Religiosity* in Conversations – *The Journal of the Institute for Jewish Ideas and Ideals*, Spring, 2010/5770, 66–82.

28. See *Eruvin* 13b.

29. See, for example, Shemot 19:5–6; Yeshayahu 42:6. See my book Between Silence and Speech: Essays on Jewish Thought (Northvale, NJ and London: Jason Aronson, 1995) chapters 3 and 5.

We must continue to be different and marry only among ourselves, or with those who have joined our people. We should make our own wines and not drink those produced by our Gentile friends, because wine is a sacred drink that needs to be sanctified by the beliefs of different religious communities. I would even suggest that each monotheistic religion produce its own wine, since it is not the liquid itself that is sacred but the winemaker's intentions that have suffused the wine.

It is nonsensical to believe that the world would be a better place if all differences would be eliminated. Distinctiveness is a most important aspect of our society. It gives it color and allows people to belong. But it should not lead to a form of separation, which serves no real goal and is the outgrowth of something that was meant for a different time.

Should the law of *yayin nesekh* be abolished altogether? Definitely not! We should not drink kosher wine that has been handled by anti-Semites, terrorists, rapists, financial swindlers, men who refuse to grant divorces to their wives, self-hating Jews, and the like.

After all, the purpose of the law is to protest, not to discriminate.

It is high time that the rabbis consider revisiting this ancient law and adapting it to our new reality.

My brother would agree.

Halakhah as an Ethic of Power: Yitz Greenberg and the War in Vietnam

Rabbi Dr. Joshua Feigelson

In the mid-to-late 1960s, Rabbi Yitz Greenberg was at the center of a cultural debate at Yeshiva University (YU) about how to be an American Orthodox Jew, and how to be an American Orthodox Jewish community. At the heart of that debate were competing understandings of *halakhah,* which were rooted in diverging views of the dangers and possibilities of experiencing a relationship with the Divine in historical terms. Rabbi Joseph Soloveitchik and the majority of people at YU understood *halakhah* as philosophical, idealized, and formal. For Greenberg, *halakhah* was historical, material, and dynamic.

In this chapter, I explore how Greenberg evolved from a cautious, if critical, position on the Vietnam War in 1966 to become an outspoken critic and anti-war demonstrator by 1969, and ultimately an articulate representative of anti-war clergy to the Senate Foreign Relations committee in 1970. I will explain how the articulation of his notion of *halakhah* evolved in tandem with his evolution on the war. In particular, I will examine how Greenberg understood *halakhah* to involve and suggest an ethics of exercising political and military power, rooted in the biblical notion of human beings created in God's image. I will also show how Greenberg applied this ethic to power structures in institutions and communities both religious and secular, and used it to blur the distinction between them.

Greenberg at the Synagogue Council of America Conference on Vietnam (1966)

Greenberg's first public statements on Vietnam came in February 1966 at a conference under the auspices of the interdenominational Synagogue Council of America, held at Columbia University. During the early 1960s, Orthodox participation in the SCA became increasingly fraught with Haredi rabbis castigating YU President Samuel Belkin, Soloveitchik and their Modern Orthodox followers over their cooperation, through the SCA, with non-Orthodox rabbis on matters of social policy, arguing that even acknowledging Reform and Conservative rabbis granted their views legitimacy. The YU-oriented rabbis disagreed, as they saw cooperation with their non-Orthodox colleagues as an important activity in representing a unified Jewish community to the non-Jewish world. In 1961, the Union of Orthodox Jewish Congregations debated whether to continue in the SCA, and decided overwhelmingly (74–16) to do so. But the dissension would fester and grow over the decade; Greenberg's remarks need to be understood against this backdrop.

While Reform rabbis, who historically had been instrumental in founding the SCA, continued to be outspoken defenders of liberal positions on civil rights and against the Vietnam War, interdenominational and interfaith cooperation became much more attenuated within YU Orthodoxy as the Orthodox community generally became more politically conservative. These shifts reflected the dissolution of "a liberal political consensus, one that once united much of the Jewish community and pointed to particular policy positions." As we will see, Vietnam, in particular, would prove a source of deep division.

The 1966 SCA conference was intended to explore "the conflict in Vietnam, and the overall relevance of religion to the search for world peace." A month earlier, the council had issued a policy statement calling on the Johnson administration to resist pressure to escalate military involvement. Greenberg was one of a number of speakers representing the various denominations as well as relevant scholarly disciplines.

At the time of the conference, the majority of Americans still supported the administration's policy of escalation. Criticism of the administration was still confined to a growing, but minority, group on the political left, mostly on university campuses such as the University of Michigan and the University of California, Berkeley. The tenor of the SCA conference and its statement put it clearly on the liberal side. Among the presenters, prominent Reform congregational Rabbi Arthur Lelyveld of Cleveland was the staunchest in calling for America to "desist" from its activity in what was clearly a civil war. Lelyveld had been a conscientious objector during World War II, and achieved notoriety for his work in the Civil Rights movement, including suffering a concussion at the hands of segregationists while registering voters in Mississippi during Freedom Summer in 1964. "The majority of the population of South Vietnam support the [Communist] National Liberation Front," he claimed, and thus the United States had no business sending troops there. Seymour Siegel, a young rabbi-professor of Jewish Thought at the Conservative movement's Jewish Theological Seminary, presented a more moderate position, calling for the United States to hold the conflict "within controllable bounds" while "actively and sacrificially seeking means to terminate the conflict." The Jewish Telegraphic Agency reported that the outcome of the conference was a consensus that cessation of conflict and "an intensive peace effort" should be American policy.

Though the SCA included the Orthodox Rabbinical Council of America as one of its constituent members, and despite the participation of other Orthodox rabbis besides Greenberg, the Orthodox community as a whole still followed the conservative attitude of the general public. The Orthodox participants in the conference were, thus, outliers in their own community. Reflecting this, the more conservative Rabbinical Alliance of America (perhaps better known in Orthodox circles by its Hebrew name, *Iggud HaRabbonim*) issued its own statement in the form of a letter to President Johnson conveying its support of the administration's policy. "The Rabbinical Alliance deplores the rash of critical statements being issued against the Government in the name of religion and morality," they wrote. "These declarations are detrimental to the security of these blessed United States, and are inimical to the best interest of our beloved country."

The gap between the academic and intellectual community, which was overwhelmingly against the war, and his own Orthodox community, which was for it, seemed to create some pressure for Greenberg, as he was both a university academic and an Orthodox rabbi. "It is my impression . . . that the bulk of the Orthodox Jewish community backs President Johnson's policy," he observed in his remarks at the conference. "I fear that this support may well reflect its relative lack of cultural and political sophistication or its tendency to render unto Caesar that which is Caesar's, rather than an analysis of the situation – but this does not change the fact of its attitude." Greenberg thus distanced himself from Orthodoxy, saying that he could not claim to speak as its representative, "but rather as one who speaks from within the framework of the classic Jewish position." This preamble to Greenberg's remarks on Vietnam reflected an early acknowledgment of his position within the community and at YU – a position at odds with the prevailing attitude.

Nevertheless, Greenberg was no pacifist. "Judaism seeks peace but does not exclude the possibility of war," he said. "War is a possible or even necessary instrument of policy under certain circumstances." How was one to tell whether a given war was necessary? "Judaism seeks utopian goals – such as peace – but its method is *halakhah*. It is the essence of *halakhah* that it seeks to realize broad absolutes – even divine ones – only in the concrete specificity of human situations." Notably, Greenberg spoke in the language of *halakhah*. In this particular formulation, he did not diverge from Soloveitchik, who likewise taught that *halakhah* was an attempt to enact timeless ideals in specific, real-world situations. In the particular setting of an inter-denominational rabbinic conference, Greenberg's embrace of *halakhah* as an operative category reflected the reality that he had more in common with Soloveitchik and Orthodoxy than he diverged from them, at least in comparison with avowedly non-*halakhic* ideologies like that of the Reform movement.

Greenberg entitled his talk "Judaism and the Dilemmas of War – An Essay in *Halakhic* Methodology." The body of his remarks were devoted to a review of Maimonides's legal distinction between "war as a possible response," or *milhemet reshut*, and "war as an appropriate or necessary response," *milhemet mitzvah* or *milhemet hova*. Whereas in later years Greenberg's writings on power would largely draw on biblical references, which would be more accessible to Christians and non-Orthodox Jews, in this talk he referred to rabbinic and later Jewish legal sources, including *Tosafot*, the twelfth century Talmudic commentaries, and the *midrash* Genesis Rabba, that would have been generally familiar to educated Orthodox Jews and some non-Orthodox rabbis, but foreign to non-Orthodox laity and many of their rabbinic and scholarly leaders. In this setting, an inter-denominational conference, the likely effect was to establish Greenberg as a genuine voice of Orthodoxy, making a claim to authenticity – "the classic Jewish position," as he put it – particularly in the eyes of the non-Orthodox rabbis who were present.

Greenberg began to articulate his policy recommendation by first claiming the political realm as terrain for clergy. The "search for the relevance of god's [sic] word," he said, "bespeaks a new vitality and earnestness in those who witness to God's address to man." Here Greenberg was speaking to his own Orthodox community, which not only supported Johnson's policy but seemed culturally averse to its rabbis engaging in political activity. Just the previous week, Greenberg had debated Abraham Hecht, president of the Rabbinic Alliance, at a meeting of the men's club of Shaaray Tefilla synagogue in Far Rockaway, New York, on the question, "Should Orthodox leaders speak out on controversial issues?" moderated by the synagogue's Rabbi Emanuel Rackman. Greenberg argued yes, and that "we need trained people to do it." Hecht disagreed, saying "there are laws that govern all and eventually they will have to be obeyed so there is no need for discussions."

Nevertheless, in arguing for clergy to speak out at the SCA conference, Greenberg cautioned they "should eschew sweeping moralisms." Clergy should make "informed judgments" about political issues, not offer impulsive reactions. "Because the liberal protest on civil rights was correct, it does not automatically follow that it is right – or has the whole truth – in Vietnam," he said. It could be that Ho Chi Minh's brand of Communism was just cause for American military intervention. "In some of its aggressive forms, Communism is not just another political or social order, but a basic denial of human dignity which seeks to cut men off from the ground of their spiritual source," he said. "The crucial judgment," which Greenberg argued was modeled by Jewish law, "is whether the National Liberation Front or Ho Chi Minh is such a form." If North Vietnam were found, upon close inspection, to be this kind of dignity-denying political entity, then according to Greenberg, the war would be justified. If it were found to be something less, then the war would be unjustified, and clergy should lead the opposition. But here, in February 1966, Greenberg expressed genuine doubt about the answer, and intoned that "religious groups should bend all their efforts to a full airing of these issues. Clergy concerned about Vietnam should be less coy in demanding this review and, at the same time, should be less fellow traveling with secular liberals, and should present at their meetings, in all their force, *both* opposing political viewpoints."

Greenberg also challenged those to his right. "Even if the war is found to be justified," he said, "we must be open to the elements of evil in such a necessary judgment and seek to minimize them." Greenberg reminded his audience that, in the real world, they could not demand moral purity. At the same time, all could agree that minimizing civilian casualties was the right course. Here he offered not only concern for the poor – "After all, the agony of Vietnamese peasantry calls to us" – but an understated evocation of what would become one of his signature phrases about the Holocaust: "Who more than Jews should be shattered by the sight of burnt children?"

In this picture of Greenberg in 1966, we see a rabbi-professor not yet 33 years old, working simultaneously to be careful and forceful, thoughtful and critical, a representative of Orthodoxy critiquing both his own community and communities beyond. We see him adopting – not yet challenging – the *halakhic* formalism of Soloveitchik and applying it to a pressing political challenge. *Halakhah* was a model, Greenberg argued, because it "refused to abandon the secular by setting forth absolute claims or policy statements which are so above the operating standards of the world that responsible and irresponsible statesmen alike can ignore them as out of the realm of plausibility." By doing so, "Halacha was able to change society – not denounce it." Greenberg did not see himself as a revolutionary. He believed in the possibility of positive change without a major political or social rupture.

The Anti-War Movement Reaches YU (1969)

Over the next three years, however, the situation changed. The United States continued its troop buildup, and by 1967, a half-million American troops were in Vietnam. As the war escalated, the anti-war movement gained strength, drawing much of its energy from university faculty, and their students who were subject to the military draft. As noted above, the Orthodox community generally supported Johnson, and, later, Nixon. At YU, the lack of major protests was undoubtedly related to the requirement that YU students be dually-enrolled in seminary courses, which meant that every male undergraduate at YU qualified for a draft exemption. When over six thousand faculty who signed a multi-page ad in the *New York Times* in March 1967 under the banner of the Inter-University Committee for Debate on Foreign Policy calling for an immediate cease-fire and withdrawal, thirty YU professors signed. But none taught in the rabbinical school and only a handful taught in Yeshiva College. Greenberg was not among the signatories.

The Tet Offensive of early 1968 shocked many Americans who had previously been assured that the North Vietnamese were incapable of winning the war. By 1969, the student protest movement made substantive inroads at YU, as anti-war students, with Greenberg's active encouragement, succeeded in getting the university to participate in a nationwide teaching moratorium on October 15. While only secular studies courses, held in the afternoon, were cancelled, even during morning religious courses "the atmosphere of Moratorium Day was evident." Enacting Soloveitchik's vision of *Torah u-Maddah,* many of the rabbis used their classes that morning to discuss "the *halakhic* overtones of American involvement in the war." A generational divide appeared, as "a great majority" of students seemed to want disengagement, while among the faculty – at least those who spoke in the morning – there were more supporters of continued American involvement, particularly on the basis of commitment to Israel: Like South Vietnam, Israel was an American ally, and if the Vietnamese could be abandoned by the United States, then Israel could be as well. Greenberg was evidently unpersuaded by such arguments, as he was the concluding speaker at a better-attended rally in the afternoon – that is, during hours when secular studies courses normally occurred – organized by the Yeshiva College Student Council, at which faculty were clearly against the war. Greenberg called on "American Jews to actively voice opinion against any further needless sacrifice of lives."

It is difficult to pinpoint what led Greenberg to change his position from 1966 to 1969, though it would seem he was like many others at the time whose thinking evolved as the war escalated. Greenberg was an increasingly active participant in interfaith and interdenominational dialogues during these years, and these encounters led to developments in his theology and thinking about *halakhah*. It is certainly plausible that his more frequent contacts with non-Orthodox and non-Jewish – and generally liberal – interlocutors had an influence on him. It could also be that Greenberg's Vietnam activism coincided with his increasing activism on behalf of other causes beyond the parochial concerns of the Jewish, and particularly the Orthodox, community. Greenberg was an activist in the early 1960s – not in the Civil Rights movement, but in the nascent movement to assist the emigration of dissident Soviet Jews. As early as 1961, during his Jerusalem sabbatical, Greenberg became involved with Yaakov Birnbaum, an English activist who, with Greenberg's aid, moved to Washington Heights in 1963 to establish an activist base in and around YU. Over the next decade, Greenberg would be a prominent public activist rabbi on behalf of the Soviet Jewry movement, joining in rallies, demonstrations, and protests. Thus, we can surmise that Greenberg's evolution from cautious critic to outspoken protestor from the mid- to late-1960s tracked with the evolution of his identity beyond the Orthodox community.

Whatever his motivations, Greenberg embraced the role of anti-war activist rabbi-professor. In November 1969, a month after the Moratorium Day rally, Greenberg accompanied a group of thirty-five YU students as they traveled to Washington, DC for a major anti-war rally that drew a quarter-million marchers to the national mall. There they joined Jewish students from other universities, representing a wide array of Jewish backgrounds, who organized at the Jewish Movement Center, staffed by the National Jewish Organizing Project, a confederation of Jewish activist groups. As Joseph Telushkin, a YU undergraduate and participant in the group, wrote, for the YU students, their encounter with the general protest movement, and with the other Jewish protesters, was formative. Since the rally was scheduled for Saturday, the students had to make accommodations for Shabbat, including finding kosher food and a Torah scroll for services. When they marched to the White House on Saturday morning, they carried no placards and accepted no pamphlets, as there was no *eruv* in Washington at the time that would enable carrying on Shabbat according to *halakhah*. They had to explain why. As they did, and as they sang Hebrew songs of peace, they drew admiring comments from the others in attendance. "It's great to have you here," one girl said, "to know you people care too."

And the effect not only touched the Orthodox protesters; it also reached the non-Orthodox Jews marching that weekend. As one of them wrote, the event "showed them that there is a very real alternative to the kind of Judaism they had known from their parents." In place of what they viewed as their parents' bland, suburbanized Judaism that emphasized the empty performance of ritual, the Orthodox students showed them that a ritually-thick, embodied Jewish practice could be a force that expressed their deepest moral and political commitments.

For Greenberg, this was an enactment of the kind of *halakhic* engagement in American life he had espoused in his writing and teaching throughout the decade. Here were Orthodox Jews living out a public commitment to *halakhah,* and showing both non-Orthodox Jews and Americans at-large that *halakhah* could be a moral force on the street, a model for American political and ethical life. The religious was not confined to the private sphere, but brought its voice into the public square. Greenberg and the student protesters thus embodied, in a literal sense, the overlapping domains of secular and religious, public and private.

Reflecting on the events in his *Commentator* column, Telushkin remarked on Greenberg's influence. Describing it as "the most beautiful *Shabbat* I can remember," Telushkin observed that "I, at least temporarily, synthesized the values most significant to me." Telushkin found that the participation of YU students alongside their non-Orthodox Jewish counterparts to be tremendously significant:

> As Irving Greenberg (who spent the weekend with us, and gave it *ruchniyut*, a pervasive spirituality it would otherwise have lacked) suggested, these people are telling us something. Right now Orthodoxy is not an option to them, for they view Orthodox Jews as being generally morally insensitive people, caught up in private concerns that are irrelevant to the students' world. Their deepest concerns, they feel, are ignored by us. But when Orthodox Jews tangibly show them that they share their moral concerns, that suffering touches them equally, then they'll regard Orthodoxy as a possible approach to life, something that can at least be considered without involving one in moral compromise. And then, if we can show a superior family life, a finer communal life, a greater ability to satisfy the existential problems of modern man (that is,

> that laws between man and God have practical ramifications) they might be willing to adopt it as a way of life.

The general attitude among Orthodox Jews, Telushkin observed, was to reject non-Orthodox Jews. Yet, Telushkin found that after the march experience this attitude was wrong. The protesters he had encountered were "often more advanced than we are in their concepts of *Tzelem Elokim.*"[1] The non-Orthodox protesters were "performing religious acts in a non-religious context, to a large extent because they feel that the religious context excludes the possibility of moral concern." The YU students, and Orthodoxy in general, thus had an opportunity to show non-Orthodox Jews that *halakhah* could, in fact, respond to the things that mattered to them.

It is important to note here how the self-image of the YU students participating in the anti-war rally was inflected by their encounter with people beyond their own community – something Greenberg likely highlighted in his Shabbat talks with the students. In the context of relationship, the YU students were forced to explain themselves, to generate a narrative, in a way they had not previously done. They had to articulate why they observed the *halakhah* that prohibited carrying objects in the public domain on Shabbat, or the *halakhah* that required them to eat only kosher food. And in the same breath, they had to explain why, as Jews who experienced their lives as bound by *halakhah*, they were in Washington, protesting the war. In the act of encounter, the students articulated and experienced a discourse of *halakhah* that was not only legally restrictive, but morally expansive.

Yet like Telushkin, Greenberg was on the outspoken fringe of the YU community, at this point – an energetic voice of conscience, but one that ultimately made little impact within the YU community itself, a result of a number of factors. The comparison of Israel to South Vietnam was a compelling one for many in the YU community. The official Haredi leadership continued to support Nixon, and the culture at YU increasingly seemed inclined to follow the lead of the ultra-Orthodox rabbinate on matters of social policy. But where Greenberg's views failed to capture the imagination of many in the Orthodox community,

1. The Jewish theology that all human beings are created in the image of God.

they would ultimately take root beyond the community of Orthodox Jews, as the non-Orthodox students of the late 1960s became the adult leaders of synagogues, Jewish federations, and Jewish philanthropies in the 1970s and 80s. The encounter between the YU students and the non-Orthodox students at the 1969 rally would provide a template for Greenberg in the years to come: representing his activist brand of Orthodoxy to non-Orthodox Jews who were thirsty for an approach to Jewish life that allowed them to live in a thick relationship with Jewish tradition and participate whole-heartedly in public life.

Speaking *Halakhah* to Power: Greenberg's Testimony to the Senate Foreign Relations Committee (1970)

Six months after the anti-war rally, Greenberg was back in Washington, this time to testify to the Senate Foreign Relations committee, at a hearing on May 7, 1970, entitled "Moral and Military Aspects of the War in Southeast Asia." By this time, Sen. J. William Fulbright, the committee chair, was the leading critic of American war policy. In 1966, and again beginning in 1969, Fulbright's committee held regular hearings at which opponents of the war, ranging from businessmen to returning soldiers, voiced their critique of the continuing military campaign. At the May 7th hearing, Fulbright's committee invited three clergymen to speak: one Protestant, one Catholic, and one Jew. The Christian representatives had distinguished resumes: John C. Bennett, the Protestant, had been president of Union Theological Seminary in New York since 1964, and was a leading figure in the anti-war movement; Bishop John J. Dougherty, the vice chair for international affairs of the U.S. Catholic Conference, had recently stepped down as president of Seton Hall University. By contrast, the Jews were represented not by a gray-haired institutional leader, but by 36-year-old Irving Greenberg.

That Greenberg was the Jewish representative at the hearing was both surprising and unsurprising. One might have expected a figure like Abraham Joshua Heschel, the white-maned philosopher-theologian of the Jewish Theological Seminary, to speak, as he was a leading voice in the anti-war movement, on par with Bennett and Martin Luther King. Heschel was recuperating from a heart attack during the early months of 1970, and was likely unavailable to testify. Whatever the reason, it was Greenberg who spoke before the Fulbright Committee. By 1970, Greenberg had already begun working beyond the Orthodox community, traveling the country to speak at synagogues, Jewish education conferences, and interfaith gatherings, and receiving regular press coverage in both Jewish and general circulation papers. He was developing a reputation among both his liberal Orthodox constituency and, increasingly, among non-Orthodox Jews as "a brilliant young professor,"[2] "who has been making a name for himself with proposals for a fresh new look"[3] at Jewish life. For him to be cast alongside Christian clergy-scholars at a Senate hearing was thus not wholly unexpected, but nevertheless unusual.

By the time of Greenberg's appearance before the committee, Johnson had been forced not to seek re-election under pressure from anti-war supporters of Eugene McCarthy and Robert F. Kennedy, and Richard Nixon had been elected President. The 1968 Democratic convention in Chicago, as well as numerous protests, laid bare the deep divisions in the country. The student protest movement had succeeded in changing public opinion, and the country was now closely divided between supporters and opponents of continued military action. In the days immediately preceding the May 7th hearing, Nixon announced a new strategy of bombing Cambodia, which had provided safe haven for Viet Cong forces. And on May 4th, National Guard troops shot and killed student demonstrators at Kent State University.

Greenberg's statement, and the subsequent question-and-answer session with members of the committee, articulated many of the key themes of Greenberg's teaching. First among these was the idea of human beings created in God's image to support a notion of inherent human dignity – particularly on behalf of Vietnamese civilians – and the related power of media to shape the way people honored or diminished the Image of God in the world. Additionally, Greenberg offered a significant early articulation of what he would later come to call "holy secularity," inverting accepted understandings of the categories of holy and secular by telling government officials that they had a duty to see

2. Ann Robinson, "On the Go," *Jewish Standard*, March 25, 1966.

3. "Orthodox Refusing to Leave Ghetto, Says Yeshiva Prof.," *National Jewish Post and Opinion*, June 10, 1966.

themselves as moral exemplars. And he rooted this argument in an ethic of power and agency developed out of his understanding of *halakhah*, along the lines we have explored until now: that *halakhah* provided a blueprint for how citizens in a liberal democracy could and should understand political power. I will explore each of these dimensions in turn, and then step back to analyze the broader ways in which this moment reflected some important inversions to received understandings of religion and secularism in both American Jewish Orthodoxy and American public life.

The last of the three clergy to speak, Greenberg began his remarks by reflecting on the role of mass media in creating the cultural climate. The amplification and reverberation of the images of the war through broadcast media were creating a "moral disaster," Greenberg said. The Vietnamese became dehumanized in the eyes of Americans, Vietnamese soldiers and civilians were not seen as images of God, and therefore God's presence in the world was diminished. Massive aerial bombardments, the use of napalm, and the continued futility of the war effort – all of these combined to desensitize American soldiers and civilians alike to "the human qualities of the enemy," and the innocent civilians being killed in such great numbers. "Every image of prisoners pushed out of a helicopter, or children napalmed, becomes a hideous moral example," he said.

In a society dominated by images broadcast on television, projected on film, and printed in newspapers, political leaders were powerful agents in generating a national moral sensibility. "Public life is the primary moral example in the United States today," he said. The messages conveyed through media "are perceived by everyone and learned environmentally, which means they are more likely picked up, internalized, and influence the actions and standards of everyone." In light of the enormous power of media, it was not only clergy, but even more so government officials, who would shape American cultural values. "All the sermons and classes in America reach a fraction of the people reached by one action of the U.S. Army or one speech of the President," he said. Greenberg pressed this point throughout his testimony, complicating the neat separation between political leaders and voices of conscience. Political leaders were moral pedagogues, and by the same token moral and religious leaders were also political figures. While their respective primary areas of expertise would remain distinct, Greenberg suggested a significant blurring of boundaries: clergy (including, he argued to his own community, Orthodox rabbis) had a duty to act politically, and political figures had a duty to act morally.

Building on this, Greenberg told the senators that the country's leaders, like all human beings, needed to recognize their wrongs and admit their errors. By way of explaining his own evolution, Greenberg argued that in the early to mid-1960s, there were good reasons to believe that intervention in Vietnam was not only strategically correct, but morally right. "There was a phase," he said, "in which we saw communist China, then in its commune period which seemed to deny the elemental dignity of man," and North Vietnam as its satellite. Evoking his own ambivalence about the war four years earlier, he observed, "In this phase the fear of another Munich and the conviction that we dare not sell out or be indifferent lest World War II repeat itself colored the judgment of many." But when those assumptions were revealed to be false, Americans should have heeded the example of the Biblical King David, who "could recognize and confess his errors and in most powerful contrition turn from his ways and redress injustice." The Johnson and Nixon administrations had done precisely the opposite, continually escalating the conflict on the assumption that one more battle, one more bombardment, would bring capitulation. The inability to admit error out of a misguided sense of pride was the ultimate failure of moral leadership and a perversion of the ethics of power that underlay both Judaism and Christianity. Connecting the theme of leadership with the concept of the Image of God, Greenberg said the "inability to accept the tragic, the ironic, the possibility of mistake and failure, is to be less than fully human. Perhaps this is our national problem."

It should be emphasized that none of these critiques were original. Liberal clergy had been voicing them for years. But the significance of Greenberg's testimony lies not so much in the originality of his comments, as in the fact that he was offering them from a Jewish perspective, one which he understood and presented as rooted in a traditional, rather than radically new, understanding of Judaism, and particularly an *halakhic* understanding rather than Heschel's prophetic one. As in the anti-war rally and march the previous November, Greenberg's Senate testimony provided an occasion for him to show, to himself, to

YU, and to the world, that the Jewish legal tradition could be applied to the most pressing political problems in the present, that *halakhah* was up to the task of modernity. Where Orthodox rabbis had testified before government officials in the past, these testimonies were about and for the sake of intra-communal issues, particularly the effects of government regulation on the kosher food industry. With his testimony to the Foreign Relations Committee, Greenberg was applying *halakhah* to current American problems for the sake of America, not only for the sake of the Jewish community.

And yet, as much as he conceived of himself as simply applying the *halakhic* tradition to the present, there was nothing simple about that. In translating traditional Jewish legal ideas into moral and political positions in present-day America, Greenberg was inherently engaging in a radically new activity, enacting a discourse of *halakhah* that took note of modern conceptions of subjectivity and agency, the political architecture of democracy, the phenomenon of mass media, and the destructive potential of modern military technology. It is important to elaborate for a moment on these dimensions before proceeding to Greenberg's testimony itself. As Greenberg began to teach and write in the years leading up to his Senate appearance, if each individual is created in God's image, then s/he is infinitely valuable, unique, and equal to every other human being. If God is understood to be free, creative, and powerful, then the Image of God is likewise meant to be free, creative, and powerful. The Image of God thus aligned well with modern Western conceptions of individual autonomy, agency, and freedom. And as Greenberg observed frequently in the late 1960s, including during his Senate testimony, in the context of modern mass communication, the Image of God can be represented and shaped, enhanced or diminished, through portrayals in art, television, and film. And in a nuclear age, a single individual could potentially destroy every Image of God – but could also develop technologies to enhance life and alleviate suffering. All of these dimensions informed the idea of *halakhah* as an ethic of power that Greenberg brought to the Foreign Relations Committee.

It is important to spell out as clearly as possible what I mean when I say that Greenberg saw *halakhah* as an ethic of power, because Greenberg himself is not entirely clear on the matter. Greenberg used the term in two ways: "the *halakhah*" described accepted, conventional Jewish law; but, *halakhah*, when not denoted as a proper noun, was also a process whereby the idealistic vision of the biblical prophets – and the contemporary voices that echoed the prophetic call – could be made real in the world. It was primarily in this latter usage that Greenberg understood it as an ethic of power, applicable both to individual ethics about matters like interpersonal relations and business affairs, and to collective questions like the status of women in Jewish law or government social welfare policy. Significantly, in this sense it was a human system, subject to the dynamics of all human power systems: on one end, the potential to do good, or as Greenberg would put it, to increase the recognition of the Image of God in the world through serving humanity and enhancing the equality and uniqueness of each Image of God; and on the other, to become an instrument for reifying existing power structures, and thereby diminishing the capacities of the Image of God through systems of inequality, tyranny, and death.

To navigate between these poles was the fundamental challenge of humanity, the challenge to which *halakhah* responded, particularly through an unceasing dialectic between ideal and real. Greenberg explained this, among other places, in a 1967 lecture at YU's Wurzweiler School of Social Work:

> The basic thesis of the halakhah is very simple: norms, whatever their intrinsic worth, cannot be realized in real life in one step, if they can be realized at all. Then the crucial question of the moral state of society becomes: how to move, *step by step*, toward the overcoming of an evil without thereby collaborating with the system, that is, in the process selling out to the system. The classic tension of being either in the underground or the establishment – with nothing in between – has been the besetting problem of reformers and of revolutionaries throughout history. Judaism felt that the only resolution of this tension is to try a two level approach: the prophetic holding up of the generality and the constant renewal of exposure to that total demand – whether it be 'freedom now' or 'social justice immediately' – must be combined with the halakhah [to achieve] the proximate and partial realization of the good possible at this moment. There is a crucial,

> ongoing role for the rabbi or the individual in deciding what is the next step to be taken. By taking only this step, one does become a de facto collaborator with the existing system. But without this 'collaboration' nothing would be achieved.

Greenberg saw *halakhah* as a way to negotiate between lofty ideals and pragmatic realities. In this, he echoed Soloveitchik. Yet where Soloveitchik understood real-world application to be a concession to reality by a perfect, ideal *halakhah*, Greenberg saw *halakhah's* this-worldliness as a virtue, not a concession. To the senators in May 1970, Greenberg put it this way: "What we need in our time is not the dismantling of power but greater and greater precision, calibration, and proper direction in its use." Power itself was neither good nor bad – it was a feature of being created in God's image.

History, *Halakhah*, and Politics: Reconsidering the Religious and the Secular

The modern shift to see individual human beings as endowed with human rights to the powers of thought and expression has been conventionally understood to have emerged out of a challenge to the authority of religious institutions. As theorists of secularism have observed, in Western Europe as in America, that project was generally inflected by a blend of Protestant theology and free-market capitalism that aimed to circumscribe religion and limit it to the private sphere. Orthodox Judaism self-defined this way: In all its forms, from Haredism to the Modern Orthodoxy of 1960s YU, Orthodox Jews maintained a notion of separate spheres between the public-secular and the private-religious. In the dominant formulation at YU at the time, the two did not need to be in serious conflict, but could be pleasantly harmonized, as *halakhah* could be applied to modern medicine, and the values of traditional Jewish thought could be brought into dialogue with modern philosophy.

Joseph Soloveitchik had begun to articulate a more totalizing possibility, in which *halakhah* became the discursive lens through which "*Halakhic* Man" encountered the world in all its parts. Greenberg understood Soloveitchik to mean that *halakhah* could inform all areas of life – even those which were generally presumed to be secular, and even the most challenging parts of those areas. He used this conceptual opening to press against the veneer of compatibility between religious and secular, *Torah* and *Madda* which was espoused at YU, pushing Orthodoxy to consider how modern developments – particularly individual autonomy for all human beings – could, and in his view must, lead to a renegotiation of Jewish tradition.

Critically, Greenberg emphasized that that negotiation must take place not only in areas that were private, or in private conversations, but in public issues and through public media. In so doing, he challenged not only the prevailing ethos at YU, but the basic assumption of the theory of secularism that religion was confined to the private realm. Beyond this, he also demonstrated that *halakhic* Judaism, a legal framework that governed embodied practice, had a place in the American public square. Anti-war marchers who wouldn't carry placards because it was Shabbat, rabbis who wore *kippot* on their heads when they testified to Congress – these were tangible expressions of not only a new dimension of American Orthodox Jewish life, but an emerging openness to embodied religious expression in public life. They also contributed to an atmosphere in which non-Orthodox Jews became more interested in recovering traditional practices, texts, and language as their own conceptions of what was appropriate in public, and what was valuable in private, shifted.

Religious and secular, public and private, were undergoing Greenberg's hoped-for reconsideration. The spheres were overlapping, and did not work in isolation from each other. Rather, they each contributed to a larger discursive frame in which individual Images of God made decisions – a frame that was amplified into a collective self-image through mass media. Morality was thus a common project of religious and political leadership, and each informed the other. This argument was most dramatically played out in the following exchange:

> SENATOR [CLAIBORNE] PELL [RI]: I do think we have to be more eloquent. Otherwise we will be yawned at or booed off the stage by the young people in their search. The churches, the moral leaders, have the responsibility here. You have the moral responsibility to make the people upon whom you depend for bread and butter take effect in the general community.

> Dr. Bennett: But a lot of ministers lost their livelihoods.
> Senator Pell: A lot of men are losing their lives.
> Senator Case: It is not for Mr. Bennett, but for the young priest or rabbi out in the grounds it is.
> Dr. Greenberg: But each act provokes other acts. When I read in the paper of the senator who risks his future in reelection to cast a certain vote, next time I say it to affect my leadership or the board of trustees. I can say if the senator can do it, how can I look myself in the mirror as a rabbi and not do it.

It is worth parsing this statement of Greenberg's closely, because it contains within it all the elements of his testimony in general. In the scenario he draws, the fact that Greenberg reads of a senator acting with courage in the newspaper – that is, mass media – gives the act an added weight and reality that prompts Greenberg to want to act likewise. Just as the senator confronted those on whom he depends for his livelihood – his constituency – with a courageous act, the rabbi can now confront his source of subsistence – his community – with his own need to act courageously. Greenberg defines that courage as the rabbi, or the senator, being able to recognize the Image of God in himself as he looks in the mirror.

For Greenberg, these gaps – between what the rabbi or senator wants to do and what he actually has the courage to do – were mirrored in the gaps between historical reality and human aspirations for history. "There is such a great gap between what ought to be and what actually is," he observed. This fact implied lessons for leaders: "Therefore any moral leader, whether he is temporal or spiritual, must continually be in conflict with both sides of the argument because we cannot get them both together for a while." Importantly, the leader served to keep the conflict between the two sides of the dialectic from erupting into violence. Holding this nexus point, where the push and pull of forces of change and forces of stability met, formed the essence of not only policy-making, but *halakhah*. If the religious was political, and the political was religious, then *halakhah* itself was a dynamic, political process – not a strictly formal, idealized process as Soloveitchik construed it.

Greenberg articulated this understanding in numerous ways during the late 1960s. In a 1968 interview in the Jewish student activist magazine *Response*, he defined *halakhah* in socio-political terms: "I believe that this is what the *halakhic* process has always been, really: the Jewish methodology of mastering life, by reconciling the conflicting claims of which all life consists – individual and society, in-group and out-group, justice and law and order. There is a legitimate, constant dialectic of these claims." Greenberg added that, in recent centuries, *halakhah* had ceased to be as dynamic a system, becoming "more abstract and more rigid." He therefore saw the task of his generation as performing "a restoration" of what *halakhah* had been once and could be again.

For Greenberg, this ethic of power – whether applied to matters within the Jewish community, or to broad political and social problems affecting society at large – was linked to his understanding of living in history. As Greenberg put it to Fulbright during their final exchange, "There are two choices in history. Either you let the historical forces dominate you as our Presidents, three of them, have allowed momentum forces to dominate them instead of exercising control. Or you have the choice of human will and leadership exercising a creative momentum of taking charge of destiny." Greenberg feared that the failure of leaders "to take charge and pull out and admit our error raises the real possibility that the momentum of history will get us out the other way – through the breakdown of legitimacy of our institutions. I think that would be a disaster of global proportions, not only to Vietnam but to the world."

Greenberg could apply this diagnosis to American political leadership, as well as to his own Orthodox community. Leaders, like all human beings, could be anchored down by the weight of the past, by their fear of appearing to break with it. In Vietnam, that resulted in further and further escalation by American military and political leadership: to de-escalate would mean that past policy had been mistaken, and would thus constitute a rupture with and rejection of past leadership. In Orthodoxy, it meant a greater and greater resistance to new legal formulations and practices, as moving in such directions would seem like breaking with tradition and the rabbis, parents, and ancestors who conveyed it.

But Greenberg argued that, in both cases, the unwillingness of leaders to exercise agency and responsibility in the present would result in institutions, whether the American government, the Orthodox rabbinic establishment, or, as he also observed in his testimony, the Catholic church, losing credibility in the eyes of their constituents. As he put it in his final remarks to the committee, *halakhah* could learn from politics as much as it could teach:

> Society is made up of rationality, history, pride, moralism, all of these things coming together. What we need now is some leadership that can pull all these trends together and really formulate this point. If I had to formulate it, I would say: there is a worldwide challenge to authority and to force – but it is not a challenge to the principle of authority. It is asking that authority justify itself, that power justify itself by serving. Authority can no longer maintain itself by simply being there or by using its power because it has it. Once you understand the challenge is to serve, this explains how devout Catholics can ask their leadership to re-think its role, or how devout Jews can challenge their leadership to reinterpret their law to serve mankind.

Greenberg saw religious institutions confronting the same problem as political institutions: how to exercise authority in a modern world in which individuals were themselves bearers of authority. The challenge required a fundamental reconsideration of previously-held assumptions about what it meant to be a person and a community. As I have shown in this essay, those assumptions were not limited to questions of the scope of Jewish law and tradition, but partook of and implicated broader questions about the contours of religious and secular spheres in American life.

Four Modern Orthodox Dissenters: Yitz Greenberg and his Contemporaries

DR. STEVEN BAYME

Introduction

On a family trip to Connecticut in the 1950s, I carefully listened as adults discussed Jewish life in Hartford. Informed that nine new synagogues had opened within the past year, all either Conservative or Reform, I innocently inquired: "none Orthodox?" "Young man," a relative responded: "Orthodoxy is destined to disappear in 20th century America."

Indeed, this was the conventional wisdom of the times. Nathan Glazer and Marshall Sklare, the leading scholars of American Judaism of the era, allocated little, if any, continuing function for American Orthodoxy. While Orthodox synagogues remained operational, they were perceived as the province of elderly men nostalgic for a world that had vanished. One relative went so far as to advise me that by the time I would be ready for marriage, no caterer would permit observance of the dietary regulations in his establishment.

Similarly, the Orthodox landscape appeared bleak. Most Orthodox synagogues were comprised of non-observant individuals whose progeny were far more likely to become Conservative or Reform. The phenomenon of the "*hashkamah minyan*" connoted early morning Shabbat prayers for those reciting the Mourner's *Kaddish* and then eager to get to their offices in pronounced contrast to the latter-day phenomenon of learned individuals anxious to get to their post-*minyan shiur.* The day school movement remained fledgling while *Haredi* yeshivot struggled to rebuild the world of Torah scholarship destroyed in the Shoah.

Beneath the surface appearances, however, one could detect signs of change: Orthodoxy was redefining itself into three distinct groupings. *Haredi* Orthodoxy, intellectually centered in Lakewood, New Jersey, was determined to claim the mantle of Torah scholarship and renew it for American Jewry. Modern Orthodoxy, headquartered in Washington Heights's Yeshiva University, aimed to transform an East European-style yeshiva into a first-class university in which the synthesis of the two civilizations of Torah and Western culture would herald Modern Orthodoxy as the wave of the future. These two groupings differed on questions of the permissibility of secular education for non-vocational purposes, cooperation with the liberal Jewish religious movements, and, perhaps most profoundly, religious Zionism. Overriding these disagreements was the ethos of "*daas Torah*," or rabbinic authority in non-*halakhic* areas of custom, culture, or politics, such as college courses, intra-denominational cooperation, and support for a secular Israeli government. Between these two intellectual poles, and observing them with curiosity, the majority of Orthodox Jews constituted a third grouping, the religiously non-observant, what the late Prof. Charles Liebman referenced as the "residual Orthodox."

This portrait of an Orthodoxy struggling to survive would quickly vanish in favor of a Modern Orthodox ascendancy. By the 1960s, and especially after Israel's victory in the 1967 War, the level of Orthodox observance rose sharply. Twelve years of day school education became normative followed by a gap year in Israel, and the leading intellectual lights of Orthodoxy rallied around the Modern Orthodox banner, particularly Yeshiva University that then served as home for the "new Orthodox Left." The residual Orthodox, as predicted, largely found their way into the Conservative and Reform movements while the *Haredim* struggled to hold their own. The weight of the future appeared solidly in the hands of the Modern Orthodox, whose most impressive spokespersons largely came out of its most liberal wings.

This chapter explores and compares the thinking of four of these Modern Orthodox intellectuals: Eliezer Berkovits, Emanuel Rackman, David Hartman, and Yitz Greenberg. Each pursued a distinctively modern approach in the face of enormous criticism both from *Haredi* leaders and even from the more "Centrist" Modern Orthodox. (By the 1970s, the term "Centrist Orthodoxy" had largely replaced "Modern Orthodoxy." In the 1990s, Rabbi Avi Weiss coined the term "Open Orthodoxy.") Over the course of decades, these men battled for the soul of Modern Orthodoxy. Their teachings survived and continued to influence their legions of admirers despite their failure to reclaim the leadership of the major institutions of Modern Orthodoxy. In many ways, however, they served as the intellectual and architectural backdrop for many of the most exciting developments within Modern Orthodoxy today.

Eliezer Berkovits

The most senior of this group was noted philosopher and *halakhist*, Eliezer Berkovits. Born in 1908 in Hungary, Berkovits attended the Hildesheimer Seminary in Berlin and completed his doctorate at the University of Berlin with a dissertation on Scottish philosopher David Hume and Deism. In 1939 he fled Germany and subsequently occupied pulpits in Britain, Australia, and Boston, Massachusetts. In 1958, he relocated to Chicago and accepted an academic post in Jewish philosophy at the Hebrew Theological College in Skokie, Illinois. He remained a major figure through the 1980s ultimately retiring to Israel. He authored nineteen books on theology and *halakhah*, many of which are either still in print or being reissued by the Shalem Institute in Jerusalem.

Berkovits' philosophical interests were both and deep. In his early volume *God, Man, and History,* he sought to bring Judaism into a critique of Western culture and ethics. Central to his theology was his concept of revelation which for him connoted memory of a divine-human encounter through which we come to know God. In turn, the God of history cares deeply about human fate. Most importantly, as did his younger colleagues David Hartman and Yitz Greenberg, Berkovits underscored the importance of covenant as man increasingly assuming responsibility for creation.

A more tightly-composed and cogently-presented work was Berkovits' volume on theological responses to the Holocaust titled *Faith after the Holocaust*. Berkovits invoked the concept of *hestar panim*: The Holocaust occurred during a period of God's "hiding His face" or

Divine absence from human events. Were God present, belief would be compelled rather than freely chosen. By contrast, human freedom entails the freedom to be demonic. The Holocaust, in short, represents the ultimate triumph of human freedom and autonomy.

Given this reading of the Holocaust as God's absence making for human freedom, Berkovits weighed Christianity and found it guilty. The churches did not mitigate, much less prevent, the Holocaust's occurrence. Therefore, Berkovits was ambivalent about Jewish-Christian dialogue, arguing that Christianity stood in greater need of it than Judaism. Dialogue could proceed only upon Christian acceptance of criminality for the sin of the Holocaust. This ambivalence, in effect, stood in contrast to Rav Soloveitchik's restriction of dialogue to social and political rather than theological matters and Yitz Greenberg's full-throated embrace of a theologically-based Jewish-Christian encounter. Moreover, if the Holocaust represented *hester panim*, the birth of Israel signaled *gilui panim*, or God revealing His face and offering a life-line to the Jewish future. For Berkovits, Israel connoted the return of the Jews to "power history" after two millennia of statelessness and absence of sovereignty.

With power, of course, went responsibility. Contemporary Judaism must be grounded in a this-worldly faith consisting of ethics and justice. Put simply, religion must be counted upon to articulate the ethical uses of human power rather than passive faith in divine intervention in history. To the contrary, divine intervention would destroy the basis for ethics by undermining human freedom. In effect, the capacity for evil became God's gift to humanity – to be free to make ethical choices. Secularization becomes a religious good in that human beings come of age, no longer relying on divine intervention; secularization lays the foundation for building a new relationship with the Deity, a relationship grounded in faith in God and in harnessing human freedom for ethical purposes.

But perhaps Berkovits' most daring and significant work was a short but compelling volume, *Not in Heaven*. Beginning with the Talmudic narrative of the "oven of *Achnai*" as a Talmudic statement that human beings must take responsibility for decision-making and not rely upon a voice from heaven, Berkovits distinguished between that which the Torah taught and that which the Torah tolerated. Much as Maimonides understood sacrifices as something that the Torah tolerated because the Jews were not ready to see them abolished, so Berkovits wished to extend such a doctrine to the tolerance the Torah exhibited for slavery and for second-class status for women, especially in matters of personal status, i.e. marriage and divorce. In effect Berkovits was making the case for historicization. Certain elements were found within Torah not because the Torah preferred or extolled them but rather because they could not be abolished given the historical conditions of the time. The implication was clear: The *halakhic* process needs to continue, particularly if the values of Torah would be subverted were the *halakhah* permitted to become rigid and ossified.

Such development had occurred historically in rabbinic times. The *prozbul*[1] of Hillel, permitting collection of debts during the sabbatical year given the needs of a credit economy, illustrated how rabbinic legislation upheld the values of the Torah but had modified their implementation given changing historical conditions. Similarly, the *lex talionis* prescribing capital punishment for the owner of an ox that repeatedly had gored human beings had evolved to compensation for the victim. Put differently, the *halakhic* conscience could not abide killing the owner of the ox. Nonetheless, the owner was guilty because he had been warned about the dangers his ox had posed yet had failed to take adequate precautions. But compensation rather than execution made the punishment fit the crime – upholding the principle yet adapting it to moral conscience.

Berkovits offered a radical theological justification for these changes. Not only had the Jews themselves gone into exile, but so had the *halakhah* itself – an exile from reality and real-life conditions. Codification of the law had locked *halakhah* into a straightjacket rather than preserve the process of *halakhic* development. The chief expression of the straightjacket in contemporary times was the modern state of Israel. Theoretically, Israel constituted a wonderful laboratory to test how *halakhic* principles may be applied in a modern nation-state. Yet rather than seek to apply such principles to real-life conditions of Jewish sov-

1. A legal innovation created by Hillel the Elder which ensured that lenders were protected when making interest-free loans to the poor before a sabbatical year.

ereignty, Israel's *halakhic* authorities had tightened the straightjacket isolating more liberal and inclusive *halakhic* opinions.

Nowhere was this more evident for Berkovits than on issues of personal status. He urged that *halakhic* authorities nullify the status of *mamzerim,* children born out of adulterous or incestuous unions, and thereby forbidden to marry. In contrast, he invoked the principle that in the Messianic Era all *mamzerim* would be made pure. Even more daringly, he advocated less restrictive and more inclusive positions on conversion to Judaism, a challenge to Israel that has increased exponentially with the onset of Russian Jewish immigration. Berkovits argued that the criterion of *kabbalat ol mitzvot,* acceptance of the commandments, consisted of belief in God, acceptance of circumcision, and purification in a *mikveh,* a ritual bath. Beyond these three requirements, for Berkovits, the very act of abjuring one's faith and joining the Jewish people sufficed to secure conversion to Judaism. Similarly, he saw no reason why non-Orthodox clergy ought to be barred from performing rabbinical functions in Israel arguing that Conservative and Reform rabbis were mistaken (*to'im,*) but hardly were apostates (*mumarim.*)

For Israel's Chief Rabbinate and for many of Berkovits' Orthodox colleagues in the U.S., these positions were deeply disturbing. Some claimed that he was really a Conservative rabbi in Orthodox garb. Berkovits replied that, for him, morality was Torah morality rather than the morality of contemporary culture, and he took Conservative Judaism to task on those grounds. He believed that all modern problems had solutions, a position approximating Blu Greenberg's aphorism, "where there is a rabbinic will, there is a *halakhic* way." Berkovits argued for a human dimension in *halakhic* decision-making, claiming that Orthodox Jews all too often stood in awe of the *Shulḥan Arukh* rather than in awe of God. He noted in particular how the Talmud alleviated disabilities placed upon women, but that process had become frozen, leaving women whose husbands had refused to grant a bill of divorce in a permanent limbo state of *igun* or "chained" marriage.

In that sense, Berkovits was largely marginalized within the Orthodox world he aspired to lead. Rav Soloveitchik did not oppose him publicly but in effect disavowed his proposals by arguing that *halakhah* stood on autonomous ground, independent of particular historical conditions. Similarly, as the Skokie Yeshiva moved rightward, particularly after the retirement of Dean Oscar Fasman, Berkovits found himself increasingly isolated within his home base.

Today, Berkovits' writings are experiencing a rebirth and renewal of interest, particularly in Israel. The issues of personal status he addressed have become even more pressing, and liberal-minded Israeli Orthodox rabbis are searching for creative solutions within the parameters of *halakhah.* Berkovits' prediction that all problems may be resolved provided we realize that Torah is "not in heaven" may well materialize posthumously.

Emanuel Rackman

Rabbi Emanuel Rackman likely influenced the Orthodox establishment far more than the others examined in this chapter. In large measure, Rackman effectively became identified with that establishment. In 1976, the *New York Times* pronounced him the "dean" of Orthodox rabbis. Past President of the Rabbinical Council of America, Editor of *Tradition,* long time Vice President of Yeshiva University and subsequently President of Bar Ilan University, Rackman held virtually every leadership position within the Orthodox establishment. Yet, he too became marginalized, initially by *Haredi* groupings, and subsequently his candidacy for President of Yeshiva University was derailed in favor of the more "Centrist" Norman Lamm.

Rackman enjoyed considerable support at YU, particularly among key trustees. The *Roshei Yeshiva* largely opposed his candidacy, especially after Rav Soloveitchik dismissed his views on the *agunah* question at the 1975 RCA convention. Like Berkovits, Rackman maintained that the *halakhic* process had become frozen in contemporary times and sought to free *agunot* through religious court action. Soloveitchik pointedly dismissed these proposals as trivializing marriage, a sacred institution.

To his credit, however, Rackman persevered in his activism and advocacy. He transformed Bar Ilan University into a first-rank institution of higher education. At the close of his career, he returned to the question of *agunot,* creating a Beit Din that would actualize his proposals. Intellectually, Rackman sought limitation rather than expansion of the role of dogma in Orthodoxy allocating room for plurality of opinion.

He saw no necessity for excessively restrictive practices and criticized over-reliance upon *gedolim*. The shift in authority to *Roshei Yeshiva*, who were far removed from the realities of Jewish life, troubled him especially. His quest for a more liberal brand of Orthodoxy abhorring fanaticism and certainty, while encouraging doubt and questioning, became his calling card. Thus, for example, he urged that the RCA refrain from attacks on Conservative and Reform colleagues.

Rackman's views on Biblical criticism in many ways were quite conservative. He acknowledged that different portions of the Torah likely were written by different people at different times. Nonetheless he assigned final authorship and editorship to Moses, a position that likely satisfied neither biblical scholars nor *Haredi* critics. Yet in his views on *halakhic* jurisprudence, Rackman adopted quite innovative and even radical positions. His view of *halakhah* was "functional" in nature. It was given over to man to fulfill its function, purposes, and values. *Halakhah*'s overriding principle, according to Rackman, was preservation and enhancement of human life, "and [to] live by them," a position developed considerably further by Yitz Greenberg.

Most important, he maintained that *halakhic* development must occur as historical circumstances and conditions change. He argued, for example, that childless women no longer undergo "*yibum*" or marriage to a brother-in-law after their husband dies. Similarly, he observed that the laws pertaining to burial and mourning after a suicide no longer were implemented. Both cases suggested ongoing *halakhic* development. By contrast, however, Rackman noted that his opponents seemed to leave no room for development save in a more restrictive and extreme direction. He hoped that the State of Israel would provide a laboratory to demonstrate how *halakhah* may be applied in a sovereign Jewish democracy. The *Haredi* establishment in Israel largely frustrated these aspirations, insisting on maintaining the religious status quo, thereby freezing the *halakhic* process. By the same token, a Modern Orthodox leadership unwilling to challenge *Haredi* dominance meant that the face of Judaism in the Jewish state would appear reactionary rather than humanitarian. Thus, Rackman lost the battles both for leadership of Yeshiva University and for transforming Israeli Orthodoxy into a distinctive synthesis between Judaism and democratic humanitarian values.

What then are Rackman's significance and legacy? Of these four leaders, he was arguably the one most feared by the *Haredi* world because of his central position and influence within the Modern Orthodox establishment. Some of his positions have morphed into the Open Orthodoxy of the International Rabbinic Fellowship and Yeshivat Chovevei Torah. Certainly his ethos of open questioning, doubt, and dialogue match the values of Open Orthodoxy. Similarly, many of his proposals for *halakhic* development, especially on *agunot*, have attracted renewed attention, particularly since the 2013 Agunah Summit. Although never accepted *in toto*, Rackman's proposals paved the way for subsequent contemporary efforts at liberating *agunot*.

In effect, then, Rackman served both as ideologist and elder statesman (or *eminence grise*) of Modern Orthodoxy. Even as Orthodoxy drifted rightward, he stood his ground, maintaining involvement, active membership, and leadership within Modern Orthodox groupings. He insisted upon Orthodox participation in inter-denominational bodies such as the Synagogue Council of America and the New York Board of Rabbis. Most importantly, his younger contemporaries looked to him as mentor and role model for his courage in resisting his detractors and his willingness to act in accordance with his convictions notwithstanding the abuse coming from so many of his opponents and the relative neutrality of many who might otherwise have been ideologically sympathetic.

David Hartman

Arguably, the most daring of these individuals was philosopher David Hartman, who in many ways became Israel's leading public intellectual. Hartman responded to the challenge of the meaning of Jewish tradition in the Jewish state. Perhaps his most profound influence lay in his capacity to bring together diverse groupings within Israeli society and the Diaspora to study Jewish texts together.

More specifically, Hartman understood God's covenant with the Jewish people as empowering the Jews to forge their own destiny. Conversely, Divine restraint made room for human power. God could be found not in supernatural miracles so much as in the warp and woof of daily life. In this context of God allowing space for human endeavor,

Hartman argued, a more activist approach to covenant was necessary – one that, for example, addressed the tensions between *halakhic* imperatives and human conscience.

This position largely placed Hartman at odds with his revered former teacher, the intellectual icon of Modern Orthodoxy, Rabbi Joseph B. Soloveitchik. The "Rav," as he was known affectionately to followers, defined covenant as surrender to Divine Will. The *agunah*[2] problem, for example, constituted a personal *Akedah*[3] requiring obedience to a law that could not be rationalized. Hartman rejected this definition of covenant as surrender. He noted that rabbinic Judaism had virtually eliminated the laws of *mamzerut*, the rebellious son, and the idolatrous city (to be sure, the Talmud recorded a certain Rabbi Yonatan who claimed to have witnessed both a rebellious son and an idolatrous city – either a statement of "never say never" or the Talmud's own way of preserving a dissenting voice). Hartman urged that the *halakhic* process must continue and that some limited *halakhic* change must ensue – e.g. on questions of marriage between a *kohen* and a convert, among other areas.

To be sure, Hartman encountered great opposition. Some of his contemporaries charged that change would undermine the *halakhic* system and its claims to authority. Hartman criticized Soloveitchik for taking *halakhah* out of the realm of human experience. To the contrary, he argued, a true covenant meant a divine/human partnership, and one which, over the course of human development, assigned humanity greater and greater responsibility for the conduct of human affairs.

Interestingly, Hartman differed similarly with Prof. Yeshayahu Leibowitz, otherwise best known as an advocate for religion-state separation in Israel. Yet Leibowitz too had argued that Judaism entailed submission to divine command and had little to do with human self-fulfillment. For Leibowitz, Isaac's *akedah* connoted the primacy of God over ethics. In turn, Hartman differentiated between the Abraham who pleaded on behalf of the residents of Sodom yet submitted

2. When a woman is trapped in a marriage because her husband refuses to grant a gett (divorce document.)

3. Literally: the story of the binding of the Isaac. Contextually, this refers to supporting a Divine law that seems to contract one's moral intuition.

to the sacrifice of his son. The former case suggested a covenant of divine-human partnership with God going so far as to query "Will I hide from Abraham that which I am doing?" The latter case pointed to human terror and submission to Divine Will. Put another way, the same Rabbi Akiva who taught an Oral Law in the name of Moses that Moses himself could not fathom accepted martyrdom at the hands of the Romans rather than forgo the teaching of Torah.

As noted, Hartman applied his theology of covenant to the reality of Israel as a modern nation-state. Israel offered an enormous opportunity to demonstrate what a viable Jewish state could do provided she was willing to adapt and apply *halakhic* teachings to a contemporary context. Like Leibowitz, however, Hartman feared that Israel was evolving into a rather narrow nationalism in which *halakhic*-minded Jews mistook chauvinism for Jewish moral teachings while secular Israelis demonstrated only the most minimal and sentimental attachments to Torah and tradition. As a result, he invited Israelis to engage Jewish tradition as an educational experience rather than as a legal system of permitted and forbidden behaviors. This effort to transmit Judaism to a secular Israeli society – opening the Jewish library to an educated yet Jewishly impoverished audience – constitutes perhaps his singular and most universally applauded legacy.

Yet Hartman also hoped to engage the religious Zionist community in which he himself had been nurtured, but which he now perceived as pursuing a path of dangerous messianism; the Religious Zionist youth movement, B'nai Akiva, now largely identified with Gush Emunim, the West Bank settlers movement, while its more liberal-minded alumni, e.g. Hartman's close collaborator Prof. Aviezer Ravitsky, effectively had been marginalized.

Hartman returned to the theme of covenant, arguing that Jews had survived by dint of adherence to covenant rather than by messianism. He looked to Maimonides, his favorite Jewish philosopher, who preferred the paths of moderation to those of messianism. Like Maimonides, he argued that our focus must be on enhancing our lives in the here and now, and that it was best to regulate messianic activism to a dim and largely unknown future.

Ironically, this lack of emphasis on messianism brought Hartman remarkably closer to the views of Rav Soloveitchik than did those of his close colleague Yitz Greenberg. For the latter, the miracle of Israel's rebirth did suggest a messianic dimension. Although Greenberg had little sympathy for the messianic activism of Gush Emunim, he perceived Israel's rebirth as a revelatory moment inaugurating a new redemptive era in Jewish history. Both Hartman and Soloveitchik were considerably more restrained, seeing Israel in positive terms – Hartman himself had uprooted his family and moved there – yet both were quite wary of the price that messianism exacted in political and moral terms.

Rather than embrace Israel as messianic realization, Hartman preferred to see Israel as emanating from Jewish historical experience. At the moment of the Exodus, the Jews were dependent upon Divine intervention and redemption. At Sinai, Jews were elevated into a covenantal partnership with the Deity. Israel today, after the detours of ghettoization in the medieval world and universalism in the modern one, was now poised to enact the Sinaitic covenant by demonstrating the meaning of a Jewish state. To do so, however, necessitated embracing covenant as an act of love rather than out of fear of punishment.

In that embrace of covenant, the entire Jewish people had a role to play. Reform Judaism stood to remind us that nationhood did not connote exclusivity. To the contrary, we retain universal responsibilities to humanity generally, and Reform Judaism correctly reminds us of the meaning of *tikkun olam*. Similarly, Conservative Judaism – with its emphasis upon historical development – demonstrated the possibilities of *halakhic* development as a process over time. To be sure, Hartman's embrace of religious pluralism rejected relativism. Thus, he chastened Reform Judaism for undermining the covenant by accepting patrilineal descent even as he criticized the Orthodox for recourse to Knesset politics to mandate the *halakhic* position on Jewish personal status. The problem of defining who is a Jew constitutes a real dilemma, but not one to be decided upon by coercive state power so much as by juxtaposing historical Jewish teachings with the real-life needs of the Jewish people.

What then constitutes Hartman's legacy? The Shalom Hartman Institute, which he founded, continues as a force for teaching Jews worldwide and has now expanded to engage American Jewish leadership on both rabbinic and lay levels. His covenantal theology resonates greatly with Reform and Conservative thinkers and theologians although rarely if ever with Orthodox ones. Yet some of the most exciting developments within Israeli Orthodoxy owe their origin to ideas first crystallized within the Shalom Hartman Institute. Moreover, Hartman set forth the humanistic face of Judaism, one badly needed in the Jewish state where the dominant image of Judaic heritage was often perceived as primitive and reactionary.

Yitz Greenberg

Where Hartman focused upon Israeli society as forming the core of the Jewish future, Yitz Greenberg devoted the bulk of his career to enhancing American Jewry and trying to shape the course of American Judaism.

In many ways, Greenberg is both indebted to and built upon the work of the other three thinkers touched upon in this essay. Hartman was arguably his closest colleague and soulmate, sharing with him his emphasis upon covenantal theology and Jewish religious pluralism. Like Berkovits, Greenberg addressed the implications of the Holocaust for theology and belief. Both rejected the "punishment for sin" classical teaching in search of alternate theological models. Like Rackman, Greenberg engaged vigorously in a long, frustrating, and continuing struggle to capture the ethos and soul of Modern Orthodoxy. Other influences on his thinking included Franz Rosenzweig's emphasis upon a dual covenant concluded, respectively, with Judaism and Christianity, and Elie Wiesel's articulation of a shift in roles between God and man during the Holocaust years. As one might imagine, Greenberg's lifelong partner, his spouse Blu, heavily influenced his attitudes toward Orthodoxy and feminism, ironically the one area in which the struggle for a truly Modern Orthodoxy culminated in victories for the Modern Orthodox camp rather than for its detractors. Needless to add, of course, Greenberg was by no means interchangeable with any of these figures. Rather he learned from, built upon, and modified each of their contributions.

Greenberg's most seminal theme concerned his covenantal theology. He stressed how all of humanity had been created in God's image and, therefore, human life possessed infinite value. Moreover, all groups have a role to play in human redemption. The Divine Covenant, first with humanity through Noah after the Great Flood, and subsequently with the Jewish people, asserted a divine/human partnership to realize the purposes of creation. In turn, Jews as a people specifically were chosen to assist all in attaining perfection. The *halakhah* of the Jews served as guide in that quest. The purpose of the law must always be kept front and center, "in order to live by them." *Halakhah* must preserve and advance human life.

Greenberg was perhaps most daring in extending the covenant theology to Christianity. Affirming multiple covenants connoted theological validity for other religions, a point suggested initially by Rosenzweig but limited by him to Judaism and Christianity. Greenberg, writing generations later, was prepared to consider allocating covenantal status to faiths outside the Jewish and Christian traditions. He looked to an alliance with Christianity that would serve as a check upon and corrective to the excesses of modernity.

Yet Greenberg erred tactically in deeming Jesus a "failed" rather than a "false" messiah. He compared Jesus to Simon Bar-Kochba, a man who had the right ideas but who failed in his mission as messiah. Christians, of course, could not relate to this position. To them, Jesus did not fail. Rather, he died for the sins of humanity and through his death provided vicarious atonement for all. Conversely, and this was perhaps Greenberg's most serious misjudgment of his own Modern Orthodox community: Liberal-minded Jews, otherwise embarrassed by the contempt for Christianity heard so frequently in Orthodox circles and who sought a more positive relationship with Christianity as religion, were dismayed by Greenberg's full-throated embrace of Christianity as Divine Revelation. Thus, hoping to arrive at a new Jewish perception of Jesus, Greenberg ended up dismaying both Jews and Christians. His efforts to separate Jesus from the Pauline/Augustine doctrine of supersessionism in which Jewish survival served only as witness to the truths of Christianity certainly could be fruitful were they pursued through alternate vehicles. But his reading of Jesus as "failed messiah" did not enhance the discussion so much as undermine his credibility in Orthodox circles. Eliezer Berkovits spoke with greater force to the effect that Christianity needed Jewish-Christian dialogue far more than did Jews given Christian complicity and guilt for the Holocaust. Similarly, Joseph B. Soloveitchik, although approving inter-faith dialogue for limited social and political purposes, opposed theological dialogue as demeaning to both faiths and trivializing the theological integrity of each.

By contrast, Greenberg's ideas met greater resonance with respect to Holocaust theology. For one thing, Greenberg singularly introduced awareness of the Holocaust to American campuses and the university curriculum, where it quickly became a widely-taught course offering attracting both Jews and gentiles. More importantly, Greenberg understood the Holocaust as a direct challenge to many Jewish assumptions about modernity. Liberalism, universalism, secular education, and the idea of progress all failed to avert the occurrence of the Holocaust. Greenberg's revision of Lord Acton's dictum became the clarion call for Jewish self-reliance in a post-Holocaust world: "Power corrupts, absolute power corrupts absolutely, but absolute powerlessness corrupts the most."

Most importantly, Greenberg, like Berkovits and Richard Rubinstein, questioned the validity of the punishment for sin model as Holocaust theology. To their minds, no sin possibly could explain such a nefarious act of genocide. Greenberg put it sharply that "one should make no theological statement unless one is prepared to say it in the presence of burning children."

Thus, Greenberg engaged in a search for alternate theological models to the punishment for sin approach. Job's anger against God and rejection of the counsel of his friends that he was being punished for his sins represented, at least on an individual level, one possibility. Moreover, the Holocaust as national tragedy might be read through the eyes of the Book of Lamentations. Where chapter one of Lamentations expressed the traditional punishment for sin theology the book's second and third chapters gave voice to a Jobian model of anger against God as adversary of the Jewish people. The conclusion to the book synthesized both models: To the Jews the message was one of "Return us O Lord, and we shall return." By contrast, to God the message was "If you have despised us so greatly, your anger has exceeded all proportionality."

Most daringly, Greenberg turned to the kabbalistic concept of *tzimtzum* or divine contraction thereby making human evil possible. Sixteenth century Kabbalists had defined *tzimtzum* as a necessary contraction of God leaving room for human freedom and for the world to come into existence. Berkovits understood the Holocaust as the price of human freedom. But Greenberg went further arguing for a more limited conception of the Deity given the fact of *tzimtzum*. In his novel *Gates of the Forest*, Elie Wiesel posited an exchange of roles – God had become man and man had become God. Greenberg defined this exchange in roles in covenantal terms: Jews had now become senior partner in the covenant. God retreated to a more passive role. As senior partner, Jews now had to take the lead in implementing the terms of the covenant, which he now termed as "voluntary" rather than obligatory. The Jews, wounded as a people by the Holocaust, could not be blamed were they to abandon the covenant. Rather, they now needed to embrace it as entirely a voluntary act. In another novel *Dawn*, Wiesel defined Israel as a symbol of the Jewish people reaffirming the covenant after the Holocaust. That entailed getting one's hands dirty and taking responsibility for what occurs in history, themes common to both Hartman and Greenberg.

Yet the theme of a voluntary covenant virtually completed Greenberg's isolation from the Modern Orthodox establishment. Orthodox leaders of all stripes decades earlier objected to his participation in Jewish-Christian dialogue and to an interview he gave in the undergraduate Yeshiva University newspaper in which he advocated limited *halakhic* change, particularly with respect to premarital gender relations, popularly known as the laws of *negi'ah*. *The Jewish Observer*, organ of the *Haredi* Agudath Israel, queried whether this was Modern Orthodoxy or "Orthodox Modernism." The "voluntary" covenant concept widened the breach with Orthodox leaders. Centrist and *Haredi* leaders alike rejected the voluntarism as legitimating discarding the covenant and its obligatory nature. In all likelihood they now perceived Greenberg as one who claimed that observance of *mitzvot* had now become a matter of personal choice rather than of Jewish imperative.

Generally, however, the Orthodox shift rightward over the past five decades left Greenberg isolated within a world that had once constituted his base of operations and spiritual home. The shift toward greater isolationism and decreased engagement with modern culture, to be sure, occurred independently of Greenberg although he became one of its primary targets. Moreover, in assessing the causes of the rightward shift, Greenberg by no means exempted the liberal movements. In his view, leftward trends prevalent within the Conservative and Reform movements maximized the distance between them and that of Orthodoxy and thereby weakened Greenberg's call for religious pluralism.

Yet Greenberg's successes within Orthodoxy also should not be minimized. He founded the SAR Academy in Riverdale, which has since become a paradigm of Modern Orthodox education at its finest. An entire generation of Yeshiva University students looked to him as their intellectual beacon and, decades later, continue to cite his influence. Some carried his ideas into major precincts of Jewish communal life, particularly within academic Jewish studies and Jewish communal organizations. Modern Orthodox feminism followed the leadership of Blu Greenberg, who established JOFA as a grassroots organization that persevered in its commitments to a Modern Orthodoxy notwithstanding condemnations from noted *Roshei Yeshiva*. In more recent times, Rabbi Avi Weiss established a Modern Orthodox rabbinical school and a parallel women's yeshiva to train women leaders as *maharats* under the rubric of an incipient and growing "open" Orthodoxy building upon many of Greenberg's ideas. Put simply, the struggle for the future of Modern Orthodoxy remains unresolved. While the numbers of Open Orthodox Jews may pale by comparison to the Centrist and *Haredi* groupings, their intellectual heft and influence have become quite formidable.

Conclusion

The four Modern Orthodox leaders described in this chapter share much in common. All formed part of the emerging Orthodox Left of the 1960s. Most claimed the tutelage of Rav Soloveitchik as intellectual dean of Modern Orthodoxy and went considerably beyond his thinking in advocating significant albeit limited *halakhic* change. Last, all underscored the significance of a covenantal partnership in which Jewish religious leaders, i.e. the *Poskim*, can and should be playing activist roles in development of *halakhah* and its implementation in contemporary society, particularly on questions of liberating *agunot* and facilitating conversion to Judaism.

As noted, widely considered moribund in the 1950s, Modern Orthodoxy by the 1960s appeared on the cusp of assuming leadership. The day school population had mushroomed from seven thousand in 1945 to over 50,000 students by 1960, reflecting in part the Baby Boom but also, more substantively, the conviction that both Jewish and American civilizations could coexist and be transmitted simultaneously to the next generation. At Yeshiva University, the idea of synthesis prevailed as an institutional goal. Rabbi Soloveitchik served as intellectual dean and archetype of such a synthesis, and his teachings impacted directly upon Orthodox individuals, many of whom attempted to define themselves in his image even as they adopted positions considerably to his left. As Yeshiva University expanded, the conviction grew that Modern Orthodoxy had developed a highly attractive ideology and value system, had built an incredible network of institutions for educating its young, and was poised to assume the mantle of leadership for the American Jewry of the future.

Sustaining this hope was the vibrancy and verve that characterized the intellectual leadership of the Orthodox left. The four dissenters engaged both themselves and their more traditionalist colleagues in exciting debates and symposia on Orthodoxy's future directions. They all articulated distinctively modern approaches to both *halakhah* and theology. For each, modern culture posed a wonderful opportunity both in Israel and in the Diaspora. If Jews now enjoyed the blessings of affluence and power they argued, the time had come for Orthodox Judaism to demonstrate the salience and compelling message of Judaic teachings in the modern world.

The agenda of Modern Orthodoxy in the 1960s consisted of four major challenges:

1. Secular education as a value in itself that could also be harnessed as a vehicle to comprehend Jewish text and tradition. For Yitz Greenberg, in particular, this connoted the challenge of engaging modern Biblical scholarship and how Orthodoxy would both participate in and respond to it.
2. Religious Zionism as an opportunity to define the nature of the Jewish state in authentically Judaic yet non-coercive forms. Emanuel Rackman and Eliezer Berkovits were particularly intent on engaging *halakhah* functionally with the demands and requirements of a modern nation-state.
3. Pluralism and intra-denominational cooperation: Yeshiva University's president, Dr. Samuel Belkin, to the dismay and conster-

nation of his *Haredi* detractors, had participated actively in the Synagogue Council of America, the leading body for intra-Jewish religious dialogue. Yeshiva University alumni served on mixed boards of rabbis in cities throughout the country. The Rabbinical Council of America had limited such intra-Jewish dialogue to external matters – the defense of Israel, Soviet Jewry, and anti-Semitism. Yitz Greenberg and David Hartman called for much broader engagement with rabbis of all the movements, joint learning programs, and according greater validation and legitimacy to the non-Orthodox streams and their religious leaders.

4. Women and Jewish feminism: This challenge emerged only in the latter years of the 1960s and the early 1970s, stimulated primarily by the feminist movement generally and, subsequently, by calls for greater involvement and leadership roles for women within the Conservative and Reform movements. Yeshiva University did create opportunities for Orthodox women to engage in serious study of the Talmud. But it was Blu Greenberg in particular who developed the banner and agenda of Orthodox Jewish feminism. Where *Roshei Yeshiva* condemned women's prayer groups, Modern Orthodox feminists persevered, and the number of such independent prayer groups grew exponentially. Greenberg's male sympathizers – particularly Rackman, Hartman, and, of course, her spouse Yitz – served in supportive roles rallying at her side.

With the notable exception of Jewish feminism, however, Modern Orthodoxy largely ceded ground on the major issues of its 1960s agenda, and its leading intellectual voices effectively were marginalized. With respect to secular education, Modern Orthodoxy abandoned its bold view of synthesis in favor of a far more modest coexistence at best between two value systems of Torah and secular culture. To be sure, Modern Orthodoxy rejected in principle *Haredi* Orthodoxy's vision that secular education might be justified only for purposes of earning a living. In practice, however, that is largely what occurred. Modern Orthodox students, now mostly alumni of one-year GAP programs at Israeli yeshivot, flocked to pre-professional programs in their undergraduate education, neglecting humanities and social sciences, to say nothing of the challenges those disciplines posed to traditionalist understanding of Jewish texts. The man of synthesis gave way to the "learner-earner" as ideal product of Jewish education.

In Israel, religious Zionism post-1967 increasingly became identified with Gush Emunim, the movement of West Bank settlers. This grouping, although in principle committed to exploring the application of Jewish law in the modern nation-state, largely emphasized the sanctity of land and the impermissibility of returning any part of the historical land of Israel to Palestinians or to Arab neighbors. More dovish Modern Orthodox voices, e.g. David Hartman and Aviezer Ravitsky, were largely relegated to the sidelines of Modern Orthodox discourse although both persevered in their engagement with such questions as public intellectuals in Israeli society. To be sure, Rav Aharon Lichtenstein added the voice of a giant in Torah in support of returning territories.

Similarly, by the 1980s intra-religious cooperation had largely given way to polarization between the movements. The liberal movements, as noted, had moved sharply leftward on issues of women's equality, patrilineal descent, intermarriage, and homosexuality, causing many within the Modern Orthodox camp to deride them as having abandoned Torah in favor of assimilation and contemporary fads. The Synagogue Council of America collapsed of its own weight in 1994, by which time mixed boards of rabbis had largely evanesced within most cities. The Modern Orthodox in particular largely had forfeited their function as a bridge between the religious movements. Greenberg mounted a valiant yet ultimately failed effort at sustaining intra-Jewish dialogue. Hartman was somewhat more successful in attracting rabbis of all denominations to study jointly at his institute in Jerusalem. But these seminars too, by the 21st century, largely lacked Centrist Orthodox participants.

As Adam Ferziger recently demonstrated, a realignment of forces occurred within American Orthodoxy over the past five decades. Ironically *Har okedi* sectors became less insular. *Haredi* women in fact took on more activist roles, especially in outreach to non-Orthodox Jews. Ironically, some *Haredi* voices were heard in praise of positive currents within Reform Judaism even as they vigorously condemned Open Orthodoxy. Conversely, Centrist Orthodoxy was becoming more insular at times adopting *Haredi* positions and thereby blurring boundaries between the two dominant wings of American Orthodoxy.

Leading the way in this retreat from the bold and forward-looking

Modern Orthodoxy of the 1960s, were developments at Yeshiva University. The leadership of YU instituted new nomenclature, defining themselves as "Centrist Orthodox" and eschewing the term "Modern Orthodox," a change President Norman Lamm, to his credit, regretted by the time of his 2003 retirement. "Modern Orthodoxy" connoted a distinctive synthesis and engagement between the values of modern culture and those of Judaism and assigning concrete positive value to both. Centrism, by contrast, was ideologically vague defining the modern camp as located somewhere on a spectrum between *Haredi* Orthodoxy and Yitz Greenberg. Compounding this weakness within Centrism was the absence of any significant "left" Orthodoxy at YU, an absence that refuted any claim of the Centrist camp to be inclusive of diverse Orthodox expressions. All this meant that the modern camp had lost its verve and independence, and looked rightward towards the *Haredi* world, which was growing dramatically both demographically and in intellectual influence.

The major exception, as noted, to Modern Orthodoxy's forfeiture of verve and independence was located within Orthodox feminism. Only here did women committed both to Torah and principles of gender equality stand their ground and insist upon maximizing women's roles in Jewish public life and ritual and resolution of issues patently unfair to women such as *agunot*. In the face of strident criticism from *Roshei Yeshiva*, including many of those within the Centrist camp, women's prayer groups multiplied considerably despite a ban placed upon them by leading YU *Roshei Yeshiva*. The Jewish Orthodox Feminist Alliance (JOFA) sustained itself over two decades in contrast to other Modern Orthodox groupings which flamed out after several forays. More tangibly, JOFA could claim limited success on questions concerning *halakhah* and women's equality.

To be sure, Yitz Greenberg's ideas on Modern Orthodoxy failed to take hold and comprised what some historians have called "the road not traveled." In some cases he was too far ahead of his constituency, violating his own leadership principle that one cannot be more than 10–15 percent ahead of one's followers. To some extent his ideas did find resonance beyond the parameters of Orthodoxy. For example, Greenberg became the unofficial rabbi of the Federation world infusing it with Jewish content and sensitizing federation leaders to the significance of Jewish education and the relevance of Jewish teaching to their personal lives. Similarly, Greenberg successfully introduced the Holocaust to American public culture particularly through the U.S. Holocaust Memorial Museum, which he was instrumental in founding in 1993.

Within Orthodoxy, however, Greenberg remained a marginalized voice even as he remained an inspirational one for some, particularly, those identified with the Open Orthodoxy that is open to all Jews and to diverse perspectives championed by Rabbi Avi Weiss. More generally, Greenberg functioned brilliantly as rabbi, professor, and role model for countless Jews, Orthodox and non-Orthodox alike, who felt privileged to attend his seminars and classes. These disciples continue to struggle in the conviction that Jewish tradition is intellectually rich and vibrant, remains compelling, and has much to say to the challenges of modernity.

Rabbi Yitz Greenberg and American Orthodoxy: The Crisis of 1966–67

Dr. Lawrence Grossman

Rabbi Yitz Greenberg has written movingly about how he "remained personally in love with the Orthodox community and its way of life, its thick texture of observance, its strong family and communal bonds, its learning and its passion for Israel," elements that "nurtured my soul and my family's." That observation, however, raises the central paradox of his life's work. As one observer has put it, "He personally identifies with Orthodoxy and is *halakhically* observant; yet, he is embraced by large segments of the American Jewish population who eschew *halakhic* commitment, while he is rejected by large segments of those who share his commitment to *halakhic* observance."

Born into an Orthodox family in Borough Park, Brooklyn in 1933, educated in Orthodox day schools, and ordained by Bais Yosef, an Orthodox yeshiva, Greenberg spent the crucial years from his late 20s through his late 30s – a period coinciding with the turbulent 1960s – in Modern Orthodox settings. Upon receiving his doctorate in history from Harvard in 1959, he started teaching at Yeshiva University, Modern Orthodoxy's flagship educational institution; he played a key role in founding Yavneh, an organization for Orthodox college students across the country, and held an important advisory role there; and in 1965 Greenberg became rabbi of the Riverdale Jewish Center, making it into a model Modern Orthodox synagogue, and in that capacity later founding the SAR Academy, one of the finest Jewish day schools in the country.

But the intellectual and institutional initiatives for which Greenberg attained national, even international, renown, namely Jewish denominational pluralism, unfettered Jewish-Christian dialogue that led him to go so far as to define Jesus as a failed, rather than a false messiah, Holocaust theology with its corollary that Jews have now entered a new, post-Holocaust third stage of history in which obedience to their covenant with God is no longer mandatory but "voluntary," and gender egalitarianism, all flowered after he severed his professional ties with these Orthodox institutions in the early 1970s. Moving into the nondenominational Jewish sphere, he first established and chaired the Jewish Studies Department at the City College of New York, and in 1973 he launched the National Jewish Conference Center, later called the National Jewish Resource Center, and finally CLAL, which promotes a kind of "civil Judaism" by providing Jewish experiences and educational resources for predominantly non-Orthodox federation leaders.

Much of mainstream Orthodoxy viewed Greenberg's programmatic and ideological breakthroughs over the years as irrelevant if not pernicious. Greenberg has been of two minds about the reason for his weakness in his own home community. Looking back in 1998, he attributed it to a shift within Orthodoxy, arguing that it "has become synonymous with fundamentalism." And he wrote, "I never dreamed that the Modern Orthodox position from which I was jumping off was going to be so weakened and even disintegrated by pressure from the *ḥaredim.*" Greenberg acknowledged that if he could "do it all over again," before launching his controversial initiatives he would try to "build a Modern Orthodox base in a much more thorough fashion, instead of assuming that it was going to maintain itself." Yet in the same volume Greenberg acknowledged that it was he who had changed, moving beyond Modern Orthodoxy to "be a Postmodern Orthodox Jew."

Physicists tell us that under some conditions motion is relative – when two bodies move apart, which one is moving away from the other is no more than a matter of perspective. So too, it may be a meaningless exercise to ponder whether the estrangement between Greenberg and institutional Orthodoxy was due to the rabbi moving left or his religious grouping moving right – or even both simultaneously. The estrangement, though, is a fact, and the open break can be traced in a crucial series of events in 1966–67 that sheds light both on the evolution of

Greenberg's thought and on developments in American Orthodoxy.

Through the early 1960s, Greenberg provided a fresh voice representing an American-born Orthodoxy that came of age after World War II. Yet he was hardly revolutionary. His general approach appeared in line with initiatives taken by the emerging Modern Orthodoxy of the time to promote an intellectually sophisticated Orthodox worldview open to contemporary realities. Some signposts of this evolving trend were the Rabbinical Council of America's launch of *Tradition* magazine in 1957; Yeshiva University's publication series *Studies in Torah Judaism,* begun in 1959; the writings of Rabbi Emanuel Rackman (1910–2008) and Professor Eliezer Berkovits (1908–92); and most important, the growing prominence of Rabbi Joseph B. Soloveitchik (1903–93), the unchallenged authority at the Rabbinical Council of America (RCA) and the Yeshiva University Rabbinical School, who was a Talmudic prodigy, a Ph.D. in philosophy, and a charismatic orator who seemingly embodied the "synthesis" of Torah and general culture that Modern Orthodoxy advertised.

If Greenberg at that point wanted to push the envelope, he did so gently; themes that would emerge full-blown in later years were expressed subtly and inoffensively. His key message, delivered before Orthodox, non-Orthodox, and non-Jewish audiences, was the need for the Jewish community to adjust to a new social and intellectual reality that blurred old ethnic and religious boundaries that had previously maintained Jewish identity.

In a talk delivered to the new Yavneh Orthodox student group in September 1962, Greenberg argued that "emancipation and westernization," followed by "the extermination of six million Jews" (the word "Holocaust" was not yet in vogue) and the inauguration of the State of Israel had together "radically changed being a Jew." Orthodox Jews had to "broaden our philosophy and understanding of Torah" and "relate ourselves anew to non-religious Jews" who shared the same "common destiny" with the Orthodox. He urged Yavneh to involve itself in social justice causes, and called on the Orthodox day schools to reduce the curricular stress on Talmud and teach more Bible, Jewish philosophy, and Jewish history.

Invited to speak at the convention of the RCA in 1965, Greenberg had a similar message: "Orthodoxy must become an integral part of the

American fabric, which involves Jew and non-Jew in every phase of the nation's social, educational, political and economic life."

In a paper he delivered at a meeting of the American Historical Association that year, subsequently published under the title "Adventure in Freedom – Or Escape From Freedom?" Greenberg spoke of American Jewish identity to a far broader audience, one that he believed needed to be warned about excessive acceptance of trends in the greater society. While the assimilatory dangers that American prosperity pose for Jews are common wisdom today, Greenberg was one of the first to gauge the impact of postwar Jewish economic success, the decline of anti-Semitism, and the new picture (first identified by Will Herberg) of "a tri-faith" American culture consisting of Catholics, Protestants, and Jews. While Jews were then just 2.9 percent of the population, they constituted a virtual third of religious America. But this success, Greenberg noted, loosened the bonds of group identity.

Most important, the crumbling of university quotas and the acceptance of large numbers of Jewish students at prestigious colleges threatened Jewish loyalty through "the 'cool style' of the academic world" and its "emphasis on universalism and affective neutrality." Rising intermarriage, Greenberg believed, was sure to follow, and declining Jewish fertility rates were already in evidence. He therefore foresaw a shrinking Jewish community, but one "more pious, more committed Jewishly, more unabashedly particularistic." In a nod to his own favored version of American Judaism, Greenberg commended those who "seek to assimilate American experience and culture critically rather than merely adjusting Judaism passively. . . ."

During the summer of 1965, however, even before the article appeared in print, Greenberg underwent an experience that shifted his orientation dramatically in the direction of Jewish pluralism. He was invited to participate in a new program – a retreat for young Jewish intellectuals held in the Laurentian Mountains hosted by his friend, Rabbi David Hartman. This interdenominational program would continue annually as the I. Meier Segals Centre for the Study and Advancement of Judaism, until Hartman's move to Israel in 1971. At that first retreat Greenberg gave a paper on "God's Acts in History" and, for the first time, got to know non-Orthodox thinkers who were serious about their Jewishness: Emil Fackenheim, Jacob Petuchowski, Eugene Borowitz,

Steven Schwartzchild, and others. Orthodox figures beside Hartman took part as well, including Eliezer Berkovits, Aharon Lichtenstein, Michael Wyschogrod, and Walter Wurzburger. Greenberg developed considerable intellectual respect for these men and came to see them – and not the conventional Orthodox rabbis and yeshiva teachers he had known – as his peer group.

The new, outspokenly interdenominational Greenberg went public that winter, making crystal clear how his views had shifted. He participated as the Orthodox voice in a symposium, held in January 1966, titled "Toward Jewish Religious Unity." The others on the program were Petuchowski (Reform), Mordecai Kaplan (Reconstructionist), and Seymour Siegel (Conservative). Presenting his familiar argument that modernity had radically altered Jewish life, Greenberg now suggested that the crisis opened up possibilities for a "thaw" of the barriers that separated Jew from Jew. Practically speaking, said Greenberg, if non-Orthodox rabbis would show a willingness to abide by the basics of Jewish marriage and divorce law, the Orthodox rabbis should explore "the full range of the *halakhah* to eliminate situations like *agunot,* husbands who abuse their superior rights in the *get* process, brothers who take advantage of *chalitzah,* etc." But in order to attain such an accommodation Orthodoxy "must train men who can perform these procedures in intellectually and culturally appealing terms" and find a way to include the non-Orthodox referring rabbi in the ceremony.

Greenberg also issued a broad challenge to Orthodoxy, declaring at the symposium that it "must change its identity from a fundamentalism to a religion, from preserving Judaism to affirming it and its sovereignty in modern culture. In short it must go through the modern experience." He was not calling for the abandonment of *halakhah,* said Greenberg, rather "for the renewal of the process of imbuing the contemporary experience with religious import by applying religious values and practices to all areas of secular life." He was realistic enough to concede that this process could "take generations." During the subsequent discussion, he said that each of the denominations, not just Orthodoxy, had to rethink its positions in the light of recent events. Since "all of us are survivors of Auschwitz," he proclaimed, no Jewish group should humiliate or judge other Jews on the basis of "institutional slogans." Reform and Conservative Judaism, he continued, "were two excellent, or at least significant, attempts to rethink Judaism as the first responses to modernism," but they, together with Orthodoxy, would "now have to be evaluated in the second round, in the hope that they can come closer to each other." Greenberg expressed some understanding for those he called Orthodox "fundamentalists," who would never consider rapprochement with modernity or with non-Orthodox forms of Judaism. They might be correct that contemporary Western culture "may actually be sick, diseased, even dead," but Greenberg disagreed; he would "stake my life and my faith" that they were wrong.

Greenberg's newly articulated revolutionary position within Orthodoxy was best appreciated by one of his dialogue partners, Seymour Siegel, a professor at the Jewish Theological Seminary. Siegel announced: "I am happy to welcome Professor Greenberg to the ranks of Conservative Judaism, because the things he has said this afternoon I find in absolutely no publication I have ever read coming from any official or even semi-official institution of Orthodoxy."

Siegel was right: Greenberg had strayed far off the Orthodox reservation. More than a decade earlier – in 1954 – Rabbi Soloveitchik, whose word was authoritative for the Modern Orthodox, had set guidelines for relations with the non-Orthodox groups. While the Orthodox would stand shoulder-to-shoulder with them on issues affecting the Jewish community as a whole – such as anti-Semitism, Israel, or relations with government bodies – there would be no such solidarity when it came to internal religious matters since, in Soloveitchik's view, non-Orthodox forms of Judaism were Jewishly illegitimate. He sought particularly to clarify the previously blurred boundary between Orthodoxy and the Conservative movement both on theological grounds – acceptance of revelation from Sinai as an Orthodox *sine qua non* – and in practical terms, rejecting all modifications of Jewish law. At the RCA convention that year Soloveitchik said that synagogues where the rabbi spoke into a microphone on Shabbat and holidays, and those that had men and women seated together were not bona fide houses of Jewish worship. From that point on separate seating, in particular, became the way to distinguish an Orthodox from a Conservative synagogue, and a newly militant Orthodoxy launched lawsuits to prevent nominally Orthodox synagogues from instituting mixed seating and campaigned for the installation of physical partitions (*meḥitzot*) between men and women in synagogues that had not previously had them.

Despite Greenberg's clearly pluralistic divergence from the path Orthodoxy was taking, his remarks at the symposium on Jewish unity drew no immediate reaction other than a report in Yeshiva University's student newspaper because the transcript of the symposium was not yet publicly available. By the time it was, Greenberg was embroiled in another controversy closer to home in which Jewish religious pluralism was just one element.

In late April, the student newspaper printed a long interview with Greenberg under the heading "Dr. Greenberg Discusses Orthodoxy, YU, Viet Nam & Sex." Greenberg opened up in the interview – he would later claim that he spoke more rashly than he should have because he thought it was off the record – by delineating exactly what an Orthodoxy that had undergone the modern experience would look like. While identifying as Orthodox and stipulating that this community had "the largest number of people who do take the covenant idea seriously," Greenberg said "it doesn't matter to me" which denomination a Jew espoused. Orthodoxy's major problem was that it had "lost all connection with modern life." It had "escaped into the purely ritualistic realm of *halakhah* . . . and has made a routine out of it." Greenberg set down three tasks Orthodoxy had to undertake to achieve relevance: apply *halakhic* values to current American issues such as civil rights, the Vietnam War, and poverty; develop an approach to Scripture that took seriously the findings of Biblical criticism; and conduct a "thorough reexamination" of the *Shulḥan Arukh* (Code of Jewish Law), an endeavor that he claimed contemporary rabbinic authorities were neglecting. He called Yeshiva College "a cultural backwater" that instead of producing people with spiritual values, turned out "secularly oriented students who are overlayed with an abundant practice of Orthodox ritual." Greenberg daringly declared sex to be the most important area of life that Jewish law did not adequately cover. The current emphasis on avoiding all physical contact with anyone of the opposite sex who is not one's spouse, he argued, reflected a negative view of sex; a revised law code should be based on the principle that for a man "to experience a woman as *tzelem Elohim* [image of God] is a *mitzvah* just as much as praying in Shul."

A torrent of criticism – Greenberg called it a "furor" – prompted him to send a detailed letter of clarification to the paper, which published it in the next issue. Striving to tone down any radical implications that readers might have drawn, he explained that his purpose was only "to point out the possibility of a position operating with the classic *halakhic* framework that would be willing to relate symbolically and sympathetically to the modern experience and shape it with the categories of *halakhah.*" He claimed that 70 percent of the original interview "is unexceptionable and is agreed with by a number of *Roshei Yeshiva* [members of the Talmud faculty] in principle, if not in specifics of judgment in each case." The bulk of his clarification addressed the section about sex, which upset many readers by seeming to advocate an end to the laws barring premarital intimacy. Greenberg rejected these "sensationalistic interpretations," insisted he was only referring to sex between married couples, and apologized "for not having clarified the language." Greenberg concluded with a plea for the open discussion of controversial issues: "There must be leeway for exploring views which may ultimately be rejected. The net hysteria generated has done much to foreclose serious consideration of these problems by students who would profit from such consideration."

Greenberg could not have expected his clarification to shield him from the attacks of sectarian Orthodoxy. The monthly organ of the Agudat Harabonim (Union of Orthodox Rabbis of the United States and Canada) editorialized in favor of revoking the ordination of "the young rabbi" who had called for "a new approach to the 'subject of sex,'" something that should not even be discussed in public. *The Jewish Observer,* the primary English-language magazine representing hardline Orthodoxy, published a sharp condemnation that used the interview as well as the January symposium on Jewish unity to cast aspersions not only on Greenberg, but also on what it considered a larger danger. The article identified Greenberg with Yavneh and with "a decided trend among certain Orthodox intellectuals" who preached an "Orthodox Modernism" and were "expert in the jargon and vagaries of modern theologians like Barth, Tillich and Buber" rather than in the classic Jewish sources. The author called this "pseudo-Orthodoxy." A letter from Greenberg defending himself provided the author a second opportunity to castigate Greenberg and his alleged ideological allies.

At Yeshiva University, Greenberg's own turf, Rabbi Soloveitchik told him, of being subjected to pressure, to denounce his views, but promised Greenberg "that no matter what they do, I will never denounce you publicly," a promise that he kept. But the promise did not extend to the rabbi's family. His younger brother, Rabbi Aaron Soloveitchik (1917–2001), who also taught Talmud at Yeshiva, gave an hour-and-three-quarters lecture responding to Greenberg on the day the original interview came out. Without mentioning Greenberg's name, the younger Soloveichik declared that Jewish law was immutable, that the strictures on sexual conduct were prerequisites for a life of holiness, and that the field of critical Bible studies was the work of German anti-Semites. Some weeks later, the student newspaper's final issue of the semester included an open letter to Greenberg from the highly respected Rabbi Aaron Lichtenstein, Rabbi Joseph Soloveitchik's son-in-law and also a member of the school's Talmud faculty, which sharply contested Greenberg's views. In later years, the two protagonists as well as scholars of the period would write about their polemical duel in detail, but its impact on Greenberg's relations with Orthodoxy deserves further clarification.

Greenberg and Lichtenstein had much in common. Both were born in 1933. Their years of graduate study at Harvard overlapped, the former attaining a Ph.D. in American History and the latter in English literature. Through advising the Yavneh Orthodox campus organization, teaching at Yeshiva University, and providing leadership to the Student Struggle for Soviet Jewry (SSSJ), both furnished role models all through the 1960s for the newly emergent Orthodox Jewish intellectual-activist "type." And the similarity went even further: Lichtenstein, like Greenberg, participated in the early Laurentian Mountains retreats organized by David Hartman, and the two were also part of a group of young faculty members at Yeshiva that met together periodically "to discuss the current state of American Orthodoxy and the direction in which its future lies," and to "confront the *halakhic* leaders of Judaism with the more relevant questions and problems that emerge from the American experience."

The extent of what the two men had in common made Lichtenstein's barbs particularly painful for Greenberg. Agreeing that students needed guidance in navigating between the worlds of Torah and secular knowledge, that there should be "more intensive and extensive application of *halakhah* to the social and political realm," and that Greenberg's critique of the atmosphere at Yeshiva was "generally sound," Lichtenstein nevertheless found plenty to criticize. He charged that Greenberg was far too accepting of contemporary American values – "I do not think that we should immerse ourselves in American society to the extent you seem to advocate" – and insufficiently appreciative of the cautious approach much of the Orthodox world took toward elements of the surrounding culture. Some of Greenberg's statements on matters requiring care and sensitivity were "by you own admission . . . either exaggerated or misleading," Lichtenstein asserted, and warned of the "spiritual casualties" that might result. He went on to mock Greenberg's second article responding to criticism of the first as evincing "pained martyrdom and pious shock": ". . . if you knew much of it was controversial . . . why the surprise over the controversy?" And while stopping short of charging Greenberg with lying in his explanation that the call for change in Jewish law referred only to relations between spouses, he pointed out that Greenberg's original language certainly left a different impression.

The split with Lichtenstein revealed a significant fault line within Modern Orthodoxy. Both Greenberg and Lichtenstein wanted Orthodoxy to face up to modernity, but the challenge and the appropriate response to it meant different things to the two men. Lichtenstein espoused humanistic study for developing a sense of the complexity of the human experience, sought to devise approaches to contemporary issues rooted in the classical Jewish sources, and was open to dialogue with those holding other points of view. After moving to Israel in 1971, he would attain renown as the co-head of Yeshivat Har Etzion until his death in 2015, winning the Israel Prize for contributions to Torah scholarship and projecting a rare voice of political and religious moderation within religious Zionism. Emphatically unlike Greenberg, however, he was extremely cautious about *halakhic* change, insisted, like Soloveitchik, on Orthodoxy's monopoly on Judaic authenticity, would not countenance religious pluralism, and considered biblical criticism beyond the pale. Lichtenstein's approach, which began to be called Centrist Orthodoxy in the late 1970s, would become dominant at Yeshiva University and the Rabbinical Council of America, leaving Greenberg's version of Modern Orthodoxy marginalized.

The final stage in distancing Greenberg from institutional Orthodoxy came in the spring of 1967 over the issue of Jewish-Christian dialogue. Greenberg's study of the Holocaust during his stay in Israel as a Fulbright fellow in 1961–62 made him "aware of the pathological images of Jewry and Judaism that Christianity had injected into the bloodstream of European culture," in turn triggering his interest in engaging Christians on the topic. His enthusiastic participation in interreligious programs upon returning to the U.S. coincided with the work of the Second Vatican Council called by Pope John XXIII in 1960 to rethink Catholic doctrine, an historic initiative that would result five years later, during the pontificate of his successor Paul VI, in the historic document *Nostra Aetate* that removed the charge of deicide from the Jewish people and inaugurated a new era in Catholic-Jewish relations. "Our timing," Greenberg would later recall about his and his wife's involvement in interfaith work, "was impeccable."

Interreligious dialogue was in the air, but Orthodox Jewish leaders were decidedly cool to it. The sectarian Orthodox – those who today would be called *Haredi* – dismissed it out of hand as just the latest Christian tactic to convert the Jews. Modern Orthodox rabbis, more acculturated and Americanized and less likely to assume that all Christians harbored inimical motives, looked to Rabbi Joseph B. Soloveitchik for guidance. Beside his impressive Talmudic scholarship, Soloveitchik was a profound religious thinker and a man both acquainted with and influenced by Christian theology.

In 1964, while the Vatican Council's projected document on the Jews was under intense discussion in Rome, Soloveitchik gave a talk, subsequently published as an article under the title "Confrontation," which set out parameters for Jewish-Christian dialogue. These were primarily concerned with ensuring that Christian participants come to the table recognizing Judaism as an independent, unique faith, and that the dialogue partners posit from the start that each faith community is separate and unique, neither having the right to demand that the other modify or eliminate any element of its theology or practice. Of immense importance for Modern Orthodox Jews interested in dialogue, Soloveitchik declared certain theological issues out of bounds. In a subsequent communication to the RCA he spelled out what he meant.

"In the areas of universal concerns," he wrote, "we welcome an exchange of ideas and impressions" but "in the area of faith, religious law, doctrine, and ritual," which Soloveitchik described as "personal" and reflecting "an intimate relationship" to God, dialogue was "improper." He did concede, however, that in talking about universal concerns such as "War and Peace, Poverty, Freedom, Man's Moral Values, the Threat of Secularism, Technology and Human Values, Civil Rights, etc." Jewish and Christian people of God would naturally express themselves "in universal religious categories" that could well be "incomprehensible to the secularist."

The RCA adopted the Soloveitchik guidelines at its 1964 convention, and the primary Modern Orthodox synagogue body, the Union of Orthodox Jewish Congregations of America (OU), followed suit. Both were member organizations of the Synagogue Council of America (SCA), an umbrella body created in 1926 that was supposed to provide a unified voice for the various streams of American Judaism, although the sectarian Orthodox, refusing to grant even implicit recognition to non-Orthodox Judaism, remained outside. To satisfy its Orthodox constituent organizations, the SCA adhered to the Soloveitchik restrictions on dialogue with Christians, and would maintain that policy until the group's dissolution in 1994.

In 1967, the SCA, the National Council of Churches (its mainline Protestant equivalent), and the National Council of Catholic Bishops' Committee on Interreligious Affairs announced a path-breaking ecumenical initiative: piloting a major interreligious conference. It was to take place in Boston on May 7–8, funded by the Ford Foundation, with "The Role of Conscience" as its theme. As Greenberg would recall, this was "the apex of the hopes and innocent aspirations" of those interested in the new field of Christian-Jewish dialogue. Sensitive, of course, to the special concerns of its two Orthodox member organizations, the SCA made sure that the program dealt with broad universal concerns rather than theological points: "[T]he role of conscience in our society, the process whereby it comes into being, and its application to specific social situations," such as racial justice, war and peace, state aid to religious education, the authority of law, and society's economic obligation to its citizens – thus adhering to Soloveitchik's requirements. Greenberg was one of the Jewish thinkers invited to participate.

However, a front-page article in *The New York Times* by religion editor Edward B. Fiske upset the carefully arranged plans for the conference by heralding it in a way that would make it anathema to Soloveitchik and the Orthodox. While previous Christian-Jewish discussion had been restricted to secular matters, Fiske wrote, he misleadingly went on to say that religious subjects would be on the agenda in Boston. Fiske explained that, up to then, Orthodox leaders had restricted the agenda for such meetings out of "fear that such talks could lead to a watering-down of the faith." Not surprisingly, the sectarian Orthodox issued a public protest: on March 23, the Agudat Harabonim (Union of Orthodox Rabbis) and four smaller groups issued a joint resolution condemning all interreligious dialogue and specifically mentioning the Boston conference. That same day Rabbi Moshe Feinstein, the prime *halakhic* authority of the Union and arguably the leading authority on Jewish legal matters in the United States, wrote to Soloveitchik urging him to join in their ruling, a request he ignored.

But Soloveitchik did take action on his own. In a letter to the president of the RCA, he wrote: "I request the Executive Committee of the Rabbinical Council of America to refrain from participating in, sponsoring or endorsing the interreligious conference on conscience to be held in Boston during May." While he had no objection to the agenda since the "vast majority" of it was "within the sphere of social morality" and therefore open for interreligious discussion, "the unfortunate manner in which this conference has been arranged and publicized," he argued, gave the impression "that Orthodoxy has revised its attitude to ecumenism and plunged into the mainstream of dialoguing and debating the most delicate and intimate theological ideas, which will neither contribute to mutual understanding of the Jew and non-Jew nor toward the promotion and strengthening of the religious cause in general." It was important, Soloveitchik concluded, "to be cautious and careful, even as regards problems of social morality, not to become unintentionally involved in the type of dialogue which is presently in vogue."

Taking their cue from their rabbinic leader, the RCA and the OU announced that they were pulling out of the conference. The SCA proceeded with plans for the event without official Orthodox participation. Greenberg, who had been invited as an individual scholar and not as a representative of any group, had to decide on his course. Orthodox leaders pressured him to withdraw, even threatening that his career prospects within the community could be hurt by a refusal to bow to the decision of Rabbi Soloveitchik. Greenberg, though, saw the option of backing out as a betrayal of his Christian dialogue partners. He was one of the few Orthodox Jews to ignore Soloveitchik's ruling and attend.

Besides placing him starkly outside the Modern Orthodox consensus, the incident affected Greenberg's view of Soloveitchik, whom he had long considered a mentor and source of inspiration. Since the outset of his involvement in interreligious dialogue in the early 1960s, Greenberg had discussed the subject with Soloveitchik, and after the publication of "Confrontation" conveyed his dissent from the rabbi's limitations on dialogue, arguing, first, that the line between social and theological issues was a distinction without a difference, and second, that the Christian interlocutors he dealt with were sincerely interested in learning about Judaism and had no conversionary intentions. These conversations gave Greenberg the distinct impression that Soloveitchik, deep down, agreed with him but felt compelled to place conditions on dialogue to protect himself and the organizations with which he was associated from attack by the sectarian Orthodox. Greenberg assumed he had a green light from Soloveitchik to continue work in this area.

While Soloveitchik made no public comment about Greenberg's involvement in the Boston conference, Greenberg saw the older man's caving in to political pressure even after all his conditions for dialogue – which Greenberg considered unnecessary in any case – were met as a demonstration of weakness that detracted from his capacities as a leader. A disillusioned Greenberg would ever after insist that Soloveitchik really had no principled objection to interreligious dialogue or to religious pluralism, but that he had no stomach for the controversy that would ensue:

> Personally, I had an overwhelming urge to say to him: But if only you had said openly what was really on your mind, then Jews could prepare properly for dialogue. Now the Orthodox will interpret your view as stating that dialogue is not permitted, and the Jewish community will be even less capable of maintaining a

> high-quality conversation. However, I did not have the heart or the courage to challenge him any more than I had.

The break with Soloveitchik implicit in the decision to participate in the Boston conference, following so soon after the open disagreement with Lichtenstein, marked the final stage of Greenberg's divergence from the path that mainstream Orthodoxy took; the disillusionment with Soloveitchik had a long-lasting effect. At a conference in 2003, marking ten years since Soloveitchik's passing, held at the Van Leer Institute in Jerusalem, Greenberg spoke about "Two Doors Rav Soloveitchik Opened and Did Not Walk Through: The Future of Modern Orthodoxy." These "doors" were religious pluralism and the historical-critical approach to Jewish religious texts, both of which Greenberg believed were necessary to make Orthodox Judaism part of the modern intellectual world. Soloveitchik hesitated to walk through to the other side of either, a task Greenberg claimed still needed to be done.

By 1968, Greenberg's references to Orthodoxy were more negative and less nuanced than they had been before, an apparent indication that he was envisioning the broader Jewish horizons that would open up for him once he cut his professional ties with Orthodox institutions. "Jewish Orthodoxy," he said, "stands today where the Catholic Church stood seventy years ago in the pre-theological phase . . . the triumph of authoritarianism, siege mentality, and fundamentalism." At Yeshiva University, he wrote, "the more intensively religious circles tend increasingly towards intellectual and cultural withdrawal." Orthodox day schools, in his view, were "deeply stamped with the psychology of the closed world" and governed by "an unnecessarily authoritarian tone." Orthodoxy, Greenberg declared, had come to stand for "dogmatic assertion, intellectual surrender of judgement" and the "cult of *Gedolim*. . . .".[1]

In later years – long after establishing CLAL outside the Orthodox orbit – Greenberg continued to call for rebuilding Modern Orthodoxy, even preparing a grant proposal, budgeted at $98,750, for a "Modern Orthodox Forum" under CLAL auspices. But the plan never material-

1. Rabbis with large followings that demand complete adherence to their views and legal positions.

ized, and for, some three decades, Greenberg would have virtually no impact on developments within Orthodoxy, which, in the absence of challenging voices like Greenberg's, grew increasingly rigid, ideologically complacent, and monochromatic.

It took a while, but the emergence of Open Orthodoxy and the establishment of Yeshivat Chovevei Torah Rabbinical School in the late 1990s – both reflecting a sense that establishment Modern Orthodoxy had drifted far off course – revived Greenberg's approach and today stand as his vindication. Without mentioning Greenberg's name, Rabbi Avi Weiss's formulation of Open Orthodoxy's principles in 1997 echoed Greenberg's call three decades earlier for Orthodox Judaism to fully address the modern experience. Weiss stressed both the ethical import and practical flexibility of *halakhah*; acknowledged the importance of secular studies as "potential aspects of Torah:" rejected an absolutist or authoritarian model of rabbinic authority; espoused Jewish religious pluralism and cooperative relations with other religions; and called for a reevaluation of the role of women in Orthodox Jewish life – an issue barely on the horizon in the 1960s that Greenberg, and even more so his wife, Blu Greenberg, had pioneered since then. And at Yeshivat Chovevei Torah, founded by Weiss, rabbinical students are exposed to "historical and source-critical methodologies," yet another plank from the Greenberg platform.

Indeed if, as time passes, current demographic trends continue and Orthodoxy constitutes a growing share of American Jewry, Greenberg's efforts to reshape it, so decisively rejected in 1966–67, may, ironically, prove his most lasting legacy.

From Prostitution to Marriage and Back Again: An Interpersonal Sexual Ethic from Rabbinic Sources

Dr. Jennie Rosenfeld

> "Sex has come to be considered a secular activity only because Poskim have abdicated their responsibility in examining its true meaning. Sex is a religious activity and we abuse it by ignoring it."

In an interview published in the Yeshiva University student newspaper *The Commentator* (April 28, 1966), Rabbi Yitz Greenberg commented on the absence of a contemporary Jewish discourse surrounding sexuality. Fifty years after Rabbi Greenberg's interview with "The Commentator," after his call for contemporary Judaism (and specifically the *Poskim*) to grapple with sexuality on both the *halakhic* and ethical levels, there has still not been an adequate response. This is one of the reasons, I believe, why even otherwise observant Jews struggle with and often abandon the attempt to integrate their Judaism into their sexual practice. No one is speaking to their conflict. Reb Yitz was decades ahead of his time in noting this lacuna and its negative impact within the Jewish community. In this chapter, I wish to take up Reb Yitz's challenge to "promulgate a new value system" which would have as its basis the concept of *Tzelem Elokim*.[1]

*

1. The Jewish theology that all human beings are created in the image of God.

Several years ago, while in the throes of writing my doctoral dissertation "Talmudic Re-readings: Toward a Modern Orthodox Sexual Ethic" on the conflict faced by Orthodox Jewish singles between the *halakhic* sexual restrictions and the cravings of the human soul, and the need to articulate a sexual ethic which could help them to navigate this conflict, I had a conversation with a non-Jewish colleague at work. In trying to explain to her the unique conflict faced by Orthodox Jewish singles, she cut me off to say that the Orthodox and the Jews and the singles are not the only ones in need of a sexual ethic and that as, a married non-Jew and atheist, she knows she would benefit from a sexual ethic – just because the sexual ethic was based in Jewish tradition didn't mean that it had nothing to say to her. And so, with a bit of trepidation and her voice in my head, I begin. . . .

The Sexual Revolution of the 1960s and 1970s abandoned all the old laws – religious and social – relating to sexuality. Today, more than forty years later, there are no new laws. However, though people may not want laws, they are still searching for guidance on how to order their sexual lives. And, with the lack of guidance in this context, individuals are left to struggle alone with their sexual decision-making, perhaps wanting to make moral choices, but lacking any moral compass to help them in this difficult endeavor.

One social ill that emerged in the aftermath of the sexual revolution is the complete void of guidance related to sexual decision-making; the "antiquated" guidelines of religion have been overturned and no new guidelines have been written. People are, therefore, left floundering in search of a meaningful framework in which to locate their sexual decisions. This void often leads people into sexual behaviors that are risky – physically, medically, and emotionally. And sexuality often remains apart from the rest of the person's identity because people don't hold themselves to the same standards of behavior that they would demand from themselves in other realms.

The Jewish feminist theologian and professor of religious studies, Judith Plaskow, articulates the problem as follows: "The simplest is the gap – indeed, one might say the abyss – between contemporary practices and traditional sexual mores" (*Decentering*, 23–4). Plaskow argues that it cannot be that the majority of Jews feel abandoned by tradition in this critical area of life; the tradition must respond and we must search to hear a voice from tradition that will resonate with life today.

Plaskow continues:

> The enormous variety in forms and values in human sexual expression cross-culturally points to the need for frameworks within which people can think and make decisions about sexuality. Despite what the old song says, sex is not just a matter of "doing what comes naturally." We always require, and indeed always find ourselves in, some context within which we negotiate this area of our lives. As things now stand, however, many Jews who try to integrate their Judaism into their daily experience don't even make the attempt when it comes to sexuality. This means that they are left without meaningful guidance from tradition in a significant area. It also means that at least some of the large numbers of synagogue members who find themselves or their children living at odds with traditional norms feel ashamed, and/or angry, and/or isolated. They experience themselves as abandoned by institutions that ought to serve as sources of sustenance.

Plaskow claims that individuals need frameworks within which to negotiate their sexual decision-making. And while Plaskow writes as a Jew, the crisis of the gap between tradition and practice of which she writes is not just a Jewish crisis – it is really a crisis for the larger Western world: "Although our culture is saturated with sexual images, there is an enormous gap between media fixation on sexuality and pressures toward sexual activity, and the capacity for individuals to speak comfortably about and claim responsibility for their own sexuality." These various gaps – the gap between tradition and practice, the gap between a hypersexual culture and personal comfort with sexuality, and the gap between the ideal and the real – create confusion in Jew and non-Jew alike about the role of sexual values in their lives.

Empirical evidence on the void of sexual values and the ensuing confusion that it serves to create is hard to come by as sexuality surveys focus more on practice than on beliefs. However, in the margins of public debate, the issue of sexual values looms large. In *Invented Moralities:*

Sexual Values in an Age of Uncertainty, Jeffrey Weeks – an academic in the fields of history and sociology with a focus on sexuality and also a gay activist in Britain – argues that:

> . . . values have shot to the top of the political agenda on both left and right. As traditional ways of life fragment under the revolutionary changes of our times, as social identities are reshaped and remade, as well-established political alignments collapse and new alliances are painfully constructed, as the public sphere is redefined, and the boundaries between public and private shift, as epidemic disease returns to haunt the imagination of the postmodern world, and as the flame of love flickers in the cold drought of various forms of hate, debates over values encapsulate our uncertainties about how we should live.

One example of this occurred in the debates that raged in the United States during the George W. Bush Administration over abstinence-only versus comprehensive sexual education. Both sides of the debate grappled with questions of values and the disconnect between Christian standards of morality and modern experience, while differing on how to deal with them. Weeks continues:

> We live in a world of uncertainty, where good guides and firm guarantees that we can reach any particular destination are in short supply, and where the goals themselves are cloudy and indeterminate. Nowhere is this uncertainty more acute than in the domain of sexuality, which has been the subject in the recent past of apparently endless panics, controversies, anguished moralizings and the rebirth of the value issue. . . . Today, the question of values has reached the centre of the political and cultural agenda, with sexuality as the magnetic core.

Weeks writes about the prevalence of confusion and uncertainty in the postmodern world – the postmodern world is a place where choice is glorified, and yet we are given no guidance in how to choose. In such circumstances, choice becomes more of burden than freedom:

> Choice has become the ruling morality both of the political right (at least in economic matters) and of the liberal left. Yet how, and with what criteria, we should choose is less clear. Is it surprising then that a sense of ending, the closure of narrative certainties, presages ethical confusion?

It is "ethical confusion" that motivates me to write and to bring to the fore a taste of Judaism's rich offerings in the realm of sexual ethics. The Talmudic text – when read beyond the level of law – contains a wealth of sexual values which speak to even the most ardent hedonist.

I believe that a return to the Talmudic text, along with a reading of the Talmudic text that seeks to appropriate it in ways relevant in the postmodern world, provides redemption from the "ethical desert" that presides over sexuality today. In so doing, Jew and non-Jew alike can find the tools that will empower them to make positive choices in their sexual lives.

Beginnings of a Jewish Response

Looking to the Jewish tradition for sexual values can help to provide a meaningful framework for all people and not just Jews. When focusing exclusively on the legal side within the rich Jewish tradition of law and lore, the teaching may be more particular to the community that observes these laws. However, exploring the ethical teachings within our tradition, which can stand independently of the law, has the potential to speak more broadly.

In this chapter I explore two passages from the Babylonian Talmud that focus on the interpersonal realm and how to treat the other in the midst of a sexual encounter and in the broader relationship. I believe that the sexual ethic that emerges from this reading can have universal relevance, though it is certainly not a comprehensive sexual ethic. There are dozens of other relevant Talmudic passages that would need to be analyzed in order to address the totality of sexual ethics and what follows is only a beginning. Reading these two stories makes a point about the way an interpersonal sexual ethic can be relevant in relationships of different natures; from the casual sexual encounter to marital sexuality.

My reading of these rich and multivalent sources is focused; my goal is to mine texts for contemporary relevance. I, therefore, aim towards appropriation, not historical reconstruction, of the sources. I am influenced by a literary approach and will sometimes use various avenues of literary theory (i.e. deconstruction) when they help further my goal of allowing this ancient text to speak to modern ears.

A word about "The Talmud" is in order before I begin: The Talmud is a multi-vocal text that presents many different and contradictory voices, often without adjudicating between them. I do not believe that the Talmud has one view of sexuality or sexual ethics, though some would have it that way. The Talmud contains hundreds of discussions of sexuality in both law and lore. While I don't wish to claim that the narratives that I will read are representative of the Talmud as a whole, neither are they all that exceptional or unique. Nevertheless, the present analysis stems from my desire for a literary appropriation of the Talmudic text to the current moment, rather than an attempt to reconstruct the "original intent" of the authors.

While marriage is certainly the desired norm within the Talmudic framework, the Talmudic literature certainly did not ignore situations involving non-marital sexual relationships. Similarly, while the story of the married rabbi depicts asceticism within marriage that is not encouraged – as sexual relations are part of the husband's marital duty to his wife – many Talmudic stories valorize scholars who leave their homes and wives for extended periods of sexual abstinence in order to travel to a center of Torah scholarship.

a. Between Subject and Object: Respecting the Other

In searching for an ethic of interpersonal interaction, we will examine two Talmudic stories of intimate male-female relationships, whose striking differences make a universal point about what it means to be in an ethical relationship. One story involves illicit sexuality in the context of prostitution and the other involves licit sexuality within the marital context. Seen side by side it emerges that sometimes the "forbidden" relationship is the one that deserves to last since it is more ethical.

The first story (*Menaḥot* 44a) involves a Torah scholar whose only given identifying information is his scrupulosity in performing the *mitz-*

vah of *tzitzit* (fringed garments), and revolves around his assignation with a particular prostitute:

> There was an incident with a man who was very scrupulous about the commandment of *tzitzit* (wearing fringes): He heard of a certain harlot in one of the towns by the sea who accepted four hundred gold [coins] for her hire, and he sent her four hundred gold [coins] and made an appointment with her. When the day of his appointment arrived, he came and waited at her doorway, and her maid came and told her, 'That man who sent you four hundred gold [coins] is here and waiting at the door'; to which she replied 'Let him come in.' He came in and she prepared for him seven beds, six of silver and one of gold; and between one bed and the other there were steps of silver, but the last were of gold. She then went up to the top bed and sat down upon it naked, and he too went up to sit next to her naked – but the four fringes [of his garment] struck him across the face, whereupon he escaped and sat upon the ground, and she too slipped off and sat on the ground. She said to him, 'By the love of the Romans, I will not leave you until you tell me what blemish you saw in me.' He replied, 'By the [Temple] service, I [swear] I have never seen a woman as beautiful as you are, but there is one precept that the Lord our God has commanded us and it is called *tzitzit* – and with regard to it *I am the Lord your God* is written twice, signifying that I am He who will exact punishment in the future, and I am He who will give reward in the future – and now [the *tzitzit*] appeared to me as four witnesses [testifying against me].' She said to him, 'I will not leave you until you tell me your name, the name of your town, the name of your teacher, and the name of your school where you learn Torah.' He wrote it down and handed it to her. Then she arose and divided all of her possessions; one third to the government, one third to the poor, and one third she took with her in her hand, in addition to the bedclothes. She then came to the house of study of R. Hiya, and said to him, 'Master, give instructions about me that they make me a convert.' He replied, 'My daughter, maybe you have fallen in love with one of the students?' She thereupon took out the note and gave it to him. He said to her, 'Go and enjoy

> your acquisition!' The same bed-clothes that she had spread for him for an illicit purpose she now spread for him lawfully [on their marriage bed]. This was that man's reward in this world and as for the reward in the world to come I do not know how much.

The story is strange on a number of levels, not least of which is the unlikely marriage between Torah scholar and prostitute. After hearing that there is a prostitute who demands four hundred gold coins as her price and after premeditating the sin to the point of even sending the money in advance and setting an appointment, in the moment of truth the Torah scholar is unable to actualize his fantasy. After the voyage and the extravagant expenditure, and as he is climbing to the highest of the seven beds, while taking off his clothes, suddenly he reaches his *tzitzit* and he stops mid-action and falls to the floor. Any hope of a sexual encounter is over, and yet the student sits on the floor. Reading the story, I would have expected him to run right out of the room once he realizes what he was about to do and decides that he is not going to do it. There is nothing that mandates that he stay, and caution would dictate that he leave as quickly as possible.

By sitting down on the floor, however, the man indicates simultaneously that their intended sexual congress is over while also making it clear that something has been left unfinished. He cannot simply leave the prostitute naked and alone on the top bed. Until this point there has been no direct communication between the man and the prostitute, though the context of their encounter has been laden with meanings for both; on his side, premeditation, advance payment, and the journey into a fantasy, and on her side the receiving of these attentions and the need to justify her reputation. And the scholar just can't leave; he needs conversation and closure, and he wants to speak, feeling that he owes it both to himself and to her to give an explanation.

The conversation that ensues is completely unexpected in the retinue of standard communication between man and prostitute. It is also fairly unique that the Torah scholar and the prostitute engage in conversation beyond negotiating a price. And here there is no haggling over money, nor any bawdiness or banter. The couple speaks, face to face, whether naked or clothed the text does not say. The scholar speaks to the prostitute – human being to human being – and shares with her the epiphany that brought him running to the floor. Naked, the prostitute hears the words of Torah that can speak to this man from within the throes of desire, and can keep him doing what he feels is right even as his desire for her remains. He tells the prostitute about the *mitzvah* of *tzitzit*, about the concepts of divine reward and punishment and about the way in which the *tzitzit* appeared to him as witnesses of his actions. He shares the Torah with her as he might share it with a learned study partner. In that moment of speech, of revelation, of sharing, the differences between them are erased and all that remains is the basic humanity of each. This woman revealed herself to him and he owes her an explanation. She is not Jewish and not learned, she is a prostitute who routinely agrees to the objectification that sex for money entails and who routinely reveals herself in this manner, she swears by a Roman deity and she is naked – and yet, he owes her an explanation and shares with her the motivating force that is closest to his heart. And she learns his name, while we who read the story never learn his name. She has the discretion to conceal it. The fact that there is open conversation between them defines the encounter and relationship as one of individuals – of subjects communicating with one another through speech, rather than a subject using an object for a limited purpose.

The story has a fairytale ending of the prostitute's conversion and marriage to the student, and life happily ever after with the same beds that she suggested to him illicitly now being used as the sanctified marital bed. It is a marriage of integrity. Both the scholar and the prostitute felt desire and had a forbidden encounter on some level. Yet rather than turn away from that past due to shame, they embrace it while transforming it. The events of the story and the rabbi's relationship with the prostitute are ethical from both sides. The prostitute treats the rabbi as a human being when she gets off the bed and sits with him on the floor as an equal. And the rabbi treats the prostitute as a human being in speaking with her, face to face, and in giving her his name, breaking the anonymity of prostitute and client. Theirs is an ethical relationship throughout, despite the elements of transgression within it; the context of transgression in no way impacts the ethical treatment that they give to each other, as it potentially could. We will return to this point after examining a very different story.

Elsewhere, the Talmud (*Kiddushin* 81b) tells the story of a married rabbi who ends up having an illicit sexual encounter with his own wife:

> R. Hiya b. Ashi was in the habit of saying 'May the Merciful One save us from the evil inclination,' every time he fell upon his face [for the prayers of supplication]. One day his wife heard him and said, 'Since it has already been so many years since he has separated from [having sexual relations] with me, what is the reason that he says this [prayer]?' One day, while he was studying in the garden, she adorned herself and repeatedly walked back and forth before him. He said to her, 'Who are you?' She said, 'I am Heruta and have returned today.' He solicited her [for sex]. She said to him, 'Bring me that pomegranate from the top of that tree'; he jumped up, went, and brought it to her. When he returned to his house his wife was firing the oven, and he ascended and sat in it. She said to him, 'What does this mean?' He told her what had happened. She said to him, 'It was me [and you therefore did no wrong]'; but he didn't believe her until she gave him proof. He then said to her, 'Nevertheless, my intention was to sin.' That righteous man fasted all his life, until he died from it.

This story is about licit sexuality and asceticism gone awry. We see a Torah scholar, R. Hiya b. Ashi, engage in an illicit sexual relationship with his wife. After several years of avoiding intercourse with his wife and praying about it daily, he finally succumbs to her advances when she dresses up and pretends to be a prostitute. From the outset, the relationship between R. Hiya b. Ashi and his wife is cast in secrets, suspicion, and guesswork, rather than open and clear communication.

The story opens with the wife overhearing her husband praying for salvation from the evil inclination; we don't know how long he has been reciting this prayer and neither does she. Instead of confronting him directly, the wife questions his actions in her own mind – if he hasn't slept with her for years, then why does he need this type of prayer? – and takes matters into her own hands. She connives to trick R. Hiya b. Ashi into having sex with her, presumably to test whether his evil inclination is at all present and whether she still has the power to arouse him, which she does. Only after he returns home and sits in the oven remorsefully, do they first speak to each other directly as man and wife; until now, we have never seen the couple communicate as a married couple, as the limited verbal exchange between them occurs only when R. Hiya b. Ashi is still under the assumption that he is dealing with Heruta the prostitute, and is negotiating a price with her.

Though, to his credit, R. Hiya b. Ashi's remorse and confession of his "adultery" to his wife, is immediate, there is still a wide gulf between them. The real communication about their relationship, about why this happened, about why R. Hiya b. Ashi hasn't had sex with his wife in years despite his virility and/or desire, about the wife's feelings in being denied the intimacy to which marriage entitles her – is absent. And though she finally convinces him that it was her whom he slept with, the wife doesn't succeed in assuaging her husband's guilt or in reigniting their sexual relationship, as he fasts in penance for the rest of his days until death brings him respite.

Though this relationship is a sanctified marriage that is never actually violated through illicit sexuality, there is something disturbing about the level and type of interaction between husband and wife. In all that is barely said, in all the deception, guesswork, and loneliness, there is something lacking in this relationship. There is something that the prostitute and the student of the previous story had that this rabbi and his wife do not: While R. Hiya b. Ashi can remain celibate within marriage for years without a word on the subject to his wife (from what we see in the text), the student feels a moral obligation to explain to the prostitute, whom he has just met, why he cannot go through with their planned sexual encounter. While R. Hiya b. Ashi is ascetic to the point that he can't even forgive himself for a sin that was never actually committed and move forward in the relationship with his wife, the student is aware enough of his own humanity to forgive himself and be able to build a life with his partner in sin. At its root, open communication is about respecting the other, and respecting the divine spark (*Tzelem Elokim*) within them. Being aware of the divinity within the other at all times, including during the sexual act itself, mandates honesty and direct communication.

b. Between Wives and Prostitutes: Practical Implications

Reading these two stories in conversation with each other opens up aspects of an interpersonal sexual ethic that neither story would yield when read alone; and, pushing the limits of interpretation will yield even more. In one instance, the Torah scholar views the prostitute as a human being and is able to see his future wife within the prostitute. In the other, the married rabbi sees the prostitute within his wife and is therefore unable to relate to her as a full human being. The communication between the Torah scholar and prostitute in *Menahot* 44a is more open and real than the communication between husband and wife in *Kiddushin* 81b – and the differences are striking when seeing the two juxtaposed. Another important point found in the juxtaposition is that being in an ethical relationship does not always correlate to the *halakhic* legitimacy of the relationship. The Talmud shows that just as a relationship between spouses can be unethical and dehumanizing, so too can a forbidden relationship be ethical and uplifting, though it remains forbidden.

The ethics of interpersonal relations are never an absolute and are not susceptible to the same clear lists of rules and regulations that define a body of law. Ethics always need conflict to be interesting and can never be spelled out to the same extent as laws can. The sexual ethic that emerges from these stories is grounded in certain broad guidelines, such as maintaining awareness of the divine spark of the other person and treating both oneself and the other with the dignity which that entails. Ethics is about a real respect for the other person, even when circumstances and differences in rank and station and religion might have us think otherwise – each and every human being is created in the image of God and that fact overrides all others. Ethics is about treating the other as a subject and not as an object – the image of God within elevates the status of each individual. Ethics is about open communication, about giving a person the answers they deserve to be able to move forward in life – our words can have the power to make or break those people who are intimately connected with us. Ethics is about the face to face encounter with the other – the vulnerability that it engenders and the respect and care that are therefore mandated.

The French Jewish philosopher Emmanuel Levinas wrote:

> 'Thou shalt not kill' or 'Thou shalt love thy neighbor' not only forbids the violence of murder: it also concerns all the slow and invisible killing committed in our desires and vices, in all the innocent cruelties of natural life . . . even in the haughty obstinacy of our objectifying and our thematizing . . . .

This passage points the way towards an ethical imperative to treat the other as a subject at all times, as "objectifying" and "thematizing" the other are alike forms of murder; the ethical obligation to the other entails seeing him or her as a human being to whom we have a responsibility. However, the details of the actions that correspond to this ethical awareness need to be determined in the situation and in the moment. There is no blanket ethical behavior, for what is ethical in one situation may be its antithesis in another. Especially within the context of violation where boundaries of different types are being blurred, determining the ethical course of action may not be easy to navigate or to pin down. However, I think that if these two stories can serve as the voices in our head when entering a sexual encounter – be it with a lifelong partner or with an anonymous stranger – the characters within will help guide us in the hard work of navigating situational ethics. Respect can mean different things in different contexts, but treating the other as a subject, as an equal, and as a "Thou" in Buber's language, can go a long way in terms of shaping our sexual decision-making as well as our treatment of the other in any given sexual encounter.

The Torah scholar in the first story goes so far in his concern for the other that he is close to forgetting himself in the process. In sitting down in the prostitute's bedroom at a point when he has decided not to pursue the encounter, the scholar puts his religious values in jeopardy. In staying in that space, he remains at risk of being re-seduced. And yet, he takes that risk without batting an eyelash, because what stands on the other side – what would happen if he just left – is the humiliation of the prostitute. As a subject and as an equal, she deserves answers for his behavior, even though giving her an answer simultaneously brings him closer to her. Decisions like that involve putting the other first and occasionally jeopardizing one's own selfish interests – what Levinas calls our "infinite" or "unlimited" responsibility toward the other and the stranger – and they stand at the heart of an interpersonal sexual ethic.

In light of and despite my belief that ethics cannot be quantified, I will end with a few practical implications:

1. Even within a long-term marriage, the sexual relationship cannot be taken for granted. Ongoing communication is essential in order to maintain the relationship over the years and through changing circumstances. Simply getting married does not guarantee respect or satisfaction; to make marriage work over time requires work!
2. Even within a short-term relationship or a "one night stand," treating the other as a subject rather than an object is important. Respect and clear communication have the power to transform what could otherwise become a commercial relationship into something deeper, and into a potentially life-changing encounter. While I do not wish to imply that the Talmud encourages or condones prostitution or casual sex, the story of the prostitute teaches us that even within the context of prostitution, the potential exists for moving beyond money into a relationship of "I–Thou." By extension, I would argue that the Talmudic mandate to always treat the other as fully human exists equally in any type of sexual relationship – from the committed to the casual. I recognize that this reading is not the only one, and that one can legitimately argue the story the opposite way as well – namely, that the very fact that the scholar refrained from sex with the prostitute was precisely because he recognized their relationship as one of "I–Thou" and that such a relationship by its definition precludes a commercial sexual encounter.
3. An outside observer to other people's relationships should never really pass judgment, since an outsider does not know the intimate nature of a couple's relationship and its meaning for them. While some may smile upon marriage (assuming that simply being married indicates one is in an ethically sound relationship) and frown upon non-marital sexuality, the above stories challenge our ability to be sanguine about the assumption that marriage or the lack thereof is an indicator of the ethics of the relationship. In an era in which many people are forming less-committed relationships, it is essential that we do not ignore this truth and articulate an ethical framework that speaks to the need for human dignity and validation. And while such relationships may be proscribed

by Jewish law, the outsider should still refrain from passing judgment. People who are involved in a sexual relationship of any type (be it within marriage or not), need to work to make that relationship as ethical and respectful as possible.

*

Safer sex, despite the well-known hazards, difficulties and 'backslidings' that make it often problematic, can be taken as symbolic of a wider need for a sense of caring responsibility that extends from sexual behavior to all aspects of social life. Love as responsibility means accepting that we are not isolated monads, sufficient unto ourselves. Our humanity is dependent on our caring and responsible involvement with others. This in turn means respecting the other.

For Weeks, respecting the other can translate into safer sexual practice. However, it is a mistake to leave that as the only translation. Rabbi Yitz Greenberg suggested using the principle of *mi-devar sheker tirhak* 'thou shall remain far from any falsehood' (Exodus 23:7) as the foundation for a sexual ethic in which people's sexual activity reflects the truth of the relationship rather than the totality of their desire. In this context, respect is also about setting appropriate boundaries, and even when those boundaries do not conform to the mandates of *halakhah,* they should at least conform to what he calls the truth of the relationship.

Incorporating Jewish values into the public discourse can transform the nature of how we view and experience sex. The value that underlies the aforementioned Talmudic stories – namely treating the other in the sexual relationship with respect, whether in a casual or a life-time relationship – has the potential to give people of all backgrounds a meaningful framework for this most important realm of human experience.

Hebrew Source A

מעשה באדם אחד שהיה זהיר במצות ציצית, שמע שיש זונה בכרכי הים שנוטלת ד׳ מאות זהובים בשכרה, שיגר לה ארבע מאות זהובים וקבע לה זמן. כשהגיע זמנו, בא וישב על הפתח. נכנסה שפחתה ואמרה לה: אותו אדם ששיגר ליך ד׳ מאות זהובים בא וישב על הפתח, אמרה היא: יכנס, נכנס. הציעה לו ז׳ מטות, שש של כסף ואחת של זהב, ובין כל אחת ואחת סולם של כסף ועליונה של זהב, עלתה וישבה

על גבי עליונה כשהיא ערומה, ואף הוא עלה לישב ערום כנגדה, באו ד׳ ציציותיו וטפחו לו על פניו, נשמט וישב לו ע״ג קרקע, ואף היא נשמטה וישבה ע״ג קרקע. אמרה לו: גפה של רומי, שאיני מניחתך עד שתאמר לי מה מום ראית בי. אמר לה: העבודה, שלא ראיתי אשה יפה כמותך, אלא מצוה אחת צוינו ה׳ אלהינו וציצית שמה, וכתיב בה +במדבר ט״ו+ אני ה׳ אלהיכם שתי פעמים, אני הוא שעתיד ליפרע ואני הוא שעתיד לשלם שכר, עכשיו נדמו עלי כד׳ עדים. אמרה לו: איני מניחך עד שתאמר לי מה שמך ומה שם עירך ומה שם רבך ומה שם מדרשך שאתה למד בו תורה, כתב ונתן בידה. עמדה וחילקה כל נכסיה, שליש למלכות ושליש לעניים ושליש נטלה בידה, חוץ מאותן מצעות, ובאת לבית מדרשו של ר׳ חייא. אמרה לו: רבי, צוה עלי ויעשוני גיורת, אמר לה: בתי, שמא עיניך נתת באחד מן התלמידים? הוציאה כתב מידה ונתנה לו, אמר לה: לכי זכי במקחך, אותן מצעות שהציעה לו באיסור הציעה לו בהיתר, זה מתן שכרו בעה״ז, ולעה״ב איני יודע כמה.

Hebrew Source B

רבי חייא בר אשי הוה רגיל כל עידן דהוה נפל לאפיה, הוה אמר: הרחמן יצילנו מיצר הרע. יומא חד שמעתינהו דביתהו, אמרה: מכדי הא כמה שני דפריש ליה מינאי, מאי טעמא קאמר הכי? יומא חדא הוה קא גריס בגינתיה, קשטה נפשה חלפה ותנייה קמיה. אמר לה: מאן את? אמרה: אנא חרותא דהדרי מיומא, תבעה, אמרה ליה: אייתי ניהליה להך רומנא דריש צוציתא, שוור אזל אתייה ניהלה. כי אתא לביתיה, הוה קא שגרא דביתהו תנורא, סליק וקא יתיב בגויה. אמרה ליה: מאי האי? אמר לה: הכי והכי הוה מעשה, אמרה ליה: אנא הואי. לא אשגח בה, עד דיהבה ליה סימני, אמר לה: אנא מיהא לאיסורא איכווני. כל ימיו של אותו צדיק היה מתענה, עד שמת באותה מיתה.

The Journey To Pluralism: A Modern Orthodox Narrative and Plea

Rabbi Irving (Yitz) Greenberg

1. Coming of Age as a Modern Orthodox Jew

I grew up in an immigrant liberal Modern Orthodox home. My mother was deeply devout. My father was a *Talmid Chakham,* and an *ilui,* a *musmach* of Rav Chayim Brisker. His greatest love was learning and teaching *gemara.* He was the Rav of the *Chevrah Shas* of Temple Beth El of Borough Park, the leading Modern Orthodox Shul, which featured world-class *chazanim* and the English speaking Rabbi in the main Minyan and a *Chevrah Shas*/daily Talmud class given by my Yiddish speaking father downstairs. My father was an independent thinker who strongly emphasized *bein adam la'chaveiro* and the importance of morality.

As a student, I attended Modern Orthodox all-day schools: elementary Yeshiva Etz Chayim and Talmudical Academy and Yeshiva University High School for Boys in Brooklyn. I planned to attend Yeshiva College but was diverted to a European refugee *Mussar* Yeshiva, Beth Joseph Rabbinical Seminary (Novardok). Although they were not modern, the school leadership accepted my going to Brooklyn College. They focused educationally on *middot, kavvanah*/integrity in ritual, the importance of *zikui harabim* (upgrading the masses through Torah study) and *bein adam lachaveiro* behavior rather than on ideological issues of modernity. The college studies opened me up intellectually more than my classmates who attended Yeshiva College, while Bais Yosef's piety turned me more intensely religious than my peers. I studied and received *Semikhah* there. Out of all this interaction, I came out a Modern Orthodox Jew, fulfilled in it and convinced of its divinity.

I accepted and took for granted Modern Orthodox assumptions. Orthodoxy was the only valid form of Judaism. To fulfill *davening* and perform all other *mitzvot,* I went exclusively to Orthodox shuls and ate only in places certified by Orthodox rabbis. I never attended a Reform Temple. Although my father told me that Christians in America were different from Poland and were respectful of Jews, I never entered a church. Certainly, I never thought of Christianity as a valid religion, let alone a covenantal partner of God.

Every religious group lived in its own cocoon in the 1950s. There was little first-hand contact with non-group members that might shake the stereotyped dismissal of other faiths/denominations as inferior. Not surprisingly, all religions continued to present themselves as absolute, with exclusive monopolies on God and revelation, possessing truths that offered the primary (if not only) way to salvation. Of course, the urban setting, the expanding media, the growing percentage of people who went to college/university were bringing more people into contact with each other and exposing more and more religions and ways of life to everyone else in society. The geographic, communication, and cultural infrastructure of absolutism was breaking down, but the critical mass of encounter and exposure had not yet been attained. I remained a liberal, but unselfconscious and complacent Modern Orthodox Jew who assumed Orthodoxy's adequacy and superiority. I was happy and quite fulfilled in this religious way of life – and dismissed the alternatives.

2. Encounter with the Holocaust

While on a Fulbright visiting professorship in Israel in 1961, I encountered the Holocaust for the first time in a direct, personal way. I was overwhelmed. Studying, reading, wrestling with the event took over my life. The endless cruelty and death shattered my faith that life and good were destined to win out in this world. I could not reconcile the fact that there was no visible intervention to stop the destruction with my belief in God and the covenant which the Lord and the people of Israel had jointly established. There were days when all my religious declarations rang hollow and I fell silent. There were offsetting factors – a lifetime of religious fulfillment, my wife's love, our newborn first child's life, the miracle of Jerusalem thriving. Daily, I saw the ongoing creation of Israel and the covenant being renewed before my eyes. But the incubus of rampant evil and meaninglessness would not let go either. I went forward, deeply conflicted, but shifted my life priorities to serve Jewry. I promised myself to work to reconcile with God, and to incorporate the orienting events of the Shoah and Israel into the religious life and the way forward for the Jewish people.

The Holocaust decisively changed the inner equilibrium of my religious life. Since my faith had barely survived, the certitude that God controlled everything – and that the Lord had decreed Orthodoxy and *halakhah* (so all nonobservant people were seriously lacking) – was materially weakened. The claim of absolute authority of the Torah, as understood by my traditional teachers, suddenly lacked credibility. I noticed that the Nazis had targeted all Jews for destruction. The enemy understood that as long as any Jew and the message he embodied survived, Nazi idolatry was contradicted. I concluded that I needed to take seriously the whole range of Jewish movements and views to understand their witness to God and redemption, which the Nazis so loathed.

I further saw that the Orthodox understanding of God and of humans' role in history had led them to their disastrous opposition to Zionism as well as to repeated bad policy decisions during the Shoah. Although no movement had adequately dealt with the unfolding Holocaust, the secular Zionists and modern movements provided faith saving alternatives afterwards. The traditional Orthodox were incapable of running a society or creating a political haven in which Jewry could live. I came to see the courage of all Jews who chose to go on living as Jews after the Shoah. Their amazing heroism in stepping up and taking responsibility for Jewish history moved me to the core. Emotionally, I experienced them as partners and as indispensable leaders, not as people handicapped by their religious views or shortcomings.

I even understood the paradox that secular life and creations were the most credible testimony that God and the covenant were still alive. Even more, I grasped that the totality of the Holocaust grew out of modern culture's combination of generating increasing force in every area of life – much of it for good – while enabling the concentration and deployment of that power to a single purpose (in this case for an evil goal) as never before. In time, I came to see that pluralism – breaking up and diffusing power in every political, military, cultural, religious form – was an essential tactic to assure that never again would such a single-minded crime be carried out. However, at the end of that first year, I had no clue how to act on these insights or to translate them into a shift from absolutism to pluralism.

3. Interfaith Pluralism: The Case of Christianity

Pluralist understanding crept up on me emotionally before I could understand it logically. It was the unlikely and unexpected outcome of an early involvement in dialogue.[1] Shocked by the catastrophic cruelty of the Holocaust, and concerned that traditional Christian anti-Semitism provided the infrastructure for the Nazis' singling out the Jews, my wife and I resolved to engage in Jewish-Christian dialogue. Our goal was less to encounter Christianity and more to convince Christians that their faith was serving as the seed bed for the longest-running and most total and vicious hatred on the planet – anti-Semitism.[2] In the process of dialogue, we met remarkable human beings, who were as determined as we were that Christianity would repent. They insisted that it live up to the standard of love that it proclaimed so that it would never again give aid and comfort to this hatred. As I met these people I came to know their ethical intensity, their passion for redeeming humanity – and their religious roots. Ultimately it sank in that Christianity deserved credit for being a primary nurturer of people of such moral grandeur.

One life-transforming moment came in the backwoods of Sri Lanka. I encountered there a whole community of Christians who had left a life of wealth, ease, and fame in Norway to follow Jesus and take up the cross. They cared for a village of brain-damaged children who were abandoned by their parents. I was stunned by the raw encounter with

1. For a comprehensive and detailed exposition see "On the Road to New Encounter between Judaism and Christianity: A Personal Journey" in Greenberg, *For the Sake of Heaven and Earth; the New Encounter of Judaism and Christianity,* 3–48.

2. See Robert Wistrich, *A Lethal Obsession: Anti-Semitism from Antiquity to the Global Jihad* (New York, Random House, 2010).

the Divine One "who dwells with the oppressed and lowly in spirit" (Isaiah 57: 15). I was no less moved by the power of this faith to inspire unlimited sacrificial love of God and humans alike. Such experiences and further exposure to Christian religious life changed my religious understanding. I came to see that in the church or a Christian prayer community that "surely the Lord is in this place; and I did not know" (Genesis 28:16).

To my surprise, I discovered that another religion – which had important elements that contradicted my Torah's teaching and which I judged were wrong – nevertheless was a true channel of connection between the God of Israel and humanity. In my youth, I believed that it was a show of disrespect for my religion to imply that some religiously valid divine worship was going on in a church, for this was the worship of a no-God [i.e. human]. Now I experienced to the depth of my being that God was active among Christians with a profound power that I encountered all too rarely even in my own community. I could not go on believing that Christians' prayers were not efficacious. Nor could I deny what I saw with my own eyes, that Christian ethics were guiding people to work for redemption. Thus, I came to understand that this was a valid and true religion by my (Jewish) standards, i.e., that it was a channel to connect humans to partner with God and it taught people to live a covenantal life of *Tikkun Olam.*

Gradually, it dawned on me that I was no longer an absolutist – one who believes that his religion is true and godly and that it had 100 percent of truth and a monopoly on relationship with God. Now I saw that if I trusted in God and the Torah, the fact that God entered into relationships with other faith communities was not a betrayal of my community's covenant. Nor did it mean that Jewry had received a false signal when it was instructed "to walk after the Lord your God" (Deuteronomy 13:5) on its distinctive paths. I determined to live in the tension of this knowledge rather than deny either of my contradictory true experiences. This made me a pluralist – one who acknowledges that sometimes there are plural (i.e., more than one) truths. They may disagree, even substantially, but they do not invalidate each other. Since I continued to reject elements of Christianity as wrong and saw still other religions as invalid, I had not become a relativist who believes that any and all religions were equally true (or false). As I deepened in my pluralism, I continued to believe that my religion was true and authoritative but recognized that it does not have a monopoly of all truth; nor does its life contain all of God's revelation.

The experience of the validity of Christianity did not communicate to me – or convince me – that Jesus is actually part of the Godhead. As a Jew, I continue to experience this aspect of the Trinity as a departure from the "purity" of putting all one's trust and faith in God alone. However, I came to understand this Christian affirmation more lovingly and respectfully. They saw Jesus as an "outreach" from God, who brings all the prayers and trust and faith expressed in him to the Creator, the God of Israel, the One to whom I feel covenanted. Therefore, I happily acknowledged that the Christian religion partners and prays to the same God that I do. This led me to understand that Jesus plays a role much like intermediaries in Jewish tradition. From the angels and prophets to wonderworking rabbis, Hasidic rebbes, and Sephardic "saints," Jews have turned to such figures throughout Jewish history to help close the enormous gap they saw between their finite, flawed mortal selves and the infinite, uncontrollable, beyond-all-conceptions of the Divine.

I also understood that in their religious experiences, Christians experienced Jesus as God "in the flesh." I do not. But even here I came to understand this phenomenon in a more respectful, generous spirit. I now interpret the classic statement of the medieval Tosafists in new perspective. They wrote that Christians "associate" Jesus with God. This is not *avodah zarah* (idolatry) that is to be treated as utterly without merit or right to exist. For Jews, such association would be considered such a great departure from monotheism that it is judged and treated as idol worship. But Gentiles are not commanded to live by such a "pure" standard of abstraction in understanding the Divine. Therefore, Christianity should not be defined or treated as idolatry. I see this approach, not as a patronizing Jewish affirmation that given Gentiles' religious limitations, Christianity is close enough to monotheism to be treated kindly. Rather, I interpret the Tosafists' insight to mean that out of the history of the Jewish encounter with God and the ongoing categories of understanding articulated in the tradition, Jews have come to experience the Divine Presence in an unmediated form – in which God did not need (or see fit) to be present in actual human form in order to covenant with the people. In the unfolding covenantal relationship with Gentiles, which Christianity represents, the Gentiles experience their contact with God through the channel of Jesus Christ. Without plighting their faith away from God, their categories incorporated Jesus as part of the actual experience of God. The Tosafists are trying to tell us that this is not idolatry, that is, the substitution of a human construct for God and placing one's trust in a finite form.

Jews neither needed nor experienced such an encounter with God. This is not, as triumphalist Christians falsely claimed, because the Jews were blind to this phenomenon or because God appeared within Christianity in a higher form. By the grace of God, Jews experienced the Divine directly. I no longer feel a need to argue with Christians' claim that God actually appeared in the flesh in Christianity and to insist that they acknowledge this understanding is the outcome of Christian culture suffused with Hellenist categories and interpretation, which seeks to "insert" a human component into the Divine.

Let me add: Revelation comes from an Infinite Boundless One, Who transcends all capacities of finite mortals to grasp. All Torah reflects a Divine self-limiting, self-anthropomorphizing outreach to humans. Inevitably humans are able to grasp only some fraction thereof in their understanding. The argument between Christianity and Judaism is not a war between idolatry and monotheism or a fight between truth and error. It is an argument about the boundaries and actual experiences within the loving, covenantal outreach between God and humanity, as experienced in these two communities. If we treat the issue this way, we can learn from and even correct and strengthen each other. This display of mutual respect can help us come closer and to work together to achieve the ultimate goals of redemption, which we share.

As a pluralist, I did not stop believing that the dominant, Judaism-negating teachings of Christianity in past millennia were wrong, or that they were expressed in evil and sinful behaviors. (Over the years, Catholicism and other mainstream Christian churches fundamentally revised their understanding of Jews and corrected the teachings that led to hatred and violence. They came to recognize Jewry's irrevocable covenant.) Nor did I stop disagreeing with the Christian shift toward emphasizing the spiritual role of salvation, and consequently giving less weight to the need and efforts to achieve material and political redemption. I remain critical of excessive reliance on intermediaries with God and of certain ascetic regimens and denial of this world which gained currency in Christianity. Only I acknowledge that some of the same tendencies were active (and sometimes even dominant) in Judaism.

Thus, another aspect of pluralism became clear. Judgments of right and wrong can (and must) still be made. However, the pluralist acknowledges the limits of his/her absolutism. Her truth/faith may not cover all people, all circumstances, all times. There may be additional absolutes out there that are not covered in my own faith. My/His truth/faith may include elements of error, of sins, of over/under emphasis. Some of these may be corrected by encountering and learning from other truths/faiths with contradictory/complementary emphases.

Some of the goals of *Tikkun Olam* may be advanced by work that my faith cannot do, but the other faith can. This is another dimension of pluralism: a willing acknowledgment that my own faith/community alone cannot achieve all of God's goals, i.e. complete *Tikkun Olam*. The pluralist phenomenon (i.e. faith/worldview/meaning system) may be not just a mystery that I must live with or an error which I cannot correct. It may be making a contribution to the world for which I and my fellow believers show, even if historically I saw the other faith/s as competitors or outright opponents of my religion.

4. Intrafaith Pluralism: The Case of Judaism

a. The Encounter that Made Me a Pluralist

My conversion to intra-Jewish pluralism came through a different route. A dear friend and spiritual soulmate, David Hartman, received a grant from a Jewish lay leader in Montréal and he invited me to plan a program with him for a summer Institute. This would enable us to study Torah together – and with as many rabbinic colleagues as we could afford to bring. After we exhausted the list of Orthodox rabbis whose work and writings had generated an appetite to learn with them, we invited another minyan of Conservative and Reform rabbis. The Reform included Emil Fackenheim, Jakob Petuchowski, Gene Borowitz, Herman Schaalman, and Dudley Weinberg, who made the strongest impression on me. There was a Holocaust factor in this experience. Elie Wiesel came in our first year. He moved the group. I presented a paper on the theological implications of the Holocaust that ignited a fusion reaction between Emil, myself, and the topic. Eliezer Berkovits, a participant, also came to grips with the subject in his way. Responding to the Shoah became the animating force in my life. Seeking an outlet led me to the rabbinate. Seven years later, I returned to academia full time, looking for a project that would enable me to focus on drawing forth the implications of the Holocaust. Two years later Elie Wiesel, Steve Shaw, and I founded CLAL to communicate to Jewish community leadership how self-understanding, public policy, and religious relationships must be transformed in light of the Shoah and the State of Israel.

Back then in the 1960s, the encounter with a high-powered group of liberal Rabbis who were such serious Jews was transformational. They were religiously vital, ethically powerful, wrestling with many of the questions that concerned me. They were also speaking to modernity as equals, not as spiritual mendicants begging to be admitted. I will never forget a long walk with Jakob Petuchowski in which we talked about *halakhah* and, in particular, about *gittin* (Jewish divorce law). Never had I had a long conversation involving *gemara* and *halakhah* with a Reform rabbi who was knowledgeable in details all the way through. I was stunned to realize that his critique was right. Women were legally inferior to their husbands, who had the absolute right to issue or refuse a *get* to his wife. Due to their unequal legal standing, women were subject to abuse in the process. Therefore the *halakhah* that I loved and upheld did need *tikkun*. Thus I learned another foundation of pluralism: recognition that one's own tradition, however valid and sacred, contained flaws that need correction. This recognition undercut another foundation of absolutism – the temptation to resort to apologetics and to explain away the flaws in one's own tradition on the (unspoken) grounds that there were no alternatives out there or that the alternatives were worse.

The outcome of that summer Institute was that my *stereotypes* and dismissals of liberal Judaism fell away. I came to see these individuals as truly embodying *Tzelem Elokim*[3] – dignified, equal and unique people living inspiring religious lives. Note again that the pluralism started with the discovery of the other's *Tzelem Elokim* first. Then comes taking their views and their spiritual ground seriously. Any movement that

3. The Jewish theology that all human beings are created in the image of God.

raises people of this quality had to be treated with respect. More than that: I came to see that Conservative and Reform were channels to connect and partner with God. They taught people to live a covenantal life, dedicated to *Tikkun Olam*. I did not become a Conservative or Reform Jew – because many of my stereotypes/criticisms accurately described people in the movements as well as weaknesses in those approaches. I concluded that my Orthodox movement, with its specific mix of strengths and weaknesses, could, on balance, contribute more to me and to Jewry overall. Nonetheless, by their existence, these liberal exemplars made a strong case that it was worthwhile to work with them to improve their movements – rather than to attack them. With this recognition, my excuses to deny and stand by flaws in my own community fell away. I would add that much of my community at Yeshiva University was moving to the right and breaking ties with the non-Orthodox. Had I not encountered and bonded to this pluralist group, I doubt that I would have had the resources to resist withdrawing from the rest of the Jews.

b. Practicing and Preaching Pluralism: the Case of CLAL

Almost a decade later, CLAL was created to reformulate and educate for a religious worldview in light of the Holocaust and Israel – and to enrich Jewish identity so that Jews would be equipped to join the rapidly opening up American society without assimilating. The ascending *haredim* (fervently Orthodox) pushed for separation and internal strengthening. I judged that Orthodoxy could not make it on its own – and should not: It needed to work with liberal religious movements and secular Jews to strengthen the community. CLAL was designed to be a place where Torah could be studied in the presence of every kind of Jew. Staff was recruited from every denominational background to enrich the conversation and widen the possible insights from varied perspectives. We experimented with ways of praying in a unified service. In the end, I concluded that it was a *mitzvah* to set up both traditional and liberal prayer service options – so all people could maximize their religious experience in a manner that spoke to them. By setting up CLAL as a pluralist venue, all people could feel that they were at home, not merely the guests of members of one preferred worldview or another.

The main justification for this pluralist organization was that it worked. A wider range of people came and participated than would have come to Orthodox *kiruv* (outreach). *Haredi* Jews never came because treating the liberal movements as equals was against their basic principles. As Modern Orthodoxy moved to the right under *haredi* influence, pluralism was delegitimized internally and Orthodox participation in CLAL programs diminished somewhat. Yet the Torah studied was consistently richer because of input from the wide variety of teachers and students. Participants' ability to grasp what *Kelal Yisrael* needed – rather than to appreciate only their own group's requirements – was considerably enhanced.

I was most excited to discover that many (most?) participants were set in motion by encounters with others. They were liberated from the routine acceptance of the standards of their day-to-day community. This opened them up to growing in Jewish living. Each group tended to see what the other lived and treasured and imagined taking it on to enrich themselves. People came looking to improve their Jewish lives. They used the encounter opportunity to take on the best from the others – rather than using the excuse of another model to lower their existing commitments. There were relatively few *ba'al teshuvah*[4] type outcomes where people were "born again" and made a drastic turn in lifestyle. Typically, people took on 5 to 10 percent more of whatever that more was – more learning, more observance, more *tzedakah*, more activism. Nevertheless, like the bumblebee whose wings are according to the laws of physics purportedly too small to support the flight of its large body, I struggled to find a credible explanation of the legitimacy of pluralism as a policy. Was I not betraying my Orthodox commitment to Torah as divine and implicitly binding on every Jew? If many Jews were not observant, then that was not my responsibility. But how could I set up or enable programs that appeared to operate at a lesser level of observance?

Especially in response to the plural religious services offered, my Orthodox friends and colleagues repeatedly asked how I could sponsor liberal prayer services when in my personal life I did not *daven* with such liturgies because some of their practices breach the *halakhah* to which I was committed. How could I pair a rabbi who believed in *Torah*

4. One who becomes ritually observant.

min ha-Shamayim [the divine nature of the faith] with a rabbi who affirmed that the Torah was sacred but – in part or all together – was created by humans? Intuitively, I knew that what CLAL was doing was right – but as an Orthodox rabbi, I struggled to find the rationale for pluralism by Orthodox standards. In the first round, I turned to great figures in the tradition whose thinking might be applied to validate the situation. The Talmud says: if you want to hang [i.e. attach your views], attach them to a tall tree.[5]

My first tall tree was the Chazon Ish, the leading sage of Israeli *haredi* Orthodoxy in the first half of the twentieth century, who was totally opposed to *halakhic* reform. Nevertheless, he ruled that inherited laws on *apikorsim* (i.e. heretics/willful deniers of the Torah) did not apply in his generation. This meant that one could not suppress them with severe, violent measures (traditionally including killing them). His rationale was the recognition that the *tzimtzum* whereby God had become "invisible" in modern times had changed the terms of religious belief and behaviors. In the past, ". . . [visible] miracles were prevalent. . . . The righteous ones [i.e. *tzaddikim, gedolim*] of the generation were under personal Divine Providence that was manifest to all . . ." so people saw (as a fact) that denying God and disobeying the law led to direct punishments from God. Therefore heresy and willful nonobservance was a direct threat to the safety of religious people. It was a justified self-defense to stop (even kill) such heretics before they brought destruction on the nation. But, ". . . in this time of the hiddenness [of God], faith has been cut off from the masses. . . ."[6] I took this to be his acknowledgment of the impact of the Holocaust and the divine *tzimtzum*. People saw that the presence of heresy or toleration of non-observant in the community did not lead to divine punishments inflicted on the sinners and observant alike. Therefore, people now understood that non-observers were not warped people, endangering innocent lives because of their immoral need to commit heresy or their self-indulgent lust for *halakhically* forbidden fruit. In this new cultural atmosphere, to act against sinners is seen as "an act of destructiveness or violence." Such acts repel people and drive them away from Torah.

5. B.T. *Pesachim* 112A.
6. Chazon Ish, *Yoreh Deah, Hilkhot Shechitah*.

Instead, the Chazon Ish called for a policy to "bring them back with bonds of love."[7]

My application of this principle was that in this cultural setting, what was hitherto heresy and willful nonobservance were now plausible, rational conclusions and innocent behaviors. Propagating those views or living a non-observant life should not be treated as life-threatening or socially endangering. All acts of suppression and/or statements of delegitimization (like violence in the Chazon Ish's approach) would become, in his words, "not [acts of] closing breaches [in Torah] but of widening breaches."[8] I concluded that all unvarnished claims of any absolute position denying any validity to alternatives were perceived by people in postmodernity as rude boorish assaults on the other, growing out of lack of information and encounter. (This meant that liberals too should not denegrate Orthodox traditionalists – but should see such extremism as a defense in the face of the unsettling impact of God's total hiddenness.) I applied the Chazon Ish's policy of "bonds of love" to mean that one should approach alternate religious viewpoints with respect, to try to create an environment where people could learn and observe together. The policy should be guided by a desire to help people perform better and to aid in enriching their religious experience.

Then I turned to Rabbi Soloveitchik. In his classic essay, *Kol Dodi Dofek*,[9] the Rav offered an indirect defense of his recognition of anti-religious Zionists and partnering with them to build Israel. R. Soloveitchik offered a definition of legitimacy for all groups: Are they bound by the covenant of Judaism and committed to advance its goals? However, he maintained that there are two levels in the covenant. The foundation level he called *brit goral*, the covenant of fate. The legitimate person or group embraced membership in the *brit* and its partnership obligations. Partnership was defined as holding four commitments: (1) Shared historical events – they affirm that their fate is one with Jewry. They take the historical events that happen to Jews as happening to them. (Compare remembering the Holocaust and supporting the state of Israel.)

7. Ibid.

8. Chazon Ish, *Yoreh Deah, Hilkhot Shechitah.*

9. "On Yom ha-Atzma'ut, 1956, Rabbi Soloveitchik delivered a public address at Yeshiva University entitled: Kol Dodi Dofek; The Voice of My Beloved Knocks."

(2) Shared suffering – the persecution, anguish or pain inflicted on other Jews is experienced as their own. (3) Shared responsibility – the common fate generates a sense of obligation to help the other. This in turn leads to (4) Shared actions – *tzedakah* or political action to help other Jews in trouble.

The second level of the covenant, which R. Soloveitchik considers to be the higher level, was the covenant of destiny (*brit yi'ud*). This level requires identification with the beliefs and values of the Jewish people. Living the covenant of destiny means living a Jewish way of life and a commitment to Jewish expression in all areas of existence. Here is where the denominations and secular Jews are in conflict over many issues. Disagreements on beliefs and conflicts over actual observances are what lead the groups to delegitimize each other. But, says R. Soloveitchik, if an individual or group has joined in the covenant of fate, then they are legitimate partners in the Jewish covenant. Then all the arguments between the groups in areas of meaning and values should be dealt with as arguments between partners. Disagreements over destiny, religious authority and ethical values should be argued out in the framework of shared community. Delegitimization or coercion are not valid instruments in an argument with a legitimate partner. However intensely I feel on the issue – however fundamental I consider the rejected item to be – I must treat the partner with respect. I need to teach and persuade them to change or to come closer. However illegitimate nonobservance is in my eyes, I can only try to improve the quality of positive performances or I can provide an alternative model. To seek to demolish or suppress is a betrayal of partnership.

R. Soloveitchik applied the principle of partnership to non-Orthodox and secular groups in the Zionist movement. He did not officially apply this principle to the liberal religious movements. He actually ruled that one should not pray in a Conservative or Reform congregation. However, I argued that the liberal denominations do accept the covenant of fate. They preach and practice shared history, suffering, responsibility, and actions. Therefore, they should be treated as legitimate partners. They should treat the Orthodox in the same manner.

R. Soloveitchik's model taught another insight on pluralism. Pluralism does not obscure or deny ongoing strong disagreements; nor should it lead to suspension of judgments of right and wrong between groups. Pluralism grows out of recognition that there is a meta-principle, some higher unifying task held in common. This reduces the salience of the disagreement from the level of total rejection (i.e. delegitimization) to the level of intense disagreement – which the Talmud calls "an argument for the sake of Heaven." Such an argument will have a lasting positive effect.[10] Even if the opponents are totally mistaken, in my judgment, I criticize the validity of these behaviors and teachings but I do not deny the legitimacy – if you will, the dignity and the quality of the other.

The third tree that I hung on was Rav Avraham Yitzhak HaKohen Kook. Kook recognized that although the majority of the *halutzim* did not believe in God and Torah and were nonobservant in their way of life, they were nevertheless doing God's work, i.e., the most important action needed to save the Jewish people. The majority of traditional religious authorities were repelled by the pioneers' blatant rejection of Judaism and religion, and those rabbis bitterly fought the Zionist movement. Zionists and Zionism were to be given no respect or legitimacy by recognizing it, let alone joining its institutions. They condemned religious Zionists and repeatedly prohibited Orthodox Jews from participating in Zionist activity or cooperating with the movement in building Israel. Nonetheless, Kook knew that the Zionists were on the right side of history – even on details like the pioneers' emphasis on work (instead of Torah study) and exercise/bodybuilding for the needed physical labor, which were Hellenizing and assimilating Gentile behaviors according to many *halakhists*.

In *Arfalei Tohar*, R. Kook wrote:

> Sometimes there is a need to go beyond [i.e. to change or violate] the Torah's instructions – but there is no one in the generation who can show the way to do it – so the matter is achieved by a breach/breakthrough [*hitpartzut*].

He also writes:

10. Ethics of the Fathers, ch. 5, Mishnah 21.

> When prophecy was present in Israel, it was possible to fix up the situation with a "temporary ruling" [*hora'at sha'ah]*. Then it [the change] would be done in permitted fashion, as a *mitzvah*, openly. But due to the sealing off of the light of prophecy, this needed improvement is done through a long-term breach. In its external form [e.g., an open break with tradition] this breach aggravates the heart. But from the internal purpose and content, it actually gladdens the heart.[11]

Here, Kook laid down another validating factor in pluralism. Sometimes the alternative which presents (or is seen) as a breach of the tradition – and is called illegitimate – actually is an improvement needed by the tradition. The inability to incorporate the *new* represents the incapacity of the authorities to interpret the tradition with the breadth of vision and proper understanding of the historical need. Therefore, the community should admit the legitimacy of the other side and acknowledge its contribution. Even if upholding the tradition drives one to declare officially that the alternative is wrong, Kook suggests that one should *de facto* be happy and accept their behavior as a *tikkun*. One is tacitly committed to eventually developing a new understanding that will bring the delegitimized alternative, officially, into the system itself.

Kook offered a deeper, more courageous insight here. The other side is right in doing this breach and, someday, the tradition will have to catch up. To Kook, this meant treating the *halutzim* with respect and dignity as doing God's work – despite their active rejection of much of the inherited tradition. My personal application has been that the Orthodox should recognize that on matters like women's equality, covenantal homosexuality, interreligious pluralism, secular education and "integration without assimilation" into contemporary culture – the liberal movements were right. While many of their changes breached the existing *halakhah*, the Orthodox should be grateful for their positions. They should learn from them and catch up to them, where appropriate.

This is not to deny that the liberal groups may have gone too far in many judgments. Reform Jews dropping *kashrut* out of affirmation of

11. A.I. Kook, *Arfalei Tohar*, in *Shmoneh Kevatzim* [Eight Collections], (Jerusalem 2004), volume 1. 203.

social contact with Gentiles – those egalitarians who insist that equality means and follow through with assimilation – come to mind. The Orthodox turn their coming later to the table of modernity into a plus by correcting the excesses, even as they take on the improvements. However, they cannot make their corrections in the liberal positions until they put behind them the delegitimization that stems from a tradition unable to upgrade or learn new approaches. Orthodoxy errs in its failure to see that *halakhah* is an ongoing process that grows and changes under different circumstances. The tradition does the best that can be done in every time, but it must be reapplied to bring the real closer to the ideal in every era.

c. *The Logic of Pluralism: The Second Wave*

As time went on, I was less satisfied to justify pluralism out of the thought of great Orthodox spiritual figures. Therefore, I sought to find grounds for pluralism in the deep structures of Judaism – structures which all types of Jews would recognize as part of their heritage. It struck me that even people who supported pluralism tended to think of it as a modern standard – imposed on the classic religions (for their own good). Is it not that those religions that thought of themselves as true are the very ones that made absolute claims?

This assumption was strengthened by the widespread observation that willingness to practice pluralism was correlated with diminishing intensity of religious spirit. The fundamentalist reaction that denied pluralism was driven by a ratcheted up religious intensity. The public often saw this reaction as a reassertion of religion's seriousness and treated these views as a more authentic representation of the true faith. I wanted a pluralism that felt authentic to Jewish tradition. My conclusion was that pluralism was grounded in the deepest fundamental principles of Judaism – the Image of God and the core method of covenant.

The key to the resolution of my search lay in the discovery process. Once the Image of God of the Other was encountered – eventually this led to the pluralist affirmation of the legitimacy of the system that nurtured and upheld this particular Image of God. Pluralism was the outcome of the discovery of the *full* Image of God of others; hitherto these were experienced as less than that, i.e., as Others. Encounter with the full image transmitted the experience that that person had the intrinsic dignities that evoked my recognition and respect. The full Image of God is of infinite value, equal and unique. Pluralism emerges when the individual internalizes these three dignities, and then realizes that he cannot dismiss the faith/system that this awesome person incarnates. I feel respect for a religion that raises such a person.

The first step in response to this insight was to hold in tension my hitherto absolute views and the others' contradictory positions. I could not reconcile them, but neither could I simply belittle them – hence, pluralism. Pluralism became prevalent in modern times precisely because modern culture brings people of every religion and lifestyle together as never before. The urban propinquity, as well as the traditional and social media, circulated worldviews and lifestyles of every person to every other person. The Others became neighbors.

The next level of pluralism came from the realization that whatever my convictions, the person speaking the dissonant views was a person of infinite value. If so, then I must weigh those words seriously. Furthermore that person was equal to me. Even if I am convinced that he/she was wrong, I could disagree but I have no right to deny the other's right to speak – or to suppress their views. As the dignity of uniqueness sank in, it motivated me to consider that maybe these elements that differed were speaking to the different circumstances or perceptions out of the uniqueness of the other. Maybe that person had seen things that I have missed. Once I recognized the differences as outcomes from uniqueness, I consider learning from them and applying them to my own worldview.

The above statements should not be confused with the idea that any and every statement made by an Image of God is automatically true or valid. In modern culture, the discovery of the infinite value and the quality of the other has paralyzed the ability to make any judgments on others. This is an overreaction. The dignity of the speaker does give his words *gravitas*. But being spoken by an Image of God cannot by itself turn an absolutely evil statement/belief into a good one. After all, a person can willfully take their capacities and dignities as an Image of God and direct them to the service of death or to degrading others. Then one has to oppose or stop the evil words/acts. The pluralist understands the weight of the Other – but has not lost the ability to say: "No!" Judaism teaches that life is sacred and the dignities of the Image of God should be upheld. By that standard, teaching that attacks life or degrades the Image of God is wrong. Given the weight of the evil action, I must refute the words or persuade the speaker to change. However, unless they pose an immediate danger to others, I have no right to suppress them by force.

Halakhah expresses this dialectical dealing with the Image of God in the treatment of a murderer. For committing the ultimate crime – destroying an innocent Image of God – some murderers pay the ultimate penalty – execution. This terminates the infinite value, equality, and uniqueness of the murderer. Nevertheless, he has not forfeited standing as an Image of God. This respect is expressed with the requirements to give him "a beautiful [i.e. minimum pain] death."[12]

Pluralists experience the Image of God of the Other powerfully; the response is to limit the absolute claims of their own faith. Such a pluralist grasps the limits of the Image of God as well. The force of that phenomena cannot extend its dignity to the point that no judgment can be passed on its behavior anymore. The pluralist has come to understand the limits of their own previously unchecked absolutism – as well as the limits of the new dignified absolutes that are encountered. In short, "pluralism is an absolutism that knows its limits."[13] The limits that pluralists impose on their own absolute values, makes room for other faith systems to express themselves in all their validity – and limits. The consequence is that whereas an absolutist has the security of fixed boundaries [one is always right the other is always wrong], he pays the price of inability to deal with other right and valid systems. This often generates an inability to correct flaws in his own system. The pluralist struggles constantly to find the boundaries where his absolute or the *other's* are no longer functioning correctly or doing justice to the other. Since the boundaries are not fixed and unchanging, the pluralist must monitor them constantly and is concerned about making a wrong judgment. This is yet another reason to acknowledge the limitations of the pluralist position. The pluralist will welcome debate and alternative

12. B.T. *Sanhedrin* 47a; *Ketubot* 37b.

13. I. Greenberg, *Seeking the Religious Roots of Pluralism,* in the Journal of Ecumenical Studies, vol. 34, is. 3, Summer 1997, 388.

views in the hope that this will shed maximum light and reduce errors as well as call attention to the boundaries and the limits.

There is a second principle that flows from the Image of God axiom that shapes understanding of pluralism. The laws of truth, communication and speech in Jewish tradition show that all truths taught and all statements made between human beings operate in two dimensions simultaneously. One is the objective correlative: Is this factually a true statement? If I stated that today is Tuesday, one can check the calendar and ascertain if it is an objectively true or false statement. This verification is independent of the humans engaged in conversation or communication.

However, all communications between people is covenantal, i.e., it grows out of relationship. Being true (or false) is shaped by the fact that an Image of God (infinitely valuable, equal and unique person) is speaking to another Image of God (infinitely valuable, equal and unique person). As the speakers speak, ideally (s)he should factor in and adjust the words to respect that the listener is an Image of God. A comprehensive assessment of the truth of this statement factors in the Image of God of the communicator and the one with whom one is communicating. This dimension may actually move the needle on a statement from true to false or the reverse.[14]

Precisely because most intrahuman statements are relational, an idea that might otherwise be ruled out as "wrong" or "false," gets a hearing. It even may be judged to be "true" because it is spoken to or by or about an image of God. Beit Hillel rules that every wedding, we dance before the bride, singing that she is "beautiful and of good character." Beit Shammai objects. For many brides, this description is false, hence a violation of the principle "remove yourself from a false statement." The *halakhah* overrules the objection on the grounds that we see the bride through the groom's eyes. To him, she is an image of God – valuable, equal, and unique. Therefore, by definition, she is beautiful and of good character.[15] By contrast, a true statement, i.e.,

14. B.T. *Shavuot* 30B. For additional examples, see Menachem M. Kasher, *Torah Sheleymah*, vol 19, 176ff.

15. B.T. *Ketubot* 17A. See on all this, my article "Seeking On Religion Roots of Pluralism: In the Image of God and Covenant" in Journal of Ecumenical Studies, vol. 34, no. 3 (Summer 1997) 385–394, especially 390ff.

an evil report on a person, told to someone who has no need to know, is classified as *lashon hara* – bad, sinful speech. Because it degrades an Image of God and falsely denies a greater truth that the person spoken about is a being of infinite value equality and uniqueness, this truth is ruled a lie – a violation of the principle "remove yourself from a false statement."[16]

While the weight of an Image of God cannot turn murder into a good deed,[17] it can shift a relational truth/a value statement/a message of friendship/a faith affirmation into the category of true (from false) or into the category of false (from true). These laws teach us that ideas get a hearing, are treated with respect and even considered a truth – thanks to the sheer weight of the dignity of the speaker. Thus, the Image of God provides the basis for a pluralist exploration of views – even where we are convinced that the other side is wrong. Whenever an Image of God speaks, the speaker's status as such an Image gives that view weight, including the right to be heard, and even a putative truth status. When we deny the right to be heard of other views or values systems, we are attacking the Image of God of those who hold the other view. Of course, we must check out the claims. If they turn out to be those of a system preaching mass murder or the degradation of others, we must reject them – in order to protect the Image of God in general. We even have the right to suppress them if there is no other way of stopping an immediate danger to people's lives posed by their words. All in all, the Image of God principle provides the basis for religious and cultural pluralism, even in the presence of religiously mandated or absolute views. Such a pluralism is not a concession to Western values. It represents a passionate, principled, religiously-driven fulfillment of a central principle in Judaism – honoring the *Tzelem Elokim*[18] in every person.

The counterpart central mechanism of Judaism is covenant – the partnership of God and humanity to turn this planet into a Paradise for all living things. Upon analysis, the structure of the covenant is an affirmation and call to pluralism. The fact that God enters into covenant

16. See in Kasher, *loc. cit.*, 98, 99, 106.

17. I should note that killing [an Image of God] in self-defense – when there is no other way of stopping the killer – turns killing into a legitimate act, even a *mitzvah*.

18. The Jewish theology that all human beings are created in the image of God.

with humans (rather than rules them by fiat) is a statement that the Lord values human freedom. As true partners, human beings are given free will and the right to choose – even and whenever God addresses or commands. By self-binding in covenant, the Lord pledges not to coerce or intimidate humanity into submitting to the Divine Will.[19] This means that God values that humans understand the divine mission and mature into voluntary commitment to it – more than guaranteeing the right outcome, be it in thought or action. Implied is that God privileges the right to choose – for only choice and taking personal responsibility enables the full development of the dignity of equality or uniqueness in the human being. Even after seeing that freedom is abused by some and that consequently some people act in an evil manner, God does not reprogram people to be automatically good. Nor does the Lord wipe out all evil. Rather the absolute God accepts limits. God will educate, persuade, inspire – but will not coerce humans to do the right thing. Nor will the Lord wipe out evil in order to assure the triumph of good.

The Divine limits are a call to humans to partnership. These self-limits are an affirmation of mortals' dignity and freedom. In practicing pluralism (understood as an absolutism that knows and honors its own limits) we are imitating God. The free play of ideas and facts is allowed – even though we are convinced that our standards are divinely mandated. We follow this policy even though there is a risk that the wrong views, presented unchecked, will win over the public. Just as God considers the risk of wrong decisions as a valid and necessary price to pay for the free exercise of human judgment, so do we. God is prepared to take the risks of defeat of the divine goals in order to achieve this desired outcome. This freedom must be extended by humans to others – again taking the risk that the good may be defeated. Only, thus, can humans grow into responsible, infinitely valuable, equal, and unique partners and co-creators of a better world.

Absolutists justify control, coercion, and denial of others' right to speak – on the grounds that the ultimate cause that they represent must be upheld and guaranteed to win out. If this means censorship, suppression, and pressuring the believers to do the right thing, then

19. See the exposition in Genesis, chapters 6–9, especially 8 and 9, when the first, universal covenant with humanity is established.

so be it. Covenant proves that God believes the opposite. God calls on us to self-limit, to make room for others' growth, to let them learn by trial and error. This self-limitation enables us to avoid idolatry, i.e., the claim that something human (including our interpretation of the religion) is absolute. Idolatry is the act/claim of making something human [however connected to divinity and religion] and treating it as absolute, perfect, all controlling. Putting limits on such claims is the heart of pluralism.

The paradigm of entering into covenant suggests a Divine self-limitation out of love and relationship. True love discovers that it must make room for the beloved and gives him/her the freedom to become his/herself. No matter how noble my intentions and exalted my nature, if I do not self-limit and allow freedom, then the beloved will be reduced, made less. The divine prophylaxis checked even the pure Godhead from dominating and taking over all creatures. In practicing pluralism, we, the human partners, pave the way for the uniqueness of humans to express itself in a variety of multiple truths. This prevents any of our religions from expanding into a malignant growth that crowds out and destroys the alternatives.

By choosing to work through covenant and making entering into a relationship central, God pointed to binding ourselves in love and making room for others' multiple expressions of life and good. Indeed, in covenant is the insight that whereas one abstract truth can be given to all, each relationship is distinctive and unique. The Infinite God has – out of love and capacity for relationship – entered into covenant in unlimited fashion – with more than one community. Thus, covenant calls us to enter into a unique relationship with God while appreciating the making available of redemption and salvation to all. This multiplicity takes nothing away from our experience of being infinitely loved and being in an inexhaustible relationship. Covenant shows that the Boundless, the Powerful One, is self-restrained and respects people. This respect expresses itself in letting them work at their own pace and capacity; also to mature. In turn, our covenantal behavior breeds self-restraint, expressible in respect for others and working with them at their own pace, capacity, and maturity.

d. The Logic of Pluralism: When Humans Take More Responsibility in the Covenant.

As I explored the increasing human role in the covenant during the last decade, it became clear that pluralism is an organic outgrowth of the covenantal process. The rabbis themselves are the outcome of a Divine opening toward pluralism.

On the biblical stage, God is the dominant partner. Since the Lord takes care of everything, there is no room for debate or quibbling with the Divine instructions: "Theirs was not to question 'why;' theirs was but to do or die." The Israelites' assignment is to listen and obey their instructions to a "T." In the desert trek: "At the command of God they camped, and at the command of God, they journeyed" (Numbers 9:20, 23).

Quite simply, since the outcomes depend on exact obedience to God, there was no room for dissidence or even a second opinion as to what to do. These were the terms of the covenant – because God always assured fulfillment to those who obeyed the true word of God.

In this environment there could be no two legitimate interpretations of God's word. Jeremiah instructed King Zedekiah and the Judahites to accept the yoke of Babylon. Another prophet, Hananiah ben Azzur (backed by a host of other active prophets) called on the nation to revolt. The Lord's response through Jeremiah was swift and unequivocal. Hananiah was not speaking in error, or misinterpreting words that he heard. He was a *false* prophet – not sent by God, not speaking the word of God. "Therefore, you shall die – for you have spoken rebellion against God" (ibid. 28:16–16). Hananiah died that year.

The Divine *tzimtzum* that initiated the rabbinic era changed the role of the two covenantal partners. As the rabbis understood the phenomenon, God self-limited and called the humans to take on more responsibility in the covenant. The consequence was that the humans would become more active. The covenantal interchange stopped being an unequivocal divine instruction, spoken through a heavenly voice and simply obeyed by the recipient. The word of God now became available as guidance, uncovered by human discernment – including analyses of past revelations and reasoned application of past principles to this moment. Human judgment had to be exercised; it played a key role in establishing what God wanted of the covenantal partner at this moment. But each human is unique. This *tzimtzum* meant that God was inviting humans to co-create revelation. The Lord welcomed the inevitable differences of opinion and judgment that followed.

The early rabbinic masters were able to come to a full meeting of minds. The Talmud reports only a handful of different rulings between Hillel and Shammai, presumably their minds met out of their lifetime of learning and scholarly argument together. However, each raised up schools of students. Soon there were hundreds of conflicting rulings between the disciples. At first, the rabbis guessed that the disagreements reflected the fact that the students had not done their homework. They had failed to follow the great masters in all that they did. Having not paid enough attention, they understandably made errors in judgment that led to contradictory rulings.[20] Many feared that, in sum, two different Torahs were emerging. Everyone understood from the tradition that two words of God could not be contradictory. The big question – and anxiety – arose: How do we ascertain which school's Torah was the true word of God?[21]

Ultimately, deeper realization emerged, helped along by a heavenly voice. By delegating a much more shaping role to the human partner, God affirmed the inevitable variety of human judgments that followed. Two honest human beings, respecting the same sanctities, seeking the same goals, could read a common text, hear a single voice and come to two differing conclusions in good faith. The difference reflected the uniqueness of each Image of God in a differential response to the differing circumstances and constantly changing times, priorities and urgencies of both leader and community. The varied responses reflected that people had become more mature in the covenant. They were not merely taking orders, but identifying with covenantal goals and purposes and applying their minds to find the best realization. In summoning people to act as full partners, rather than as junior partners, the Lord was inviting people to do just this. This process assured that they would grow and become even more mature – which (as we have seen) is the point of the covenantal method.

As the Talmud developed, the rabbis came to realize that the varied

20. *Sanhedrin* 88b.
21. *Eruvin* 13b.

minds and judgments of the discussants were a source of insight, not confusion. The greater the variety of minds, the wider the frame of questions, answers and deliberations, the more facets of the truth were uncovered. Thus, the method of *chavruta* – learning, analyzing and reasoning together – emerged as the preferred technique of uncovering the meaning. *Machloket* (reasoned argument in which each side tried to develop its own insight and perspective to the maximum, while simultaneously challenging and exploring the counter view) became the favored process for arriving at the truth. Thus rabbinic tradition is a big step on the path of full covenantal pluralism.[22]

The rabbis felt that they had been summoned to a new level of partnership. This gave them authority so these could "permit" and these could "prohibit"; these could rule "pure" and these "impure" in the same matter.[23] They (and the Talmud generally) concluded that, although marriage was taking place in one group that would result in their children being considered illegitimate and non-marriageable *mamzerim* in the other group, nevertheless "these [Hillelites] and those [Shammaites] are the words of the living God." But the rabbis' pluralism operated within tight limits. They affirmed that they had no authority to abolish a law of the Torah. It is noteworthy that by use of legal processes and restrictive interpretations, they could in practice nullify the application of certain laws – such as capital punishment, the all-out war on the seven nations, and the execution of the wayward son.[24] Still they insisted, in principle, they could not permanently cancel a law given at the higher, e.g., earlier level of revelation. They finally allowed that,

22. David Kraemer, The Mind of the Talmud: An Intellectual History of the Bavli (New York, Oxford University Press, 1990) especially chs. 4–6. Kraemer points out that by the time we get to the Bavli, *Hazal* are more interested in the shakla v'tarya, in the debate and exchange of ideas, and less concerned to come to the final p'sak (ruling) than in the earlier Talmud and documents.

23. B.T. Hagigah 3b. "... These rule impure, these rule pure. These prohibit, these permit; these disqualify, these validate. ... the text [Torah] says, all were given from one shepherd, one God gave them."

24. On the restriction of capital punishment procedure, see B.T. *Sanhedrin*, chs. 3–9. on the wayward son, see Sifrei on Deuteronomy 21:18–21. See also *Sanhedrin* 68B–71B especially 71A where the view of Rabbi Shimon is that there never was and never will be a wayward son convicted and executed.

in a moment of emergency, they could cancel a law – but only as a "temporary ruling" (*hora'at sha'ah*).[25]

As the rabbis of the Talmud understood it, the human partner was authorized to carry out the covenant, to apply it to new circumstances, to adjust tactics to better deal with certain situations. This power of attorney could not be used to countermand the declared wishes of the senior partner. Despite all their differences, both agreed that one must believe in God, that the Torah was the word of God, that humans could not abrogate any of the laws, that it was eternally binding, that one could not legitimately deny that God had created the world or chosen the Jewish people and entered into covenant with them. The rabbis of rabbinic Judaism were pluralists but not relativists. There were other competing sects such as Sadducees, Jewish Christians, Boethusians, and Epicureans, which they delegitimized as beyond the pale. They did not consider those groups' teachings and rulings to be part of the Torah – not even to be factored in as minority opinions. How then can we apply the inclusive principle of pluralism to today's much more divergent religious groupings within and without Judaism?

e. *The Logic of Pluralism When Humans Take Full Responsibility for the Covenant*

A broadened pluralism is the outcome of further development in the *brit.* I believe that in modernity, God has again self-limited to call humans to full responsibility in the covenant. God's total hiddenness is intended to enable human judgments to come out of their own understanding, identification with and voluntary assent to the conclusions. In history, God has come closer and bound God more deeply to humanity and the human condition. The choice of the method of covenant shows God's belief that the more humans are empowered to take responsibility for the realization of the covenant, the more they will think profoundly and try creatively to achieve the goals. The divine commitment to perform all miracles only through natural means and human agents declares that when humans develop to their maximum, they discover and utilize all the powers built into Creation in order to complete it.

25. See Rambam *Mishneh Torah. Hilkhot Shemitah V'Yovel* 13:8 and Raavad's comment there.

By delegating full responsibility to human beings, God widened the parameters of pluralism, from the right to diverge on tactics to the right to offer alternative strategies. This extends even to overriding past channels and models in order to better achieve the goals. The Lord authorizes humans to exercise freely their creativity and not to hesitate to innovate in order to realize God's vision.[26]

With this grant of power, anybody who responds to this summons, consciously or unconsciously, anybody who takes on the task of repairing the world, becomes a legitimate partner in the work of finishing creation. This is true whether or not they affirm that they are joining in the covenant of redemption. Those who devote themselves to this mission become co-creators of the Torah of the triumph of life, and honored workers in the never ending task of reconciling present reality with the future perfection. This makes people with a wider range of views – some hitherto considered deviationist and beyond the pale – into active and legitimate partners in the covenant of *Tikkun Olam*. They share in generating the *halakhah*, the way of life in which every action contributes to *Tikkun Olam*.

When liberal rabbis conceive of God in far less personal terms, they should not be dismissed as breaching the commandment to believe in God, but be recognized as trying to refine the inherited concept of God and bring it closer to the "purer" less utilitarian or magical understanding of the Divine. When secular thinkers identify the Divine with the cosmic process, they should be understood as trying to make belief in God fully credible in the presence of scientific understanding and cultural consensus of the unbroken operation of natural laws. Since science gives us better understanding of creation and better capacity to heal the world, it is our responsibility to make the religious dimension of Being credible in their presence. Given that they are trying to achieve the goals of the covenant (or some part thereof) they should be welcomed as legitimate and needed partners – taking a role in articulating and in moving humans to function at a higher level in realizing the covenant.

26. My argument for the unfolding covenant and God's *tzimtzum* as a call to humans to take full responsibility is detailed at full length in two books, *The Triumph of Life* (forthcoming) and *Partnership for Life: Judaism and Meaning in Life and History* (forthcoming).

When Reform or Reconstructionist Jews drop certain classical observances – or when they bring new commandments, such as to save the environment or honor people hitherto marginalized – they should not be dismissed as anti-*halakhic*. Rather, they should be judged as using their greater legitimate autonomy to spell out additional obligations needed (or the extra steps now possible) to achieve *Tikkun Olam*. How do they arrogate to themselves the right to abrogate laws which Hillel and Shammai deemed to be beyond their capacity to question? They are saying: "As much as we love and respect the inherited tools of redemption, in our judgment, these new tools (or not using some of the old tools) will be even more effective in bringing the end closer." In an imagined conversation, I see them saying to God: "You must trust us that (in our judgment) this way is even more likely to persuade the public to accept the mission and the goals. In our times, this way is more likely to nurture the soul and increase moral growth."

The divine delegation of authority does not mean that liberal changes are never wrong. In many cases, abandoning ritual behaviors weakened the power of the religion. The elimination of the prayers for restoration and return to Israel in the prayer books was a grave misjudgment of trends in history. The mistakes of liberals should be criticized and corrected. The greater the power humans assume, the greater the negative consequences of bad decisions or misused powers. Reformers should be all the more open to guidance or to learning from others' models. Their accomplishments and their errors can be learned from by the Orthodox – precisely because they are treading new paths. Many of these roads are not yet mapped or fully understood.

When Modern Orthodox or Conservative Jews generate new leadership roles for women, they seek to apply covenantal tradition anew as part of a dynamic process of redeeming the world. They undoubtedly make errors that need to be critiqued also. But all criticisms should be constructive (which would make them more likely to be listened to) and not intended to be demolishing, which makes them more likely to be ignored.

When rabbis use academic and critical scholarship to understand canonical texts, they are not repudiating *Torah min ha-Shamayim*. They are trying to develop an understanding of the connection between the Divine and the human – and of passing messages between the Infinite and the finite – that is credible in our time. They should fully understand the risks of being totally absorbed into the present culture and the danger of losing connection with the Eternal and beyond. They should welcome help from critics to the right and the left of them. Still, they should not be asked to dumb themselves down willfully in order to stay within the boundaries of the inherited and the approved versions of revelation.

Traditional and *haredi* Jews uphold the inherited *halakhah* as it is. They should see their role as the counterculture to keep the present generation from being swallowed up in the maelstrom of post-modern culture. They make a major contribution to keeping pluralism healthy and so keep themselves legitimate in the pluralist, covenantal community. However, they must be concerned that in upholding past authority, they may be (admittedly with good intentions) failing to respond to a Divine request that they (and all humans) take on more responsibility. They must continually ask themselves, if by adhering to their traditionalism, they are upholding the goals of the covenant or holding them up.

All traditional religions need to take up the blessing and challenge of pluralism. If they simply say "no" – if they continue to uphold their traditional assumptions of superiority or of absolute status (as if the others are not present or worthy of serious consideration) – they will be perceived as clueless, as overbearing and closed-minded, and will risk losing credibility altogether.

Of course there is the option of fundamentalism – of sealing ourselves off from the world and/or shutting out the others through force, whether cultural, political, or military. However this approach is under pressure. Sometimes when it is utilized – as in *jihad* or religious persecution – it turns the religion against its own best values and violates the Images of God in the others. Moreover, a fundamentalist turn forfeits credibility in the general culture – and that culture shows no sign of weakening as it continuously spreads.

It would be wise for all religions to re-focus on the goal of *Tikkun Olam*. This highlights the great unfinished tasks standing before all religions. No one faith community can realistically hope to achieve world transformation by itself. It takes maturation, a realistic sense of one's capabilities together with an acceptance of one's own limits, to play a more constructive role in an age of humans coming into their own. Maturation leads to humility, i.e., a willingness to serve God's purposes and the greater good as one of many messengers, rather than insisting on dominating the process or getting all the credit. At every step of this way, a pluralist attitude of respect and openness to learn from others, affirmation that they have a constructive role to play and that they are needed by my group, will improve each one's own capacity and credibility. I add that religious groups should show equal respect and openness to cooperate with secular groups seeking to repair the world.

*

Postscript and a Plea

My narrative of the journey to pluralism has turned into a plea for Modern Orthodox Jews to become pluralists. I acknowledge that this means voluntarily giving up one of Orthodoxy's strongest cards – the internal and external belief that it is exclusively valid. I also admit that the *haredi* policy to strengthen Orthodoxy by becoming more countercultural to post-modernity, to dismiss the spiritual concerns and break ties with liberal denominations, has paid off in demographic and institutional growth. (The PEW Survey of 2010 showed that Jews are maximally integrating in this culture and that assimilation is surging.)

Yet in light of the Shoah and Israel, the ultra-Orthodox achievement is marginal to Jewish history. Jewry must enter post-modernity fully in order to run a modern state as well as to protect and pursue Jewish life in the Diaspora. By the same token, if we save ourselves and abandon the rest of Jewry, we are driving them further from tradition toward assimilation. In doing so, we betray the covenant of fate.

I also believe that on this path, we are turning a deaf ear to the Divine summons to take charge of the covenant – and for all humanity to take steps to move the world closer to the messianic goals. We have the capacity to lead the world toward a higher form of *avodat Hashem* (service of God), in which religious people give up their "perks" and status as God's exclusive agents and serve the Lord out of love, lishmah, humbly, as witnesses and coworkers with other Jews and non-Jews.

If we take a pluralist road, we will have to re-articulate all our beliefs and deepen our religious life to nurture the individual and to attract others in the midst of the most dynamic culture in human history. We will sustain the rest of the Jews and be sustained by them, even as we differ and we learn from each other. Since we are wrestling with the central issues facing all peoples and all religions, a pluralist Jewry can again become "a light unto the nations "(Isaiah 42:6) and a "blessing on earth" (ibid. 19:24).

Contributors

Dr. Steven Bayme serves as National Director, Contemporary Jewish Life Department, American Jewish Committee.

Dr. Erica Brown is an associate professor at George Washington University and the director of its Mayberg Center for Jewish Education and Leadership. She is the author of eleven books.

Rabbi Ariel Burger is the designer of the Adult Learning Initiative at the Harold Grinspoon Foundation.

Rabbi Dr. Nathan Lopes Cardozo is an author, a highly sought-after speaker, the Founder and Dean of the David Cardozo Academy and the Bet Midrash of Avraham Avinu in Jerusalem.

Rabbi David Jaffe is the Founder of the Kirva Institute, whose work is dedicated to helping people access Jewish spiritual wisdom for building sustainable, healthy communities.

Rabbi Darren Kleinberg, Ph.D. is Head of School at Kehillah Jewish High School, in Palo Alto.

Rabbi Dr. Eugene Korn is Academic Director of the Center for Jewish-Christian Understanding in Israel. Formerly the founding editor of *The Edah Journal*, he was blessed with the opportunity to first learn from R. Greenberg at Yeshiva College and to continue learning from R. Yitz throughout his career.

Rabbi Dr. Seth Farber is a Modern Orthodox rabbi, a historian, and the founder of ITIM, which helps people navigate the religious authorities' bureaucracy in Israel.

Rabbi Dr. Joshua Feigelson earned rabbinic ordination at Yeshivat Chovevei Torah and a Ph.D in Religious Studies from Northwestern University. He wrote his doctoral dissertation on the life and teaching of Rabbi Yitz Greenberg.

Professor Arna Poupko Fisher teaches Bible and Jewish Thought in the Judaic Studies Department of the University of Cincinnati.

Rabbi Dr. Alon Goshen-Gottstein is founder and director of the Elijah Interfaith Institute and a leading voice in Jewish theological engagement with world religions.

Rabbi Dr. Yitz Greenberg is a Modern Orthodox rabbi, an author of more than ten books, one of the leading American Jewish scholars and theologians in our time. He is the Past President of The National Jewish Center for Learning and Leadership.

Dr. Lawrence Grossman, editor of the American Jewish Year Book from 2000 through 2008, is Director of Publications at the American Jewish Committee.

Rabbi Daniel Landes is Director of Pardes. In 1982, while on sabbatical from the Simon Wiesenthal Center and Yeshiva of Los Angeles, he created with Rabbi Greenberg within the Center for Learning and Leadership (CLAL), the first inter-denominational *kollel* for faculty and students.

Rabbi Asher Lopatin is the president of Yeshivat Chovevei Torah Rabbinical School, an Orthodox rabbinical school that cultivates a love of Torah and a philosophy of inclusiveness. He is a Rhodes Scholar and previous spiritual leader of Anshe Sholom B'nai Israel Congregation, a Modern Orthodox synagogue in Chicago, where he served for eighteen years.

Rosh Kehilah Dina Najman is the Marta d'Atra of The Kehilah of Riverdale, an Orthodox congregation in Riverdale and heads the Gemara department at SAR Academy in Riverdale.

Dr. Jennie Rosenfeld serves as the Manhiga Ruchanit in Efrat and teaches Talmud and Halakha at the Pelech High School in Jerusalem. She co-authored *Et Le'ehov: The Newlywed's Guide to Physical Intimacy.*

Rabbi Joseph Telushkin is the author of *Jewish Literacy, A Code of Jewish Ethics* (two volumes) and *Rebbe.*

Rabbi Avi Weiss is the founder of the Yeshivat Chovevei Torah Rabbinical School, the founder of Yeshivat Maharat, the founder of the International Rabbinical Fellowship, the founder of AMCHA, and has been the leading Rabbi of the Hebrew Institute of Riverdale for decades.

Tanya White is a lecturer of Tanach and Jewish Thought at various institutions throughout Israel and abroad and is currently pursuing her doctoral studies at Bar Ilan University in Jewish Thought.

Rabbi Dr. Shmuly Yanklowitz is the President and Dean of the Valley Beit Midrash, the Founder and President of Uri L'Tzedek, the Founder and CEO of The Shamayim V'Aretz Institute, and the author of ten books on Jewish ethics.

Dov S. Zakheim was Under Secretary of Defense (2001–2004) and Deputy Undersecretary of Defense (1985–87). A member of several government advisory boards and the Council on Foreign Relations, and a Fellow of the Royal Swedish Academy of War Sciences, he earned his doctorate from Oxford and *semichah* from Ha-Ga'on Rav Shmuel Walkin, zt"l.